HOWARD GARRETT'S
PLANTS FOR TEXAS

University of Texas Press

Austin

Howard Garrett's
PLANTS
FOR TEXAS

First edition, 1996

Requests for permission to reproduce material from this work
should be sent to Permissions, University of Texas Press,
Box 7819, Austin, TX 78713-7819.

∞ The paper used in this publication meets the minimum
requirements of American National Standard for Information
Sciences—Permanence of Paper for Printed Library Materials,
ANSI Z39.48-1984.

Library of Congress Cataloging-in-Publication Data

Garrett, Howard, 1947–
    [Plants for Texas]
    Howard Garrett's plants for Texas. — 1st ed.
        p.   cm.
    ISBN 0-292-72787-9. — ISBN 0-292-72788-7 (pbk.)
    1. Landscape plants—Texas.   2. Plants, Cultivated—
Texas.   3. Landscape gardening—Texas.   4. Gardening—Texas.
5. Organic gardening—Texas.   I. Title.
SB435.52.T4G37   1996
635'.0484'09764—dc20   95-41757

To
my mom and dad
Jewell and Ruby Garrett

who have never fussed about
my doing things differently—

the natural way.

CONTENTS

ACKNOWLEDGMENTS

THANKING ALL THE PEOPLE who have helped me learn about plants would have to start with Dr. Robert Reed at Texas Tech University. I took a course in horticulture because it sounded easier than the other choice—chemistry. It was, and I fell in love with learning about plants because Dr. Reed made it so interesting.

Throughout my career I have been lucky enough to work with several people who helped me learn about the practical side of planting in Texas. Thanks go to Quinton Johnson, who taught me about turf management; Naud Burnett, who taught me how to consider and use unusual plants; John Morelock, who taught me about perennials; Cody Carter, who taught me how to plant trees; Phil Huey, who taught me many plant secrets; Odena Brannam, who taught me about herbs; Malcolm Beck, who taught me about agricultural crops; and Walt Davis, who taught me about forage grasses.

Special thanks go to my assistant, Tracy Flanagan, for working many long hours typing and editing the manuscript along with all her other duties at my office. Tracy also handles the advertising on my radio show on WBAP and is my office manager.

And to my wife Judy and my daughter Logan, thanks for letting me work night and day to finish this project. I promise to slow down soon.

Howard Garrett's
PLANTS
FOR TEXAS

INTRODUCTION

SOME PLANT BOOKS cover landscape plants; others cover vegetables or herbs. Some discuss grasses, and others concentrate on natives or introduced plants. This book covers 'em all. This is a Texas plant encyclopedia. It's not for the professional horticulturist as much as for the landscape contractor, nurseryman, and homeowner. If you wonder about a plant in Texas—whether a shrub, vine, flower, grass, tree, weed, or cover crop—it's probably in this book. There are more plants in more categories explained in *Plants for Texas* than in any other book written for the state. I hope you like it and find it helpful. I'm sure you will!

I think you'll find the arrangement of this book to be the best—the easiest to use and the most enjoyable to read. No punches are pulled. Some gardening authors give wimpy, noncommittal advice, leaving the main decisions up to you. Not here. You need my help and my cold, hard facts about what plants to use and what plants to avoid here in Texas.

From the East Texas piney woods to the deserts of West Texas, to the hill country of Central Texas to the tropical Rio Grande and of course through my home area of the Dallas–Fort Worth Metroplex, *Plants for Texas* is the first book and probably the last to address native and introduced plants—selection, planting instruction, and organic maintenance for the entire great state of Texas.

To have beautiful gardens in Texas that are easy to maintain, there are six essential rules:

1. Stop using artificial fertilizers and pesticides.
2. Increase the air in the soil.
3. Increase the organic matter in the soil.
4. Increase the rock minerals in the soil.
5. Mulch the bare ground.
6. Increase the biodiversity of plants, animals, insects, and soil life.
7. Select adapted plants.

Selecting adapted plants is the most important point and what this book is about. When poorly adapted plants are used, none of the other points matter. This book is designed to help you make good selections.

There is, however, only one sensible way to garden—organically! Organiphobes will argue that point, but they're wrong. Organic gardening is no longer a fad. Actually it never was. We gardeners have in the past used the chemical rescue approach and have poisoned our environment. Some people still are. We didn't invent the chemical approach. The universities did with grants from the chemical companies. Planting and maintaining plants organically has been done by a small percentage of people for a long time. Resistant people have a hard time accepting the organic philosophy. I bought into it immediately because it just made sense. Even if it hadn't worked so well, I would have fought for it because of the environmental aspects, but I have been delighted to discover that the natural alternatives really work. In fact, they work much better than the toxic-chemical approach, which isn't saying much because that approach doesn't work at all over the long haul.

We started poisoning the world in a serious way along about World War II. That's when we invented and accelerated the use of many of the synthetic pesticides and fertilizers. It's ironic that these dangerous products don't even work. Most artificial fertilizers are very salty, feed plants with too much too fast, have no organic matter, and often contain fillers that are less than "earth friendly." Fake fertilizers not only glut and stress plants, they cause a toxic buildup of nitrates and phosphates in the soil and drinking water. These laboratory-produced products aren't balanced according to nature's pattern and usually contain no organic matter, very few trace minerals, and rarely any vitamins, hormones, or enzymes. A few farmers, politicians, and garden communicators are now aware of the problem and are teaching alternative methods and products. We home gardeners should be doing the same.

Toxic pesticides are a terrible problem in that they indiscriminately destroy beneficial as well as troublesome insects. Harsh artificial products also destroy the balance of beneficial microorganisms and other life in the soil. It's all about common sense and balance. Before selecting any fertilizer, soil amendment, or pest control product, ask one simple question and let the answer be the guide as to whether you buy and use the product or not: "If I use this product, will it hurt or benefit the earthworms?" If the product is detrimental to the earthworms, it shouldn't be used. If the earthworms like what you are doing to the soil, the plants will love it.

I wrote this book because it seems logical that gardeners need one book that contains information on all types of Texas plants. I'll give you the truth about all the plants in this book—the pros and the cons. I owe nothing to the chemical companies or the big growers—that should be obvious. If a plant is a dog, I'll tell you. If a plant is great, I'll tell you. Landscaping is a major investment, and there is no need to choose high-maintenance or short-lived plants. Although no plant or horticulture technique is perfect, I have tried to give you the best advice on how to achieve the greatest success with a new or renovated garden in Texas. The Lone Star State is a big state with several different climates and soils. I hope my book helps you no matter where you live.

PLANTING DESIGN

Gardens are never static. They are complex living organisms consisting of many millions of other smaller living organisms. Gardens are dynamic and start changing from the moment of installation. A garden cannot be planted that never needs any adjustment. One of the great pleasures of gardening is the fine-tuning through the years by moving plants about, adding plants when needed, and removing those that are no longer useful or interesting.

Most gardens have at least two lives—the first is established when the plants are installed. The sec-

ond starts when the trees mature and shade the ground. When trees are young, the majority of the shrubs, ground covers, and grasses must be the kind that thrive in the full sun. As the trees grow, mature, and shade the ground, low plants and understory trees must be shade tolerant. Change in planting is then needed. Don't be afraid to experiment. The trial-and-error method is what the pros use, so why not amateurs? As plants mature, new ideas will present themselves. If you watch and listen, the garden will show you what needs to be done. Some plants will need to be pruned, some will need to be added, and some will need to be removed. The most important design point is that the garden should be enjoyable—otherwise what's the point?

People who give you rules such as "Plant tall plants at the ends of the house to frame it and lead the eye to the front door" create limitations. Don't fall for all of these recommendations. If you want to plant the biggest plants right smack in front of the front door, have at it. It's your house, not the people's who drive by or work in the government agencies. Too few people actually enjoy their gardens. They are too worried about what other people think.

Trees

Of all the plants, trees are the first and most important consideration. Statistics show that landscaping is the only home improvement that can return up to 200 percent of the original investment. The key to that increase is the trees. In addition to providing great beauty, trees create the atmosphere or the *feel* of a garden. Trees provide shade and food, house wildlife, screen bad views, frame good ones, and make us feel good. Trees increase property values rapidly as they grow. Trees save energy and money by shading our houses in the summer and by letting the sun shine through for warmth in the winter.

Choosing the right tree for the exact spot is not just an aesthetic decision but an important investment decision as well. How pretty you think the tree will look growing in that particular spot is not as important as how the tree will like growing in that particular spot. If a tree likes where and how you've planted it, you will like the effect. Understanding the horticultural needs of a tree is essential. Simple but essential. Trees need to be well aerated and growing in a living, healthy, balanced soil. Remember that all trees—ornamental and food crop trees—originally grew in the forest in healthy soil with mulch on the ground. The forest floor cross-section should be reproduced and maintained under all newly planted trees. Mulch! That's the most important word. If you want healthy trees, mulch the root zone.

There are two categories of landscape trees: shade and ornamental. Shade trees are the large structural trees that form the skeleton of the planting plan and grow to be from 40 feet to over 100 feet tall. They are used to create the outdoor spaces, block undesirable views, and provide shade. This category includes the oaks, elms, pecans, and other long-lived trees. Shade trees, if properly selected and used, will do more to improve the quality and value of property than any other natural improvement.

Ornamental trees are used to add beauty, texture, color, and scale and to create focal points; they grow to be 8 feet to 30 feet tall. Trees such as Mexican plum, crabapple, hawthorn, and crape myrtle are used primarily for their spring or summer flower color. Others, such as yaupon or wax myrtle, are used for their evergreen color or berries. Some, such as Japanese maple, are used for their distinctive foliage color and interesting branching characteristics. Ornamental trees are also used as understory planting trees to help create a more natural effect.

Shrubs

Shrubs are secondary plants. They are used to form evergreen masses or large splashes of color, to provide food for wildlife, and to screen bad views. Some shrubs bloom in the spring or summer; others have lovely fall color. Shrubs should be selected on the basis of adaptability. Horticultural requirements should have priority over aesthetic considerations. If the plant won't live where planted, it doesn't matter what it looks like during its short life. Tall-growing varieties are used for background plantings and screens. Medium-height shrubs are used for masses, flower display, or evergreen color. Dwarf varieties are used for foundation planting, masses, and interesting bed shapes.

Ground Cover

Ground-cover plants are used to replace turf in areas that are too shady for grass. They are used for texture change and to create interesting bed shapes. They are low-growing, vinelike or grasslike materials that are primarily used to cover large areas. Ground covers are usually the best plant choices in heavily shady areas. Often ground covers become the last phase of the permanent garden installation and are planted after the trees have matured to shade out the grass. Ground-cover planting is considerably more expensive than turf.

Vines

Vines are usually fast, vertical-growing plants that twine around, cling to, or climb on walls, fences, posts, or overhead structures. They are used for quick shade, vertical softening, and inexpensive color display. Vines are an inexpensive way to get lots of greenery and color in a hurry. They are also quite good in smaller spaces where wide-growing shrubs and trees would be a problem. Vines can be used as annual plants and will even do well in pots.

Herbs

Herbs make wonderful landscape plants and should be used more in ornamental gardens even if gourmet cooking or home remedies are not in the plans. The traditional definition of a herb is a plant that is used for its food-enhancing flavor, medicinal properties, or fragrance. Others say that herbs are "plants that have specific uses." Herbs fall into several categories: trees, shrubs, ground covers, annuals, and perennials. Most herbs are easy to grow, especially with organic techniques.

Vegetables

Many varieties of vegetables will grow in Texas even though few are native. The harsh soil and climate here are usually a challenge. The best vegetables for use in Texas include asparagus, beans, beets, broccoli, cabbage, cantaloupe, carrots, chard, collards, corn, cucumbers, eggplant, garlic, onions, kale, lettuce, mustard, okra, black-eyed peas, peppers, potatoes, pumpkins, radishes, spinach, squash, tomatoes, turnips, and watermelon. Food crops are traditionally planted in dedicated "garden" areas, but more and more they are being interplanted with herbs and ornamental plants to increase biodiversity, interest, and production.

Fruits, Nuts, and Berries

Fruit trees do well in Texas under organic management. The best choices include apples, pears, pecans, blackberries, figs, peaches, plums, elderberries, and strawberries. Few are native to Texas, but many introductions can be grown here in healthy soil under thick mulch or cover crops. Interplanting and biodiversity are again very important.

Flowers

Everyone loves flowers. Annual and perennial flowers are an important finishing touch to any fine garden. Even a poorly designed garden with lots of flowers in bloom is impressive. Annuals are useful for that dramatic splash of single-season color, and perennials are valuable because of their faithful return to bloom year after year. Since replacing annual color each year is expensive, annuals should be concentrated to one or a few spots rather than scattered about. Perennial flowers can be used more randomly throughout the garden. Some perennials return better than others. Notice the notes in this regard under the entries for the specific plants being considered. The best location for flowering plants is an eastern exposure. Morning sun is magical, and the afternoon shade is appreciated by most annuals and perennials. Flowers, with their nectar and pollen, also provide food for beneficial insects.

Grasses

Turf is a beautiful and enjoyable part of the garden but is also where the most problems lie. To eliminate some of the problems, apply a little common sense. Grasses should be selected on horticultural requirements. For example, large sunny areas that will have active use should be planted in common Bermudagrass or buffalograss. Shady, less used areas should be planted with St. Augustine. Buffalograss should be chosen for areas that will not get much water. The hybrid tifgrasses should be used in areas that need a smooth, highly refined surface. Ryegrass and other winter grasses can be used to provide winter color and to eliminate early-spring weed problems. Winter grasses used for overseeding can also help speed soil improvement.

Weeds

There are good and bad weeds. If your lawn has lots of weeds, there's a reason. Weeds don't grow unless they're needed. Usually they are indicator plants that your soil is lousy. Many weeds provide trace minerals and help balance the chemistry of the soil. Some weeds exist because there is not enough air or organic matter in the soil, others because the soil is too wet or too dry. Most weeds can be gotten rid of by aeration, granite or lava sand, compost or other organic fertilizers, proper irrigation management, and some hand or mechanical work.

On the other hand, many so-called weeds are beautiful and shouldn't be worried about. I encourage clover, wild violets, blue-eyed grass, native anemones, dichondra, and other wildflowers. The notorious dandelion has all kinds of uses for salads, cookies, wine, and so forth. It and the fall-blooming road aster, two of the most worrisome turf-grass weeds, are controlled by good organic soil and turf management. My favorite turf is a mix of grasses, herbs, and wildflowers.

POISONOUS PLANTS

Many poisonous plants exist, and it's not reasonable to eliminate them all from our gardens. Children need to be taught which ones can be eaten and which are dangerous. The best policy is to teach them not to eat any plants without your approval and supervision.

Some of the most common poisonous plants are listed below, but many other plants have various levels of toxicity. Even many of our food crops can cause skin irritations and other toxic reactions. Oranges, lemons, grapefruit, onions, garlic, artichokes, spinach, beets, asparagus, potatoes, tomatoes, and pineapple have been known to cause dermatitis. Some common ornamental plants that cause poisoning when eaten include autumn crocus, avocado leaves, azalea, belladonna lily, black locust, boxwood, cardinal flower, Carolina jessamine, castor bean, cherry laurel, crow poison, English ivy, foxglove, fruit tree seeds, jimson weed, Kentucky coffee tree, lantana, larkspur, lily-of-the-valley, mistletoe, morning glory, narcissus, oleander, pennyroyal mint, periwinkle, pittosporum, sassafras, sweet pea, tansy, Texas mountain laurel, tomato leaves, umbrella plant, walnut (green shells), wormwood, and yew. The moral is to watch what you eat!

CREATING HEALTHY, BALANCED SOIL FOR TEXAS

Creating successful landscaping, vegetable gardens, herb gardens, or any other kind of garden is not difficult if certain basic steps are taken: (1) careful selection of native and well-adapted plant types; (2) creation of healthy, balanced beds; (3) establishment of excellent drainage solutions; (4) use of organic planting techniques; and (5) use of organic maintenance procedures. Take care of the first four steps and maintenance will be easy and enjoyable.

Soils

Plants need live, healthy, balanced soil for productive growth and protection against pests. Gardens have one or a combination of soil types, including clay, silt, loam, sandy loam, sand, gravel, and rock. Clay soils have the smallest particles, compact the most, and drain the least. Sand, gravel, and broken rock have the largest particles, compact the least, and drain the best. All soils have five major components: organic material, minerals, water, air, and living organisms. The seldom-discussed living organisms are very important and consist of earthworms, insects, plants, algae, bacteria, fungi, and other microorganisms.

Most Texas clay soils are deficient in two things—air and organic matter. Tightly structured clay soil is nutritious but needs to be loosened to improve drainage to allow air into the root zone in order to stimulate microbes and release tied-up nutrients. Microorganisms are a very important part of the healthy soil-building program and can only flourish if there is plenty of air and organic matter. Sandy soils are deficient in everything except sand. They might have enough air, but they rarely have enough organic matter and mineral nutrients.

Healthy soils must have a balance of mineral nutrients. A balanced soil should have approximately the following percentages of available nutrients: calcium—65–70 percent, magnesium—12–22 percent, potassium—4–5 percent potassium, and adequate amounts of sulfur, iron, copper, zinc, molybdenum, boron, manganese, and other trace minerals. If the mineral balance of the soil is right, the pH will be between 6.3 and 6.8. That's rarely achieved in Texas soils, but soil tests can give you a general idea of how far out of balance your soil is. One of the best soil tests is to dig out a piece of soil measuring 12 inches by 12 inches by 7 inches deep and count the earthworms. If there aren't at least ten, you need more air and more organic matter. Sound simple? It is! The structure of the soil at depths of 12 inches and 24 inches is important for drainage and the deep development of root systems, but the structure of the top 7 inches is the most important. That's where air, organic matter, microbes, earthworms, and feeder roots are concentrated.

Aeration

The value of punching holes in your lawn and beds is greatly underrated. Aeration opens holes or slits in the soil and allows air to enter and contact the roots of plants. It's a little-discussed fact that a plant can get 50 percent or more of its nutrients from the air instead of from the soil.

I know you've heard that nitrogen, phosphorous, and potassium are the three most important fertilizer elements for plants, but that's wrong. The guy originally responsible for this error is a German scientist by the name of Justus Von Liebig who led people to believe that the elements N-P-K were the most important elements and the only elements necessary for plant growth. Unfortunately, this idea has stuck and has been a major contributor to the misapplication and overfertilization of agriculture and landscape soils. The N-P-K ratio of elements is almost irrelevant in an organic program. Elements that are much more important to the soil are H-O-C (hydrogen, oxygen, and carbon). These elements are readily available from the environment in the form of water, air, and organic matter—if the soil is healthy. Microbes and earthworms will provide proper aeration over the long haul. Mechanical aeration simply speeds up the natural process at the beginning of an organic program.

Oxygen is a critical nutrient but not the only important component of air. Carbon dioxide and nitrogen, both essential to soil and plant health, exist in large quantities in the air. Many other mineral elements such as copper, boron, iron, and sulfur exist in small quantities in the air, too. These nutrients are available to plant roots and microorganisms if there is enough pore space in the soil. Oxygen gives the most noticeable response. It stimulates microbial activity and helps make other soil nutrients available to plant roots. Good aeration gives the same greening effect as that of applying nitrogen fertilizer to the soil. Look at the tall green grass around fire ant mounds. That response is primarily due to the aeration provided by the ants in the ground.

Mechanical aeration will allow air to circulate more easily and farther down into the root zone of lawn grasses, trees, shrubs, and other plants. Aeration will invigorate plants through increased root development and provide a greening effect as if a high-nitrogen fertilizer has been applied.

If the soil conditions are right, all biological systems will work according to nature's plan. Soil that is open, well-drained, rich in organic material, and moist will be loaded with microorganisms. These microscopic plants and animals feed on organic matter and minerals to create humus, humic acid, nitrogen, phosphorous, potassium, and other trace elements that are often locked up in the soil and not available to plant roots. The need to add high levels of traditional fertilizer nutrients is thus significantly reduced. Working with nature's systems in this manner will not only increase the health of all plantings but will save a significant amount of money in the long term. Soil will naturally become aerated by the addition of organic matter and the stimulation of microbial activity if given enough time. Just add compost and organic fertilizers and stop using harsh, synthetic products. However, most of us want the process to go faster and the answer is "punching holes" in the ground. These holes, rips, or tears can be punched with a stiff-tined turning fork or any other spiked tool. Such tools can be rented, but the most convenient method is to hire a landscape contractor to use a mechanical aerator to poke holes or cut slices all over the yard. Hand work usually has to be done in the beds.

Mechanical aerators are available in all shapes and sizes and with various features. Some just punch small holes, others cut slits, others remove cores, some inject water while punching holes. Some can even punch holes 12 inches deep. All these machines work. The deeper and closer together the holes, the better. Just choose a machine that fits your budget, because the cost varies greatly. I have personally used machines made by Bluebird, Torro, Ryan, Air-Way, and even some homemade machines, and they all do the job. The object is getting as much air into the soil as possible. When that happens, microbe populations increase, natural nitrogen cycles function properly, and nature's wonderful systems are all set in motion. It's not necessary to understand these systems in great detail—just to respect their presence and let them work for you.

Soil Amendments

Texas soils need some very basic amendments besides air. Here are some of the most important.

Sulfur is a needed amendment if your soil is too high in calcium, as most North Texas soils are. If calcium is too high, magnesium will usually be too low and most of the trace minerals will be tied up and unavailable to plants. Granulated, elemental sulfur is available and easy to apply. For a more complete sulfur fertilizer, a natural material called Sul-Po-Mag or K-Mag can be used. It contains sulfur, potassium, and magnesium.

Short of air, *organic matter* is the most important soil amendment. It helps balance the chemical and physical nature of the soil. The best organic matter for bed preparation is compost. Compost can be made from anything that was once alive. Everything that's alive is going to die, and everything that dies is going to rot. Organic matter provides humus and aids in the loosening of the soil by adding particles larger than the soil particles and by providing food for microorganisms. About 85 percent of a plant's roots are found in the first 7 inches of soil. Deeper roots are mainly in search of water and trace minerals. Therefore, there's no need to work organic material into the soil very deeply. My least favorite organic matter for bed preparation is peat moss. It doesn't last long, has little nutrient value, is the most

expensive organic material, and must be purchased from sources that are several hundred miles outside Texas and shipped across the United States. Use of peat moss also poses an environmental problem related to digging out the bogs or wetlands in Canada.

Rock powders such as greensand, glacial rock powder, granite sand, lava sand, zeolite, and soft rock phosphate provide the soil with a natural source of major elements and trace minerals. Rock powders from volcanic sources are the best because they increase the exchange capacity and energy in the soil. Lava sand is usually the most effective volcanic material.

Organic fertilizers have low levels of the elements we hear about most often. Nitrogen, phosphorous, and potassium are by far the most commonly recommended nutrients. For thirty years or more, the recommended analysis for fertilizers used in Texas has been a 3-1-2 ratio, such as 15-5-10. Those numbers represent 15 percent nitrogen, 5 percent phosphorous, and 10 percent potash. That's supposedly changing now to a 1-0-0 ratio, which is a move in the right direction. The theory of the new fertilizer recommendation is that potassium and phosphorus are supposedly not needed since our soils already have so much of these elements. A great problem with this theory is that although a soil test might show high levels of phosphorus and potassium, these nutrients may not be available to plants because of insufficient amounts of soil air, humus, and rock minerals.

Organiphobes say that plants can't tell the difference between nitrogen from an organic source and nitrogen from a synthetic source. In the final entry into plant use, that may be true, but there are other considerations. Plants need more than nitrogen, phosphorus, and potash. They probably need all the ninety-two natural mineral elements. Why? Because if we analyze healthy plant tissue, we can find traces of most or all of these elements. Guess what? Most natural organic fertilizers contain most or all the ninety-two elements. That's because these plant foods come from plants. Even if the fertilizer is animal manure, the cow first ate grass or the chicken ate the grain. The famous elements N-P-K are important, but so are carbon, hydrogen, oxygen, sulfur, magnesium, copper, cobalt, sodium, boron, molybdenum, zinc, and so on. Most of these minerals are present in composted manure fertilizers. A balance of all the necessary mineral nutrients is also present in meals such as alfalfa, cottonseed, soybean, or fish.

To show how unimportant high N-P-K numbers are, look at earthworm castings. Possibly nature's most perfectly balanced and most effective fertilizer, they have an analysis of less than 1-1-1. Some organic contractors use nothing but earthworm castings, and their gardens are always green and beautiful and the flowers are showy. Compost, nature's own fertilizer, usually has an analysis of around 1-1-1. Keep this a secret for now, but plant roots can absorb more than basic elements. They can absorb large complex molecules and even chunks of organic matter. To answer the fools who say this is impossible, remind them that herbicides have very large complex molecules. Ask them how the plant can absorb those chunks. Expect a pregnant pause.

What's wrong with synthetic fertilizers? Most contain little or no carbon, no organic matter, and few if any trace minerals. They do have high levels of salts, including nitrates, which can inhibit or destroy beneficial soil microorganisms. High-nitrogen, water-soluble fertilizers usually work too fast and glut plants with excessive amounts of nutrients. Nitrogen glut leads to thin cell walls and great susceptibility to insect and disease attack, as these unhealthy plants aren't able to withstand drought, cold stress, and salt effects. Eating too much white bread and processed sugar creates the same kind of nutrient imbalance in the human body. To metabolize raw sugar, minerals and vitamins must be borrowed from the body. When the balance is compromised, people are more susceptible to colds, flu, and more serious diseases. Just a little side note, but it's all related. Health is health in plants and animals.

Plants can get enough nitrogen easily. Nitrogen is plentiful in a properly functioning natural system. Air is almost 80 percent nitrogen. Many of the microbes in the soil can grab nitrogen right out of the air in the soil and make it available to plants. That's why aeration is so important. Nitrogen is also released in the soil by the feeding of microorganisms on organic matter. That's why compost is so important.

PLANTING PROPERLY

Bed Preparation

It doesn't matter whether you are about to plant annuals, perennials, herbs, flowers, or vegetables—the formula is the same. The planting bed should be a mixture of compost, native soil, and rock minerals. To prepare beds properly, simply mix 4 to 8 inches of compost into the existing soil and create a raised bed. Use 4 inches of compost for ground cover, 6 inches for shrubs, and 8 inches for roses and other perennials. Native plants can use less. That's all you have to do, but there are some additions that can speed up the establishment of your new plants. It's okay to add 10 to 20 pounds of cottonseed meal or other organic fertilizers. Be careful because you can easily overdo it if you aren't careful. Too much fertilizer, even organic fertilizer, can kill plants. Too much of anything is a bad idea. Add lava or granite sand at the rate of 40 to 80 pounds per thousand square feet for additional help.

Mulches

After the plants have been installed, finish the project by recreating the forest floor. Mulch it. Spread a thick layer of organic mulch over the soil. Bare soil should not be visible around the new planting. Coarse-textured, shredded hardwood bark or shredded native tree trimmings are the best choices, but any rough-textured organic mulch will work. Pine bark and peat moss are the only two choices I don't recommend because they are easily washed or blown away. My favorites are coarse-shredded mulch for annuals and perennials and partially completed compost for roses and vegetables. Other available mulches include grain straw, pine needles, decomposed sawdust, cottonseed hulls, pecan hulls, cedar flakes, and wood chips. Organic mulch keeps the soil cool during the hot summer months, prevents weed growth, and slows the evaporation of moisture from the soil. The most important function of mulch is keeping the microbes and earthworms alive and active at the surface of the soil. I don't like plastics, fabrics, or gravel as mulch. They destroy the natural interface between the mulch and soil surface where the microbes and earthworms stir things together to create a perfect soil.

A gardener once told me she was mostly organic but still had to spray chemicals for spider mites. After trying to fool me for a while that she was doing everything organic and still had the mite pests, she admitted that her garden soil was bare—not covered with mulch. Tilling organic matter into the soil is not mulching. Covering the surface with a blanket of coarse-textured organic matter is mulching. *This is not an option.* Bare soil must be covered with a permanent layer of natural mulch. The only exception is when planting seeds. In that case, pull the mulch back, plant the seed, then push the mulch back up around the plants as they grow. To sum up: install new material in native soil enriched with lots of compost, mulch all bare soil, and use organic fertilizers as often as the soil needs help. This is the basic organic program. It's that simple.

Timing

One of the biggest misconceptions is that landscape installation should be done in the spring. That is the worst time. Contractors and nurseries are busier in the spring and early summer than at any other time of the year.

Landscape installation is best done in the fall and winter. If plants are installed in the fall, they will develop root growth through the winter and be more vigorous in the spring.

Trees should be transplanted in the fall or winter. For best results, new trees should be planted then, too. Trees planted in the spring, and certainly in the summer, will just sit there and wait for the next season to really start to grow. Container-grown trees can be planted with good results year round.

There is, of course, some danger of freeze damage to small shrubs, ground covers, and grasses when planted in fall and winter. You may prefer to install these small plants in the spring. Trees and large shrubs are not usually susceptible to freeze damage. Planting in the fall or winter offers roots a chance to start growing before the foliage emerges in the spring. It's usually worth the risk.

Most plants can be planted any month of the year if several precautions are taken. When transporting plants in an open vehicle in the hot part of summer, cover them to protect them from the sun and wind and to keep the root ball moist. Always dampen the planting beds prior to planting. During freezing weather don't leave plants out of the ground without protecting the roots from possible freeze damage. Store plants in shady areas prior to planting. Always keep the plants moist and mulched during freezing weather. Once in the ground, well-adapted plants will normally survive a freeze. In mild spring or fall weather it's easy to forget to keep containers or newly planted material moist, so check them often but don't overwater.

Tree Planting

Trees are by far the most important landscape element. There's only one catch. If the trees aren't healthy and don't grow, they won't do you any good at all. To grow properly, trees must be planted properly. Since many tree-planting procedures are horticulturally incorrect, they are a substantial waste of money. My recommendations for tree planting have developed over years of carefully studying many planting techniques and trying to understand what works and what doesn't. Nature has been my teacher and as usual shows the right way.

It was 1976 when I first saw trees planted correctly. I'm sure they had been planted right before—I just hadn't seen it done. I had been commissioned to design the landscaping for a corporation's facility in Addison, Texas. The budget was tight and the site was large and uninteresting. Using the excess soil from the building excavation, we created free-flowing berms to add interest and provide sites for trees to be planted above the native white limestone, not realizing at the time the importance of the built-in drainage system the berms provided. An old friend, Cody Carter, planted all the trees on that job. Since that time, I've watched those trees, and I've watched trees on other projects planted with all kinds of techniques. Here's what I learned.

1. Dig an Ugly Hole

Tree holes should be dug exactly the same depth or slightly less than the height of the ball. Don't guess—measure the height of the ball. Dig a rough-sided hole instead of a slick-sided or glazed hole such as those made by a tree spade or auger. Slick-walled tree holes greatly restrict root penetration into the surrounding soil and limit proper root growth. A saucer-shaped hole that is narrow at the bottom but at least three times wider than the root ball at the soil surface is the best.

2. Run a Perk Test

If time allows, fill the hole with water and wait until the next day. If the water doesn't drain away overnight, the soil doesn't drain well enough. If that's the case, move the tree to another location or improve the drainage by installing a drain line full of gravel running from the tree to a lower point on the site. Another draining method that sometimes works is to dig a pier hole down from the bottom of the hole into a different soil type and fill the hole with gravel. A sump from the top of the ball down to the bottom of the ball does little if any good. Positive drainage is critical, so don't take shortcuts here.

3. Backfill with Existing Soil

Place the tree in the center of the hole so that the top of the ball is perfectly flush or slightly higher than the surrounding grade. Backfill with the soil that came from the hole—nothing else. This is a critical point. Don't add sand, foreign soil, organic matter, or fertilizer into the backfill. Adding amendments to the backfill like peat moss, sand, or foreign soils will not only waste money but hurt the establishment and growth of the tree. Roots need to start growing in the native soil from the beginning. When the hole is dug in solid rock, topsoil from the same area should be used. Some native rock mixed into the backfill is beneficial. Compost worked into the top 7 inches (but no deeper) of backfill is beneficial.

Settle the backfill with water. Don't ever do something dopey like tamping or stomping on the backfill. Settle the soil naturally with water. Water the backfill very carefully, making sure to get rid of all air pockets. By the way, putting gravel in the bottom of the hole is a total waste of money.

When planting balled and burlapped plants, leave the burlap on the sides of the ball but loosen the burlap at the trunk and remove the burlap from the top of the ball. Remove any nylon or plastic covering or string. Artificial materials won't decompose and can girdle the truck and the roots as the plant grows. Wire mesh should be removed to avoid root girdling because wire does not break down very fast in our alkaline soils. When planting from plastic containers, carefully remove plants and tear the outside roots if they have become root bound and are adhering to the container. Never leave plants in containers. Bare-rooted, balled and burlapped, and container plant materials should all be planted the same way. When planting bare-rooted plants, it is critical to keep the roots moist during the transportation and planting process.

4. Do Not Wrap or Stake

Trunks of newly planted trees should not be wrapped. It wastes money, looks unattractive, harbors insects, and leaves the bark weak when removed. Tree wrapping is similar to leaving a bandage on your finger too long. It leaves softened, weakened bark. If you're worried about the unlikely possibility of sunburn, it's much better to paint the trunk with a diluted white latex paint. Use a whitewash just like Tom Sawyer did and let the tree slowly and naturally grow it off. If the tree is weak or has damage to the trunk, spray the wound with hydrogen peroxide and leave it exposed to air.

In general, staking newly planted trees is goofy. This antiquated procedure is almost always unnecessary if the tree has been planted properly and has an earth ball of the proper size: at least 9 inches for each inch of trunk diameter. Staking most trees is a waste of money and detrimental to proper trunk development. In rare circumstances (sandy soil, tall evergreen trees, roof gardens, etc.) where the tree needs to be staked for a while, connect the guy wires as low on the trunk as possible and remove the stakes as soon as possible. Never leave them on more than one growing season. Temporary staking should be done with strong wire and metal eyebolts screwed into the trunk. Staking should be a last resort—it is unsightly and expensive, adds to maintenance costs, and restricts the tree's ability to move with the wind

and develop tensile strength in the trunk. It can also cause damage to the delicate cambium layer. Always remove all tags that the nurseries attached.

5. Do Not Overprune

Limb pruning is not necessary to compensate for the loss of roots during transplanting or planting. Most trees fare much better if all the limbs and foliage are left intact. The more foliage, the more food produced to build the root system. The health of the root system is the key to the overall health of the tree. The only trees that seem to respond positively to thinning at the time of transplanting are field-collected live oak and yaupon holly. Container-grown trees definitely need no pruning and deciduous trees never need to be thinned.

6. Mulch the Top of the Ball

After planting, create the "forest floor" over the planting hole. Mulch the top of the ball with 1 inch of compost and then 3 inches of mulch. This step is important in lawns and beds. Don't plant grass around the base of the tree until the tree is established. Water rings, which are soil dikes sometimes used to hold water on the tree ball, are unnecessary and can even become a problem to get rid of after the tree is established.

Shrub, Ground Cover, and Vine Planting

Good soil preparation is necessary when planting all shrubs, ground covers, and vines. Soils in Texas have some common deficiencies. Clay soils have a lack of organic matter and a lack of air, causing drainage problems, as well as a lack of oxygen in the root zone. Sandy soils usually have plenty of air but are severely deficient in organic matter and mineral nutrients. Both are deficient in living organisms. The following soil preparation steps will overcome these limitations:

- Scrape away all weeds and grass, including underground stems called rhizomes. A cut 2 inches deep will usually remove all the reproductive parts of the existing vegetation, even Bermudagrass. No excavation should be done in bare soil areas. *Do not rototill prior to removing grass from the planting area.* Tilling will drive the reproductive pieces down into the ground where they will become a weed problem forever.
- If needed to establish the proper grade, add topsoil to all beds to within 2 inches of the adjacent finished grade. Use native topsoil, similar to that which is on the site. I do not

recommend using herbicides to kill grass and weeds prior to excavation—ever!

- Cover areas to be planted with a 4- to 6-inch blanket of compost; then apply lava sand at the rate of 40 to 80 pounds per thousand square feet and a 100 percent organic fertilizer at the rate of 10 to 20 pounds per thousand square feet. If cotton bur compost is used, cut the fertilizer rate in half.
- Till the amendments and the existing topsoil together to a depth of 6 to 8 inches—a little deeper is okay but never deeper than 10 inches. Driving organic matter below that level can cause improper breakdown and root damage.
- After thoroughly tilling all beds, rake smooth to eliminate undulations. Put a flat top on the bed and slope the edges down to slightly lower than the adjacent grade, forming a little ditch to aid drainage.
- Moisten beds before planting, especially in hot weather. Do not plant in dry soil!
- Plants should be watered by sticking the hose down beside the ball and soaking thoroughly. Always soak root balls before planting. Plant wet root balls into moist soil. Transplant shock and death from dry roots will be eliminated if you do this.

Azalea, Dogwood, Camellia, and Rhododendron Planting

These are acid-loving plants and most of our Texas soils certainly aren't that. Here's what to do if you insist on trying to grow these high-maintenance plants:

- Excavate and remove existing soil to a depth of 4 to 6 inches. Or better still, pile the bed mix on top of the existing soil. The bed should be at least 30 inches wide for each row of plants.
- Build the bed with a mixture of 50 percent compost, 50 percent shredded hardwood bark, copperas (one pound per cubic yard), Epsom salts (one pound per cubic yard), and granulated sulfur (one pound per cubic yard). Place the mixture in the bed area to a depth of 16 inches. Be sure to thoroughly saturate this mixture in a tub or wheelbarrow prior to placing it in the bed. Peat moss can be added to the mixture, but it isn't necessary. Adding a small amount of native soil to the mixture is helpful to introduce microorganisms.
- Mound the beds so that the finished grade is at least 18 inches above the adjacent grade.

- Tear or cut the potbound roots before planting. This is very important. Without this step, the roots will never break away from the ball and the plant often dies.
- Soak each plant in a washtub or bucket filled with a 1 percent solution of liquid seaweed or natural apple cider vinegar. (Natural apple cider vinegar is made from apples. Apple cider "flavored" vinegar is distilled vinegar that has been artificially colored and flavored.)

Note: If you live in an acid-soil area, simply add 8 inches of quality compost and alfalfa meal at a rate of 30 pounds per thousand square feet and plant away. In both cases, remember to add 2 to 3 inches of organic matter to the beds every year in late winter to replace that which has decayed. If this is done, the beds probably won't have to be rebuilt more often than every seven years.

Annual, Perennial, Herb, and Vegetable Planting

Flower beds should be built the same as those for shrubs and ground covers with the addition of a little more organic material. Use at least 6 inches of compost. These beds should also be mounded or raised more than other plant beds if possible. Raised flower beds are critical for proper drainage. Flowers are often planted in the same beds as the shrubs and ground covers. Some annuals and perennials can tolerate this, but gardeners would have greater success if they would do one simple thing—raise or mound the flower beds to give the root zone more air. Flower beds can simply be mounded 6 to 9 inches by adding compost. Mixing at least some of the existing soil into the concoction is a good idea. Bulbs should always be planted in prepared beds and will do better with a tablespoon of bone meal, earthworm castings, or colloidal phosphate tossed into the bottom of the hole. Plants will be larger, longer lasting, and more showy if soaked in a 1 percent solution of Agrispon, Medina, or other biostimulants such as seaweed prior to planting. A small handful of Epsom salts tossed in the planting hole can also help flower and fruit production because most soils in Texas are deficient in magnesium and sulfur.

Transplanting

Established plants should be transplanted only during the dormant season. Fall is the best time, and winter is the second-best time. Large plants are harder to transplant than small ones. Smaller plants that have not developed an extensive root system can be moved during the growing season if watered-in immediately. Relocated plants should be installed with the same techniques as those used for new plants, as explained previously.

Mulching

All bare soil around newly planted plants should be covered with a layer of mulch. Nature doesn't allow bare soil and neither should gardeners. Mulching should be done immediately after planting is completed. Acceptable mulches are shredded tree trimmings, shredded hardwood bark, pine needles, coarse compost, hay, cocoa shells, pecan shells, or shredded cypress bark. Mulch should usually be at least 2 inches deep, but if plants are large enough, 3 to 4 inches is better. Mulching helps hold moisture in the beds, controls weeds, and keeps the soil temperature at the proper temperature—around 84 degrees. I don't use or recommend plastic sheets as mulch. The plant's root systems will cook from the heat buildup. Neither do I recommend weed fabrics or gravel as mulches. Nothing compares with a thick layer of good organic material placed in direct contact with the soil. Add about 1 inch of compost and 3 inches of mulch to all planting beds every year. Most soil structure and nutrition problems can be solved with good organic matter, specifically compost. Grass clippings left on the turf will provide the organic matter for lawn areas.

Wildflower Planting

In the past, most wildflowers were planted by scattering the seed over bare ground and crossing your fingers. As a result, few gardeners were having success with wildflowers. Here are some methods that should improve your chances.

Plant wildflowers on bare ground or in heavily scalped and aerated grassy areas. Areas with buffalograss are the best. Remove all weeds and grass tops by scalping and loosen any heavily compacted areas by mechanical aeration—no need to remove rock. A light rototilling (an inch deep) is the best bed preparation in many cases. Shallow tilling removes the top growth but leaves the roots in place, providing a long-lasting diet of organic matter. Soil amendments and fertilizers are not needed other than an optional light application of a 100 percent organic fertilizer at the rate of 5 pounds per thousand square feet.

Treat the seed prior to planting with a 1 percent solution of Agrispon, Bioform, Medina, or other biostimulant such as seaweed or apple cider vinegar. Small seeds can be spread on newspaper and misted with the solution; larger seeds can be soaked in the liquid. The seeds should then be allowed to dry to make them easier to handle. Apply the seed at the recommended rate, making sure to get good soil-seed contact by lightly raking the seed into the soil. Spring-blooming wildflowers should be planted from late summer to early fall the previous year in order to take advantage of the fall rains and to copy nature's techniques.

Apply supplemental irrigation in the fall and in the spring if the weather is unseasonably dry. If rains are normal, no watering is needed.

Grass Planting

Grass-planting techniques can be quite simple or very complicated and a huge waste of money. If you follow these simple techniques, your lawn establishment will be enjoyable and affordable.

Preparation should include the removal of weed tops, debris, and rocks over 2 inches in diameter from the surface of the soil. Rocks within the soil are no problem because they help drainage. Till to a depth of 1 inch and rake topsoil into a smooth grade. Deep rototilling is unnecessary and a waste of money unless the soil is heavily compacted. When planting grass seed, the addition of organic material is beneficial, but strong fertilizer is unnecessary and can even hurt germination. Only on solid rock areas is the addition of native topsoil needed. Imported foreign topsoil is a waste of money and can cause a perched (trapped) water table, the introduction of weeds, and other lawn problems. Mild organic fertilizers and amendments such as earthworm castings (10 pounds per thousand square feet) and lava sand (40 pounds per thousand square feet) can be helpful at planting time. Erosion protection material, such as jute mesh, should be placed on the soil in sloped areas prior to planting. Follow the manufacturer's recommendations for installation by overlapping, tucking it into the soil at the edges, and pinning it down carefully. Some people recommend and use herbicides to kill weeds prior to planting. I don't. These chemicals can be hazardous and damage the soil biology.

Planting grass by hydromulching (a water, paper, seed, and fertilizer mix) should be done so that the seed is placed in direct contact with the soil. The seed should be broadcast on the bare soil first and the hydromulch, if used, blown on top of the seed. One of the worst mistakes I see in grass planting is mixing the seed in the hydromulch slurry of paper and fertilizer. This causes the seed to germinate in the mulch, which is suspended above the soil, so many of the seeds are lost from dehydration.

Seeding Rates for Wildflowers

Common Name	Botanical Name	Flower Color	Rate per 1,000 sq.ft.	Rate per acre
Black-eyed Susan	*Rudbeckia hirta*	yellow	5–10 oz.	3 lbs.
Bluebonnet	*Lupinus texensis*	blue	1–2 lbs.	30 lbs.
Butterfly weed	*Asclepias tuberosa*	orange	1/2 lb.	10 lbs.
Coreopsis	*Coreopsis lanceolata*	yellow	6–12 oz.	10 lbs.
Coreopsis	*Coreopsis tinctoria*	red and yellow	5–10 oz.	2 lbs.
Cosmos	*Cosmos* spp.	multicolors	1/2 lb.	15 lbs.
Crimson clover	*Trifolium incarnatum*	crimson	1/2–1 lb.	15–25 lbs.
White clover	*Trifolium repens*	white	1/4–1/2 lb.	5–10 lbs.
Engelmann daisy	*Engelmannia pinnatifida*	yellow	1/4–1/2 lb.	5 lbs.
Evening primrose	*Oenothera* spp.	multicolors	3/4–2 oz.	1/2 lb.
Gaillardia	*Gaillardia* spp.	red/yellow	1/2 lb.	10 lbs.
Gayfeather	*Liatris pycnostachya*	purple	1/2 lb.	10 lbs.
Horsemint	*Monarda citriodora*	lavender	5–10 oz.	3 lbs.
Indian blanket	*Gaillardia pulchella*	red and yellow	1/2 lb.	10 lbs.
Indian paintbrush	*Castilleja indivisa*	orange	1/2–1 oz.	1/4 lb.
Indian paintbrush	*Castilleja purpurea*	purple	1/2–1 oz.	1/4 lb.
Maximilian sunflower	*Helianthus maximiliani*	yellow	5–10 oz.	2 lbs.
Mexican hat	*Ratibida columnaris*	red and yellow	5–10 oz.	2 lbs.
Oxeye daisy	*Chrysanthemum leucanthemum*	white	1/4–1/2 lb.	5 lbs.
Purple coneflower	*Echinacea purpurea*	purple	1/2 lb.	12 lbs.
Snow-on-the-mountain	*Euphorbia marginata*	white	5–10 oz.	3 lbs.
Tahoka daisy	*Machaeranthera tanacetifolia*	purple	1/4–1/2 lb.	5 lbs.
Verbena	*Verbena* spp.	purple	1/4–1/2 lb.	6 lbs.
White yarrow	*Achillea millefolium*	white	2 1/2–5 lb.	1 1/2 lbs.
Gold yarrow	*Achillea filipendulina*	yellow	3/4–2 lb.	1/2 lbs.

Night temperatures must be 65–70 degrees for Bermudagrass or buffalograss to germinate and no lower than 40 degrees in the fall and winter for fescue, rye, and other cool-season grasses. After spreading the seed, thoroughly soak the ground and lightly water the seeded area enough to keep it moist until germination is complete. Fertilize with a 100 percent organic fertilizer sometime before the first mowing. As the seed germinates, watch for bare spots. Reseed these bare areas immediately. Continue the light watering until the grass has solidly covered the area. At this time, begin the regular watering and maintenance program.

Spot sodding is done by countersinking 4- by 4-inch squares into the ground flush with the existing grade 12 to 14 inches apart after grading, then smoothing and leveling the soil. Organic fertilizer should be applied after planting at a rate of 20 pounds per thousand square feet. Regular maintenance and watering should be started at this time. This is not a planting procedure I highly recommend because it is slow to cover and often results in an uneven, weedy lawn.

To solid squares of sod should be laid joint to joint after first fertilizing the ground with a 100 percent organic fertilizer at a rate of 20 pounds per thousand square feet. Grading, leveling, and smoothing prior to planting is very important. The joints between the blocks of sod can be filled with compost to give an even more finished look.

Tifgrasses (TexTurf 10, Tifway 419, Tifgreen 328, and Tifdwarf) are dwarf forms of common Bermudagrass. They should be planted by solid sodding or hydromulching sprigs with the same procedures as used for planting Bermudagrass seed. Tifgrasses are sterile hybrids and expensive to maintain. I don't recommend these grasses for homeowners.

Cool-season grasses such as fescue, ryegrass, bentgrass, and bluegrass should be planted for best results in late September or October, although they can be planted anytime during the winter when the temperature is above 40 degrees. In all cases, the newly applied lawn seed should be watered regularly until the grass has grown to the point of covering the ground.

Seeding Rates for Grasses

Common Name	Botanical Name	Lbs. per 1,000 sq.ft.	Lbs. per acre
Barley	*Hordeum vulgare*	4–7	80–100
Bentgrass	*Agrostis* spp.	1 1/2–2	25–30
Bermudagrass, common	*Cynodon dactylon*	2	20–40
Blue grama	*Bouteloua gracilis*	1/2–2	15–20
Bluegrass, Texas	*Poa arachnifera*	1/2–2	15–20
Bluestem, big	*Andropogon gerardii*	1/2–2	15–20
Bluestem, little	*Schizachyrium scoparium*	1/2–2	15–20
Bluestem, bushy	*Andropogon glomeratus*	1/2–3	15–20
Bluestem, silver	*Andropogon saccharoides*	1/2–2	15–20
Buffalograss	*Buchloe dactyloides*	1/2–4	15–40
Centipedegrass	*Eromochloa ophiuroides*	2–4	40–50
Common reed	*Phragmites australis*	Division only	Division only
Fescue, tall	*Festuca* spp.	4–7	80–100
Gamagrass, eastern	*Tripsacum dactyloides*	1/2–2	15–20
Indiangrass	*Sorghastrum nutans*	1/2–3	15–20
Lovegrass, sand	*Eragrostis trichodes*	1/2–2	15–20
Lovegrass, weeping	*Eragrostis curvula*	1/2–2	15–20
Muhly, Gulf	*Muhlenbergia capillaris*	1/2–2	15–20
Muhly, Lindheimer's	*Muhlenbergia lindheimeri*	1/2–2	15–20
Oats	*Avena sativa*	4–7	80–100
Rye, cereal (elbon)	*Secale cereale*	4	80–100
Ryegrass, annual	*Lolium multiflorum*	3–5	50
Ryegrass, perennial	*Lolium perenne*	3–5	50
Seaoats, inland	*Chasmanthium latifolium*	1/2–2	15–20
Sideoats grama	*Bouteloua curtipendula*	1/2–2	15–20
Switchgrass, lowland	*Panicum virgatum*	1/2–2	15–20
Switchgrass, upland	*Panicum, virgatum*	1/2–2	15–20
Wheat	*Triticum* spp.	4–7	80–100
Wildrye, Canada	*Elymus canadensis*	1/2–2	15–20

Installation Mistakes

Here are some of the worst installation mistakes I see on both residential and commercial projects:

1. Planting trees improperly by digging small, smooth-sided holes, backfilling with soft foreign materials, setting trees too low, and staking and wrapping trees.
2. Planting too many plants of the same type. Biodiversity is essential, but many gardeners plant large masses and straight lines of plants. Using many different kinds of plants encourages many different kinds of beneficial insects and other helpful critters.
3. Planting plants too deep in the soil. This also causes a smothering of the root system and sometimes rots the plant stem or trunk.
4. Failing to cover all bare soil with mulch.
5. Failing to provide proper drainage.
6. Contaminating the soil with toxic insecticides, herbicides, and fungicides.
7. Wasting money on unnecessary bed preparation ingredients like peat moss, concrete sand, and artificial amendments.

PLANT MAINTENANCE

Landscape and garden maintenance can be easy or hard. In fact, it can take several routes. Poorly designed gardens can look good if maintained well. Conversely, well-designed gardens that are poorly maintained will usually look bad. The design of any landscape or garden, large or small, must include maintenance considerations in the early planning stages. Otherwise, it won't be a long-term success.

Unlike buildings or other structures, which look

their best the day they are finished, gardens look good when finished but will change every year and improve every year, or so we hope. Gardens, as opposed to architecture, are never static. Gardens are dynamic, complex living organisms that not only change seasonally but continue to grow and mature every year.

The best maintenance program is one that is as natural and affordable as possible, requires the least amount of time, and provides beauty.

Maintaining Trees

Protection of Existing Trees

Trees are the most important landscape elements and need the most carefully planned maintenance of anything in the garden. Protecting and staying away from tree root systems during construction and leaving the grade and the drainage pattern (both surface and underground) intact are essential to a tree's health. Although a tree's roots grow out far beyond the drip line of the foliage, protecting the area from drip line to trunk will give most trees a pretty good chance of survival. Installing a physical barrier such as a wire or wood fence is the only method that keeps automobile and foot traffic, fill soil, and construction debris off the tree's root system. Buying new trees is expensive. They are a major investment, so I recommend that you work hard to keep any existing ones alive. The secret? Leave 'em alone.

Pruning

In general, people prune trees too often and too heavily. Some trees need more pruning than others, but most need very little. For example, many shade trees such as bur oak and Chinese pistachio require almost no pruning. Some fruit trees such as peaches need regular pruning to encourage fruit production and to make harvesting easier, but ornamental trees rarely need more than the removal of dead wood and limbs that are in the way or growing into the roof. When a tree is drastically thinned, artificially lifted, or severely cut back, it hurts the tree. A good rule of thumb for trimming trees is to try to copy nature's pruning techniques. Pruning a tree into an artificial shape is a waste of money, has ugly results, and is usually detrimental to the health of the plant. If you can't decide whether to trim or not, don't! Remember that any cut into the tissue of a plant hurts the plant. This is especially true for trees.

A common pruning mistake is the lifting or raising of the bottom of the plant by removing lower limbs. Low limbs add grace and beauty to the tree, and removing them unnecessarily can cause stress

and lead to other health-related problems. Lifting doesn't necessarily allow more light to reach the grass or other plantings beneath. If the top of the tree has not been thinned, a solid canopy still exists and no significant increase of light to the ground plane has been created. It's best to remove only dead or damaged limbs, limbs that are rubbing, limbs with mistletoe or disease, and, in certain cases, enough of the canopy to allow shafts of sunlight all the way through the tree to the plants growing beneath.

Pruning cuts should never be made flush to the tree trunk. The small stub, the branch collar, should always be preserved. The branch collar is the part of the tree that allows the cut to heal naturally.

Pruning paint should *not* be used. Damaged living tissue will always heal faster if exposed to fresh air. Pruning paint can seal moisture and disease spores into a protected environment and actually increase the spread of problems. Some arborists still recommend painting the cuts on oak trees in oak wilt areas. I'm not sold on that idea. It's better to simply avoid pruning oaks in the spring and early summer when the insect that spreads the disease is active. If you must prune in the spring, go ahead and take their advice but use natural shellac for the pruning paint.

Cabling is another very expensive technique that in most cases is unnecessary and detrimental to the tree. Cabling simply moves the stress point from one position to another. Cables are unsightly and create an artificial tension in the tree that can actually lead to more ice breakage instead of less. The only time cabling should be used is to keep a weak crotch from splitting. Proper cabling runs horizontally between vertical limbs and keeps them from splitting the tree in half.

Aeration

Mechanical aeration of the root systems of trees is done while aerating the lawn or planting beds under the trees. Hand aerators are useful when working in a tree's root system. Another good tool is a piece of pipe connected to a water hose. With this device, you can water and aerate at the same time by pushing the pipe into the soil to a depth of 10 to 12 inches. Mechanical aeration is no longer needed when the soil is healthy and alive with earthworms and microbes. Aeration would be used again if compaction takes place for any reason.

Mulching

Trees should be mulched at the time of planting, and additional mulch should be added each fall unless a green cover crop exists. Use a 3- to 4-inch layer of mulch over the root ball to prevent the competition of grass roots, maintain soil moisture, and keep the soil temperature at the proper level. If trees are planted in beds, the entire bed should be mulched.

Fertilizing

The rate of fertilizer should be based on the surface area to be fertilized rather than the diameter of the tree trunk. Organic programs feed the soil rather than the plants, so the amount of fertilizer is related to the amount of area, not the number or kind of plants. I normally fertilize once in the early spring and again in early summer with a 100 percent organic fertilizer such as Garden-Ville Soil Food or GreenSense at the rate of 20 pounds per thousand square feet. A third application is sometimes needed in the fall. Fertilizer should be spread on the surface of the soil rather than put in deep holes around the trees. Fertilizing after thoroughly aerating the root system is a good idea. The root system of trees is much more shallow than most people realize. Most of the roots are located in the top 12 to 18 inches of soil, and, as noted earlier, most of the feeder roots are in the top 7 inches of soil. Lava sand broadcast under trees at the rate of 40 to 80 pounds per thousand square feet is also very beneficial.

Watering

Watering is the most variable function in the maintenance puzzle due to soil type, climate, plant varieties, and sun exposure. If trees are planted properly, very little supplemental watering is needed except during the heat of the summer. The idea is to keep the ground at a relatively even moisture level rather than subject plants to a wet-dry, wet-dry cycle. Newly planted trees should be thoroughly soaked every other week or so in the hot growing season and once a month in the cooler seasons. This watering should be done in addition to regular watering of the grass areas or planting areas surrounding the trees. Obviously, rain will alter this schedule. Once trees are established, a regular watering of the surrounding planting areas is normally enough. During periods of extreme drought, the soaking procedure may need to be used again.

Pest Control

Spraying for insects and diseases on a preventative basis wastes money and adds unnecessarily to the contamination of our environment. Sprays for insects and diseases should be applied only after pests are seen, and environmentally safe alternatives to toxic poisons should be used. Aphids, for example, can be controlled with a strong blast of water and the release of ladybugs. Diatomaceous earth and pyrethrum products are excellent for general insect control. Horticultural oil is another good choice. *Bacillus thuringiensis* (Bt) is an environmentally safe control for cutworms, loopers, and caterpillars. Ladybugs (ladybird beetles), green lacewings, and trichogramma wasps provide excellent control of aphids, spider mites, worms, and other small insects. Beneficial insects should be released at dusk after wetting all the foliage or at daybreak when dew is on the foliage. Most fungal problems can be controlled by spraying with baking soda spray or by applying beneficial microbes to the soil.

Harsh chemical pesticides will probably continue to be used, at least for a while, but smart gardeners are switching to the natural alternatives. Besides being extremely harmful to people and pets, strong chemicals also kill the beneficial microorganisms, earthworms, insects, lizards, frogs, and birds in the garden.

Weed Control

Herbicide application under any tree is stupid. Let me rephrase that. If you use herbicides under trees, you're a nincompoop! Improvement of soil health, hand removal, and mulch on all bare soil are usually the only measures needed. Strong vinegar can be sprayed full strength on suckers to knock them back if necessary. Hand removal is better. A mulch layer on the roots of trees is the most important ingredient in the management of healthy trees. All trees, ornamental and food crop trees, originally grew in a forest and had a thick layer of mulch over their roots. That's what we should continue to do.

Maintaining Shrubs

Pruning

No pruning is required at the time of planting, and yearly pruning should be kept to a minimum, leaving the plants as soft and natural as possible. Pick-pruning of shrubs, although somewhat time-consuming, has always been my favorite method. It is the careful removal of individual limbs versus shearing of the entire plant. Due to time constraints, a combination of light shearing and careful pick-pruning is usually the most practical. Severe shearing or boxing should be avoided except in extremely formal gardens. Flowering shrubs, especially spring bloomers, need to be pruned immediately after flowering, not later in the season and not in the winter, so that the buds for the next year's flower display aren't removed.

Mulching

Shrubs should be mulched at the time of planting. The mulch does an excellent job of preventing compaction, holding moisture in the soil, preventing weeds, and keeping the ground cool, thus aiding in the quick establishment of root systems. Because mulch slows down the rate of the rain entering the soil, it gives the soil a chance to absorb the water more efficiently. Mulch also encourages microorganisms to work nearer the surface of the soil. Mulch around shrubs should be replaced anytime it wears thin. Bare soil should never be left exposed to sunlight.

Fertilizing

Fertilize shrubs in the early spring, again in early to mid-summer, and a third time in the fall if the soil still needs improvement. As with trees, I recommend fertilizing the ground surface with a 100 percent organic fertilizer at the rate of 20 pounds per thousand square feet. Avoid a concentration of fertilizer at the trunk or main stem of the plant to avoid burn. A thorough watering should follow any application of fertilizer.

Watering

I recommend the same watering techniques for shrubs as for trees with one exception. Since shrubs are smaller and can dry out faster, they need a little more care in monitoring the watering program. In the hotter parts of the state, which is most of the state, I recommend a sprinkler system unless you have an awful lot of free time to stand at the end of a water hose. Above-ground bubblers and soaker hoses are sometimes helpful, but I would avoid below-ground drip systems. Above-ground sprinklers are usually the best choice for landscaping and vegetable crops. Rain falls on the foliage, so why shouldn't irrigation water?

Pest Control

I recommend the same pest control techniques for shrubs as explained previously for trees. Effective pest control is greatly enhanced by keeping plants as healthy as possible using 100 percent organic fertilizers and generous amounts of well-made compost and rock minerals. Insects and diseases attack primarily weak, unhealthy, stressed plants. It is not necessary to kill every bad bug in your garden—a few are no problem and an important part of nature's system. A healthy population of beneficial insects is the only pest control needed for adapted plants that have been planted in healthy soil.

Weed Control

Pull the weeds by hand and mulch heavily. Weeds won't exist in shrub beds if the soil is properly mulched with 3 to 5 inches of coarse organic matter such as shredded native tree trimmings.

Maintaining Ground Covers and Vines

Pruning

Ground cover and vines need no pruning at planting time. The only regular ground-cover pruning I recommend, other than edging as needed, is a one-time top cut in late winter or early spring. This work can be done with hand shears or with a lawn mower set at its highest setting. In large areas most ground covers other than English ivy can be mowed, saving a lot of time and money. To prevent tearing the plants, sharpen the blades of the lawn mower and, if mowing large areas, stop occasionally to resharpen. Some mowers cannot be set high enough to mow ground covers. This is a perfect job for an old non-mulching mower. Be sure to put the trimmings in the compost pile.

Vines should be kept trimmed back to the desired size. Flowering vines, however, should only be pruned immediately after they have stopped blooming. Pruning at other times can eliminate the next year's flower production.

Mulching

Mulch the bare soil after vines and ground covers have been installed. Once the ground cover is established, mulching is generally not needed because the foliage takes over that function. However, remulching should be done if any bare areas appear during the season. Thorough mulching immediately after installation is the key to the fast establishment of ground cover. Thick mulch should be maintained around all vines. A light application of compost is beneficial to establish ground-cover beds.

Fertilizing

Ground cover and vines need the same fertilization as shrubs. A 100 percent organic fertilizer will give you the best results for establishment and for long-term health. These fertilizers are released slowly, are loaded with trace minerals, will stimulate and feed soil life, and will not burn young plants.

Watering

During the establishment period, ground covers need supplemental hand watering in addition to that supplied by the sprinkler because their very small root systems can dry out quickly. The key to the quick establishment of ground cover is keeping the soil evenly moist, not sopping wet. Mulch will help greatly in this regard.

Pest Control

Use the same pest control techniques for ground cover and vines as for trees and shrubs. Watch out for caterpillars. They are a particular problem for many vines.

Maintaining Annuals, Perennials, Herbs, and Vegetables

Pruning

Spent flowers and stems of ornamental plants should be removed as they fade in order to encourage new blooms. Plants that have become damaged or diseased should be removed to the compost pile. No, you don't have to worry about contamination. The microbial activity in the compost will neutralize disease organisms, insect pests, and seed. Food crop pruning is explained in more detail for specific species.

Mulching

Mulching the exposed soil around the plants should be done at planting; remulching should be done as any bare areas appear during the season.

Fertilizing

Annuals and perennials should be fertilized along with the trees, shrubs, and lawn with 100 percent organic fertilizers. For additional flower production, use earthworm castings (10 pounds per thousand square feet) and bat guano (10 pounds per thousand square feet) or other high-quality organic fertilizers in addition to the basic fertilizer. Spray the plants at least twice per month with fish emulsion and seaweed. Epsom salts (magnesium sulfate) at a rate of 1 tablespoon per gallon can be added to the spray solution if a magnesium deficiency exists. Natural apple cider vinegar and blackstrap molasses (1 tablespoon of each per gallon) are also helpful in the spray mix. Adding lava sand (40 pounds per thousand square feet) to all planting beds also helps.

Watering

Water is needed to maintain an even moisture level. Beds should never be soggy wet or bone dry between waterings. Occasional deep waterings are much better than frequent sprinkles. Potted plants should be watered daily through hot months and as needed during the cooler months. Once the plants have filled in solidly, use the same watering schedule as

for the rest of the garden but check the pots often. Potted plants should be fertilized weekly with a diluted solution of fish emulsion, seaweed, vinegar, and molasses. The same mixture in a concentrated form can be put in a 5-gallon bucket of water and sprayed on foliage from a siphon hose connection. As a simple aid at each watering, add 1 tablespoon of natural apple cider vinegar to each gallon of irrigation water. Be sure to clean metal equipment; vinegar is highly acidic and very corrosive.

Pest Control

Use the same pest control technique as explained for trees (exceptions for specific plants are covered in the pages that follow). Garlic and neem sprays are excellent general repellents. Ladybugs do an excellent job of controlling aphids. Diatomaceous earth and pyrethrum are effective in the control of many crawling insects. *Bacillus thuringiensis* (Bt) controls cutworms, loopers, and caterpillars well. Keeping the soil healthy and nutritious using generous amounts of compost will help keep pests to a minimum. Insects and diseases primarily prey on unhealthy or stressed plants. Protect all insects and release ladybugs, trichogramma wasps, and green lacewings. Wasps, bees, dragonflies, fireflies, big-eyed bugs, minute pirate bugs, and assassin bugs are also beneficial garden insects.

Certain plants are reported to do a good job of repelling insects. The most often mentioned are artemesia, basil, marigold, lavender, pennyroyal mint, rosemary, sage, garlic, santolina, lemon balm, and thyme. What works best is biodiversity. Use lots of different kinds of plants.

Weed Control

I prefer hand pulling and mulch to control weeds. Straight vinegar—100 grain (10 percent acid) or stronger—is a good nonselective herbicide for hot-weather weeds. Superfast, a natural herbicide from Safer, is another good choice. Beds will be virtually weed free if they are mulched properly with a thick blanket of organic matter.

Maintaining Turf Grasses

Mowing

Grass maintenance is the most time-consuming and expensive part of garden maintenance. Start by using the kind of grass that is most appropriate for your property. *Mow on a regular basis and leave the clippings on the lawn.* For best results, no more than a third of the leaf blade should be removed in any one mowing. Mow grasses according to the following guidelines:

- Bermudagrass, St. Augustine, and fescue— once a week to a height of 2 1/2–3 inches
- Tifgrass—two times a week to a height of 1/2–3/4 inch
- Zoysiagrass—every other week to a height of 3–4 inches
- Buffalograss—no more than once or twice a month to a height of 3–4 inches

The spring ritual of scalping the lawn early in the spring is a waste of time and money and is detrimental to the turf. It exposes bare soil to sunlight, which destroys organic matter and microbes, repels earthworms, and stimulates the germination of weed seed. It also wastes organic matter. Common lawn grasses should never be mowed lower than 2 inches unless getting ready for overseeding. I've changed my mind about the value of overseeding in the fall. Ryegrass (annual or perennial) does improve the soil, looks pretty through the winter months, and conceals the typical spotty weed effect in late winter and early spring. Overseeding also helps with the control of nutgrass.

Fertilizing

Turf fertilization can be handled in exactly the same manner as described above for trees and shrubs. In fact, the easiest and most cost-effective technique is to fertilize everything in your garden at the same time. Never use synthetic "weed and feed" fertilizers. They have no place in good horticulture. You should also avoid the often recommended high-nitrogen synthetic fertilizers. The overuse of inorganic fertilizers contaminates the soil and water systems with salt, including cancer-causing nitrates. Organic fertilizers have lower levels of nitrogen and are naturally slow release. They have excellent buffering abilities and provide organic matter to build the humus in the soil.

Top-dressing lawns in the spring by spreading sand or loam is a mistake. Top-dressing should be done only to level low spots, and the best material to use is the same soil that exists in your lawn.

Watering

Watering is the most variable part of the puzzle and should only be used when necessary rather than on a calendar schedule. Occasional deep waterings are better than light sprinkles on a more regular basis. The amount of water to be used will vary tremendously from one site to the next, depending on soil type, sun exposure, location in Texas, and preference—that is, how green you want your grass. Consistency is the key. Once your soil is organic, bal-

anced, and healthy, less irrigation will be needed. Establish a level of moisture that you think is appropriate—one that isn't too wet or too dry—and stick with that program. Here's a general formula that will give you a good starting point, but be sure to modify it through the year for your particular situation:

- Winter—two waterings per month
- Spring and fall—one watering per week
- Summer—one watering every third to fifth day
- Newly planted material—one watering every other day in summer, one watering per week in winter
- Establishment period for seeded grass—one watering two to four times per day until established
- New sod—one watering each day until established (usually 7–10 days)

Obviously, rain, cloudy days, snow, wind, drainage, watering method, amount of water used per watering, and water bills all affect this schedule, but it's a starting point. It would be ideal to get to a point of watering no more than once per week.

Aeration

Lack of oxygen is often the most limiting factor in the soil. Aeration is an important and often overlooked technique. To aerate grass areas, simply punch holes in the ground with any kind of equipment available in your area. Landscape contractors can be hired to do the work. It is amazing what this simple procedure can produce. Grass will green up as if it has been fertilized, and the root systems of nearby shrubs and trees will appreciate the increase of air into the soil. Be sure to mark the location of the sprinkler heads and other utilities prior to the work to avoid damage.

Pest Control

Lawns rarely have insect problems if the soil is healthy and drains well. Preventative spraying is a stupid procedure because you will always kill more beneficial organisms than the few pests that might be around.

Herbicides

Chemical weed killers are very dangerous, and I recommend staying away from them. They should be used only as a last resort, if at all. Herbicides hurt soil life and can damage the roots of trees and shrubs. There's one exception, however. Corn gluten meal

Organic Pest Control Guide

Pest	Control	Application
Ants	Pyrethrum, baking soda	Dust as needed. Use baking soda indoors only.
Aphids	Water blast	Use hose nozzle or thumb to spray strong stream of water.
	Ladybugs	Release ladybugs, braconid wasps, and green lacewings.
Bagworms	*Bacillus thuringiensis*	Use as directed on label. Spray with 1 tsp. soap per gallon of water at dusk, add 1 tbsp. of blackstrap molasses per gallon of water.
		Protect native wasps.
Black spot	Baking soda spray or sulfur dust	Spray or dust lightly as needed.
	Compost	Broadcast 1/2".
Brown patch	Baking soda spray	Spray as needed.
	Actinovate	Use as directed on label.
Chiggers	Sulfur	Dust as needed. For liquid spray use 2 tbsp. per gallon of water.
Crickets	Diatomaceous earth	Dust infested area with 1 cup per 1,000 sq. ft.
	Nolo Bait	Use as directed on label.
Early blight	Compost tea	Spray tomatoes regularly.
Elm leaf beetle	*Bacillus thuringiensis* 'San Diego'	Spray at dusk as directed on label.
Fire ants	Compost tea	Drench mounds. Add pyrethrum for more power.
	Dry grits	Sprinkle on top of mound.
Fire blight	Triple Action 20	Spray as needed.
Fleas	Beneficial nematodes, diatomaceous earth, pyrethrum products	Treat infested area. Bathe pets regularly and feed with supplements.
Gray leaf spot	Baking soda spray	Spray foliage lightly as needed.
Grubworms	Beneficial nematodes	Use as directed on label and keep soil moist.
Lacebugs	Horticultural oil, garlic or pepper tea	Spray as needed.
Leafminers	Neem	Spray as necessary.
Mealybugs	Horticultural oil	Use as directed on label.
Nematodes	Citrus peelings	Save and freeze. Grind up and apply to soil just before planting.
Pecan casebearers	Trichogramma wasps	Release every two weeks during the spring, starting at pecan bud break.
Pillbugs	Beer traps	Put cheap beer or apple core into a recessed container.
	Flour, hot pepper powder	Dust around and on infested plants.
Roaches	Diatomaceous earth, boric acid (indoors only), pyrethrum	Dust infested areas lightly.
	Bait stations	Mix one part sugar, one part baking soda detergent.
Slugs	Beer trap	Put beer in plastic jar or glass sunk into ground.
	Self-rising flour	Dust as needed.
	Hot pepper powder	Dust as needed.
Sooty mold	Baking soda spray	Spray lightly as needed.
Thrips	Garlic or pepper tea, Neem	Spray every two weeks or as needed.
	Green lacewings	Release as needed.
Whiteflies	Garlic pepper tea and seaweed	Spray as needed.
	Green lacewings	Release as needed.

Note: Don't buy diatomaceous earth from swimming pool suppliers. It has been melted and chemically treated, so it is a completely different product. It doesn't work and is dangerous to breathe.

is a natural preemergent herbicide and also a very powerful organic fertilizer. It should be applied for annual weed control in turf around the beginning of March and October. If you decide to use toxic herbicides, apply them with a wick applicator directly on target weeds to avoid spray drift. Full-strength vinegar (10 percent or 100 grain) sprayed on unwanted plants acts as an effective organic herbicide. An even stronger vinegar (20 percent or 200 grain) is available commercially. The natural herbicide Superfast, which is basically soap, seems to work quite well.

Maintenance Mistakes

Good plant selection is important, but all plants need to be planted properly or failure will ensue. Here are some of the worst maintenance mistakes I see on both residential and commercial properties:

1. Failure to allow for proper drainage. Water pushes the air out of the soil. When the soil drains, air moves back into the soil and it breathes properly. When water doesn't drain away, roots die. Roots need oxygen and the other nutrients in the air.
2. Failure to mulch bare soil. Nutrients and living organisms are most critical right at the surface of the soil. If exposed to sunlight and wind, that layer will be killed. It needs to be alive and thriving. The forest doesn't allow bare soil. Neither should you.
3. Assuming that native plants are maintenance-free and need no supplemental water or care for establishment. Natives, just like introduced plants, need to be planted properly and watered carefully until established.
4. Spreading sand or loam on lawns in the spring.
5. Topping trees, overpruning, and dehorning trees.
6. Installing steel curbing at the edge of beds along sidewalks or other paving surfaces instead of properly lowering the grade of the edge of the bed.
7. Overtrimming trees and shrubs.
8. Using chemical "weed and feed" fertilizers.
9. Misusing herbicides and chemicals in general.
10. Failing to remove sick or overgrown plants.
11. Overusing artificial, high-nitrogen, salt-based fertilizers.

Water-Saving Tips

- Mulch all bare soil.
- Repair leaky faucets.
- Use a nozzle or spray gun on the hose so water can be shut off when not in use.
- Use a broom, not a hose, to clean paved surfaces.
- Collect rainfall in containers to use for landscape or pot plant watering.
- Put grass and planting beds on different sections of the sprinkler system when possible.
- Run the sprinkler system manually when needed rather than on a set schedule.
- Water during the cooler parts of the day to reduce evaporation.
- Avoid watering when windy, if possible.

Organic Pest Control

Organic pest control uses a comprehensive or wholistic approach instead of the chemical or "bigger hammer" approach. The goal is to create healthy biodiversity so that the insects and microbes will control themselves. Insect pests and diseases are not the problem; they are only symptoms of sick plants. Using natural products and building healthy soil is the best treatment over the long term for all these pests. An excellent all-purpose spray for most diseases is a mixture of garlic tea and liquid seaweed.

Weed Control

Many "weeds" are actually herbs, wildflowers, and beneficial grasses. Good cultural practices, organic fertilizers, compost, and soil activators will encourage desired plants and grasses and discourage weeds. A simple way to get rid of weeds is to chop them out with a hoe or remove them with hand tools.

Chemical herbicides should be avoided. A better method is to use vinegar (100 grain or 10 percent). Spot-spray it full strength directly on weeds on a sunny day. Commercial vinegar (200 grain or 20 percent) is even better. Remember that strong vinegar is very corrosive to metal, so clean tools and containers well after application. Corn gluten meal also makes an excellent organic herbicide. Broadcast it at the rate of 20 pounds per thousand square feet in early March and early October to control annual weeds.

PLANT MATERIALS
A to Z

A

ABELIA

Abelia grandiflora (ah-BEE-li-ah gran-dee-FLORE-ah). **COMMON NAME:** ABELIA, GLOSSY ABELIA. **TYPE:** Semi-evergreen shrub. **LOCATION:** Sun to part shade. **HEIGHT:** 6'–8'. **SPREAD:** 6'–8'. **SPACING:** 3'–8'. **BLOOM/FRUIT:** Tubular white or pink-tinged flowers from June through October. **PROPAGATION:** Stem cuttings. **HABITS/CULTURE:** Graceful, upright, arching new growth in long shoots, bronze foliage in fall. Easy to grow in any soil, drought tolerant. **USES:** Boundary hedge, screen, barrier. **PROBLEMS:** Few. **TIPS/NOTES:** This plant looks bad when sheared into hedge. Pick-prune if possible. If shearing is unavoidable, do it lightly. Dwarf varieties with heights of 3'–5' are relatively good for mass plantings and suitable for small gardens. 'Sherwood,' 'Prostrata,' and 'Edward Goucher' are a few of the choices. They are not as carefree as the large plant. Native to Asia.

Abelia grandiflora abelia

ACACIA

Acacia spp. (ah-KAY-shuh). **COMMON NAME:** WRIGHT ACACIA, HUISACHE. **TYPE:** Deciduous shrub or small tree. **LOCATION:** Sun to part shade. **HEIGHT:** 10'–30'. **SPREAD:** 8'–15'. **SPACING:** 8'–15'. **BLOOM/FRUIT:** Most have clear yellow flowers in spring or summer and beanlike seed pods. **PROPAGATION:** Seed, cuttings. **HABITS/CULTURE:** Spreading shrubs or small trees with delicately textured leaves. Generally drought tolerant. Some varieties are thorny. Fast-growing, generally short-lived. **USES:** Specimen, small tree, screen plant. **PROBLEMS:** Freeze damage in the northern part of the state. **TIPS/NOTES:** Hundreds of species are available. Most are cold tender in the northern half of the state. *Acacia farnesiana* is the huisache tree that grows in the southern part of Texas and resembles the mesquite tree in habit and culture. *Acacia wrightii* is a small tree or large shrub native to south-central Texas. It is an excellent honey plant because of the fragrant white flower spikes.

Acalypha hispida chenille plant

ACALYPHA

Acalypha hispida (ah-ka-LEE-fa HIS-pid-a). **COMMON NAME:** CHENILLE PLANT. **TYPE:** Tropical annual bedding plant. **LOCATION:** Sun. **HEIGHT:** 18"–36". **SPREAD:** 15"–18". **SPACING:** 12"–15". **BLOOM/FRUIT:** Long, fuzzy red tassels all summer. **PROPAGATION:** Cuttings. **HABITS/CULTURE:** Annual foliage and flower plant; kin to copperleaf but has long, showy flowers and green foliage. Very cold tender. **USES:** Annual beds, pots, hanging baskets. **PROBLEMS:** Freeze damage.

Acalypha wilkesiana (ah-ka-LEE-fa wilk-see-AN-ah). **COMMON NAME:** COPPERLEAF, COPPERPLANT. **TYPE:** Annual bedding plant. **LOCATION:** Sun. **HEIGHT:** 24"–36". **SPREAD:** 24"–36". **SPACING:** 12"–18". **BLOOM/FRUIT:** Insignificant. **PROPAGATION:** Cuttings. **HABITS/CULTURE:** Fast-growing tropical shrub, performs as an annual in Texas. Colorful orange-copper foliage all summer. Dies at frost. Best in full sun, prefers prepared beds with good drainage, ample water and fertilizer. **USES:** Background for other bedding plants. **PROBLEMS:** Extensive root system often competes with other bedding plants. **TIPS/NOTES:** Excellent companion for white periwinkle. Native to the Pacific Islands.

Acalypha wilkesiana copperleaf

ACER

Acer negundo (A-sir nay-GOON-do). **COMMON NAME:**
BOX ELDER, BOX ELDER MAPLE, ASH LEAF MAPLE,
RED RIVER MAPLE. **TYPE:** Deciduous tree. **LOCATION:**
Sun. **HEIGHT:** 40'–50'. **SPREAD:** 40'–50'. **SPACING:** Do not
plant! **BLOOM/FRUIT:** Small green flowers in spring. **PROPA-
GATION:** Seed or cuttings. **HABITS/CULTURE:** Differs from
other maples by having 3–9 leaflets. New growth is olive
green; mature foliage is bright pea-green. Native to the eastern half of the state. Very fast-growing. Needs lots of water. **USES:** None. **PROBLEMS:** Dry conditions, insects, heart rot. **TIPS/NOTES:** The red and black box elder bug loves this tree—you probably won't.

Acer negundo
box elder

Acer palmatum (A-sir pal-MAY-tum). **COMMON NAME:**
JAPANESE MAPLE. **TYPE:** Deciduous tree. **LOCATION:**
Shade to part shade. **HEIGHT:** 6'–20'. **SPREAD:** 10'–20'. **SPAC-
ING:** 10'–15'. **BLOOM/FRUIT:** Insignificant on most species;
bloom effect comes from the unfolding of the colorful new
growth. **PROPAGATION:** Seed, cuttings, grafting. **HABITS/
CULTURE:** Beautiful spreading branches on various-size
varieties; some are tall, others dwarf, some red, others
green. Over 400 varieties exist worldwide. Easy to grow
in any soil with normal water and fertilization. Best in

Acer japonicum
fan leaf Japanese maple

Acer palmatum 'Coral Bark,' fall

light shade or morning sun with afternoon shade. **USES:**
Specimen garden tree, understory tree, year-round color.
Smaller varieties are good in pots. **PROBLEMS:** Delicate
foliage will sometimes burn in the heat of summer, especially in western exposure. **TIPS/NOTES:** The green variety
of *Acer palmatum* is the largest-growing and toughest.
'Bloodgood,' 'Burgundy Flame,' and several other cultivars have red foliage color. 'Dissectum' is the dwarf lacy-
leaf variety. 'Coral Bark' has bright red stems in winter.
There are hundreds of choices, even variegated forms.
Native to Japan.

Acer rubrum (A-sir ROO-brum). **COMMON NAME:** RED
MAPLE. **TYPE:** Deciduous tree. **LOCATION:** Sun. **HEIGHT:**
70'–90'. **SPREAD:** 30'–40'. **SPACING:** 20'–40'. **BLOOM/FRUIT:**
Small red to yellowish green flowers in spring, winged
seeds in fall. **PROPAGATION:** Seed or cuttings. **HABITS/CUL-
TURE:** Upright growth, smooth bark, rounded crown. Red
fall color. Needs deep soil. **USES:** Shade tree. **PROBLEMS:**

Acer palmatum Japanese maple, summer

Acer palmatum Japanese maple, fall

Acer palmatum 'Coral Bark,' early spring

A

Likes a cooler climate than most of Texas offers, always does better in deep, sandy soils. **TIPS/NOTES:** *Acer rubrum* var. *tridens* or *trilobum*, trident red maple, has somewhat smaller leaves and is more tolerant of our alkaline soils. Its fall color will range from gold to light red.

Acer leucoderme chalk maple   *Acer grandidentatum* bigtooth maple

Acer rubrum var. *tridens* or *trilobum* trident red maple

Acer saccharinum silver maple

Acer saccharinum (A-sir sah-kar-RINE-um). **COMMON NAME:** SILVER MAPLE. **TYPE:** Deciduous tree. **LOCATION:** Sun. **HEIGHT:** 40'. **SPREAD:** 20'–30'. **SPACING:** Do not plant! **BLOOM/FRUIT:** Greenish yellow. **PROPAGATION:** Seed. **HABITS/CULTURE:** Fast-growing, weak-wooded, short-lived junk tree. Grows about the same in any soil. **USES:** Fast-growing temporary tree, low-quality firewood. **PROBLEMS:** Chlorosis, borers, cotton root rot, short-lived, weak wood. **TIPS/NOTES:** Trash tree. Native to the eastern United States.

Acer saccharum 'Caddo' (A-sir sah-KAR-um). **COMMON NAME:** CADDO MAPLE. **TYPE:** Deciduous tree. **LOCATION:** Sun. **HEIGHT:** 60'. **SPREAD:** 30'. **SPACING:** 20'–30'. **BLOOM/FRUIT:** Uneventful blooms in spring, samaras (winged seed) in fall. **PROPAGATION:** Seed, cuttings. **HABITS/CULTURE:** Upright to spreading, yellow to golden fall color. Easy to grow in any soil, even rocky, alkaline soil. Drought tolerant. **USES:** Shade tree, great fall color. **PROBLEMS:** Few if any. **TIPS/NOTES:** Best large-growing maple tree for alkaline Texas soils. Not used enough. *Acer leucoderme*, the chalk maple, is another good choice for Texas soils. *Acer grandidentatum*, bigtooth maple, is a Texas native.

ACHILLEA

Achillea spp. (ah-KILL-ee-ah). **COMMON NAME:** YARROW. **TYPE:** Perennial herb. **LOCATION:** Sun. **HEIGHT:** 2'–3'. **SPREAD:** 2'–4'. **SPACING:** 1'–2'. **BLOOM/FRUIT:** Flat-topped clusters of flowers in white, rose, pink, yellow, and red. **PROPAGATION:** Seed or division. **HABITS/CULTURE:** Feathery foliage with a pleasant fragrance when crushed. Very winter hardy, easy to grow in any well-drained soil. **USES:** Perennial borders, cut-flower beds, herb gardens. Attracts bees, hoverflies, and parasitic wasps. **PROBLEMS:** Some varieties grow tall and tend to sprawl. Spreads easily and can become invasive. **TIPS/NOTES:** *Achillea millefolium* has white and sometimes pink blooms. Very tough species. Plant in spring or fall. *Achillea filipendulina* has yellow flowers.

Achillea filipendulina yarrow

Acer saccharum 'Caddo' Caddo maple

AESCULUS

Aesculus glabra (ESS-kah-lus GLA-bra). **COMMON NAME:** TEXAS BUCKEYE. **TYPE:** Deciduous small tree. **LOCATION:** Sun or part shade. **HEIGHT:** 20'–40'. **SPREAD:** 10'–20'. **SPACING:** 10'–15'. **BLOOM/FRUIT:** Creamy white to yellow flowers in spring. Leathery capsule has 1–3 large shiny seeds that are poisonous. **PROPAGATION:** Seed, late-winter root cuttings. **HABITS/CULTURE:** Compound leaves with 7–9 leaflets. Very upright growth. **USES:** Ornamental tree. **PROBLEMS:** Summer defoliation. **TIPS/NOTES:** *Aesculus glabra* var. *glabra,* the Ohio buckeye, is not well adapted in Texas. *Aesculus pavia* var. *pavia,* the red buckeye or scarlet buckeye, reaches heights of 15'–25' and has red flower spikes in spring. Most buckeyes lose their foliage in the heat of summer. Don't worry—that's normal.

Aesculus glabra Texas buckeye

Aesculus pavia var. *pavia* scarlet buckeye

AGARITA—see *Berberis trifoliolata*

AGAVE

Agave spp. (ah-GAH-vee). **COMMON NAME:** AGAVE. **TYPE:** Evergreen accent plant. **LOCATION:** Sun. **HEIGHT:** 6'–13'. **SPREAD:** 6'. **BLOOM/FRUIT:** Yellowish green flowers on tall stalks after ten years or so. Some species have pinkish white flowers. **PROPAGATION:** Seed, separation of pups. **HABITS/CULTURE:** Most agaves form a rosette of thick, leathery, yellow-green leaves. Like dry, well-drained soil. **USES:** Specimen. **PROBLEMS:** Coarse texture, sharp spines, hard to work around, dangerous. **TIPS/NOTES:** *Agave americana,* the century plant, has blue-green leaves up to 6' long with hooked spines along the edges and a wicked spine at the tip. Several varieties have yellow- or white-striped leaves. More than 300 species exist.

Ageratum houstonianum ageratum

AGERATUM

Ageratum houstonianum (ag-er-RA-tum huse-tone-ee-AN-um). **COMMON NAME:** AGERATUM, FLOSS FLOWER. **TYPE:** Annual bedding plant. **LOCATION:** Morning sun or part shade. **HEIGHT:** 8"–12". **SPREAD:** 12"–15". **SPACING:** 9"–12". **BLOOM/FRUIT:** Round, fluffy lavender or white flowers all summer. **PROPAGATION:** Seed. **HABITS/CULTURE:** Rounded overall shape, heart-shaped leaves. **USES:** Small groupings or borders. Good in pots. **PROBLEMS:** Spider mites in the heat of summer. Likes cool weather best.

AILANTHUS

Ailanthus altissima (eye-LAN-thus). **COMMON NAME:** TREE OF HEAVEN. **TYPE:** Deciduous tree. **LOCATION:** Sun. **HEIGHT:** 50'. **SPREAD:** 20'–40'. **SPACING:** 20'–30'. **BLOOM/FRUIT:** Inconspicuous green flowers, followed by large clusters of reddish brown winged seeds from September to October. **PROPAGATION:** Seed. **HABITS/CULTURE:** Upright, extremely tolerant of the harshest conditions, including drought, heat, wind, and lousy soil. **USE:** Grows where nothing else will grow. **PROBLEMS:** Can become an obnoxious weed. Also listed as *Ailanthus glandulosa.*

Ailanthus altissima tree of heaven

AJUGA
Ajuga reptans (ah-JOO-ga REP-tans). **COMMON NAME:** AJUGA, CARPET BUGLE. **TYPE:** Evergreen ground cover. **LOCATION:** Shade. **HEIGHT:** 3"–6". **SPREAD:** 12"–18". **SPACING:** 6"–9". **BLOOM/FRUIT:** Blue flower spikes in spring. **PROPAGATION:** Division. **HABITS/CULTURE:** Low-growing, leafy ground cover that spreads by runners. Green or bronze-purple leaves and purple flowers on short stalks. Needs extremely healthy beds with good drainage. Best in sandy, acid soil. High water and fertilizer requirements. **USES:** Ground cover for small areas. **PROBLEMS:** Nematodes, soil-borne diseases. **TIPS/NOTES:** Do not invest much money in this plant. It's pretty when healthy but rarely stays that way over a long period of time. Native to Europe.

Ajuga reptans ajuga

Albizia julibrissin mimosa

ALBIZIA
Albizia julibrissin (al-BIZ-ee-ah jul-leh-BRY-sin). **COMMON NAME:** MIMOSA. **TYPE:** Deciduous tree. **LOCATION:** Sun. **HEIGHT:** 20'. **SPREAD:** 30'. **SPACING:** Do not plant! **BLOOM/FRUIT:** Fluffy pink flowers in summer, followed by beanlike pods. **PROPAGATION:** Seeds. **HABITS/CULTURE:** Spreading limber branches that droop to the ground. Lacy foliage with small leaflets that close at night. Shallow, destructive root system. Needs lots of room and lots of water. **USES:** Not even good for firewood. **PROBLEMS:** Short-lived with destructive roots that crowd out good plants. **TIPS/NOTES:** Luckily it is dying out from disease. The ultimate junk tree. Native to India and Nepal.

ALCEA
Alcea rosea (AL-see-ah RO-see-ah). **COMMON NAME:** HOLLYHOCK. **TYPE:** Biennial or short-lived perennial bedding plant. **LOCATION:** Partial shade. **HEIGHT:** 2'–8'. **SPREAD:** 2'–3'. **SPACING:** 2'. **BLOOM/FRUIT:** Purple, red, pink, white, or yellow flowers on tall spikes in summer. **PROPAGATION:** Seed. **HABITS/CULTURE:** Early to midsummer flowers on coarse-textured vertical stems. **USES:** Background perennial garden color. **PROBLEMS:** Rust, aphids. **TIPS/NOTES:** Grows best in morning sun and afternoon shade.

Allamanda allamanda

ALLAMANDA
Allamanda spp. (al-ah-MAN-da). **COMMON NAME:** ALLAMANDA. **TYPE:** Tropical vine. **LOCATION:** Sun to part shade. **HEIGHT:** Climbing vine. **SPREAD:** Wide-spreading vine. **SPACING:** 3'–5'. **BLOOM/FRUIT:** Fragrant yellow trumpet-shaped 3" flowers. **PROPAGATION:** Stem cuttings. **HABITS/CULTURE:** Slow-vining, sprawling. Requires moderate water and fertility. Nonclinging. **USES:** Summer color. **PROBLEMS:** All parts are poisonous. **TIPS/NOTES:** Best in coastal regions.

ALLIUM
Allium spp. (A-lee-um). **COMMON NAME:** GARLIC, ONION, LEEK, CHIVES, SHALLOT. **TYPE:** Perennial bulb. **LOCATION:** Sun or dappled shade. **HEIGHT:** 8"–30". **SPREAD:** 8"–12". **SPACING:** 4"–8". **BLOOM/FRUIT:** Round clusters of small flowers on hard stems. **PROPAGATION:** Cloves, bulblets. **HABITS/CULTURE:** Straplike leaves, underground bulbs with many cloves. *Tulbaghia violacea* is society garlic and has narrow foliage and beautiful blue-purple flowers in summer. *Allium scorodoprasum*, giant or elephant garlic, is a leek that has a milder flavor than true garlic and produces a fist-size bulb that sometimes does not produce individual cloves. Its culture is the same as for common garlic. **USES:** Home remedy to prevent and relieve arthri-

Allium ophioscorodon garlic

Allium schoenoprasum garlic chives

Tulbaghia violacea society garlic

tis and regulate blood pressure. Excellent flavoring agent for vegetables, meats, sauces, gravies, soups, and just about anything else. Deters many insect pests. Tea made from garlic juice is used to repel insects and prevent diseases. Decorative ornamental plant. **PROBLEMS:** None serious. **TIPS/NOTES:** For bigger bulbs, cut the flowers off before they open. Subspecies of garlic (often called varieties) are *Allium sativum,* common garlic, which usually has no flower stalk, and *Allium ophioscorodon,* with a flower stalk. Wild garlic or wild onion is *Allium canadense* var. *canadense.* It blooms mostly in the spring, forming white, yellow, pink, red, and purple umbels atop slender stalks. The seeds are black and white and wrinkled. *Nothoscordum bivalve,* crow poison, is the dangerous look-alike and has white to cream-color flowers with a dark stripe on the outside. Crow poison blooms in spring and sporadically year round. Pedicels of each flower are longer than the wild onion's. The presence of either of these plants in the lawn means that the soil has a chemical imbalance, low humus, and a predominance of anaerobic microbes. Cultivated onion is *Allium cepa.* It should be planted in fall or very early spring. Easy to grow in healthy soil. Set out transplants, seed, or sets in fall or early spring. Problems include cutworms, nematodes, thrips, and various soil diseases. Chives are *Allium schoenoprasum.* Garlic chives have white flowers in August, and onion chives have purple flowers in the spring. Egyptian onion, *Allium cepa* var. *proliferum,* also called upside-down onion, tree onion, or walking onion, is very easy to grow—once planted, you'll have it forever. It produces up to 16 small onions on top instead of flowers.

ALMOND—see *Prunus amygdalus*

ALOCASIA

Alocasia spp. (al-oh-KAY-see-a). **COMMON NAME:** ELEPHANT EAR. **TYPE:** Perennial accent plant. **LOCATION:** Sun or filtered light. **HEIGHT:** 3'–5'. **SPREAD:** 3'–4'. **SPACING:** 2'–3'. **BLOOM/FRUIT:** Flowers similar to the calla lily's but unimpressive. **PROPAGATION:** Corms, division. **HABITS/CULTURE:** Huge caladium-like leaves on 3–5 stalks. Needs loose, moist, highly organic soil for best results. **USES:** Large foliage texture, tropical effect. **PROBLEMS:** Few; freeze damage in the northern part of the state. **TIPS/NOTES:** See *Colocasia esculenta* for photo.

ALOE

Aloe vera (al-low VER-a). **COMMON NAME:** ALOE VERA. **TYPE:** Tender succulent perennial. **LOCATION:** Sun to part shade. **HEIGHT:** 18"–3'. **SPACING:** 1'–2'. **PROPAGATION:** Division, cuttings. **HABITS/CULTURE:** Upright, succulent rosette. Needs dry to moist well-drained soil. Easy to grow in pots or in beds in the warm part of the state. **USES:** Potted plants. Juice from leaves used primarily on burns but also recommended by many for internal uses. **PROBLEMS:** Freeze damage. Roots will rot if overwatered. **TIPS/NOTES:** More than 300 species. No home or business should be without one. Plant from spring to fall.

Aloe vera aloe vera   *Aloysia triphylla* lemon verbena

ALOYSIA

Aloysia triphylla (a-lo-ISS-ee-a tri-FIL-la). **COMMON NAME:** LEMON VERBENA. **TYPE:** Tender perennial herb. **LOCATION:** Full sun to part shade. **HEIGHT:** 3'–5'. **SPREAD:** 3'–5'. **SPACING:** 2'–3'. **BLOOM/FRUIT:** Insignificant lemon-scented white flowers in late spring. **PROPAGATION:** Cuttings, seed. **HABITS/CULTURE:** Shrublike herb with woody stems. Leaves are rough-textured and pointed. Needs well-draining soil on the dry side. Full morning sun and afternoon shade is the best exposure. **USES:** Flavoring for fish and other meats, relaxing herb tea high in vitamin C. **PROBLEMS:** Spider mites, white flies unless grown in totally organic conditions. Aphids and caterpillars occasionally. **TIPS/NOTES:** Also known as *Lippia citriodora.* Lemon verbena has one of the most pleasant lemon scents and flavors of all herbs.

ALTHEA—see *Hibiscus syriacus*

AMARANTHUS

Amaranthus tricolor (am-ah-RAN-thus TRI-color). **COMMON NAME:** JOSEPH'S COAT. **TYPE:** Annual bedding plant. **LOCATION:** Sun to part shade. **HEIGHT:** 1'–2'. **SPREAD:** 1'–3'. **SPACING:** 12"–18". **BLOOM/FRUIT:** Tiny unimportant flowers. **PROPAGATION:** Cuttings, seed. **HABITS/CULTURE:** Decorative leaves, usually blotched with a variety of colors from yellow to deep maroons. **USES:** Summer color for borders on masses. **PROBLEMS:** Slugs, cutworms. **TIPS/NOTES:** Grown in the Orient as a green vegetable. 'Splendens' has deep red foliage with brilliant light red

Amaranthus tricolor Joseph's coat

upper leaves. *Amaranthus cruentus* is one of the many edible amaranths that are extremely delicious and healthy to eat.

AMARYLLIS—see *Hippeastrum* spp.

AMERICAN BEAUTYBERRY—see *Callicarpa americana*

AMORPHA

Amorpha fruticosa (a-MOR-fah froo-teh-COH-sah). **COMMON NAME:** FALSE INDIGO, INDIGOBUSH, RIVER LOCUST. **TYPE:** Deciduous shrub or small tree. **LOCATION:** Sun to part shade. **HEIGHT:** 8'–10'. **SPREAD:** 10'–12'. **SPACING:** 6'–15'. **BLOOM/FRUIT:** Dark purple 6"–8" vertical spikes with bright orange anthers. **PROPAGATION:** Seed, cuttings. **HABITS/CULTURE:** Grows well in wet soils but can adapt to normal garden soil. Usually has many stems from the ground but can be trimmed into a small tree. **USES:** Excellent for creek banks and poorly drained soils. Can be used in the landscape as a specimen plant for wet-soil areas and for erosion control. Extracts from the leaves and seeds can be used to control aphids, grain moths, cotton bollworms, and other pests. Crush 1 part leaves with 25 parts water, filter, and spray on food and ornamental crops. It is harmless to beneficial insects and animals. It also repels pests when interplanted with other food crops or garden plants. 'Dark Lance' is a good-looking cultivar. **PROBLEMS:** Few if any because it contains natural insect repellents. **TIPS/NOTES:** The herb known as false indigo is *Baptisia australis* and is a dye plant.

Amorpha fruticosa false indigo

ANACUA—see *Ehretia anacua*

ANEMONE

Anemone coronaria (ah-NEM-oh-nee core-oh-NAIR-ee-ah). **COMMON NAME:** ANEMONE, WINDFLOWER. **TYPE:** Annual flower. **LOCATION:** Sun to part shade. **HEIGHT:** 6"–15". **SPREAD:** 6"–12". **SPACING:** 3"–4". **BLOOM/FRUIT:** Multicolored flower on long slender stems. Colors include white, red, pink, purple, and rose. Single and double forms available. **PROPAGATION:** Seed, bulbs. **HABITS/CULTURE:** Lacy foliage and colorful poppylike flowers in spring. Actually a tuberous root but performs as an annual. Plant in late winter in full sun or partial shade with the claws pointed down. Soak in mixture of 1 tablespoon liquid seaweed per gallon of water before planting just under the soil surface. Must be replanted each year in Texas. **USES:** Multicolored spring flowers. **PROBLEMS:** Aphids, cutworms. **TIPS/NOTES:** Use a knife or clippers to pick anemones because pulling may tear the crown of the tuber. *Ranunculus repens* is a very similar plant but taller.

Anemone coronaria anemone
Photograph by August A. De Hertogh

Anemone hupehensis Japanese anemone

Anemone hupehensis (uh-NEM-oh-nee hew-pee-HEN-sis). **COMMON NAME:** JAPANESE ANEMONE. **TYPE:** Perennial flower. **LOCATION:** Morning sun to shade. **HEIGHT:** 15"–24". **SPREAD:** 12"–15". **SPACING:** 12". **BLOOM/FRUIT:** Lovely pastel flowers on long stems growing from rosettes of dark green foliage. **PROPAGATION:** Division. **HABITS/CULTURE:** Likes healthy, moist soil. **USES:** Perennial beds, fall color. **PROBLEMS:** Slugs, snails. **TIPS/NOTES:** Often sold under the name *Anemone japonica*.

ANETHUM

Anethum graveolens (a-NAY-thum gra-VAY-oh-lenz). **COMMON NAME:** DILL. **TYPE:** Annual herb. **LOCATION:** Sun. **HEIGHT:** 3'. **SPREAD:** 18". **SPACING:** 12". **BLOOM/FRUIT:** Yellow flowers or umbels on tall shoots. **PROPAGATION:** Seed. **HABITS/CULTURE:** Upright hollow shoots, fernlike foliage. **USES:** Sleep-inducing tea and seasoning for salads, breads, potatoes, butter, and vinegar. **PROBLEMS:** Caterpillar of the beautiful swallowtail butterflies. Don't kill them all.

ANGEL'S TRUMPET—see *Datura wrightii*

ANISACANTHUS

Anisacanthus quadrifidus var. *wrightii* (ah-nee-sah-CAN-thus kwah-DRIF-eh-dus var. RIGHT-ee-eye). **COMMON NAME:** FLAME ACANTHUS. **TYPE:** Deciduous shrub. **LOCATION:** Sun to part shade. **HEIGHT:** 3'–4'. **SPREAD:** 3'–4'. **SPACING:** 2'–3'. **BLOOM/FRUIT:** 1 1/2"–2" red, orange, or yellow flowers from midsummer to frost. **PROPAGATION:** Seed, cuttings. **HABITS/CULTURE:** Easy to grow in well-drained soil in sun or dappled shade. Cut back in late winter to promote full growth and heavy flowering. **USES:** Summer color to attract hummingbirds and butterflies. **PROBLEMS:** Possible freeze problems in the far northern

parts of the state. No pest problems. **TIPS/NOTES:** Good low-maintenance plant, should be used more often. Several other species available from West Texas are more upright and shrubby.

ANTIGONON

Antigonon leptopus (an-TIG-oh-nom LEP-to-pus). **COMMON NAME:** CORAL VINE, QUEEN'S WREATH. **TYPE:** Deciduous vine. **LOCATION:** Sun or light shade. **HEIGHT:** 20'–30'. **SPREAD:** 10'–20'. **SPACING:** 5'–10'. **PROPAGATION:** Cuttings or seed. **HABITS/CULTURE:** Large-growing vine with dark green foliage and bright pink flowers from late summer through fall. **USES:** Colorful fast-growing vine. **PROBLEMS:** Freeze damage in far North Texas. **TIPS/NOTES:** Evergreen in frost-free areas. Freezes to the ground in most of Texas.

Antigonon leptopus coral vine

Anisacanthus quadrifidus var. *wrightii* flame acanthus

Antirrhinum snapdragon

ANTIRRHINUM

Antirrhinum spp. (an-tee-REE-num). COMMON NAME: SNAPDRAGON. TYPE: Annual bedding plant. LOCATION: Sun to part shade. HEIGHT: 12"–36". SPREAD: 9"–12". SPACING: 9"–12". BLOOM/FRUIT: Upright flower spikes, available in many colors: red, pink, orange, bronze, and white. Good annual color for fall or from late winter to early spring. PROPAGATION: Seed. HABITS/CULTURE: Plant in sun or semishade. Likes alkaline soil, moderate water, regular fertilization. Grows best in cool weather and can take some freezing temperatures. USES: Cool-season color, borders, cut flowers. PROBLEMS: Rust, cutworms, hot weather. TIPS/NOTES: Plant in late winter or early spring. Native to the Mediterranean.

APPLE—see *Malus pumila*

APPLE, MAY—see *Podophyllum peltatum*

APRICOT—see *Prunus armeniaca*

AQUILEGIA

Aquilegia spp. (ah-kwi-LEE-ji-ah). COMMON NAME: COLUMBINE. TYPE: Perennial flower. LOCATION: Shade to part shade. HEIGHT: 12"–24". SPREAD: 12"–18". SPACING: 12"–18". BLOOM/FRUIT: Delicate but dramatic late-spring and summer flowers in blue, red, purple, yellow, and white. Flowers are trumpetlike with long spurs. PROPAGATION: Seed. HABITS/CULTURE: Delicate, woodsy plant, blooms on long stems with blue-green lacy foliage. Evergreen in all but the northern part of the state. Goes dormant in the heat of summer if not irrigated. Likes loose, well-drained, moderately fertile soil and light water. USES: Color in shady areas. Delicate texture. PROBLEMS: Few if any, somewhat slow to establish. TIPS/NOTES: *Aquilegia canadensis* is the red and yellow native and is very carefree. *Aquilegia longissima* has long-spurred pure yellow flowers and grows to 24"–3' tall. *Aquilegia hinckleyana* is native to far West Texas; it has been rediscovered and labeled 'Texas Gold' because of its yellow flowers.

ARABIAN JASMINE—see *Jasminum sambac*

ARALIA—see *Fatsia japonica*

ARBORVITAE—see *Thuja occidentalis*

ARBUTUS

Arbutus texana (ar-BYOO-tus tex-AN-ah). COMMON NAME: MADRONE, TEXAS MADRONE. TYPE: Evergreen tree. LOCATION: Sun to light shade. HEIGHT: 20'–30'. SPREAD: 20'–30'. SPACING: 15'–25'. BLOOM/FRUIT: White to pale pink flowers in spring. Raspberrylike fruit clusters in fall. PROPAGATION: Seed. HABITS/CULTURE: Spring-blooming ornamental, usually multitrunked, with thin, flaky bark and leathery, dark green leaves. Slow growth in any well-drained soil. USES: Ornamental tree. PROBLEMS: Wet feet, root fungi, and other problems related to poor drainage. Hard to transplant. TIPS/NOTES: Beautiful tree that should be used more. Much more cold hardy than reported.

Aquilegia columbine

Arbutus texana madrone
Photograph by Andy Wasowski

Ardisia japonica Japanese ardisia

Artemisia abrotanum southernwood

Arundo donax cane, winter

ARDISIA

Ardisia japonica (ar-DIS-ee-ah jah-PON-ih-kah). **COMMON NAME:** JAPANESE ARDISIA. **TYPE:** Evergreen ground cover. **LOCATION:** Morning sun to shade. **HEIGHT:** 12"–15". **SPREAD:** 36" or more. **SPACING:** 12". **BLOOM/FRUIT:** Small white flowers in clusters in fall, followed by red berries from fall through winter. **PROPAGATION:** Division. **HABITS/CULTURE:** Slow-growing, moisture-loving, clumping ground cover. Spreads by underground stems. **USES:** Ground cover for shaded areas in the warmer parts of Texas. **PROBLEMS:** Will freeze below 15 degrees. **TIPS/NOTES:** Risky to use in the northern half of Texas. Dies to the ground but usually returns in the spring.

ARIZONA CYPRESS—see *Cupressus arizonica*

ARTEMISIA

Artemisia abrotanum (ar-tay-MIS-ee-ah a-BROT-an-um). **COMMON NAME:** SOUTHERNWOOD. **TYPE:** Perennial herb. **LOCATION:** Sun. **HEIGHT:** 18"–34". **SPREAD:** 36" or more. **SPACING:** 24"–36". **PROPAGATION:** Cuttings. **HABITS/CULTURE:** Shrubby growth, feathery gray-green foliage. Tangerine-like fragrance. **USES:** Moth repellent. Tall ground cover. Good companion plant for roses. **PROBLEMS:** Few if any.

Artemisia absinthium (ar-tay-MIS-ee-ah ab-SINTH-ee-um). **COMMON NAME:** WORMWOOD. **TYPE:** Perennial herb. **LOCATION:** Full sun. **HEIGHT:** 18"–24". **SPREAD:** 24"–36". **SPACING:** 18"–24". **PROPAGATION:** Seed, division. **HABITS/CULTURE:** Easy to grow in well-drained soil. Gray foliage. **USES:** Provides gray color in the perennial garden. Repels fleas, ticks, and moths. Made into wreaths. **PROBLEMS:** Very aggressive spreader. 'Powis Castle' is an excellent choice.

Artemisia dracunculus (ar-tay-MIS-ee-ah dra-KUN-kew-lus). **COMMON NAME:** FRENCH TARRAGON. **TYPE:** Perennial herb. **LOCATION:** Sun. **HEIGHT:** 18"–24". **SPREAD:** 24"–36". **SPACING:** 12"–18". **PROPAGATION:** Root division, cuttings. **HABITS/CULTURE:** Cold tolerant, sprawling, dark green foliage. **USES:** Seasoning for fish, chicken, butter, and breads. **PROBLEMS:** Can't stand wet soil.

Artemisia annua (ar-tay-MIS-ee-ah AN-you-ah). **COMMON NAME:** SWEET ANNIE. **TYPE:** Tender perennial herb. **LOCATION:** Full sun. **HEIGHT:** 3'–6'. **SPREAD:** 36" or more. **SPACING:** 3'–4'. **PROPAGATION:** Seed. **HABITS/CULTURE:** Very easy to grow in any soil. Tiny light green foliage. **PROBLEMS:** Spreads and reseeds to a problem level sometimes. **USES:** Potpourri and dry arrangements.

ARUNDO

Arundo donax (a-RUN-doe doe-NAX). **COMMON NAME:** CANE, GIANT REED. **TYPE:** Perennial grass. **LOCATION:** Sun. **HEIGHT:** 8'–10'. **SPREAD:** Wide-spreading. **SPACING:** 3'–5'. **BLOOM/FRUIT:** Many-flowered panicles with off-white flowers. **PROPAGATION:** Division. **HABITS/CULTURE:** Tall grass that spreads by thick, knotty rhizomes. Has large summer flowers like those of pampas grass. Very aggres-

Asclepias tuberosa butterfly weed

Aspidistra elatior cast iron plant

sive and easy to grow. **USES:** Tall screen, erosion protection. **PROBLEMS:** Can become invasive. **TIPS/NOTES:** Grows very well in soil too moist for other plants.

ASCLEPIAS

Asclepias tuberosa (az-KLEP-ee-us too-ber-OH-sah). **COMMON NAME:** BUTTERFLY WEED. **TYPE:** Perennial herb. **HEIGHT:** 1 1/2'–2'. **SPREAD:** 2'. **SPACING:** 2'. **BLOOM/FRUIT:** 2"–4" clusters of yellow or orange blooms from April to September. **PROPAGATION:** Seed, root cuttings. **HABITS/CULTURE:** Relatively easy to grow in any soil. Slow-growing. Does not grow well in pots. **USES:** Summer color to attract butterflies. **PROBLEMS:** Aphids on new growth. Can die out from too much water. Hard to transplant. **TIPS/NOTES:** Plant a few, but don't invest a lot of money in this plant.

ASH, ARIZONA—see *Fraxinus velutina* 'Arizona'

ASH, GREEN—see *Fraxinus pennsylvanica*

ASH, MARSHALL SEEDLESS—see *Fraxinus pennsylvanica*

ASH, PRICKLY—see *Zanthoxylum clava-herculis*

ASH, TEXAS—see *Fraxinus texensis*

ASH, WHITE—see *Fraxinus americana*

ASIAN PEAR—see *Pyrus pyrifolia*

ASIMINA

Asimina triloba (a-SIM-in-ah tri-LO-ba). **COMMON NAME:** PAWPAW, CUSTARD APPLE, WILD BANANA. **TYPE:** Deciduous tree. **LOCATION:** Shade to part shade. **HEIGHT:** 15'–30'. **SPREAD:** 15'–20'. **SPACING:** 10'–15'. **BLOOM/FRUIT:** Purplish green flowers in April. Fruit is banana-shaped, green when young, brown or black when mature; edible in the fall. **PROPAGATION:** Cuttings, layering. **HABITS/CULTURE:** Tropical-looking. Native to the deep acid soils of East Texas. Very large fan-shaped leaves turn yellow in the fall. Young shoots and leaves covered with rusty down. **USES:** Edible fruit, distinctive tropical-looking foliage texture. **PROBLEMS:** Leaf-eating ants. Hard to transplant large specimens, small plants are fairly easy. **TIPS/NOTES:** *Asimina parviflora* is the dwarf pawpaw. Keep fruit in cold storage until fully ripe for sweet taste.

ASPARAGUS

Asparagus officinalis (uh-SPARE-ah-gus oh-fis-ih-NAH-lis). **COMMON NAME:** ASPARAGUS. **TYPE:** Perennial vegetable. **LOCATION:** Sun. **HEIGHT:** 4'–5'. **SPREAD:** 6' and more. **SPACING:** 18"–24". **BLOOM/FRUIT:** Insignificant flowers. Small red fruit on female plants. **PROPAGATION:** Crowns or division. **HABITS/CULTURE:** Shoots produced in early spring from rhizomes. Foliage is tall, graceful, lacy, and fernlike. **USES:** Edible shoots. **PROBLEMS:** Harvesting too early after planting. Snails, slugs, cutworms, and fungal diseases in poorly drained soil. **TIPS/NOTES:** Plant in beds 3'–4' wide in late winter. Place crowns in a trench 10"–12" deep and slowly cover the roots with rich soil, manure, and mulch. Or, alternatively, place roots on top of healthy soil and cover with 8"–12" of mulch. Plant one- to two-year-old crowns in a double staggered row for the most efficient production. Harvest very sparingly until after two years of growth. For better production, allow two or three shoots to grow to maturity early. Germination takes 7–21 days at 68–86 degrees. Cold weather makes for larger spears.

ASPIDISTRA

Aspidistra elatior (as-pi-DIS-tra ee-LAY-she-or). **COMMON NAME:** ASPIDISTRA, CAST IRON PLANT, BARROOM PLANT. **TYPE:** Evergreen accent plant. **LOCATION:** Shade. **HEIGHT:** 24". **SPREAD:** 24". **SPACING:** 18". **BLOOM/FRUIT:** Inconspicuous brown flowers close to the ground in spring. **PROPAGATION:** Division. **HABITS/CULTURE:** Dark-green, large-leafed foliage. Leaves sprout from the ground. Spreads by rhizomes. Easy to grow in any well-drained soil. Likes shade and plenty of water. **USES:** Tall ground cover, coarse texture, low-light area, container plant. **PROBLEMS:** Edges of foliage get ragged, especially in windy areas. Grasshoppers occasionally. **TIPS/NOTES:** Named for its toughness. Native to Japan.

ASTER

Aster spp. (AS-ter). **COMMON NAME:** ASTER. **TYPE:** Perennial flower. **LOCATION:** Sun. **HEIGHT:** 2'–3'. **SPREAD:** 2'–4'. **SPACING:** 12"–18". **BLOOM/FRUIT:** Daisylike perennial that blooms from summer through fall. Some varieties bloom only in the fall. **PROPAGATION:** Seed or division. **HABITS/CULTURE:** Most common asters bloom in the fall with light blue or white flowers. Plant in well-prepared beds. Moderate water and fertilization requirements. Divide established plants in spring every three or four years. **USES:** Fall color, border, cutting gardens. Considered to be one of the best perennial flowers in the world. **PROBLEMS:** Cutworms, powdery mildew, and root rot. Can be overwatered easily. **TIPS/NOTES:** Plant in fall or early spring. The hardy blue aster is the common fall-blooming variety. Many other varieties and colors are available. Roadside aster is considered a noxious weed by many people, a beautiful wildflower by others. I like it. It has white or light purple flowers in the fall. If you want it to go away, just aerate, fertilize, and water a little more. This little annual flower loves lousy soil.

Aster aster

Aucuba japonica aucuba

ASTER, ROADSIDE—see Weeds

ASTER, STOKES—see *Stokesia laevis*

ASTILBE

Astilbe spp. (a-STIL-bee). **COMMON NAME:** FALSE GOATSBEARD. **TYPE:** Perennial flower. **LOCATION:** Shade to partial sun. **HEIGHT:** 12"–24". **SPREAD:** 24"–30". **SPACING:** 12". **BLOOM/FRUIT:** Early summer spirelike blooms in white, pink, lavender, and red. **PROPAGATION:** Seed or division. **HABITS/CULTURE:** Needs cool, moist (even boggy) soil in partial shade. **USES:** Temporary summer color. **PROBLEMS:** Does not like our hot weather. **TIPS/NOTES:** I don't highly recommend it for use in Texas.

AUCUBA

Aucuba japonica (ah-CUBE-ah jah-PON-eh-kah). **COMMON NAME:** AUCUBA. **TYPE:** Evergreen shrub. **LOCATION:** Shade. **HEIGHT:** 5'–6'. **SPREAD:** 5'–6'. **SPACING:** 3'. **BLOOM/FRUIT:** Paltry blooms and fruit. **PROPAGATION:** Stem cuttings. **HABITS/CULTURE:** Upright growth on thick green stems. Yellow spots on long oval leaves. Likes shade, moist soil, good drainage. Dwarf forms are available. **USES:** Background, coarse texture, screen or accent plant. **PROBLEMS:** Leaf edges will turn black in full sun. Scale, nematodes, mealybugs, and spider mites, although none of these are serious. **TIPS/NOTES:** Also available in green and dwarf forms. Some folks do not like the spotty ones called 'Golddust'. I think they are appropriate in some shade gardens. Native to Japan.

AZALEA—see *Rhododendron* spp.

BALD CYPRESS—see *Taxodium distichum*

BALSAM—see *Impatiens balsamina*

BAMBOO—see *Bambusa* spp.

BAMBUSA

Bambusa spp. (bam-BEW-sa). **COMMON NAME:** BAMBOO. **TYPE:** Evergreen grass. **LOCATION:** Sun to part shade. **HEIGHT:** 2'–30'. **SPREAD:** Unlimited. **SPACING:** 2'–4'. **BLOOM/FRUIT:** Rarely blooms. **PROPAGATION:** Division. **HABITS/CULTURE:** Giant varieties and low-growing ground covers. All bamboos spread like grasses because they are. New sprouts come up each spring. Best in partial shade, any soil, no special needs. **USES:** Evergreen background, container plant, or barrier. **PROBLEMS:** Spreads and invades other plants. Some varieties will freeze in winter. **TIPS/NOTES:** Spreading can be controlled by kicking over the shoots just as they emerge in the spring and chopping up the runners. This technique is effective and much less trouble than digging out the entire planting. Native to Asia.

BANANA—see *Musa* spp.

BAPTISIA

Baptisia australis (bap-TIS-ee-ah ow-STRAH-lis) **COMMON NAME:** FALSE INDIGO, WILD INDIGO. **HEIGHT:** 3'–6'. **SPREAD:** 3'. **SPACING:** 24"–36". **BLOOM/FRUIT:** Spikes of indigo blue, sweet pea–like flowers in early summer, followed by inflated seed pods. **PROPAGATION:** Seed. **HABITS/CULTURE:** Blue-green, deeply cut leaves. Beautiful blue flowers and interesting seed pods, both good for cutting arrangements. Cut back spent flowers for a second burst of flowers. Deep-rooted and drought tolerant. **USES:** Color in early summer, perennial garden, blue dye. **TIPS/NOTES:** *Baptisia tinctoria* is used to make blue dye.

Baptisia australis false indigo

BARBERRY, RED—see *Berberis thunbergii*

BASIL—see *Ocimum basilicum*

BASSWOOD—see *Tilia* spp.

BAY—see *Laurus nobilis*

BAY MAGNOLIA—see *Magnolia grandiflora*

BEAN—see *Phaseolus vulgaris*

BEAUTYBERRY, AMERICAN—see *Callicarpa americana*

BEE BALM—see *Monarda citriodora*

BEET—see *Beta vulgaris*

Begonia semperflorens wax begonia

BEGONIA

Begonia semperflorens (beh-GON-ee-ah sim-per-FLOR-enz) **COMMON NAME:** WAX BEGONIA. **TYPE:** Annual bedding plant. **LOCATION:** Sun to part shade. **HEIGHT:** 6"–15". **SPREAD:** 12"–18". **SPACING:** 9"–12". **BLOOM/FRUIT:** Red, pink, or white summer flowers. **PROPAGATION:** Seed or cuttings. **HABITS/CULTURE:** Compact, erect, or trailing growth. Soft, shiny foliage that is sometimes red. Blooms throughout the summer. Needs loose, well-prepared beds, lots of organic matter, and good drainage. Some varieties need sun, others do best in shade. **USES:** Summer color, hanging baskets and pots. Edible flowers. **PROBLEMS:** Slugs and cutworms. **TIPS/NOTES:** Plants grown in pots can be moved indoors and saved through winter, although this may not be worth the trouble. Plant after the last freeze. Cut back leggy plants in summer for renewed blooming. Native to Brazil.

BELLIS

Bellis perennis (BELL-is pe-RIN-is). **COMMON NAME:** ENGLISH DAISY. **TYPE:** Perennial flower. **LOCATION:** Full sun or morning sun. **HEIGHT:** 6"–8". **SPREAD:** 9". **SPACING:** 6". **BLOOM/FRUIT:** Blooms from winter through early spring with bunches of small flowers in pink, white, rose, and lavender. **PROPAGATION:** Seed. **HABITS/CULTURE:** Likes loose, highly organic soil in full sun. Normal water and fertilization requirements. Plant in fall for winter color. Plant in early spring in far North Texas. **USES:** Small borders, small color masses in cool weather. Grows as an annual in Texas. **PROBLEMS:** Usually hard to find in nurseries. Burns out in our hot summers. **TIPS/NOTES:** Good choice for small color areas.

BERBERIS

Berberis thunbergii (BER-ber-is thun-BERG-ee-eye) **COMMON NAME:** RED BARBERRY. **TYPE:** Semideciduous shrub. **LOCATION:** Sun or shade. **HEIGHT:** 3'–6'. **SPREAD:** 3'–6'. **SPACING:** 2'–3'. **BLOOM/FRUIT:** Yellow to orange spring flowers. **PROPAGATION:** Cuttings. **HABITS/CULTURE:** Thorny, dense red foliage in summer. Regular and dwarf forms available. Easy to grow in any well-drained soil, drought tolerant. **USES:** Colorful barrier or hedge. **PROBLEMS:** None serious. **TIPS/NOTES:** Water carefully until established. Thorns create a good barrier. The dwarf pygmy variety is an ugly little thing at first. Mentor barberry, *Berberis mentorensis*, is a larger-growing green plant with red fall and winter color. 'Rose Glow' is a pink-tinged cultivar. 'William Penn' is compact, with yellow flowers in spring and red foliage in winter. Can withstand drought and very low temperatures. Native to Japan.

 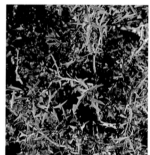

Berberis thunbergii red barberry   *Berberis trifoliolata* agarita

Berberis trifoliolata (BER-ber-is try-fole-ee-oh-LAY-tuh). **COMMON NAME:** AGARITA, DESERT HOLLY. **TYPE:** Evergreen shrub. **LOCATION:** Sun or shade. **HEIGHT:** 3'–6'. **SPREAD:** 3'–6'. **SPACING:** 3'. **BLOOM/FRUIT:** Yellow spring flowers and red berries from midsummer to fall. **PROPAGATION:** Seed, division, or layering. Cuttings are very difficult. **HABITS/CULTURE:** Spiny leaves, always in threes. Irregular branching pattern that is more open in shade, tighter in full sun. Easy to grow in any well-drained soil, drought tolerant. **USES:** Evergreen border, boundary, or background plant. **PROBLEMS:** None. **TIPS/NOTES:** Native from Central and West Texas to Mexico.

BERGAMOT—see *Monarda citriodora*

BERMUDAGRASS, COMMON—see *Cynodon dactylon*

BERMUDAGRASS, TIF (TIFGRASS)—see *Cynodon dactylon*

BETA

Beta vulgaris (BAY-ta vul-GAH-ris). **COMMON NAME:** BEET. **TYPE:** Annual vegetable. **LOCATION:** Sun. **HEIGHT:** 8"–12". **SPREAD:** 6". **SPACING:** 3". **BLOOM/FRUIT:** Insig-

nificant. The foliage and underground storage roots are the edible parts. **PROPAGATION:** Seed. **HABITS/CULTURE:** Cool-season annual vegetable. Plant seed 1" deep 4–6 weeks before the average last killing frost. Grows best in rich, healthy soil. Fertilize with organic food when plants are 6" tall. Seeds germinate in 3–14 days at 68–86 degrees. **USES:** Edible foliage and root. **PROBLEMS:** Nematodes, wireworms, grubworms, cutworms, flea beetles, and leaf diseases. Boron deficiency. **TIPS/NOTES:** Succession plantings can be made throughout the summer, but protection from hot summer sun is needed. Beets do best in flat-topped raised rows. Thin closely growing beet seedings to get larger beet roots. By the way, beet greens are delicious raw or cooked. *Beta vulgaris cicla*, Swiss chard, is a close relative.

BETULA

Betula nigra (BET-ew-la NI-gra). **COMMON NAME:** RIVER BIRCH. **TYPE:** Deciduous tree. **LOCATION:** Sun. **HEIGHT:** 30'–50'. **SPREAD:** 15'–20'. **SPACING:** 20'–25'. **BLOOM/FRUIT:** Unimportant. **PROPAGATION:** Softwood cuttings. **HABITS/CULTURE:** Usually has multiple trunks. Young bark is smooth and pinkish, bark on older trees is brown, flaky, and curling. Diamond-shaped leaves. Needs plenty of moisture. Very fast-growing but not long-lived. Yellow fall color. **USES:** Shade tree or specimen tree. **PROBLEMS:** Does not do well in heavy alkaline clay soils and hot climates. **TIPS/NOTES:** Interesting tree but not highly recommended in Texas.

Betula nigra river birch

B

BIGELOW OAK—see *Quercus sinuata* var. *sinuata*

BIGNONIA

Bignonia capreolata (big-NO-nee-ah kap-ree-oh-LATE-ah). **COMMON NAME:** CROSSVINE, IRONCROSS. **TYPE:** Evergreen vine. **LOCATION:** Sun to part shade. **HEIGHT:** High-climbing vine. **SPACING:** 4'–8'. **BLOOM/FRUIT:** Yellow and red trumpet-shaped spring flowers. **PROPAGATION:** Cuttings or seed. **HABITS/CULTURE:** Climbs aggressively by tendrils. Easy to grow in any soil in either sun or shade.

Moderate water and fertilization requirements. Relatively easy to control. **USES:** Vine for fences, overhead structures, and decorative screens. **PROBLEMS:** Few if any. **TIPS/NOTES:** Interesting vine because it hasn't been used much. Native to Texas and the southern United States.

Bignonia capreolata cross vine

BINDWEED—see Weeds

BIRCH, RIVER—see *Betula nigra*

BIRD OF PARADISE—see *Caesalpinia* spp.

BLACKBERRY—see *Rubus* spp.

BLACK CHERRY—see *Prunus serotina*

BLACK-EYED SUSAN—see *Rudbeckia hirta*

BLACKFOOT DAISY—see *Melampodium leucanthum*

BLACK GUM—see *Nyssa sylvatica* var. *sylvatica*

BLACKHAW—see *Viburnum rufidulum*

BLACKJACK OAK—see *Quercus virginiana*

BLACK WILLOW—see *Salix babylonica*

BLANKET FLOWER—see *Gaillardia pulchella*

BLUEBEARD—see *Caryopteris* spp.

BLUEBELL—see *Eustoma grandiflorum*

BLUEBERRY, RABBITEYE—see *Vaccinium ashei*

BLUEBONNET—see *Lupinus texensis*

BLUE-EYED GRASS—see *Sisyrinchium* spp.

BLUE GLAUCAGRASS—see *Festuca ovina* 'Glauca'

BLUE GRAMA—see *Bouteloua curtipendula*

BLUEGRASS, TEXAS—see *Poa arachnifera*

BLUE MIST—see *Caryopteris* spp.

BLUE OAK—see *Quercus virginiana*

BLUE SPIRAEA—see *Caryopteris* spp.

BOIS D'ARC—see *Maclura pomifera*

BONESET—see *Symphytum officinale*

BORAGE—see *Borago officinalis*

BORAGO

Borago officinalis (bo-RA-go oh-fis-ih-NAH-lis). **COMMON NAME:** BORAGE. **TYPE:** Annual herb. **LOCATION:** Sun to part shade. **HEIGHT:** 24"–36". **SPREAD:** 18"–30". **SPACING:** 18". **BLOOM/FRUIT:** Bright blue starlike flowers with black anthers, sometimes pink or white flowers. **PROPA-**

GATION: Seed. **HABITS/CULTURE:** Flowering herb. Easy to grow from seed, fast-growing. Fuzzy leaves 6"–8" long. Cut back hard from time to time to maintain compactness. **USES:** Herb vinegars, cucumber flavoring. Use the flowers in drinks and teas—they're delicious. **PROBLEMS:** Grasshoppers occasionally.

Borago officinalis borage

BOTTLEBRUSH—see *Callistemon citrinus*

BOUGAINVILLEA

Bougainvillea spp. (boo-gan-VIL-lee-ah). **COMMON NAME:** BOUGAINVILLEA. **TYPE:** Tropical vine. **LOCATION:** Sun. **HEIGHT:** 15'. **SPACING:** 5'–6'. **BLOOM/FRUIT:** Purple, red, gold, pink, orange, and white flowers called bracts. **PROPAGATION:** Stem cuttings. **HABITS/CULTURE:** Climbing and sprawling vine with thorny stems. Permanent only in the extreme southern part of Texas. Fertile soil not important, but good drainage is. **USES:** Summer color, best in

Bougainvillea bougainvillea

pots or hanging baskets so it can be moved indoors in winter. **PROBLEMS:** Freeze damage. **TIPS/NOTES:** Seems to bloom better if kept root bound and not consistently moist. Cussing 'em sometimes helps to set the flowers. Stanley Marcus taught me that.

BOUNCING BET—see *Saponaria officinalis*

BOUTELOUA
Bouteloua curtipendula (boo-tuh-LOO-ah ker-tuh-PEN-dew-lah). **COMMON NAME:** SIDEOATS GRAMA. **TYPE:** Perennial grass. **LOCATION:** Sun. **HEIGHT:** 2'–4'. **SPREAD:** 18"–24". **SPACING:** 15–20 lbs. of seed per acre, 2–2 1/2 lbs. per thousand sq. ft. Space transplants 3' apart as a garden accent. **BLOOM/FRUIT:** Small oatlike seeds hang down uniformly on one side of the stem. **PROPAGATION:** Seed. **HABITS/CULTURE:** Leaf blades are flat with hairs and bumps along the edges. **USES:** High-quality, nutritious forage for livestock. Blue grama is *Bouteloua gracilis*.

Bouteloua curtipendula sideoats grama

BOX ELDER—see *Acer negundo*

BOXWOOD—see *Buxus microphylla*

BRASSICA
Brassica oleracea (BRA-si-ka o-le-RAH-see-ah). **COMMON NAME:** BROCCOLI, CABBAGE, COLLARDS, KALE. **TYPE:** Annual vegetables. **LOCATION:** Sun to part shade. **HEIGHT:** 12"–24". **SPREAD:** 12"–18". **SPACING:** 6"–12". **BLOOM/FRUIT:** Insignificant. **PROPAGATION:** Seed. Plant 1/2" deep. **HABITS/CULTURE:** Cool-weather annuals that need healthy,

Brassica oleracea kale   *Brunfelsia australis*
                                 yesterday, today, and tomorrow

moist soil for best results. Mulching is critical. Germination in 3–10 days at 68–86 degrees. **USES:** Delicious foliage and immature flower heads on broccoli, foliage on other varieties. **PROBLEMS:** Harlequin bugs, cutworms, aphids, green worms, flea beetles, loopers, and boron deficiency. **TIPS/NOTES:** Broccoli is an extremely nutritious vegetable, and cabbage ain't bad. Best to plant from transplants in the spring. Start from seeds or transplants in the fall. Other varieties include *Brassica juncea*, mustard greens; *Brassica rapa*, turnip greens; *Brassica napus*, rutabaga.

BRAZIL PLUME—see *Justicia* spp.

BRIDAL WREATH—see *Spiraea* spp.

BRUNFELSIA
Brunfelsia australis (brun-FELLS-ee-ah aw-STRAY-liss). **COMMON NAME:** YESTERDAY, TODAY, AND TOMORROW. **TYPE:** Tender perennial or tropical. **LOCATION:** Sun to part shade. **HEIGHT:** 3'–4'. **SPREAD:** 3'–4'. **SPACING:** 3'. **BLOOM/FRUIT:** Three colors of flowers on the plant at the same time: dark blue-purple blooms age to a lavender and then turn white before falling off. **PROPAGATION:** Cuttings. **HABITS/CULTURE:** Bushy semitropical. Easy to grow in healthy, well-drained potting soil. **USES:** Excellent potted plant for patio or terrace. **PROBLEMS:** Only one flush of flowers in the spring, but I think it's worth it. **TIPS/NOTES:** Can take some frost if located in a protected area. No promises, but it's tougher than you might think. *Brunfelsia americana*, lady of the night, has white flowers only and blooms all summer.

BUCHLOE
Buchloe dactyloides (BUCK-low dac-ti-LOY-dees). **COMMON NAME:** BUFFALOGRASS. **TYPE:** Warm-season turf grass. **LOCATION:** Sun. **HEIGHT:** 3"–6" (mown). **SPREAD:** Wide-spreading by rhizomes. **SPACING:** 5–7 lbs. of seed per thousand sq. ft. in spring or summer. **PROPAGATION:** Seed. For hybrids, solid sod only. **BLOOM/FRUIT:** Hybrids have none. Native has flaglike flower heads on male plants; female plants have large burrlike seed pods at ground level. **HABITS/CULTURE:** Low-growing, blue-green foliage, decorative flower heads (which most people think are the seeds). Very easy to grow in any soil except wet areas.

Buchloe dactyloides buffalograss

Bumelia lanuginosa chittamwood

Low fertilizer requirements. **USES:** Low-maintenance turf, large natural areas. **PROBLEMS:** Slow to establish, but this is not a problem. **TIPS/NOTES:** This is our only native lawn grass and the most drought-tolerant and maintenance-free of all. Don't water too much. Native from Texas to Minnesota and Montana. Sterile hybrids include 'Prairie,' '609,' and 'Stampede,' which is a very low-growing selection.

BUCKEYE, MEXICAN—see *Ungnadia speciosa*

BUCKEYE, SCARLET—see *Aesculus glabra*

BUCKEYE, TEXAS—see *Aesculus glabra*

BUCKTHORN, CAROLINA—see *Rhamnus caroliniana*

BUDDLEIA
Buddleia spp. (BUD-lee-ah). **COMMON NAME:** BUTTERFLY BUSH. **TYPE:** Deciduous shrub. **LOCATION:** Sun to part shade. **HEIGHT:** 3'–8'. **SPREAD:** 4'–6'. **SPACING:** 3'–4'. **BLOOM/FRUIT:** Fragrant flowers, mostly in spring. Many colors. **PROPAGATION:** Cuttings or seed. **HABITS/CULTURE:** Arching, open-branching growth, usually thinly foliated. Blooms in spring on second year's growth. Prune after flowers have faded. Drought tolerant. **USES:** Summer color attracts butterflies. **PROBLEMS:** Can suffer freeze damage.

TIPS/NOTES: *Buddleia alternifolia* and *Buddleia davidii* have lilac flowers. The native *Buddleia marrubiifolia* has orange flowers. Cultivars available in several colors.

Buddleia butterfly bush

BUFFALOGRASS—see *Buchloe dactyloides*

BUMELIA
Bumelia lanuginosa (boo-ME-lee-ah lay-noo-gee-NO-sah). **COMMON NAME:** CHITTAMWOOD, GUM ELASTIC TREE. **TYPE:** Deciduous tree. **LOCATION:** Sun. **HEIGHT:** 60'. **SPREAD:** 30'. **SPACING:** 20'–40'. **BLOOM/FRUIT:** Small

off-white to yellow flowers in spring, blue-black drupes in September and October. **PROPAGATION:** Seeds or cuttings. **HABITS/CULTURE:** Slow, upright, dark stiff branches, small leaves similar to those of live oak, yellow fall color and thorns. Resembles live oak at a distance. Easy to grow in any well-drained soil. **USES:** Shade tree. Good bird plant. **PROBLEMS:** Thorns on juvenile growth. Borers can be a serious problem. **TIPS/NOTES:** Not often used as a landscape plant. I usually try to keep them alive if already existing on a site, but I don't plant new ones. Native to the southern and southwestern United States.

BUR CLOVER—see Weeds

BUR OAK—see *Quercus macrocarpa*

BUTTERFLY BUSH—see *Buddleia* spp.

BUTTERFLY WEED—see *Asclepias tuberosa*

BUTTONWOOD—see *Platanus occidentalis*

BUXUS
Buxus microphylla (BUX-sus mike-ro-FILL-ah). **COMMON NAME:** BOXWOOD, LITTLELEAF BOXWOOD. **TYPE:** Evergreen shrub. **LOCATION:** Sun to part shade. **HEIGHT:** 3'–5'. **SPREAD:** 3'. **SPACING:** 18"–24". **BLOOM/FRUIT:** Unimportant. **PROPAGATION:** Cuttings. **HABITS/CULTURE:** Compact shrub with rounded leaves. Medium to light green color and soft texture. Shallow roots. Grows in any well-drained soil. Water and fertilizer needs are moderate. **USES:** Border, low hedge, foundation planting. **PROBLEMS:** Nematodes, leaf miners, scale, soil fungus, and freeze damage. **TIPS/NOTES:** Not recommended unless a short clipped hedge is needed. Can be kept trimmed to 12" in height. Dwarf yaupon holly and germander are better choices. Native to Japan, Asia, Europe, and North Africa.

Buxus microphylla boxwood

CABBAGE—see *Brassica oleracea*

CAESALPINIA

Caesalpinia spp. (kie-sal-PEEN-ee-ah). **COMMON NAME:** BIRD OF PARADISE BUSH, MEXICAN POINCIANA. **TYPE:** Tropical bush or small tree. **LOCATION:** Sun. **HEIGHT:** 8'–15'. **SPREAD:** 10'–15'. **SPACING:** 8'–10'. **BLOOM/FRUIT:** 3"– 6" yellow or red racemes from spring to fall. **PROPAGATION:** Seed. **HABITS/CULTURE:** Small, delicate ornamental tree with upright growth, lacy foliage, and long-lasting summer flowers. Needs sun, good drainage, and protection from freezing weather. **USES:** Ornamental tree, yellow summer flowers. **PROBLEMS:** Will freeze easily in the northern half of the state. **TIPS/NOTES:** *Caesalpinia mexicana* is a yellow-flowering Texas native that grows wild in the far southern tip of the state. *Caesalpinia gilliesii* has tiny leaflets and yellow flowers with distinctive long red stamens. In Dallas mine have frozen to the ground but returned in spring—usually.

Caesalpinia bird of paradise bush

Caladium × hortulanum caladium

CALADIUM

Caladium × hortulanum (kuh-LAY-dee-um hor-too-LAN-um). **COMMON NAME:** CALADIUM. **TYPE:** Annual. **LOCATION:** Shade to part shade. **HEIGHT:** 1'–2'. **SPREAD:** 12"– 18". **SPACING:** 8"–12". **BLOOM/FRUIT:** Lilylike flowers should be cut away to keep the energy in the foliage. **PROPAGATION:** Bulbs. **HABITS/CULTURE:** Brightly colored leaves on tall stems from tubers. White varieties seem to be more sun tolerant. Plant tubers in well-prepared beds after the soil temperature has warmed to about 70 degrees in late spring. Dies at frost. Not worth trying to save the tubers through the winter. Mix 1 tablespoon fish meal, zeolite, Epsom salts, or colloidal phosphate into hole before planting tuber. **USES:** Summer color in ground cover areas, flower beds, or containers. **PROBLEMS:** Wind damage. **TIPS/NOTES:** The whites are my favorites, such as 'Candidum,' 'Arron,' and the strap varieties like 'White Wing' and 'Jackie Suthers.' Mother plants are native to the riverbanks of the Amazon.

CALENDULA

Calendula officinalis (ka-LEN-dew-la oh-fis-ih-NAH-lis). **COMMON NAME:** CALENDULA, POT MARIGOLD, ENGLISH MARIGOLD. **TYPE:** Annual bedding plant and herb. **LOCATION:** Sun or light shade. **HEIGHT:** 12"–15". **SPREAD:** 15". **SPACING:** 12". **BLOOM/FRUIT:** Composite

orange or yellow daisy-like flowers. **PROPAGATION:** Seed. **HABITS/CULTURE:** Cool-season annual flower and herb. Set out transplants in the fall or early spring in the northern part of the state. Sow seed in mid- to late summer in flats. Plant in healthy, well-drained soils. **USES:** Annual flower color for the cooler months, good in pots. **PROBLEMS:** Can't stand hot weather. **TIPS/NOTES:** Used as a pot herb.

Calendula officinalis calendula

CALLICARPA

Callicarpa americana (cal-eh-CAR-pah a-mer-ee-KAHN-ah). **COMMON NAME:** AMERICAN BEAUTY-BERRY. **TYPE:** Deciduous shrub. **LOCATION:** Sun or shade. **HEIGHT:** 4'–8'. **SPREAD:** 5'–8'. **SPACING:** 3'– 5'. **BLOOM/FRUIT:** Clusters of small yellowish flowers in spring. Clusters of purple or

Callicarpa americana white American beautyberry

white berries in late summer through fall. Each berry contains four seeds. **PROPAGATION:** Seed or cuttings. **HABITS/CULTURE:** Sprawling native shrub with insignificant pink flowers in spring and extremely showy purple or white berries in fall that last into the winter. Likes well-drained soil but adapts to any soil type. Very easy to grow but needs moist soil. **USES:** Free-form shrub or mass planting. Fall berry color. Excellent bird attractant in late fall and early winter. **PROBLEMS:** Few if any. **TIPS/NOTES:** Versatile, carefree plant. Does not work well for cutting—berries fall off. Native from the eastern United States to Texas.

CALLIOPSIS—see *Coreopsis tinctoria*

CALLIRHOE
Callirhoe involucrata (kal-ih-ROH-ee in-voh-loo-KRAY-tah). **COMMON NAME:** WINECUP. **TYPE:** Perennial wildflower. **LOCATION:** Sun to part shade. **HEIGHT:** 6"–12". **SPREAD:** 2"–4". **SPACING:** 18"–24". **BLOOM/FRUIT:** Wildflower with 2" wine-red, late-spring blooms. **PROPAGATION:** Seed. **HABITS/CULTURE:** Grows from turniplike tubers. In irrigated gardens the plant will bloom all summer. Grows wild in Texas in open woods, on prairies, and along roadsides. Likes dry conditions. **USES:** Wildflower. **PROBLEMS:** Few if any. **TIPS/NOTES:** Should be used more.

Callistemon citrinus bottlebrush

Callirhoe involucrata and *Oenothera speciosa* winecup and evening primrose

CALLISTEMON
Callistemon citrinus (kal-LIS-ta-mon ki-TREE-nus). **COMMON NAME:** BOTTLEBRUSH. **TYPE:** Evergreen shrub. **LOCATION:** Sun. **HEIGHT:** 8'–12'. **SPREAD:** 4'–8'. **SPACING:** 4'–5'. **BLOOM/FRUIT:** Showy red bushlike flowers in spring, sporadic through summer. **PROPAGATION:** Cuttings. **HABITS/CULTURE:** Large upright-growing shrub with red flowers throughout the growing season. Long, slender, medium green leaves. **USES:** Colorful hedge or screen plant for the South. **PROBLEMS:** Freeze damage in most of Texas. Not reliably hardy above Houston.

CALOCEDRUS
Calocedrus decurrens (cal-oh-SEED-rus day-KER-enz). **COMMON NAME:** INCENSE CEDAR. **TYPE:** Evergreen tree. **LOCATION:** Sun. **HEIGHT:** 70'–90'. **SPREAD:** 20'–30'. **SPACING:** 15'–30'. **BLOOM/FRUIT:** Small brown cones that look like duck bills when open. **PROPAGATION:** Seed or cuttings. **HABITS/CULTURE:** Tall-growing, symmetrical, straight-trunked like arborvitae. Dense foliage. Adaptable to a wide range of soils. Emits pleasant fragrance in summer. **USES:** Specimen, windbreak, tall screen. **PROBLEMS:** Availability and slow growth. **TIPS/NOTES:** *Libocedrus* is the old genus name.

CALYLOPHUS
Calylophus spp. (kal-ee-LOH-fuss). **COMMON NAME:** YELLOW PRIMROSE. **TYPE:** Perennial flower. **LOCATION:** Sun to part shade. **HEIGHT:** 12"–18". **SPREAD:** 18". **SPACING:** 12". **BLOOM/FRUIT:** Yellow buttercup-type flowers from March to November. **PROPAGATION:** Seed in the fall. **HABITS/CULTURE:** Easy to grow in any well-drained soil. Similar growth habit to the pink evening primrose, but has narrower leaves. Flowers open in the late afternoon and last all the next day. Likes hot spots and must have excellent drainage. Evergreen in the southern part of the state. **USES:** Summer color, perennial beds, wildflower areas.

CALYPTOCARPUS
Calyptocarpus vialis (ka-lip-toe-CAR-pus vie-AL-iss). **COMMON NAME:** HORSEHERB. **TYPE:** Deciduous to semi-evergreen ground cover. **LOCATION:** Shade. **HEIGHT:** 8"–10". **SPREAD:** 18"–36". **SPACING:** 12"–15". **BLOOM/FRUIT:** Everblooming tiny yellow flowers. **PROPAGATION:** Division or seed. **HABITS/CULTURE:** Very easy to grow in any soil. Evergreen in the southern half of the state. Freezes to the ground in the northern areas but returns each spring. Drought tolerant and pest free. **USES:** Natural ground cover. **PROBLEMS:** None. **TIPS/NOTES:** Should be used more. Looks terrific when planted with wild violets. Some people still consider it a weed—that's too bad.

Calyptocarpus vialis horseherb

CAMELLIA
Camellia spp. (ka-MEAL-ee-a). **COMMON NAME:** CAMELLIA. **TYPE:** Evergreen shrub. **LOCATION:** Part shade. **HEIGHT:** 6'–8'. **SPREAD:** 3'–6'. **SPACING:** 3'–5'. **BLOOM/FRUIT:** Showy single and double flowers that bloom from fall through spring, depending on the variety. **PROPAGATION:** Cuttings. **HABITS/CULTURE:** Dark glossy foliage on bushy growth. Slow-growing. Needs loose, well-drained acid soil and protection from winter winds for best performance. Filtered light is best sun exposure. Full sun in the afternoon will burn foliage. Begin fertilizing with organic fertilizers such as fish emulsion or cottonseed meal just after blooms fade in spring. **USES:** Evergreen accent plant, border or container plant. **PROBLEMS:** Scale, aphids, winter damage, and iron deficiency. **TIPS/NOTES:** Native to China and Japan. Over 5,000 varieties. *Camellia sasanqua* 'White Dove' is a good choice for Texas. *Camellia japonica* has larger leaves and the showiest flowers. Sasanquas are easier to grow than japonicas.

CAMPHOR TREE—see *Cinnamomum camphora*

Camellia japonica camellia

Campsis radicans 'Flava' and 'Madame Galen' trumpet vine

Canna generalis canna

CAMPSIS

Campsis radicans (KAM-sis RAD-ee-kans). **COMMON NAME:** TRUMPET VINE, TRUMPET CREEPER. **TYPE:** Deciduous vine. **LOCATION:** Sun to part shade. **HEIGHT:** Tall-growing vine. **SPACING:** 5'–8'. **BLOOM/FRUIT:** Orange, yellow, or red 3" trumpet-shaped summer flowers. **PROPAGATION:** Cuttings. **HABITS/CULTURE:** Large sprawling vine with showy orange and red trumpetlike flowers that bloom all summer. Climbs by aerial roots. Bare in winter. Easy to grow in any soil, relatively drought tolerant. Prune back to the main trunk if needed after leaves fall in the autumn. **USES:** Climbing vine for fences, arbors, screens, or poles. Summer color. **PROBLEMS:** Spreads badly, causing a maintenance problem. Can destroy old structures. **TIPS/NOTES:** Native to the East Coast, Florida, and Texas. 'Madame Galen,' introduced by French nurseries, doesn't spread as much as the native plant. *Campsis radicans* 'Flava' has pure yellow flowers, 'Crimson Trumpet' pure red.

CANARY BIRD FLOWER—see *Tropaeolum* spp.

CANDLETREE—see *Cassia alata*

CANDYTUFT—see *Iberis sempervirens*

CANNA

Canna generalis (CAN-ah jen-er-ALL-is). **COMMON NAME:** CANNA, CANNA LILY. **TYPE:** Perennial flower. **LOCATION:** Sun. **HEIGHT:** 2'–6'. **SPREAD:** 3'–6'. **SPACING:** 18"–24". **BLOOM/FRUIT:** Flowers bloom from late spring to fall. Colors include red, pink, orange, yellow, salmon, and multicolors. **PROPAGATION:** Division of rhizomes. **HABITS/CULTURE:** Coarse perennial that spreads from underground stems. Large, coarse-textured leaves and flowers. Most popular is the dwarf red variety. Dies to ground at frost, returns the next spring. Needs full sun, loose soil, plenty of water, and healthy amounts of fertilizer for good blooms. **USES:** Use as a background flower or in large open beds. **PROBLEMS:** Leaf rollers, wind damage, coarseness. **TIPS/NOTES:** Easy to grow, but too coarse for most small gardens. Native to the tropics. The red foliage selections tend to have smaller flowers but are better-looking plants. To encourage more flowers, cut back after stalks finish blooming.

CANTALOUPE—see *Cucumis melo*

CAPSICUM

Capsicum spp. (CAP-see-cum). **COMMON NAME:** RED PEPPER, CHILE. **TYPE:** Tender perennial vegetable and herb. **LOCATION:** Sun to shade. **HEIGHT:** 12"–6'. **SPREAD:** 18"–36". **SPACING:** 18"–24". **BLOOM/FRUIT:** Small white flowers followed by fruit in many sizes, colors, and flavors. **PROPAGATION:** Seed or transplants. **HABITS/CULTURE:** Grows in almost any soil but best in healthy raised beds. Despite what you may have heard or read, peppers grow and produce very well in sun or shade. I've had excellent production in fairly heavy shade. Plant transplants after threat of last frost, usually two weeks after tomatoes are planted. Soil temperature should be at least 60 degrees. Sidedress with organic fertilizer when the plant first flowers. Germination in 6–14 days at 68–86 degrees. **USES:** Interesting potted plants, food. Peppers are loaded with trace minerals. They aid circulation and digestion. **PROBLEMS:** Sunburn on fruit, leaf miners, spider mites, leaf diseases, and nematodes. None are serious in an organic program. **TIPS/NOTES:** All capsicum peppers turn red when ripe. Always cut the peppers from the plant; breaking them off can severely damage the stems. Cayenne pepper is long, thin, bright red, and hot. Chili piquin or birdseye pepper is very hot and a favorite food of mockingbirds. It perennializes in the southern half of the state. 'Habanero' is a beautiful, bright orange pepper that looks like a small shriveled pumpkin. It has a distinctive taste and is extremely hot and will even burn your skin. 'Jalapeño' is a good hot standby. 'Serrano' is similar to jalapeño but smaller. 'Tabasco' is slow to mature but very hot and delicious. Spanish Spice, a big, long sweet pepper, is very productive. Other good sweet peppers include 'Big Bertha,' 'Sweet Banana,' 'Large Red Cherry,' 'Gypsy,' and 'Bell Tower.' Two good decorative peppers are 'Squash' and 'Purple Peruvian'; both are very hot. Black pepper, *Piper nigrum,* is harder to grow in Texas.

CARDINAL CLIMBER—see *Ipomoea* spp.

CARDINAL FLOWER—see *Lobelia cardinalis*

CARDINAL VINE—see *Ipomoea* spp.

Capsicum 'Habanero' Habanero pepper

Carissa macrocarpa natal plum

CARISSA

Carissa macrocarpa (ka-RISS-ah mac-row-CAR-pa). **COMMON NAME:** NATAL PLUM. **TYPE:** Evergreen shrub. **LOCATION:** Sun to part shade. **HEIGHT:** 4'–6'. **SPREAD:** 4'–6'. **SPACING:** 2'–3'. **BLOOM/FRUIT:** Very fragrant white flowers throughout the summer, followed by red plume-shaped edible fruit. **PROPAGATION:** Seed or cuttings. **HABITS/CULTURE:** Easy-to-grow, salt-tolerant plant for the lower third of the state. Thick dark green leaves, spines on branches and at the end of each twig. Thick and bushy. Dwarf variety 'Minima' grows only to 24" or so. Needs loose healthy soil and moderate water and fertilizer. **USES:** Screen or hedge, fragrance. **PROBLEMS:** Will freeze except in the far southern part of Texas. **TIPS/NOTES:** *Carissa macrocarpa* 'Boxwood Beauty' has no thorns.

CARISSA HOLLY—see *Ilex cornuta* 'Burfordii Nana'

CARNATION—see *Dianthus* spp.

CAROLINA BUCKTHORN—See *Rhamnus caroliniana*

CAROLINA JESSAMINE—see *Gelsemium sempervirens*

CAROLINA SNAILSEED—see *Cocculus carolinus*

CARPET BUGLE—see *Ajuga reptans*

CARROT—see *Daucus carota*

Capsicum ornamental pepper

CARICA

Carica papaya (KAR-ih-cah pah-PIE-yah). **COMMON NAME:** PAPAYA. **TYPE:** Tropical fruit tree. **LOCATION:** Sun. **HEIGHT:** 8'–10'. **SPREAD:** 5'–6'. **SPACING:** 4'–6'. **BLOOM/FRUIT:** Inconspicuous cream-colored flowers. **PROPAGATION:** Seed. **HABITS/CULTURE:** Straight trunks, crown of very large, deeply cut leaves on long stems. Fruit on female plants. Both male and female plants are needed for fruit production. Papaya plants have the ability to change sex. Fruit production is best when plants are started from seed in the winter and set outside in beds after the last frost. **USES:** Tropical effect, fruit production in the southern half of the state. **PROBLEMS:** Can't take any frost. **TIPS/NOTES:** Best to start new plants every year rather than trying to overwinter established plants in a greenhouse.

CARYA

Carya spp. (CARE-ee-ah). **COMMON NAME:** HICKORY. **TYPE:** Deciduous tree. **LOCATION:** Sun. **HEIGHT:** 50'–140'. **SPREAD:** 30'–50'. **SPACING:** 20'–30'. **BLOOM/FRUIT:** Spring catkins, fall egg-shaped nuts. **PROPAGATION:** Seed. **HABITS/CULTURE:** About eight species in Texas, hard to tell apart. They have very similar characteristics and hybridize freely between species. Generally like moist, acid soils of East Texas. *Carya glabra*, pignut hickory, likes well-drained ridges. *Carya texana*, black hickory, likes dry, granite-rock hillsides. *Carya ovata*, shagbark hickory, has the sweetest nuts. Foliage looks similar to that of pecan, but the leaflets are bigger. **USES:** Shade tree, edible nuts. **PROBLEMS:** Won't grow in alkaline soils. **TIPS/NOTES:** Hickan is a grafted cross between pecan root stock and hickory top.

Carya illinoinensis pecan

Carya illinoinensis pecan

Caryopteris blue mist

Carya illinoinensis (CARE-ee-ah ill-ih-noy-NEN-sis). **COMMON NAME:** PECAN. **TYPE:** Deciduous tree. **LOCATION:** Sun. **HEIGHT:** 100'. **SPREAD:** 100'. **SPACING:** 30'–50'. **BLOOM/FRUIT:** Male flowers in drooping catkins, female flower clusters when the leaves break out or just before. Nuts ripen in the fall. **PROPAGATION:** Seed, cuttings, or grafting. **HABITS/CULTURE:** Irregularly spreading, extremely graceful, yellow fall color, very long-lived and deep-rooted. Easy to grow anywhere. **USES:** Shade tree, pecan crop. **PROBLEMS:** Hickory shuckworm, pecan casebearer. Webworms are mainly an aesthetic problem. Somewhat messy most of the time. **TIPS/NOTES:** Great choice for the state tree. The native varieties make better landscape trees than those bred for soft-shell pecan crops; they also have the highest-quality nuts, although they are usually small and thick-shelled. Native to North America. Good hybrid choices for Texas include 'Caddo,' 'Desirable,' 'Chocktaw,' 'Kiowa,' and 'Cheyenne.' Do not plant 'Stuartz,' 'Mahan,' 'Burkett,' or 'Success.' Zinc is often recommended as a foliar spray, but I have found it to be unnecessary in a totally organic program.

CARYOPTERIS

Caryopteris spp. (ka-ree-OP-te-ris). **COMMON NAME:** BLUE MIST, BLUEBEARD, BLUE SPIRAEA. **TYPE:** Perennial bedding plant. **LOCATION:** Sun to part shade. **HEIGHT:** 2'–4'. **SPREAD:** 2'–3'. **SPACING:** 2'–3'. **BLOOM/FRUIT:** Deep blue to lavender flowers in summer. **PROPAGATION:** Cuttings or seed. **HABITS/CULTURE:** *Caryopteris clandonensis* is low-growing, usually about 2' high and 2' wide. 'Azure' and 'Heavenly Blue' are available cultivars. *Caryopteris incana* is taller-growing, usually up to 4'. Dies to the ground in winter and usually returns in spring in the northern half of the state. Makes a bushy evergreen in the southern part of the state. **USES:** Summer color. Excellent for use with white flowering plants. **PROBLEMS:** May freeze out in harsh winters. **TIPS/NOTES:** Hasn't been used much in the past. Should be planted more often.

CASHMERE BOUQUET—see *Clerodendrum bungei*

Cassia alata candletree

Castilleja indivisa
Indian paintbrush

CASSIA

Cassia alata (CASS-ee-ah ah-LAY-tah). **COMMON NAME:** CANDLETREE. **TYPE:** Tropical used as an annual bedding plant. **LOCATION:** Sun. **HEIGHT:** 6'–8'. **SPREAD:** 6'–8'. **SPACING:** 3'–4'. **BLOOM/FRUIT:** Showy yellow flowers in spiked clusters that bloom in late summer. Fruit is a dark pod containing several seeds. **PROPAGATION:** Seed or cuttings. **HABITS/CULTURE:** Open, spreading growth in summer. Large compound leaves. Becomes large in one season. Needs sun, loose organic soil, and moderate water and fertilizer. Prune back after flowering. **USES:** Dramatic accent plant, late summer color, background and annual color for large open areas. **TIPS/NOTES:** Parks departments use together with cannas for a carefree colorful show. Native to the tropics. *Cassia corymbosa* is the native common tree senna.

CASTOR BEAN—see *Ricinus communis*

CAST IRON PLANT—see *Aspidistra elatior*

Castilleja purpurea yellow Indian paintbrush

Catharanthus roseus periwinkle

Catalpa bignonioides catalpa

CASTILLEJA

Castilleja spp. (kass-teh-LAY-ah). **COMMON NAME:** IN-DIAN PAINTBRUSH. **TYPE:** Annual and perennial wild-flowers. **LOCATION:** Sun. **HEIGHT:** 6"–12". **SPREAD:** 9"–12". **SPACING:** 1/4 lb. per acre. **BLOOM/FRUIT:** Vertical spikes bloom from March to May. **PROPAGATION:** Seed. **HABITS/CULTURE:** Very small seed, usually hard to establish. **USES:** Wildflower. **PROBLEMS:** Harder to establish than other wildflowers. **TIPS/NOTES:** *Castilleja indivisa* is the annual red-orange Indian paintbrush. *Castilleja purpurea* is the perennial that blooms in red, yellow, white, pink, and orange. All paintbrushes are said to be parasitic on grass roots.

CATALPA

Catalpa bignonioides (kuh-TALL-puh big-none-ee-OID-ees). **COMMON NAME:** CATALPA, INDIAN BEAN. **TYPE:** Deciduous tree. **LOCATION:** Sun. **HEIGHT:** 60'. **SPREAD:** 40'. **SPACING:** 30'–40'. **BLOOM/FRUIT:** Showy white orchidlike flowers that bloom heavily in late spring. Fruit is a long bean containing many compressed and papery thin seeds. **PROPAGATION:** Seed or cuttings. **HABITS/CULTURE:** Large, fast-growing, open-branching. Smooth bark, very large light green leaves. Easy to grow in any soil, rarely needs pruning. Grown in East Texas to attract black caterpillars for fishing. **USES:** Shade tree for large estates, parks, and golf courses. Early summer flowers. **PROBLEMS:** Messy flowers and catalpa worms in summer. **TIPS/NOTES:** Great climbing tree. I like this tree more than most people do. When I was a kid, there were two large catalpas in our yard. I climbed them a lot. Native to the southern United States.

CATHARANTHUS

Catharanthus roseus (ca-tha-RAN-thus ro-SAY-us). **COMMON NAME:** PERIWINKLE, VINCA. **TYPE:** Annual bedding plant. **LOCATION:** Sun. **HEIGHT:** 9"–18". **SPREAD:** 12"–15". **SPACING:** 9"–12". **BLOOM/FRUIT:** Phloxlike white, pink, or rose flowers from early summer to fall. **PROPAGATION:** Seed. **HABITS/CULTURE:** Low, compact annual for dry areas. Very heat tolerant. Plant in any well-drained soil in full sun after the weather turns permanently warm in spring. **USES:** Summer color. **PROBLEMS:** Watering too much, planting too early in the spring, or using high-nitrogen synthetic fertilizer causes *Phytophthora* stem disease. **TIPS/NOTES:** Always plant the dwarf varieties so they won't droop over. Photo shows the most popular, 'Bright Eye.' Native to Madagascar. 'Pink Panther' has petals of dark pink or light red with white undersides, reddish stems. The disease problems that often plague periwinkle are usually eliminated in a totally organic program.

CATMINT—see *Nepeta* spp.

CATNIP—see *Nepeta* spp.

CAULIFLOWER—see *Brassica oleracea*

CEDAR, DEODAR—see *Cedrus deodara*

CEDAR, EASTERN RED—see *Juniperus virginiana*

CEDAR, INCENSE—see *Calocedrus decurrens*

CEDAR, MOUNTAIN—see *Juniperus virginiana*

CEDAR, RED—see *Juniperus virginiana*

CEDRUS

Cedrus deodara (SEE-drus dee-oh-DAR-a). **COMMON NAME:** DEODAR CEDAR. **TYPE:** Evergreen tree. **LOCATION:** Sun. **HEIGHT:** 50'. **SPREAD:** 30'. **SPACING:** 20'–40'. **BLOOM/FRUIT:** Unimportant. **PROPAGATION:** Cuttings or grafting. **HABITS/CULTURE:** Moderate growth rate, large conical shape, pointed top. Foliage reaches to the ground. Small pinelike needles. Fairly easy to grow in well-draining soil. Needs plenty of room. **USES:** Parks, large estates, evergreen backdrop. **PROBLEMS:** Too large at the base for most residential gardens; freeze damage, disease, bagworms, and red spider. **TIPS/NOTES:** Sometimes called "California Christmas Tree." Graceful when healthy, but I wouldn't invest much money in this plant. Native to the Himalayas.

Cedrus deodara deodar cedar

CELOSIA

Celosia spp. (sey-LOW-see-ah). **COMMON NAME:** COCKSCOMB. **TYPE:** Annual bedding plant. **LOCATION:** Sun. **HEIGHT:** 12"–24". **SPREAD:** 12"–18". **SPACING:** 10"–12". **BLOOM/FRUIT:** Bright red, pink, orange, or yellow flowers in summer. **PROPAGATION:** Seed. **HABITS/CULTURE:** Bold-textured summer color. Red is the most common flower. Some varieties also have red foliage. Plant in spring from transplants after last frost. Plant in midsummer for fall color. Cutting back to stimulate more flowers is not recommended. **USES:** Low border, dramatic color splashes. **PROBLEMS:** Slugs and snails. **TIPS/NOTES:** Dry by hanging upside down in a paper bag. Color will last all winter.

Celosia cockscomb

CELTIS

Celtis occidentalis hackberry

Celtis occidentalis (SEL-tis ok-si-den-TALL-is). **COMMON NAME:** HACKBERRY. **TYPE:** Deciduous tree. **LOCATION:** Sun. **HEIGHT:** 50'. **SPREAD:** 40'. **SPACING:** Do not plant! **BLOOM/FRUIT:** Inconspicuous flowers appear with the new leaves. Fruit is a round black drupe that ripens in the fall. Birds love 'em. **PROPAGATION:** Seed. **HABITS/CULTURE:** Fast-growing, short-lived. Self-propagates from seed every spring all over the place. *Celtis laevigata* is a less common variety. Any soil, any condition. **USES:** None. **PROBLEMS:** Galls, borers, weak roots, brittle wood, short life. **TIPS/NOTES:** Do not plant, and cut down the ones that sprout up! Native to North America. *Celtis sinensis,* Chinese hackberry, is supposedly much better—with longer leaves and no gall problem.

CENIZO—see *Leucophyllum frutescens*

CENTAUREA

Centaurea cineraria (sin-TAU-ree-ah sin-er-RARE-ee-ah). **COMMON NAME:** DUSTY MILLER. **TYPE:** Perennial herb and bedding plant. **LOCATION:** Sun. **HEIGHT:** 18"–24". **SPREAD:** 18"–24". **SPACING:** 12". **BLOOM/FRUIT:** Yellow flowers in early summer. **PROPAGATION:** Seeds or cuttings. **HABITS/CULTURE:** Distinctive plant with fuzzy, silver-gray foliage. Plant in full sun in any well-drained soil. Needs moderate water and fertilizer. **USES:** Color contrast, drought-tolerant gardens, stone walls, pots. **PROBLEMS:** Few if any. **TIPS/NOTES:** Plant from containers anytime. Native to southern Europe.

CENTURY PLANT—see *Agave* spp.

Centaurea cineraria dusty miller

Cercis canadensis eastern redbud

Cercis canadensis 'Oklahoma'
Oklahoma redbud

CEPHALANTHUS

Cephalanthus occidentalis (seff-ah-LAN-thus ox-eh-DEN-tal-is). **COMMON NAME:** BUTTONBUSH. **TYPE:** Deciduous shrub. **LOCATION:** Sun to part shade. **HEIGHT:** 10'–12'. **SPREAD:** 10'–12'. **SPACING:** 6'–8'. **BLOOM/FRUIT:** White or pale pink summer flowers in 1"–2" globes. Fruit in heavy brown clusters. **PROPAGATION:** Seed, root cuttings, root division. **HABITS/CULTURE:** Bush or small tree with round, fragrant pale pink to white flowers that bloom all summer in the sun, off and on in the shade. Will grow in wet soil and even in shallow water. **USES:** Attracts bees, butterflies, and waterfowl. **PROBLEMS:** Few if any.

Cercidiphyllum japonicum katsura

Cephalanthus occidentalis buttonbush

CERCIDIPHYLLUM

Cercidiphyllum japonicum (ker-ki-dee-FILE-um jah-PON-ih-come). **COMMON NAME:** KATSURA. **TYPE:** Deciduous tree. **LOCATION:** Best in morning sun and afternoon shade. **HEIGHT:** 30'–40'. **SPREAD:** 20'. **SPACING:** 10'–15'. **BLOOM/FRUIT:** Inconspicuous, slow-growing flowers. **PROPAGATION:** Cuttings. **HABITS/CULTURE:** Delicate branching and leaf pattern. Lovely blue-green foliage shows tints of red through the growing season. Red or yellow fall color. Slow-growing with nearly round 2"–3" leaves spaced in pairs along arching branches. Plant in deep, healthy soil in filtered light or in morning sun with afternoon shade. **USES:** Understory ornamental tree. **PROBLEMS:** Leaves will burn in hot afternoon sun. **TIPS/NOTES:** Worth a try. 'Pendula' is a weeping form.

CERCIS

Cercis canadensis (SER-sis kan-ah-DEN-sis). **COMMON NAME:** EASTERN REDBUD. **TYPE:** Deciduous tree. **LOCATION:** Sun or shade. **HEIGHT:** 20'–30'. **SPREAD:** 20'–30'. **SPACING:** 15'–20'. **BLOOM/FRUIT:** Rose, pinkish purple, or white flowers on bare branches in early spring. Fruit is a thin bean with several dark, hard seeds. **PROPAGATION:** Seed or cuttings. **HABITS/CULTURE:** Wide-spreading ornamental, purple or white spring color, yellow fall color. Easy to grow in any soil, drought tolerant. **USES:** Ornamental garden tree, understory spring color. **PROBLEMS:** Borers, leaf rollers. **TIPS/NOTES:** White variety seems healthier than the purple native. Crinkled-leaf Mexican variety is the most drought tolerant. 'Oklahoma' has dark green, glossy foliage; 'Forest Pansy' has red-purple foliage in summer. Flowers of all varieties are edible and delicious in salads or as a garnish.

CEREAL GRASSES—see Grasses

CHAENOMELES

Chaenomeles japonica (key-NOM-me-lees ja-PON-eh-cah). **COMMON NAME:** FLOWERING QUINCE. **TYPE:** Deciduous shrub. **LOCATION:** Sun to light shade. **HEIGHT:** 4'–6'. **SPREAD:** 4'–6'. **SPACING:** 3'–4'. **BLOOM/FRUIT:** Flowers are various shades of red, pink, and white in early spring. **PROPAGATION:** Cuttings. **HABITS/CULTURE:** Often the first shrub to bloom each year in late winter. Grows best in prepared beds but tolerates a wide range of soils. Will grow in sun or shade but blooms better in sun. Relatively drought tolerant. **USES:** Spring flower display. **PROBLEMS:** Leaf spot, chlorosis, heat. **TIPS/NOTES:** This is not a fruit tree. I use this plant more as a source of cut flowers than

as a shrub since it looks so bad in the summer months. Native to China. *Chaenomeles speciosa*, common flowering quince, is the larger-growing variety. *Cydonia oblonga* is the fruiting quince.

Chaenomeles japonica flowering quince

Chamaemelum chamomile

Chasmanthium latifolium inland seaoats

CHAMAEMELUM

Chamaemelum spp. (ka-mee-MAY-lum). **COMMON NAME:** CHAMOMILE. **TYPE:** Annual herb. **LOCATION:** Sun to part shade. **HEIGHT:** 12"–18". **SPREAD:** 18"–24". **SPACING:** 12". **PROPAGATION:** Seed. **BLOOM/FRUIT:** Small, daisylike white flowers. **HABITS/CULTURE:** Delicate fernlike foliage. Likes morning sun and afternoon shade. Can tolerate some light frost. **USES:** Sleep-inducing tea from the foliage and flowers. Lovely summer-flowering plant for the perennial garden. Good in pots. **PROBLEMS:** Caterpillars and slugs. **TIPS/NOTES:** Plant transplants in the spring. Plant seed about February 1, but protect plants if temperature drops below 25 degrees.

CHAMOMILE—see *Chamaemelum* spp.

CHARD—see *Beta vulgaris*

CHASMANTHUM

Chasmanthium latifolium (chas-MAN-thee-um lah-teh-FOLE-ee-um). **COMMON NAME:** INLAND SEAOATS, BAMBOOGRASS. **TYPE:** Perennial grass. **LOCATION:** Shade. **HEIGHT:** 2'–4'. **SPREAD:** Unlimited. **SPACING:** 2'–3'. **BLOOM/FRUIT:** Insignificant flowers, followed by very decorative pale tan seed pods. **PROPAGATION:** Division or seed. **HABITS/CULTURE:** Easy to grow in any soil in shady areas. Can tolerate morning sun. Looks like dwarf bamboo. **USES:** Great plant for erosion control in the shade. **PROBLEMS:** Spreads aggressively by seed and rhizomes, so be careful where you plant it. **TIPS/NOTES:** In large areas, sow 1/2–2 lbs. seed per thousand sq. ft. Stems with dry seed heads can be cut for long-lasting dry flower arrangements. Cutting the seed heads off before they mature helps to prevent spreading.

CHASTE TREE, LILAC—see *Vitex agnus-castus*

CHEIRANTHUS

Cheiranthus cheiri (ki-RAN-thus KAY-ree). **COMMON NAME:** WALLFLOWER. **TYPE:** Perennial. **LOCATION:** Sun to part shade. **HEIGHT:** 24". **SPREAD:** 24". **SPACING:** 18". **BLOOM/FRUIT:** Yellow, red, orange, or purple flowers in spring. Purple is most common. **PROPAGATION:** Seed or cuttings. **HABITS/CULTURE:** Gray-green foliage, fairly drought tolerant. Likes well-drained soils and plenty of mulch for best results. **USES:** Masses or borders. **PROBLEMS:** Doesn't like high humidity and heat. **TIPS/NOTES:** 'Bowles Mauve,' the best choice for Texas, has lavender flowers and a compact rounded shape.

CHENILLE PLANT—see *Acalypha hispida*

CHENOPODIUM

Chenopodium spp. (chin-no-PO-dee-um). **COMMON NAME:** EPASOTE, EPAZOTE, LAMB'S-QUARTER, WORM-SEED, JERUSALEM OAK. **TYPE:** Annual or perennial herb. **LOCATION:** Sun to light shade. **HEIGHT:** 3'–5'. **SPREAD:** 3' and more. **SPACING:** One is plenty. **BLOOM/FRUIT:** Tiny flowers, spikes of tiny green seeds in the fall. **PROPAGATION:** Seed. **HABITS/CULTURE:** Serrated leaves with camphorlike fragrance, multiple stems from the base, sprawling form with age. Very easy to grow in any soil in any location. No fertilizer necessary other than compost and mulch. **USES:** Food, flavoring agent, insect repellent. *Chenopodium album*, lamb's-quarter or pigweed, has leaves that are whitish underneath, smooth pale green above. Leaves can be eaten in salads or cooked like spinach. *Chenopodium ambrosioides*, epasote or Mexican tea, has strongly scented foliage and is used to flavor Spanish dishes. **PROBLEMS:** These plants can spread by seed and become serious pests; they sprout up anywhere. **TIPS/NOTES:** I make a sun tea by putting a large handful of epazote, comfrey, and rosemary in a 5-gallon bucket of water, covering it with clear plastic, and leaving it in the sun for one day. It's an excellent flea repellent and good for the skin of dogs and cats. Epasote is the bean herb. Toss a couple of leaves or two teaspoons of the dried herb into any bean dish during the last 15 minutes of cooking to eliminate the gas. That's what they say!

CHERRY, WILD BLACK—see *Prunus serotina*

CHERRY, SOUR—see *Prunus cerasus*

CHICKWEED—see Weeds

CHILE—see *Capsicum* spp.

Chilopsis linearis desert willow

CHILOPSIS

Chilopsis linearis (KY-lop-sis lin-ee-ERR-is). **COMMON NAME:** DESERT WILLOW. **TYPE:** Deciduous tree. **LOCATION:** Sun. **HEIGHT:** 30'. **SPREAD:** 25'. **SPACING:** 15'–20'. **BLOOM/FRUIT:** Fragrant, tubular, snapdragon-like summer flowers. Colors range from white to pale pink, deep rose, and purple. Fruit is long, hard capsule with many flat, oval, feathery winged seeds. **PROPAGATION:** Seed or cuttings. **HABITS/CULTURE:** No fall color to speak of. Easy to grow in any soil. Drought tolerant. Does better with more water. Prune often for dense growth and more flowers. **USES:** Specimen garden tree, summer color. **PROBLEMS:** Root rot if overwatered. **TIPS/NOTES:** Lovely small tree that should be used more. Native to the southwestern United States. Has a high tolerance of chlorinated water.

Chilopsis × Catalpa (KY-lop-sis kuh-TALL-puh). **COMMON NAME:** CHITALPA. **TYPE:** Deciduous tree. **LOCATION:** Sun. **HEIGHT:** 30'. **SPREAD:** 30'. **SPACING:** 20'–30'. **BLOOM/FRUIT:** Pink or white catalpa-like or orchidlike flowers that bloom all summer. **PROPAGATION:** Cuttings. **HABITS/CULTURE:** Cross between catalpa and desert willow. Very open-branching tree. Leaves are 6"–8" long and 1"–2" wide. Smooth, light-colored bark. Easy to grow in any soil. Rarely needs pruning. **USES:** Distinctive garden or small-area tree. **PROBLEMS:** Root rot if overwatered. Catalpa moth caterpillar. **TIPS/NOTES:** This hybrid cultivar is relatively new to the scene, and its health is questionable.

Chilopsis × Catalpa chitalpa

CHINABERRY—see *Melia azedarach*

CHINESE ELM—see *Ulmus parvifolia sempervirens*

CHINESE FRINGE TREE—see *Chionanthus virginica*

CHINESE JUJUBE—see *Ziziphus* spp.

CHINESE PARASOL TREE—see *Firmiana simplex*

CHINESE PARSLEY—see *Coriandrum sativum*

CHINESE TALLOW—see *Sapium sebiferum*

CHINESE WISTERIA—see *Wisteria sinensis*

CHINKAPIN OAK—see *Quercus muhlenbergii*

Chionanthus virginica fringe tree

CHIONANTHUS

Chionanthus virginica (key-oh-NAN-thus ver-JIN-eh-kah). **COMMON NAME:** FRINGE TREE, CHINESE FRINGE TREE. **TYPE:** Deciduous tree. **LOCATION:** Partial shade. **HEIGHT:** 15'–30'. **SPREAD:** 15'–20'. **SPACING:** 10'–25'. **BLOOM/FRUIT:** Lacy, fragrant white flower clusters in spring just before foliage appears and immediately after the dogwoods bloom. Both male and female flowers are beautiful. Female plants have dark blue clusters of berries that ripen in late summer to fall. **PROPAGATION:** Seed, soft-wood cuttings. **HABITS/CULTURE:** Gorgeous, slow-growing, ornamental native tree. Does best in sandy, acid soils but will grow in soil with a neutral pH—in Houston, for example. Yellow fall color. Moderate water requirements. Can grow in wet soil. **USES:** Ornamental understory tree, spring color. **PROBLEMS:** Not adapted to alkaline soil. **TIPS/NOTES:** Flowers form on year-old growth, so prune only after blooming.

CHISOS OAK—see *Quercus shumardii* or *texana*

CHITALPA—see *Chilopsis* × *Catalpa*

CHITTAMWOOD—see *Bumelia lanuginosa*

CHIVES—see *Allium* spp.

CHOKE CHERRY—see *Prunus serotina*

CHLOROPHYLLUM

Chlorophyllum spp. (cho-lor-PHI-lum). **COMMON NAME:** FAIRY RING, TOADSTOOL. **HEIGHT:** 4"–6". **SPREAD:** 3'–12'. **BLOOM/FRUIT:** Mushrooms. **PROPAGATION:** Spores. **HABITS/CULTURE:** Fruiting bodies of fungi growing on decaying organic matter. White caps that looks like golf balls when young expand to 4"–8" in diameter at maturity. Usually appear in lawns in summer after rainy periods. Caps are white at first, then turn gray-green and have distinctive green spores, reddish brown "scales" on the cap, and a ring on the smooth stalk. Fairy rings usually grow in soil where wood is decaying, such as roots or an old stump. **USES:** None. **PROBLEMS:** Visual only, no problem for the turf. **TIPS/NOTES:** Very toxic! Known for their tendency to collect heavy metals from the air and soil.

CHRISTMAS AMARYLLIS—see *Hippeastrum* spp.

CHRYSANTHEMUM

Chrysanthemum spp. (kruh-SAN-thuh-mum). **COMMON NAME:** CHRYSANTHEMUM, MUM. **TYPE:** Perennial bedding plant. **LOCATION:** Sun. **HEIGHT:** 12"–36". **SPREAD:** 18"–36". **SPACING:** 12"–18". **BLOOM/FRUIT:** Fall-blooming perennials with lots of colors and combinations. Some bloom in spring, some in fall. **PROPAGATION:** Cuttings or division. **HABITS/CULTURE:** Attractive foliage that looks good most of the year. Likes loose soil, good drainage, ample water, and regular fertilization. For best blooms, pinch the new growth off until August 1. Stop fertilization when the buds show color. Light shining on the plants at night retards blooms. **USES:** Perennial gardens, borders, pots, and cutting gardens. **PROBLEMS:** Aphids. **TIPS/NOTES:** The National Chrysanthemum Society has established 13 different categories: Spoon, Reflexing Incurve, Semidouble, Decorative, Anemone, Spider, Single, Reflex, Pompom, Thistle, Laciniated, Quill, and Incurve. They are all beautiful. Native to Europe, Asia, and South Africa.

Chrysanthemum cinerariifolium (kruh-SAN-thuh-mum sin-er-rare-ee-eye-FOLL-ee-um). **COMMON NAME:** PYRETHRUM, INSECT FLOWER, PAINTED DAISY. **TYPE:** Perennial bedding plant. **LOCATION:** Sun. **HEIGHT:** 12"–36". **SPREAD:** 12"–36". **SPACING:** 12". **BLOOM/FRUIT:** White or yellow 1 1/2" summer flowers. **PROPAGATION:** Seed. **HAB-**

Chrysanthemum chrysanthemum

Chrysanthemum leucanthemum oxeye daisy

ITS/CULTURE: Foot-long foliage with a silvery, silky, hairy underside. Colorful daisylike, long-stemmed summer flowers. **USES:** Summer color, pyrethrum organic insecticide. **PROBLEMS:** Toxic to handle. **INSIGHT:** *Chrysanthemum coccineum,* more commonly called painted daisy, is also a source of pyrethrum and has white, yellow, pink, and red flowers.

Chrysanthemum leucanthemum (kruh-SAN-thuh-mum loo-KAN-thuh-mum). **COMMON NAME:** OXEYE DAISY. **TYPE:** Perennial bedding plant or wildflower. **LOCATION:** Sun. **HEIGHT:** 12"–36". **SPREAD:** 18"–36". **SPACING:** 12"–18". **BLOOM/FRUIT:** Large, showy white flowers from early June to August. **PROPAGATION:** Seed, cuttings, or division. **HABITS/CULTURE:** Returns very well each year. Easy to grow in any well-drained soil. Low water and fertilizer requirements. Established plants should be divided every few years. **USES:** Summer flowers, perennial gardens. **PROBLEMS:** None serious. **TIPS/NOTES:** Cut flowers have a bad odor. This plant is similar to *Chrysanthemum × superbum*, shasta daisy, but tougher and more drought tolerant. 'Silver Princess' is a good shasta daisy choice. *Machaeranthera tanacetifolia*, Tahoka daisy, is a Texas native that blooms all summer with blue flowers. *Aphanostephus skirrhobasis*, lazy daisy, is a low-growing annual.

CIGAR PLANT—see *Cuphea* spp.

CILANTRO—see *Coriandrum sativum*

CINNAMOMUM

Cinnamomum camphora (sin-ah-MO-mum cam-FORE-rah). **COMMON NAME:** CAMPHOR TREE. **TYPE:** Evergreen tree. **LOCATION:** Full sun. **HEIGHT:** 40'–50'. **SPREAD:** 30'. **SPACING:** 20'–30'. **BLOOM/FRUIT:** Clusters of very small, fragrant white flowers in late spring, followed by small black fruits. **PROPAGATION:** Cuttings. **HABITS/CULTURE:** Beautiful shiny fragrant leaves that smell like camphor. Needs protection in winter and excellent drainage. **USES:** Potpourri, specimen tree. **PROBLEMS:** Roots are very competitive. May freeze at 20 degrees and below. Possible root rot. **TIPS/NOTES:** Use from San Antonio south.

Cinnamomum camphora camphor tree

CITRUS

Citrus spp. (SIT-rus). **COMMON NAME:** ORANGE, GRAPEFRUIT, LEMON, LIME. **TYPE:** Tender evergreen. **LOCATION:** Full sun. **HEIGHT:** 5'–20'. **SPREAD:** 5'–20'. **SPACING:** 8'–20'. **BLOOM/FRUIT:** Fragrant flowers in spring, followed by decorative and delicious fruit. **PROPAGATION:** Seed, grafts to trifoliate orange rootstock. **HABITS/CULTURE:** Glossy evergreen foliage, fragrant flowers, colorful summer fruit. **USES:** Potted plants, fruit production. **PROBLEMS:** Freeze damage in most of the state. **TIPS/NOTES:** All the citrus species can be grown in the far southern part of the state, but it's sometimes risky even there. Satsuma orange seems to be the most cold tolerant of all the citrus, but still needs winter protection in most of the state. In the northern half of the state, be sure to grow citrus plants in a pot so you can move them inside during freezing weather.

CITRULLUS

Citrullus vulgaris (sit-RUL-us vul-GAIR-is). **COMMON NAME:** WATERMELON. **TYPE:** Annual fruit. **LOCATION:** Sun. **HEIGHT/SPREAD:** Very large vine, will climb and spread to over 20'. **SPACING:** 4'–10'. **BLOOM/FRUIT:** Small yellow flowers, followed by extremely large yellow- or red-meated fruit. **PROPAGATION:** Seed. Germination occurs in 4–14 days at 68–86 degrees. **HABITS/CULTURE:** Large-growing, deep-rooted annual that loves sandy soil, although it will grow in any healthy soil. **USES:** Food crop. **PROBLEMS:** Poor pollination, downy mildew, blossom-end rot from uneven soil moisture, cutworm, and white heart caused by overfertilization. **TIPS/NOTES:** Watermelons are ripe when the tendril nearest the fruit has turned dry and brown.

Clematis paniculata sweet autumn clematis

CLEMATIS

Clematis paniculata (KLEM-ah-tis pa-nik-ew-LAH-ta). **COMMON NAME:** CLEMATIS, FALL CLEMATIS, SWEET AUTUMN CLEMATIS. **TYPE:** Perennial vine. **LOCATION:** Sun to shade. **HEIGHT:** High-climbing. **SPREAD:** 8'–20'. **SPACING:** 3'–6'. **BLOOM/FRUIT:** Small white flowers in late summer. The fruit that follows is very lacy and long lasting. **PROPAGATION:** Seed, cuttings. **HABITS/CULTURE:** Vigorous semi-evergreen climbing vine with profusion of fra-

C

Clematis pitcheri native clematis

grant 1" white flowers in the late summer. Easy to grow in any well-drained soil. Needs little to moderate water and light fertilizer. Don't prune the first year. **USES:** Climbing vine for fences, arbors, and decorative screens. Late-summer color. **PROBLEMS:** Somewhat aggressive. **TIPS/NOTES:** The correct botanical name is *Clematis maximowicziana*. Native to Japan. *Clematis × jackmanii* also does pretty well here in filtered light. *Clematis texensis,* scarlet clematis, is native and has small unusual red flowers. *Clematis pitcheri* is the purple-flowering native.

CLEOME

Cleome spinosa (CLAY-oh-mee spin-OH-sa). **COMMON NAME:** SPIDER FLOWER. **TYPE:** Annual bedding plant. **LOCATION:** Sun to part shade. **HEIGHT:** 3'–5'. **SPREAD:** 3'–4'. **SPACING:** 2'–3'. **BLOOM/FRUIT:** White, pink, and purple flowers in summer. **PROPAGATION:** Seed. **HABITS/CULTURE:** Plant in morning sun for best results. Needs healthy, well-drained soil. Plant transplants or sow seed directly into garden soil after soil has warmed in the spring. Will re-seed readily. **USES:** Background summer color. Interesting texture. **PROBLEMS:** Wet soil will do it in. **TIPS/NOTES:** Dramatic summer color—should be used more often.

CLERODENDRUM

Clerodendrum bungei (kle-ro-DEN-drum BUNG-gee-ee). **COMMON NAME:** CASHMERE BOUQUET. **TYPE:** Perennial herb. **LOCATION:** Sun to shade. **HEIGHT:** 3'–6'. **SPREAD:** 6' and more. **SPACING:** 3'. **BLOOM/FRUIT:** Fragrant pink to red 1/2" flowers in 6"–8" clusters. **PROPAGATION:** Division. **HABITS/CULTURE:** Large dark green leaves with fuzzy undersides. Showy summer flowers. Spreads aggressively by underground suckers. Cut back severely in the spring and pick-prune through the growing season to maintain interesting summer color and texture. **USES:** Attracts hummingbirds. Good with other aggressive plants like perilla, houtouynia, and hojo santa where spreading is not a worry. **PROBLEMS:** Is very invasive. *Clerodendrum paniculatum* is the pagoda flower. *Clerodendrum speciosissimum* is the dramatic java plant.

CLEYERA—see *Ternstroemia gymnanthera*

CLOVER, BUR—see Weeds

CLOVER, CRIMSON—see *Trifolium repens*

CLOVER, WHITE—see *Trifolium repens*

Cleome spinosa spider flower

Clerodendrum bungei Cashmere bouquet

Cocculus carolinus Carolina snailseed

COCCULUS

Cocculus carolinus (COKE-cue-lus kar-oh-LINN-us). **COMMON NAME:** CAROLINA SNAILSEED, MOONSEED, SNAILSEED. **TYPE:** Perennial vine. **LOCATION:** Sun to part shade. **HEIGHT:** 10'–15'. **SPREAD:** 10'–15'. **BLOOM/FRUIT:** Small off-white flowers from July to October, clusters of red berries in the fall. **PROPAGATION:** Seed. **HABITS/CULTURE:** Twining native vine with heart-shaped leaves and unspectacular flowers, followed by showy clusters of bright, shiny red berries. Vine looks like greenbriar but has no lobes. **USES:** Native vine, food for wildlife. **TIPS/NOTES:** Considered a weed by many but actually a pretty nice-looking vine.

COCKSCOMB—see *Celosia* spp.

CODIAEUM

Codiaeum variegatum (ko-dee-EYE-um var-ee-ah-GAH-tum). **COMMON NAME:** CROTON. **TYPE:** Tropical evergreen shrub. **LOCATION:** Sun to part shade. **HEIGHT:** 3'–6'. **SPREAD:** 3'. **SPACING:** 24". **PROPAGATION:** Stem cuttings. **HABITS/CULTURE:** Tender evergreen shrub used as an annual for foliage color. Large colorful leaves with yellow and red variegations. Plant in well-prepared beds. Color is better in full sun than in shade. **USES:** Summer color, potted plants to be moved indoors in winter. **PROBLEMS:** Red spider mites on stressed plants, root rot in poorly drained soils.

Codiaeum variegatum croton   *Coleus* coleus

COLEUS

Coleus hybrids (COLE-ee-us). **COMMON NAME:** COLEUS. **TYPE:** Annual bedding plant. **LOCATION:** Shade. **HEIGHT:** 18"–24". **SPREAD:** 18"–24". **SPACING:** 12"–18". **BLOOM/FRUIT:** Insignificant purple flower stalks. **PROPAGATION:** Cuttings. **HABITS/CULTURE:** Colorful leaves of red, yellow, orange, green, and various combinations. Dies at frost, very tender to cold. Needs shade, drainage, moisture, and protection from wind. Keep flowers pinched off to benefit foliage. **USES:** Summer color. Border or mass plantings. Containers or hanging baskets. **PROBLEMS:** Slugs, snails, mealybugs, and aphids. **TIPS/NOTES:** Roots easily in water and can be grown indoors. Coleus produced from cuttings are more colorful, flower less, and can take more sun. They are often sold as sun coleus. Native to the tropics.

COLLARDS—see *Brassica oleracea*

COLOCASIA

Colocasia esculenta (col-oh-KASS-ee-ah ESS-cue-len-ta). **COMMON NAME:** ELEPHANT EARS. **TYPE:** Perennial bulb. **LOCATION:** Sun to part shade. **HEIGHT:** 3'–6'. **SPREAD:** 2'–4'. **SPACING:** 2'–3'. **BLOOM/FRUIT:** Insignificant. **PROPAGATION:** Corms or division. **HABITS/CULTURE:** Very large leaves on long stems. Looks like a big caladium. **USES:** Texture change, especially effective near water. **PROBLEMS:** Will sometimes freeze out in the northern part of the state.

Colocasia esculenta elephant ears

COLUMBINE—see *Aquilegia* spp.

COMFREY—see *Symphytum officinale*

CONEFLOWER—see *Rudbeckia hirta*

CONEFLOWER, PURPLE—see *Echinacea angustifolia*

CONEFLOWER, YELLOW—see *Heliopsis scabra*

CONSOLIDA

Consolida ambigua (kon-SO-li-da am-BIG-you-ah). **COMMON NAME:** LARKSPUR, DELPHINIUM. **TYPE:** Annual bedding plant. **LOCATION:** Sun or part shade. **HEIGHT:** 18"–36". **SPREAD:** 18"–24". **SPACING:** 12". **BLOOM/FRUIT:** Pink, salmon, blue, white, rose, or purple blooms in spring or early summer. **PROPAGATION:** Seed. **HABITS/CULTURE:** Upright annual that reseeds easily to return year after year. Lacy foliage and dense vertical flowers. Blooms best in the cooler part of the growing season. **USES:** Good annual in perennial beds. **PROBLEMS:** Poisonous. **TIPS/NOTES:** Seed should be planted in fall for best results but can be planted through February.

Consolida ambigua larkspur

COPPERLEAF—see *Acalypha wilkesiana*

COPPERPLANT—see *Acalypha wilkesiana*

CORALBERRY—see *Symphoricarpos orbiculatus*

CORAL VINE—see *Antigonon leptopus*

Coreopsis coreopsis

Cornus drummondii rough-leaf dogwood

COREOPSIS

Coreopsis spp. (ko-ree-OP-sis). **COMMON NAME:** CORE-OPSIS. **TYPE:** Perennial bedding plant and wildflower. **LOCATION:** Sun to light shade. **HEIGHT:** 12"–36". **SPREAD:** 24". **SPACING:** 12"–24". **BLOOM/FRUIT:** Yellow daisylike flowers from late spring through summer. **PROPAGATION:** Seed. **HABITS/CULTURE:** Perennial that looks good most of the year and great while in bloom from May to August. Primarily yellow flowers. Easy to grow in any soil, minimal water and food needs. **USES:** Summer color, perennial beds, cut flowers. **PROBLEMS:** Few if any. **TIPS/NOTES:** *Coreopsis lanceolata* is a pure yellow native. Several hybrids such as 'Sun Ray' and 'Baby Sun' are available. *Coreopsis tinctoria* is an annual with a red center. There are many other choices, and almost all of them are good. *Coreopsis verticillata* 'Moonbeam' is an excellent fern-leafed perennial.

CORIANDER—see *Coriandrum sativum*

CORIANDRUM

Coriandrum sativum (ko-ree-AN-drum sa-TEE-vum). **COMMON NAME:** CORIANDER, CHINESE PARSLEY, CILANTRO. **TYPE:** Annual. **LOCATION:** Full sun or morning sun with afternoon shade. **HEIGHT:** 18"–24". **SPREAD:** 18"–24". **SPACING:** 12"–15". **BLOOM/FRUIT:** White or mauve flowers in summer, followed by umbels of round seed. **PROPAGATION:** Seed. **HABITS/CULTURE:** Easy to grow from seed. Original leaves are flat and green, resembling Italian parsley. As the plant matures, the leaves become feathery and the flowers start to appear. **USES:** Culinary herb. Foliage and seeds are used to flavor many dishes. **PROBLEMS:** None serious if planted at the proper time. **TIPS/NOTES:** Plant seeds or transplants before the last frost in spring or in September for a fall crop. Coriander likes cool weather.

CORNUS

Cornus drummondii (KOR-nus druh-MUN-dee-eye). **COMMON NAME:** ROUGH-LEAF DOGWOOD. **TYPE:** Deciduous small tree. **LOCATION:** Sun or shade. **HEIGHT:** 15'. **SPREAD:** 15'. **SPACING:** 6'–12'. **BLOOM/FRUIT:** Creamy white flower clusters in late spring, hard white fruit in fall. Fruits

Cornus florida flowering dogwood   *Cornus florida* flowering dogwood

disappear quickly because birds love them. **PROPAGATION:** Seed or cuttings. **HABITS/CULTURE:** Small tree, blooms after leaves have formed in late spring. Seed pods are white in late summer and purple in fall. Plant spreads easily by seeds and suckers and can become a pest. Stems are reddish and very decorative in winter. Easy to grow in any soil. Drought tolerant. **USES:** Background mass, understory tree, seeds for birds. **PROBLEMS:** Leaf fungus. Can be invasive. **TIPS/NOTES:** Many have been cut down by people thinking they are weeds. This plant is graceful and tough, should be used more in natural gardens. Native from the eastern United States to Texas.

Cornus florida (KOR-nus FLOR-eh-duh). **COMMON NAME:** FLOWERING DOGWOOD. **TYPE:** Deciduous tree. **LOCATION:** Shade to part shade. **HEIGHT:** 20'. **SPREAD:** 20'. **SPACING:** 15'–20'. **BLOOM/FRUIT:** Lovely white or pink spring flowers. Red seeds (drupes) in the fall. **PROPAGATION:** Seed or cuttings. **HABITS/CULTURE:** Graceful, layered structure. Pink or white flowers in spring. Red fall color. Needs loose, acid, highly organic, well-drained soil and plenty of moisture. Will do best in beds of mostly organic material. **USES:** Ornamental tree, spring flowers, red fall color. Oriental gardens. **PROBLEMS:** Cotton root rot, soil alkalinity, borers. **TIPS/NOTES:** This tree is native to acid, sandy soils like those in East Texas. Many improved cultivars available.

C

CORONILLA

Coronilla varia (ko-row-NIL-ah VAR-ee-ah). **COMMON NAME:** CROWN VETCH. **TYPE:** Perennial ground cover. **LOCATION:** Sun to part shade. **HEIGHT:** 24". **SPREAD:** Wide-spreading. **SPACING:** 20–30 lbs. of seed per acre. **BLOOM/FRUIT:** Lavender-pink flowers in 1" clusters, followed by brown seed pods. **PROPAGATION:** Seed. **HABITS/CULTURE:** Legume that spreads aggressively by creeping roots and rhizomes. Very easy to grow in any part of the state. **USES:** Ground cover for cut banks, erosion control on slopes. **PROBLEMS:** Rank growth habit, invasive. Once established, it's difficult to eliminate.

CORTADERIA

Cortaderia selloana (core-ta-DER-ee-ah sell-oh-AN-ah). **COMMON NAME:** PAMPAS GRASS. **TYPE:** Perennial grass. **LOCATION:** Sun. **HEIGHT:** 8'. **SPREAD:** 8'. **SPACING:** 8'–10'. **BLOOM/FRUIT:** Tall white flower plumes from late summer through fall. **PROPAGATION:** Division. **HABITS/CULTURE:** Fountainlike grass clumps with long, slender, sharp-edged blades of foliage. White flower plumes in late summer that last long into the winter. Foliage turns brown in harsh winters and should be cut back. Easy to grow in any soil. Minimal water and food requirements. Needs good drainage. **USES:** Accent plant, border for roads, drives, or parks. Good for distant viewing. **PROBLEMS:** Few if any. **TIPS/NOTES:** White plumes are good for interior arrangements. Female plants have the showiest plumes. Native to South America. The Texas native *Muhlenbergia lindheimeri*, Muhlygrass, is similar but more natural-looking.

Cortaderia selloana Pampas grass

CORYLUS

Corylus avellana 'Contorta' (KO-ril-us ah-ve-LAH-na). **COMMON NAME:** HARRY LAUDER'S WALKING STICK, WALKING STICK FILBERT. **TYPE:** Deciduous ornamental tree. **LOCATION:** Sun to part shade. **HEIGHT:** 8'–10'. **SPREAD:** 8'–10'. **SPACING:** 6'–8'. **PROPAGATION:** Cuttings. **HABITS/CULTURE:** Dramatically gnarled and twisted branches and twigs, with smaller leaves than the mother plant's. Very slow-growing. **USES:** Special feature, potted plant, courtyard tree, novelty. **PROBLEMS:** Tends to sucker from root stock. **TIPS/NOTES:** Kin to regular filbert and hazelnut.

Cosmos sulphureus cosmos

COSMOS

Cosmos spp. (KOS-mos). **COMMON NAME:** COSMOS. **TYPE:** Annual bedding plant. **LOCATION:** Sun. **HEIGHT:** 12"–18". **SPREAD:** 2"–4". **SPACING:** 12"–18". **BLOOM/FRUIT:** Open branching effect. Daisylike flowers, double and single in yellow, white, purple, pink, and red. **PROPAGATION:** Seed. **HABITS/CULTURE:** Lacy foliage and flowers on long stems. Multicolored flowers in summer. Easily grown from seed in any well-drained soil. Plant in late spring or early summer. **USES:** Masses, borders, backgrounds, summer flowers, bird attractant. **PROBLEMS:** Few if any. Prone to fungus if planted too early in the season. **TIPS/NOTES:** Plant from seed directly in beds after last frost. Native to Mexico. *Cosmos bipinnatus* has thicker stems, grows taller, and comes in several colors. *Cosmos sulphureus* is the mostly yellow variety.

COTINUS

Cotinus spp. (co-TIN-us). **COMMON NAME:** SMOKETREE. **TYPE:** Deciduous shrub. **LOCATION:** Sun to part shade. **HEIGHT:** 10'–15'. **SPREAD:** 10'–15'. **SPACING:** 10'. **BLOOM/FRUIT:** Off-white to light purple 12" panicles from mid to late spring. **PROPAGATION:** Cuttings, seed, or layering. **HABITS/CULTURE:** Upright and open, beautiful round leaves. Several cultivars are available with a wide range of yellow, red, and purple color in spring, summer, and fall. Smokelike false flowers in spring or early summer. Tough plant, easy to grow in any soil, drought tolerant. Needs excellent drainage. **USES:** Specimen, foliage color, unique flowers. **PROBLEMS:** Few if any in well-drained soil. **TIPS/NOTES:** *Cotinus coggygria* is the introduction from

Europe and Asia. Two good purple-leaf cultivars are 'Royal Purple' and 'Velvet Cloak.' *Cotinus obovatus* is the native plant. It has green summer foliage, grows larger, and has lovely apricot-gold and sometimes red fall color.

Cotinus smoketree

Cotinus smoketree

COTONEASTER

Cotoneaster glaucophyllus (co-ton-ee-AS-ter glau-co-FILE-us). **COMMON NAME:** GRAY COTONEASTER. **TYPE:** Evergreen shrub. **LOCATION:** Sun. **HEIGHT:** 3'–4'. **SPREAD:** 3'–4'. **SPACING:** 2'–3'. **BLOOM/FRUIT:** Lots of tiny white flowers in spring, red-orange berries in late summer and fall. **PROPAGATION:** Cuttings. **HABITS/CULTURE:** Low mass, color contrast. Likes any well-drained soil. Tolerates extreme heat and reflected light. Needs full sun. **PROBLEMS:** Fireblight, too much water. **TIPS/NOTES:** Not as healthy as *Cotoneaster horizontalis*. Native to China.

Cotoneaster glaucophyllus
gray cotoneaster

Cotoneaster horizontalis
rock cotoneaster

Cotoneaster horizontalis (co-ton-ee-AS-ter hor-eh-zon-TALL-is). **COMMON NAME:** ROCK COTONEASTER. **TYPE:** Deciduous shrub. **LOCATION:** Sun. **HEIGHT:** 2'–3'. **SPREAD:** 5'–6'. **SPACING:** 2'–3'. **BLOOM/FRUIT:** Small pink flowers in late spring. **PROPAGATION:** Cuttings. **HABITS/CULTURE:** Low, horizontal, spreading branches are layered and arch downward. Very graceful. Reddish purple fall color and bare branches in winter. Must have good drainage. Well-prepared beds are best, and it likes being on the dry side. **USES:** Mass planting, accent, distinctive texture. **PROBLEMS:** Several insects and fireblight can attack this plant if in stress. **TIPS/NOTES:** *Cotoneaster dammeri* resembles rock cotoneaster but is smaller and has larger flowers in the spring. Native to China.

COTTON—see *Gossypium* spp.

COTTONWOOD—see *Populus deltoides*

COVER CROPS

Buckwheat—*Fagopyrum* spp. Plant at a rate of 30 lbs. seed per acre after the last killing frost in spring.

Clover—see *Trifolium repens*

Elbon rye—*Secale cereale.* Plant in October at a rate of 2 1/2–4 lbs. seed per thousand sq. ft. or 25–50 lbs. per acre as a winter cover crop and deterrent to harmful nematodes.

Hairy vetch—see *Vicia* spp.

Oats—*Avena sativa.* Plant in October at a rate of 30–40 lbs. seed per acre. Works well as a winter crop, especially when used with hairy vetch.

Peas—see *Pisum sativum* or *Vigna sinensis*

CRABAPPLE—see *Malus floribunda*

CRABGRASS—see *Digitaria* spp.

CRAPE MYRTLE—see *Lagerstroemia indica*

CRATAEGUS

Crataegus mollis (krah-TEEG-us MAH-lis). **COMMON NAME:** NATIVE HAWTHORN. **TYPE:** Deciduous tree. **LOCATION:** Sun to shade. **HEIGHT:** 25'–40'. **SPREAD:** 20'–30'. **SPACING:** 20'. **BLOOM/FRUIT:** White spring flowers, red fall fruit. **PROPAGATION:** Seed, cuttings. **HABITS/CULTURE:** Gorgeous white flowers in spring. Delicate foliage and red berries in fall. Flaky bark and usually multiple trunks. Easy to grow in any well-drained soil, drought tolerant. **USES:** Understory tree, specimen garden tree. **PROBLEMS:** Cedar apple rust, aphids and other insects. **TIPS/NOTES:** Found mostly in higher, well-drained rocky soils. Native to Central Texas and Oklahoma. *Crataegus texana*, Texas hawthorn, is quite similar. Mayhaws are *Crataegus aestivalis* and *Crataegus opaca*. Parsley hawthorn is *Crataegus marshallii*, and *Crataegus reverchonii* is the reverchon hawthorn. Green hawthorn is *Crataegus viridis*.

Crataegus mollis
native hawthorn

Crataegus phaenopyrum
Washington hawthorn

Crataegus phaenopyrum (krah-TEEG-us fa-no-PIE-rum). **COMMON NAME:** WASHINGTON HAWTHORN. **TYPE:** Deciduous tree. **LOCATION:** Sun to part shade. **HEIGHT:** 25'. **SPREAD:** 15'. **SPACING:** 10'–15'. **BLOOM/FRUIT:** White flowers in spring, small red berries in fall. **PROPAGATION:** Seed, cuttings. **HABITS/CULTURE:** Upright, densely branching with thorns. Clusters of white flowers in spring, blooms later than most spring-flowering trees. Red berries from fall through winter. Yellow fall color. Easy to grow and less susceptible to rust than other varieties. **USES:** Specimen garden tree. **PROBLEMS:** Some folks don't like the thorns, but they don't bother me. **TIPS/NOTES:** Should be used more in this area. Native to the eastern and northeastern United States.

CREEPER, TRUMPET—see *Campsis radicans*

CREEPER, VIRGINIA—see *Parthenocissus quinquefolia*

CRINUM
Crinum spp. (CRY-num). **COMMON NAME:** CRINUM LILY. **TYPE:** Perennial wildflower. **LOCATION:** Sun to part shade. **SPREAD:** 24"–40". **SPACING:** 24"–40". **BLOOM/FRUIT:** Some bloom in early summer, others in late summer. Lilylike flowers in white, pink, and rose. **PROPAGATION:** Seed or offshoots from mother plants. **HABITS/CULTURE:** Clumping perennial with long stalks, 4"–6" lily-shaped, fragrant flowers. Thick fleshy roots from large bulbs. Plant in spring or fall in rich, healthy soil. **USES:** Perennial garden, bold foliage texture. **PROBLEMS:** Slugs and snails. **TIPS/NOTES:** Flowering is more prolific if clumps are left undisturbed for several years.

CROCOSMIA
Crocosmia pottsii (crow-KOS-me-ah POTS-ee-ee). **COMMON NAME:** CROCOSMIA. **TYPE:** Perennial flowers. **LOCATION:** Sun to part shade. **HEIGHT:** 18"–24". **SPREAD:** 24"–36". **SPACING:** 12"–18". **BLOOM/FRUIT:** Red-orange flowers in early summer. **PROPAGATION:** Division. **HABITS/CULTURE:** Spreading perennial with sword-shaped leaves. **USES:** Perennial garden color, cut flowers. **PROBLEMS:** Tends to sprawl.

CROCUS
Crocus spp. (CROW-kus). **COMMON NAME:** CROCUS. **TYPE:** Perennial bulb. **LOCATION:** Sun to part shade. **HEIGHT:** 4"–8". **SPREAD:** 4"–8". **SPACING:** 3"–6". **BLOOM/FRUIT:** Blooms in many colors, mostly from late winter through early spring. Some bloom in the fall. **PROPAGATION:** Corms. **HABITS/CULTURE:** Leaves are basal and grasslike, often with a silver midrib. Purple, blue, yellow, and white flowers are available. Plant corms in the fall. **USES:** Low-growing perennial color. **PROBLEMS:** Squirrels, rabbits, gophers. **TIPS/NOTES:** *Sternbergia lutea,* a yellow fall-blooming crocus, naturalizes better and lasts longer than most other crocuses. *Crocus sativus,* saffron, blooms with gorgeous purple flowers and bright red stigmas, the source of the delicious and valuable spice. Plant in the spring for fall flowers.

Crinum crinum lily   *Croscosmia pottsii* crocosmia

Crocus crocus

CROSSVINE—see *Bignonia capreolata*

CROTON—see *Codiaeum variegatum*

CROWN VETCH—see *Coronilla varia*

CROW POISON—see *Allium* spp.

CUCUMBER—see *Cucumis sativus*

CUCUMIS
Cucumis melo (KEW-kew-mis MAY-lo). **COMMON NAME:** CANTALOUPE, MUSKMELON. **TYPE:** Annual fruit. **LOCATION:** Sun. **HEIGHT:** 6'–8'. **SPREAD:** 3'–6'. **SPACING:** 3'–6'. **BLOOM/FRUIT:** Yellow flowers with small immature fruit behind the female blooms. **PROPAGATION:** Seed. **HABITS/CULTURE:** Raised rows or hills, healthy soil. Excellent drainage is critical. Plant in the spring when soil temperature reaches 60 degrees. Plant 3–5 seeds per hill. **USES:** Food. **PROBLEMS:** Poor flavor due to excess soil moisture. Powdery mildew, nematodes, aphids, cucumber beetles, squash bugs, flea beetles, garden flea hoppers, lack of pollination, and soil fungus. **TIPS/NOTES:** I haven't had much luck with fall crops. Best to plant in the spring.

Cucumis sativus (KEW-kew-mis sa-TEE-vus). **COMMON NAME:** CUCUMBER. **TYPE:** Annual vegetable. **LOCATION:** Sun. **HEIGHT/SPREAD:** Climbing vine. **SPACING:** 3'. **BLOOM/FRUIT:** Insignificant. **PROPAGATION:** Seed, transplants. **HABITS/CULTURE:** Easy-to-grow vegetable that produces best when started from transplants. I still plant seed—it's easier. Plant after soil temperature reaches 65 degrees. Best to grow vertically on cages. USES: Food. PROBLEMS: Foliage diseases, nematodes, moisture stress, aphids, flea beetles, garden flea hoppers, cucumber beetles, squash bugs, leaf miners, stink bugs, and powdery mildew. TIPS/NOTES: Poor fruit set results from cloudy wet springs, poor honeybee activity, and use of toxic pesticides.

CUCURBITA

Cucurbita spp. (kew-KUR-bi-ta). COMMON NAME: PUMP-KIN, SQUASH. TYPE: Annual vegetable. LOCATION: Sun. HEIGHT/SPREAD: High-climbing, widely spreading. SPACING: 24"–6'. BLOOM/FRUIT: Yellow flowers, melonlike fruit. Squash has gourdlike fruit. PROPAGATION: Seed. HABITS/CULTURE: Large-growing vines with extensive root systems. Plant in spring after danger of frost. Germination in 3–7 days at 68–86 degrees. Very fast-growing but susceptible to lots of critters. USES: Food. PROBLEMS: Garden flea hoppers, flea beetles, powdery mildew, viruses, cucumber beetles, aphids, squash vine borers, squash bugs, cutworms, and nematodes. TIPS/NOTES: Pumpkins don't like low pH, acid soil. Summer squash such as 'Yellow Squash,' 'Zucchini,' and 'Patty Pan' can be harvested at any size. Winter squash like 'Hubbard,' 'Acorn,' and 'Turban' should not be harvested until fully mature.

CUPFLOWER—see *Nierembergia* spp.

CUPHEA

Cuphea spp. (KOO-fee-a). COMMON NAME: MEXICAN HEATHER, FALSE HEATHER. TYPE: Tender tropical used as an annual. LOCATION: Sun to part shade. HEIGHT: 12"–24". SPREAD: 24"–36". SPACING: 18". BLOOM/FRUIT: Small pink, purple, or white flowers all summer. PROPAGATION: Cuttings. HABITS/CULTURE: Lacy foliage, tiny dark green leaves, and very small flowers from spring to frost. Not picky about soil, likes loose, well-drained, healthy soil best. USES: Pots, borders, summer color, delicate texture. PROBLEMS: Freezes easily in the northern half of the state. TIPS/NOTES: Performs as an annual in all but the southern half of Texas. Perrenializes in mild winters if protected and mulched. *Cuphea hyssopifolia* is the false holly. *Cuphea ignea* is the red-flowered cigar plant.

Cuphea Mexican heather

CUP OAK—see *Quercus macrocarpa*

CUPRESSOCYPARIS

Cupressocyparis leylandii (koo-PRESS-oh-sy-pear-us lay-LAND-dee-ee). COMMON NAME: LEYLAND CYPRESS. TYPE: Evergreen shrub. LOCATION: Sun. HEIGHT: 30'–40'. SPREAD: 20'–30'. SPACING: 10'–15'. PROPAGATION: Cuttings. HABITS/CULTURE: Evergreen with pyramidal over-

all shape, moderate to fast growth. Looks the same year round. Soft foliage. Adapts to most well-drained soils. USES: Background plants, evergreen screen, specimen. PROBLEMS: Root rot in poorly drained soils. Not a foolproof plant in Texas. TIPS/NOTES: Makes a decent living Christmas tree.

Cupressocyparus leylandii
Leyland cypress

CUPRESSUS

Cupressus arizonica (koo-PRESS-us air-ah-ZON-ih-ca). COMMON NAME: ARIZONA CYPRESS. TYPE: Evergreen tree. LOCATION: Sun. HEIGHT: 40'–50'. SPREAD: 30'–40'. SPACING: 20'–30'. PROPAGATION: Cuttings, easy to grow from seed. HABITS/CULTURE: Upright, aromatic blue-green evergreen foliage. Fast-growing for 30–40 years. Colorful flaky bark. USES: Specimen, windbreak. Grows best in West Texas, only fair in the rest of the state. PROBLEMS: Doesn't like the heat and humidity of typical Texas summers. TIPS/NOTES: Native to Big Bend's Chisos Mountains, where it grows to 90'. Shouldn't be used east of Dallas.

Cupressus sempervirens (koo-PRESS-us sem-per-VYE-rens). COMMON NAME: ITALIAN CYPRESS. TYPE: Evergreen tree. LOCATION: Sun. HEIGHT: 40'. SPREAD: 8'–10'. SPACING: 6'–10'. BLOOM/FRUIT: Golf-ball-size cones of shield-shaped scales. PROPAGATION: Seed, cuttings. HABITS/CULTURE: Tiny, scalelike leaves. Slow-growing, unusually upright. Very dark green juniper-like foliage. Relatively easy to grow in any well-drained soil. USES: Background, tall border, screen, specimen tree for formal gardens, windbreak. PROBLEMS: Red spider mites, bagworms, disease problems, short-lived in this area due to heat and humidity. TIPS/NOTES: Looks out of place in Texas. Unless you have formal Italian gardens, I would avoid this plant. Native to southern Europe.

CUSTARD APPLE—see *Asimina triloba*

Cupressus arizonica Arizona cypress

Cupressus sempervirens Italian cypress

CYMBOPOGON

Cymbopogon citratus (sim-bo-PO-gon si-TRA-tus). **COMMON NAME:** LEMONGRASS. **TYPE:** Tender perennial herb. **LOCATION:** Sun. **HEIGHT:** 3'–5'. **SPREAD:** 3'. **SPACING:** 2'–3'. **BLOOM/FRUIT:** Rarely flowers. **PROPAGATION:** Division. **HABITS/CULTURE:** Grows in grasslike tufts similar to pampas grass. Lemon-scented 1/2"–1" blades grow from a fleshy base. Winter hardy only in the southern tip of Texas, an annual elsewhere. **USES:** Lemon flavor for meats and other dishes, teas. Good source of vitamin A. **PROBLEMS:** Freezes easily, red spider mites, rust on leaves if over-watered. **TIPS/NOTES:** Grows well in containers and can be moved indoors during winter. Large clumps can be separated to start more plants.

Cymbopogon citratus lemongrass   *Cynodon dactylon* Bermudagrass

Cynodon dactylon cultivar tifgrass

CYNODON

Cynodon dactylon (SIN-no-don DAC-ti-lon). **COMMON NAME:** BERMUDAGRASS. **TYPE:** Warm-season grass. **LOCATION:** Sun. **HEIGHT:** 1"–4" (mown). **SPACING:** 2 lbs. seed per 1000 sq. ft. **BLOOM/FRUIT:** 3–8 slender flower heads in a cluster 6"–8" tall, tiny black seeds. **PROPAGATION:** Seed. **HABITS/CULTURE:** Narrow leaf blade, spreads by stolons and rhizomes. Brown in winter. Low maintenance except for keeping out of beds. Very aggressive grass. Grows in any soil. Does much better with ample water and food, but is quite drought tolerant. Does not develop thatch. **USES:** Lawn grass, playing fields. **PROBLEMS:** Some insects and diseases but none serious. One of the most invasive weeds in the world. **TIPS/NOTES:** Looks okay mixed with St. Augustine and some weeds. Native to warm regions around the world. Thought to have originated in Africa. Grass planting around new shrubs and trees will retard their growth. Texturf-10 is a dark green variety relatively free of seed stems and a good choice for athletic fields.

Cynodon dactylon cultivars (SIN-no-don DAC-ti-lon). **COMMON NAME:** TIFGRASS, TIF BERMUDAGRASS. **TYPE:** Warm-season grass. **LOCATION:** Sun. **HEIGHT:** 1"–4" (mown). **SPACING:** 10–15 bushels of stolons per thousand sq. ft. **PROPAGATION:** Stolons. **BLOOM/FRUIT:** Fine-textured and low-growing version of common Bermudagrass. Sterile, does not produce viable seed. **HABITS/CULTURE:** Hybrid forms of common Bermudagrass. Narrower leaf blade and finer overall texture. Tifdwarf is the finest-textured, Tifgreen 328 is slightly larger, and Tifway 419 is the largest and easiest to grow of the dwarf hybrids. High-maintenance grass because weeds and imperfections are much more visible. **USES:** Refined lawns and putting greens, golf course tees, and fairways. **PROBLEMS:** Some insects and diseases but none serious. Bad thatch buildup. **TIPS/NOTES:** Too much work for home lawns. I don't recommend it. Native to laboratory.

CYPERUS

Cyperus alternifolius (cy-PEAR-us all-ter-ni-FOAL-ee-us). **COMMON NAME:** CYPERUS, UMBRELLA PLANT. **TYPE:** Perennial sedge. **LOCATION:** Sun to part shade. **HEIGHT:** 4'–8'. **SPREAD:** 4'–8'. **SPACING:** 2'–3'. **BLOOM/FRUIT:** Dry, greenish-brown flower clusters. **PROPAGATION:** Cuttings or division. **HABITS/CULTURE:** Grasslike with three-sided solid stems. Light and graceful plant with thin upright shoots. Dies to the ground each winter but returns in the spring. Plant early in the season so root system will develop fully before freeze. More like a shrub than a flower. Likes moist, healthy planting soil, but grows well in wet areas and even under water. **USES:** Accent plant, distinctive foliage, bog or aquatic plant. **PROBLEMS:** Grasshoppers. Severe winter might kill the plant—just buy another one. It's worth it. **TIPS/NOTES:** Cut stems in late summer, remove foliage, and put stem in water upside down—will sprout and root for planting outside the following spring. *Cyperus rotundus*, the common nutgrass weed, is also a sedge with a triangular stem. *Cyperus papyrus* is the plant used to make paper by the ancient Egyptians. Native to Madagascar.

Cyperus alternifolius umbrella plant

Cyrtomium falcatum holly fern

CYPRESS, ARIZONA—see *Cupressus arizonica*

CYPRESS, BALD—see *Taxodium distichum*

CYPRESS, ITALIAN—see *Cupressus sempervirens*

CYPRESS, LEYLAND—see *Cupressocyparis leylandii*

CYPRESS, MONTEZUMA BALD—see *Taxodium distichum*

CYPRESS, POND—see *Taxodium ascendens*

CYPRESS VINE—see *Ipomoea* spp.

CYRTOMIUM

Cyrtomium falcatum (sir-TOE-me-um foul-KA-tum). **COMMON NAME:** HOLLY FERN, JAPANESE HOLLY FERN. **TYPE:** Evergreen fern. **LOCATION:** Shade to part shade. **HEIGHT:** 2'. **SPREAD:** 2'–3'. **SPACING:** 1'–2'. **BLOOM/FRUIT:** Reproduces by spores running lengthways on the back sides of fronds. **PROPAGATION:** Division, spores. **HABITS/CULTURE:** Low-growing, compact, evergreen clumps with dark green leathery fronds. Likes moist, well-drained, highly organic soil in partial or full shade. **USES:** Mass plantings, softening element. Good in containers. **PROBLEMS:** Sunburn and freeze damage, caterpillars occasionally. **TIPS/NOTES:** Native to Asia and South Africa.

DAFFODIL—see *Narcissus* spp.

DAHLBERG DAISY—see *Dyssodia tenuiloba*

DAHLIA

Dahlia spp. (DAL-ee-ah). **COMMON NAME:** DAHLIA. **TYPE:** Perennial bedding plant. **LOCATION:** Sun. **HEIGHT:** 2'–6'. **SPREAD:** 2'–4'. **SPACING:** 12"–24". **BLOOM/FRUIT:** Many flower types in all colors except true blue. **PROPAGATION:** Tubers. **HABITS/CULTURE:** Colorful flowers grown from tuberous roots. Blooms from spring to fall but does not bloom well in the hotter parts of the summer. Dwarf varieties are the best for Texas. Needs sun, rich porous soil and heavy fertilization. Plant in February or March and mulch heavily. **USES:** Summer flowers, background plant for perennial beds, cut flowers. **PROBLEMS:** Heat, red spider mites. Not well adapted to Texas gardens. **TIPS/NOTES:** Dahlia is the national flower of Mexico.

Dahlia dahlia

Dalea frutescens black dalea

Dalea bicolor silver dalea

DAISY, CUTLEAF—see *Engelmannia pinnatifida*

DAISY, DAHLBERG—see *Dyssodia tenuiloba*

DAISY, ENGELMANN—see *Engelmannia pinnatifida*

DAISY, ENGLISH—see *Bellis perennis*

DAISY, GERBERA—see *Gerbera jamesonii*

DAISY, GLORIOSA—see *Rudbeckia hirta*

DAISY, OXEYE—see *Chrysanthemum leucanthemum*

DAISY, SHASTA—see *Chrysanthemum leucanthemum*

DALEA

Dalea spp. (DAY-lee-ah). **COMMON NAME:** DALEA. **TYPE:** Deciduous ground cover or low shrub. **LOCATION:** Sun. **HEIGHT:** 1'–3'. **SPREAD:** 3'. **SPACING:** 3'. **BLOOM/FRUIT:** Small magenta flowers in late summer or early fall. **PROPAGATION:** Seed, cuttings. **HABITS/CULTURE:** Easy to grow in well-drained soil. Rounded, spreading, low-growing with tiny leaves. Very drought tolerant. **USES:** Low mass, late summer color, texture and color contrast. **PROBLEMS:** Very few if not overwatered. **TIPS/NOTES:** *Dalea frutescens*, black dalea, is widespread in Texas and has dark green foliage. *Dalea bicolor*, silver dalea, has fuzzy gray-green foliage. *Dalea greggii* is a slow-growing but excellent full-sun ground cover. All species require perfect drainage.

DALLISGRASS—see *Paspalum dilatatum*

DANDELION—see *Taraxacum officinale*

DATURA

Datura wrightii (day-TOO-rah RITE-ee-eye). **COMMON NAME:** ANGEL'S TRUMPET, JIMSONWEED. **TYPE:** Perennial shrub. **LOCATION:** Sun. **HEIGHT:** 3'–5'. **SPREAD:** 5'–6'. **SPACING:** 4'–6'. **BLOOM/FRUIT:** Fragrant white or purple night-opening flowers, 4"–6" wide. Blooms all summer the first season. **PROPAGATION:** Seed. **HABITS/CULTURE:** Large, fuzzy, dark green foliage, thick succulent stems that stink when crushed or broken. Dies to ground in winter but returns each spring. Spreads easily by seed. Native to Texas. **USES:** Dramatic color and fragrance. **PROBLEMS:** Coarse, weedy, and poisonous. It's pretty anyway. Tender skin can easily get a rash from contact with stems or foliage. **TIPS/NOTES:** Mistakenly called Moonflower, which is a nonpoisonous member of the morning glory family. *Datura metel* has double purple flowers and is naturalized here in Texas.

Datura wrightii Jimsonweed

Dianthus dianthus

DAUCUS

Daucus carota (DA-kus ka-ROT-a). **COMMON NAME:** CAR-ROT. **TYPE:** Annual vegetable. **LOCATION:** Sun. **HEIGHT:** 8"–12". **SPREAD:** 8"–12". **SPACING:** 3–4 seeds per inch. **BLOOM/FRUIT:** Insignificant. **PROPAGATION:** Seed. **HABITS/CULTURE:** Needs soft, well-prepared, healthy soil. Don't overfertilize, or you'll get a lot of top growth and not much carrot. Put a 2" mulch layer around carrots as they grow. Germination in 6–21 days at 68–86 degrees. Tolerates cool soil. Plant in late winter for a spring crop or midsummer for a fall crop. **USES:** Tremendous source of vitamins and minerals. **PROBLEMS:** Grubworms, wireworms, cutworms, rabbits, bacterial diseases, nematodes. **TIPS/NOTES:** Harvest whenever large enough to eat. Carrots can be stored in the fall and winter by leaving them in the ground. Unless the critters get 'em, they will get sweeter and tastier. Wild carrot, also known as Queen Anne's lace, is a tall weed with tiny white flowers. Control it by mowing or covering with mulch.

DAWN REDWOOD—see *Metasequoia glyptostroboides*

DAYLILY—see *Hemerocallis* spp.

DEAD NETTLE—see *Lamium maculatum*

DELPHINIUM—see *Consolida ambigua*

DEODAR CEDAR—see *Cedrus deodara*

DESERT WILLOW—see *Chilopsis linearis*

DIANTHUS

Dianthus spp. (dye-AN-thus). **COMMON NAME:** DIAN-THUS. **TYPE:** Annuals and perennial bedding plants. **LOCATION:** Sun. **HEIGHT:** 8"–12". **SPREAD:** 12"–18". **SPACING:** 9"–12". **BLOOM/FRUIT:** Delicate-looking cool-weather flowers in a variety of colors, ranging from reds and purples to pinks and whites. **PROPAGATION:** Seed. **HABITS/CULTURE:** Some are annual, others perennial. Some varieties will bloom all winter if weather is not severe. Need prepared and well-drained beds in full sun, moderate water and fertilizer. **USES:** Cool-season color. **PROBLEMS:** None serious. **TIPS/NOTES:** Plant in the fall or late winter. A good perennial variety is *Dianthus allwoodii*. Carnations, pinks, and sweet william are all variations of this genus.

DICHONDRA

Dichondra micrantha (die-CON-dra my-CRAN-tha). **COMMON NAME:** DICHONDRA, PONYFOOT. **TYPE:** Perennial ground cover. **LOCATION:** Part shade. **HEIGHT:** 2"–4". **SPREAD:** Runners. **SPACING:** 6"–12" for plugs; or sow 1 lb. seed per thousand sq. ft. in April or May. **PROPAGATION:** Seed, plugs. **HABITS/CULTURE:** Perennial lawn plant or ground cover. Very low-growing, spreads by runners. Tiny lily-pad-looking leaves. Likes partial to fairly heavy shade and moist soil. **USES:** Excellent between stepping stones. Sometimes used as turf. **PROBLEMS:** Dichondra flea beetle. **TIPS/NOTES:** Many people don't understand that *Dichondra* is a beautiful ground cover instead of a noxious weed to be sprayed with toxic herbicides. Can be killed with broadleaf herbicides, but why? If you don't like it, let the soil dry out more between waterings. Sometimes sold as *Dichondra carolinensis* or *Dichondra repens*.

Dichondra micrantha dichondra

D

DIGITALIS

Digitalis spp. (di-gi-TAH-lis). **COMMON NAME:** FOX-GLOVE. **TYPE:** Annuals and biennials. **LOCATION:** Sun to shade. **HEIGHT:** 2'–6'. **SPREAD:** 2'. **SPACING:** 2'. **BLOOM/FRUIT:** Vertical stalks with white, pink, red, and yellow flowers from May through June. **PROPAGATION:** Seed. **HABITS/CULTURE:** Prolific wildflower with tubular flowers shaped like fingers of a glove. Hairy gray-green leaves from base clumps. Likes fertile, moist soil. Sow seed in spring. Set out plants in fall or late winter in full sun or partial shade. In warm weather, water frequently. Sow seeds in the spring or set out plants in the fall for blooms the following spring and summer. Watch for snails and slugs. After the first flowering, cut the main spike so side shoots will develop and bloom. Do not plant foxglove near comfrey. The leaves are similar, and the leaves of foxglove should not be handled. Teach children to look but not to touch. **USES:** Background flower, source of a powerful heart medicine that should be administered by doctors only. **PROBLEMS:** Entire plant is toxic. **TIPS/NOTES:** Don't plant in garden where small children play.

Digitalis foxglove

Diospyros texana
Texas persimmon

DIGITARIA

Digitaria (dige-ah-TEAR-ee-ah). **COMMON NAME:** CRAB-GRASS. **TYPE:** Annual grass. **LOCATION:** Sun. **HEIGHT:** 12"–24". **SPREAD:** 24" and more. **BLOOM/FRUIT:** Seed heads like fingers. **PROPAGATION:** Seed, roots where each nodule touches the ground. **HABITS/CULTURE:** Branches grow out along the ground, then turn up after rooting at nodes. Warm-season, shallow-rooted, low-growing annual grass from Europe. Likes moist soil. **USES:** Foliage crop for cattle. **PROBLEMS:** Considered a noxious lawn weed. **TIPS/NOTES:** Let the soil dry out to get rid of it if unwanted. It indicates poor aeration and limited availability of calcium. It looks much like our normal lawn grasses; don't worry about it. In lawns, just mow it. In beds, smother it with mulch.

DILL—see *Anethum graveolens*

Diospyros virginiana common persimmon

DIOSPYROS

Diospyros texana (dye-OSS-pear-os tex-AN-ah). **COMMON NAME:** TEXAS PERSIMMON. **TYPE:** Deciduous tree. **LOCATION:** Sun to part shade. **HEIGHT:** 10'–30'. **SPREAD:** 12'–15'. **SPACING:** 12'–15'. **BLOOM/FRUIT:** Small, sweet, seedy, edible 1" fruit, black when ripe. Flowering doesn't start until after 5–6 years. **PROPAGATION:** Seed transplants, grafts. **HABITS/CULTURE:** Trunks and branches resemble crape myrtle, with pretty, peeling outer bark. Insignificant fall color. Small leathery leaves. Slow-growing but easy to grow in any soil, even rocky areas. Drought tolerant. **USES:** Ornamental garden tree, decorative bark. **PROBLEMS:** Few if any. Freeze damage. **TIPS/NOTES:** Native to South and Central Texas. Keep fruit away from horses and cattle—seeds can cause constipation in livestock.

Diospyros virginiana (dye-OSS-pear-os ver-gin-ee-AN-ah). **COMMON NAME:** COMMON PERSIMMON, EASTERN PERSIMMON. **TYPE:** Deciduous tree. **LOCATION:** Sun. **HEIGHT:** 60'. **SPREAD:** 30'. **SPACING:** 20'–40'. **BLOOM/FRUIT:** Insignificant flowers. Bright pink 1" fruit, sour until after the first sharp freeze. **PROPAGATION:** Seed, cuttings, and transplants. **HABITS/CULTURE:** Yellow fall color, dark, deeply fissured bark. Shiny foliage that gracefully droops. Fruit turns orange after first frost. Easy to grow in any soil, drought tolerant, self-pollinating. **USES:** Shade tree, food for wildlife. **PROBLEMS:** Webworms, messy fruit. **TIPS/NOTES:** An excellent shade tree. *Diospyros kaki*, the Japanese variety, is smaller but has fruit the size of apples. 'Eureka' is a flat-shaped fruit on a small, easy-to-grow tree. 'Hachiya' is a medium-size tree with a large, cone-shaped, orange-red seedless fruit. 'Tane-nashi' is a good ornamental landscape persimmon with moderately productive fruit that stores well. 'Tamopan' produces a flat fruit with a ring constriction near its middle. 'Fuyu' or 'Fuyugaki' is the nonastringent choice. It won't pucker your mouth, even if eaten green, and has the texture of an apple. It's also self-pollinating. Wooden golf clubs are made from persimmon wood. Native to Texas and the eastern United States.

Dryopteris wood fern

DODDER—see Weeds

DOGWOOD, FLOWERING—see *Cornus florida*

DOGWOOD, ROUGH-LEAF—see *Cornus drummondii*

DOLICHOS

Dolichos lablab (DOE-lee-chos LAB-LAB). **COMMON NAME:** HYACINTH BEAN. **TYPE:** Annual vine. **LOCATION:** Sun. **HEIGHT/SPREAD:** Tall-climbing and wide-spreading. **SPACING:** 4'–8'. **BLOOM/FRUIT:** Purple flowers in late summer, followed by short, deep purple seed pods. **PROPAGATION:** Seed. **HABITS/CULTURE:** Tall-climbing annual vine, planted from pretty black-and-white seeds in the spring. Fast-growing and beautiful. Very easy to grow. **USES:** Late summer color, shade for arbor or trellis. **PROBLEMS:** Black fuzzy caterpillars.

DRYOPTERIS

Dryopteris spp. (dry-OP-ter-is). **COMMON NAME:** WOOD FERN. **TYPE:** Perennial. **LOCATION:** Sun to part shade. **HEIGHT:** 18"–24". **SPREAD:** 2'–3'. **SPACING:** 12"–18". **BLOOM/**

FRUIT: Reproduces by spores, located in long rows on the underside of the fronds. **PROPAGATION:** Spores or division. **HABITS/CULTURE:** Low-spreading fern. Delicate, deeply cut, light green fronds. Needs shade or filtered light. Can grow in any soil, but likes loose, well-drained beds best. **USES:** Great for a softening effect in almost any garden, good contrast with darker greens. **PROBLEMS:** Rare grasshopper damage is about all. **TIPS/NOTES:** Mysterious dark spots under leaves are the reproductive spores—not insects. Southern wood fern is *Thelypteris kunthii*; river fern is *Dryopteris normalis*; Japanese painted fern is *Athyrium niponicum* 'Pictum.'

DUCHESNEA

Duchesnea indica (doo-CHEZ-ne-ah IN-dee-cah). **COMMON NAME:** FALSE STRAWBERRY. **TYPE:** Evergreen ground cover. **LOCATION:** Sun to part shade. **HEIGHT:** 3"–6". **SPREAD:** Wide-spreading. **SPACING:** 9"–12". **BLOOM/FRUIT:** Small yellow flowers, followed by small hard strawberry-like fruit. **PROPAGATION:** Seed or division. **HABITS/CULTURE:** Low-growing ground cover, spreads by runners and by seeds. Resembles the regular strawberry, but the fruit doesn't develop, is much smaller, and tastes like cardboard. Easy to grow in any soil, fairly drought tolerant. **USES:** Ground cover for unrefined gardens. **PROBLEMS:** Spreads badly—very invasive. **TIPS/NOTES:** I learned the hard way that this stuff takes over the entire garden by popping up everywhere. Native to the United States and South America.

DURRAND OAK—see *Quercus sinuata* var. *sinuata*

DUSTY MILLER—see *Centaurea cineraria*

DYSSODIA

Dyssodia tenuiloba (die-SO-de-ah ten-you-ee-LOW-ba). **COMMON NAME:** DAHLBERG DAISY, GOLDEN FLEECE. **TYPE:** Annual bedding plant. **LOCATION:** Sun. **HEIGHT:** 12".

Dolichos lablab hyacinth bean

Duchesnea indica false strawberry

Dyssodia tenuiloba Dahlberg daisy

SPREAD: 12". SPACING: 9"–12". BLOOM/FRUIT: Nickel-size golden yellow-orange flowers that bloom most of the summer. PROPAGATION: Seed. HABITS/CULTURE: Delicate, bright green, fragrant foliage. Likes well-drained soil. USES: Summer color. PROBLEMS: Few if any. TIPS/NOTES: Looks great when planted with copperleaf, firebush, Mexican petunia, and other bronze- or purple-leaf plants.

ECHINACEA

Echinacea angustifolia (ek-ih-NAY-see-ah an-gus-ti-FOAL-ee-ah). COMMON NAME: PURPLE CONEFLOWER. TYPE: Perennial herb. LOCATION: Sun. HEIGHT: 2'–3'. SPREAD: 2'–4'. SPACING: 1'–2'. BLOOM/FRUIT: Flowers are dark pink to light lavender with yellow centers. PROPAGATION: Seed, division. HABITS/CULTURE: Brightly flowered perennial that blooms from early to mid summer. Carefree and drought tolerant. USES: Perennial beds, natural areas, most anywhere—it's a great plant. All parts of the plant are herbal. Taken as a tea, it improves the immune system. PROBLEMS: Few if any. TIPS/NOTES: *Echinacea purpurea* is a lower-blooming variety with larger flowers. 'White Swan' is a white-flowering cultivar.

Echinacea purple coneflower

ECHINOPS

Echinops exaltatus (e-KEY-nops ex-all-TA-tus). COMMON NAME: GLOBE THISTLE. TYPE: Perennial bedding plant. LOCATION: Sun. HEIGHT: 2'–3'. SPREAD: 2'. SPACING: 2'. BLOOM/FRUIT: Round blue flower heads in late spring and summer. PROPAGATION: Seed. HABITS/CULTURE: Distinctive round flowers on vertical stems. Dark green thistle-like foliage. Likes the northern part of Texas more than the southern half. USES: Dramatic perennial color. PROBLEMS: Doesn't like extremely hot weather.

EGGPLANT—see *Solanum tuberosum*

Ehretia anacua anacua

EHRETIA

Ehretia anacua (eh-REE-shah ah-NOK-you-ah). COMMON NAME: ANACUA, SANDPAPER TREE. TYPE: Evergreen tree. LOCATION: Sun to part shade. HEIGHT: 20'–40'. SPREAD: 30'. SPACING: 20'–30'. BLOOM/FRUIT: Clusters of 2"–3" fragrant white panicles that are showiest in March, followed by orange fruit. PROPAGATION: Seed. HABITS/CULTURE: Distinctive dark green shade tree for South Texas. Leaves feel like sandpaper. Needs plenty of water to get established, then becomes drought tolerant. Rough-textured bark. USES: Great as honeybee attractant, shade tree, food for wildlife. PROBLEMS: Will freeze north of San Antonio.

ELAEAGNUS

Elaeagnus spp. (eel-ee-AG-nus). COMMON NAME: ELAEAGNUS, SILVERBERRY. TYPE: Evergreen shrub. LOCATION: Sun to part shade. HEIGHT: 6'–8'. SPREAD: 6'–8'. SPACING: 3'–4'. BLOOM/FRUIT: Tiny, fragrant, silvery fall flowers, followed by small edible fruit. PROPAGATION: Seed, cuttings. HABITS/CULTURE: Tough, gray-green plant. New growth in long, arching shoots. Fragrant fall blooms are hidden within the foliage. Fruit in spring is tasty and good for jellies. Grows in any soil, fairly drought tolerant. Responds well to shearing if necessary. USES: Border, background, screen. PROBLEMS: None except pruning requirements. TIPS/NOTES: *Elaeagnus macrophylla* 'Ebbenji' is my favorite since it seems to be the most compact form. *Elaeagnus pungens* is the larger-growing and less desirable variety—it has hidden thorns. Native to Japan, Europe, Asia, and North America.

Elaeagnus macrophylla silverberry

Elaeagnus angustifolia Russian olive

Elaeagnus angustifolia (eel-ee-AG-nus an-gus-ti-FOAL-ee-us). **COMMON NAME:** RUSSIAN OLIVE. **TYPE:** Deciduous tree. **LOCATION:** Sun. **HEIGHT:** 30'. **SPREAD:** 20'. **SPACING:** 15'–20'. **BLOOM/FRUIT:** Small yellow or silver summer flowers. Small drupes mature from August to October. **PROPAGATION:** Cuttings. **HABITS/CULTURE:** Silvery gray foliage, bushy unless trimmed. Relatively short-lived. Easy to grow in any well-drained soil, drought tolerant. Moderate fertilizer needs. **USES:** Shade tree, gray color. **PROBLEMS:** Too much water is the only serious problem. **TIPS/NOTES:** Likes the arid parts of the state best. Native to Europe and Asia.

ELBOW BUSH—see *Forestiera pubescens*

ELDERBERRY—see *Sambucus canadensis*

ELEPHANT EARS—see *Colocasia esculenta*

ELM, AMERICAN—see *Ulmus americana*

ELM, CEDAR—see *Ulmus crassifolia*

ELM, CHINESE—see *Ulmus parvifolia sempervirens*

ELM, LACEBARK—see *Ulmus parvifolia sempervirens*

ELM, SIBERIAN—see *Ulmus pumila*

ELM, WINGED—see *Ulmus crassifolia*

ENGELMANN DAISY—see *Engelmannia pinnatifida*

ENGELMANNIA

Engelmannia pinnatifida (eng-gull-MAHN-ee-ah pin-ah-TIFF-ih-dah). **COMMON NAME:** CUTLEAF DAISY, ENGELMANN DAISY. **TYPE:** Perennial wildflower. **LOCATION:** Full sun. **HEIGHT:** 1'–3'. **SPREAD:** 3'. **SPACING:** 2'–3'. **BLOOM/FRUIT:** Yellow 1" flowers from spring to fall, mostly in May. **PROPAGATION:** Seed. **HABITS/CULTURE:** Easy to grow in almost any soil. Forms rosette of lobbed foliage in winter, strong taproot, blooms well with low to medium moisture. Flower petals curl under on the ends during extremely hot weather. **USES:** Perennial color, wildflower, livestock forage. **PROBLEMS:** Sometimes hard to establish. **TIPS/NOTES:** Carefree after established.

Engelmannia pinnatifida Engelmann daisy

Equisetum hyemale horsetail reed

ENGLISH IVY—see *Hedera helix*

ENGLISH MARIGOLD—see *Calendula officinalis*

ENGLISH PRIMROSE—see *Primula vulgaris*

EPASOTE—see *Chenopodium* spp.

EQUISETUM

Equisetum hyemale (eh-kwee-SEAT-um HIM-ah-lee). **COMMON NAME:** HORSETAIL REED. **TYPE:** Perennial herb. **LOCATION:** Sun to part shade. **HEIGHT:** 2'–4'. **SPREAD:** Unlimited. **SPACING:** 18". **BLOOM/FRUIT:** Spores in conelike spikes at the end of the stems. **PROPAGATION:** Division, spores. **HABITS/CULTURE:** Slender, hollow, vertical green stems with black rings at each joint. Grows in soil or water. Does not need good drainage. **USES:** Pots. Marshy or wet areas, bog gardens, aquatic gardens. Distinctive accent. Source of herbal remedies—good for hair and fingernails. **PROBLEMS:** Can spread badly and become a serious pest. **TIPS/NOTES:** Prehistoric plant, very interesting and easy to use. Native to Eurasia and the Pacific Northwest.

ERIOBOTRYA

Eriobotrya japonica (err-eh-oh-BOT-tree-ah ja-PON-eh-cah). **COMMON NAME:** LOQUAT. **TYPE:** Evergreen shrub or small tree. **LOCATION:** Sun to part shade. **HEIGHT:** 10'–15'. **SPREAD:** 10'–15'. **SPACING:** 8'–12'. **BLOOM/FRUIT:** Extremely fragrant, off-white, late-fall flowers. Delicious orange fruit follows if weather conditions are favorable. **PROPAGATION:** Seed, cuttings. **HABITS/CULTURE:** Large shrub or small tree. Large, leathery, gray-green leaves. Likes any soil with moderate water and fertilizer, does best in well-prepared beds in areas protected from winter winds. **USES:** Screen, specimen, or background plant. Lower foliage can be trimmed off to form small ornamental tree. **PROBLEMS:** Freeze damage. Fireblight; spray with streptomycin in fall when plant is in bloom. Spraying regularly with garlic tea is a more organic approach. **TIPS/NOTES:** Many loquats died in the 1983 freeze, especially in the northern half of the state. Native to China and Japan.

EUONYMUS

Euonymus alatus (ewe-ON-eh-mus al-LAY-tus). **COMMON NAME:** FLAMELEAF EUONYMOUS, BURNING BUSH. **TYPE:** Deciduous shrub. **LOCATION:** Sun to part shade. **HEIGHT:** 8'–15'. **SPREAD:** 8'–15'. **SPACING:** 4'–8'. **BLOOM/FRUIT:** Inconspicuous flowers. Bright red-orange fruit in fall. **PROPAGATION:** Cuttings, seed. **HABITS/CULTURE:** Thick, winged stems. Excellent red fall color. Best color in full sun, but tolerates any soil in sun or shade. Moderate water and fertilizer requirements. **USES:** Specimen, accent, fall color. Can be trimmed into a small tree. **PROBLEMS:** None serious. **TIPS/NOTES:** Native to northeast Asia and China. 'Compacta' is the dwarf version and better for small gardens. 'Rudy Haag' is even smaller, grows to a height of 4'–5'. Dwarf varieties can be planted 3'–4' apart.

Euonymus fortunei 'Colorata' (you-ON-eh-mus for-TUNE-ee-eye call-oh-RAY-ta) **COMMON NAME:** PURPLE WINTERCREEPER. **TYPE:** Evergreen ground cover. **LOCATION:** Sun to light shade. **HEIGHT:** 8"–12". **SPREAD:** Ground cover. **SPACING:** 12". **BLOOM/FRUIT:** Insignificant. **PROPAGATION:** Cuttings. **HABITS/CULTURE:** Evergreen ground cover, spreads by runners; reddish fall color that lasts through winter. Sun or partial shade is best exposure. Moderate water and fertilization needs. Establishes quickly if planted properly and mulched after planting. Needs well-drained, prepared beds. **USES:** Ground cover for large areas. **PROBLEMS:** Scale insects occasionally. **TIPS/NOTES:** Avoid *Euonymus radicans* and other larger-leafed varieties. Native to China.

Euonymus japonicus (ewe-ON-eh-mus jah-PON-eh-kus). **COMMON NAME:** EVERGREEN EUONYMUS. **TYPE:** Evergreen shrub. **LOCATION:** North of the Mason-Dixon line. **HEIGHT:** 5'–8'. **SPREAD:** 4'–6'. **SPACING:** Do not plant! **BLOOM/FRUIT:** Unimportant. **PROPAGATION:** Cuttings. **HABITS/CULTURE:** Upright thick stems, thick waxy leaves. **USES:** None. **PROBLEMS:** You name it! Scale, powdery mildew, aphids, leaf spots, crown gall, anthracnose, nematodes, heat, etc. People who sell this plant should be put in the electric chair for 99 years.

Eriobotrya japonica loquat

Euonymus alatus
flameleaf euonymus

Euonymus fortunei 'Colorata'
purple wintercreeper

Euonymus japonicus
evergreen euonymus

EUPHORBIA

Euphorbia spp. (ew-FOR-bee-ah). **COMMON NAME:** SPURGE. **HABITS/CULTURE:** A large group of annuals, biennials, perennials, succulents, and shrubs. Most have a milky sap, some are poisonous. Flowers are actually a group of colored bracts. **TIPS/NOTES:** *Euphorbia lathyris* is gopher spurge. *Euphorbia marginata* is snow-on-the-mountain. *Euphorbia milii* is crown of thorns. *Euphorbia pulcherrima* is poinsettia. *Euphorbia tirucalli* is pencil tree. *Euphorbia supina* is a very low-growing annual broadleaf that likes hot weather and is considered a weed by many. It releases a milky latex when its stems are broken.

EURYOPS

Euryops spp. (YEW-ree-ops). **COMMON NAME:** AFRICAN BUSH DAISY. **TYPE:** Tender perennial or annual bedding plant. **LOCATION:** Sun. **HEIGHT:** 3'–4'. **SPREAD:** 24"–36". **SPACING:** 18"–24". **BLOOM/FRUIT:** Bright yellow daisylike flowers. **PROPAGATION:** Cuttings or seed. **HABITS/CULTURE:** Easy to grow in any well-drained soil. Needs minimal water and fertilizer. Shrubby tender perennial used as an annual except in the extreme southern part of the state. Lacy foliage and bushy growth. **USES:** Pots, summer color. **PROBLEMS:** Mostly pest free. **TIPS/NOTES:** Cut back after heavy flush of flowers to prolong blooming.

Eysenhardtia texana Texas kidneywood

Euryops African bush daisy

Eustoma grandiflora
Texas bluebell

EUSTOMA

Eustoma grandiflorum (you-STO-mah gran-dee-FLORE-rum). **COMMON NAME:** LISIANTHUS, TEXAS BLUEBELL. **TYPE:** Annual and perennial wildflower. **LOCATION:** Sun. **HEIGHT:** 1'–2'. **SPREAD:** 1'–3'. **SPACING:** 1'–2'. **BLOOM/FRUIT:** Upright plant, bell-shaped spring and summer flowers in white, pink, and blue. **PROPAGATION:** Seed. **HABITS/CULTURE:** Tolerates fairly dry, well-drained soil but likes even moisture better. Does quite well in our heat. **USES:** Annual flowers. **PROBLEMS:** Few if any. **TIPS/NOTES:** Grows wild in Texas but has been picked almost clean. The Japanese genetically altered forms, *Lisianthus*, are annual. The native *Eustoma exaltatum* lives 3–7 years, flowering best in the second and third years.

EVENING PRIMROSE—see *Oenothera* spp.

EVERGREEN OAK—see *Quercus virginiana*

EVERGREEN WISTERIA—see *Millettia reticulata*

EVE'S NECKLACE—see *Sophora affinis*

EYSENHARDTIA

Eysenhardtia texana (eye-zen-HAR-dee-ah tex-AN-ah). **COMMON NAME:** KIDNEYWOOD, TEXAS KIDNEYWOOD. **TYPE:** Deciduous shrub or small tree. **LOCATION:** Sun. **HEIGHT:** 8'–15'. **SPREAD:** 6'–8'. **SPACING:** 6'–8'. **BLOOM/FRUIT:** Wonderfully fragrant white 3"–4" flower spikes, bloom April to November after rains. **PROPAGATION:** Seed, cuttings. **HABITS/CULTURE:** Shrubby, multiple-stemmed tree with fine-textured foliage and open growth. Leaves have a citrus smell when crushed. Drought tolerant, but grows better with adequate moisture. **USES:** Attracts bees and butterflies. **PROBLEMS:** Freezes in harsh winters in the northern half of the state. **TIPS/NOTES:** Beautiful little tree, should be used more.

FAIRY RING—see *Chlorophyllum* spp.

FALSE DATE—see *Ziziphus* spp.

FALSE DRAGONHEAD—see *Physostegia virginiana*

FALSE GOATSBEARD—see *Astilbe* spp.

FALSE HEATHER—see *Cuphea* spp.

FALSE HOLLY—see *Osmanthus* spp.

FATSHEDERA

Fatshedera lizei (fats-HEAD-ra LEE-zay-ee). **COMMON NAME:** FATSHEDERA. **TYPE:** Evergreen vine. **LOCATION:** Shade to filtered light. **SPACING:** 3'–5'. **BLOOM/FRUIT:** Unimportant. **PROPAGATION:** Cuttings. **HABITS/CULTURE:** Foliage looks like large English ivy. Climbing, sprawling vine. Grows well in heavy shade, even indoors. Likes plenty of water in well-prepared, well-drained beds. Needs to be tied to a structure or it will fall over. Usually bare at the base. **USES:** Evergreen vine, coarse texture. **PROBLEMS:** Freeze damage in the northern part of the state. Aphids on new growth. **TIPS/NOTES:** This is a cross between *Fatsia japonica* and *Hedera helix.* 'Variegata' has white-bordered leaves.

FATSIA

Fatsia japonica (FAT-si-ah jah-PON-eh-kah). **COMMON NAME:** ARALIA, JAPANESE ARALIA. **TYPE:** Evergreen shrub. **LOCATION:** Shade. **HEIGHT:** 4'–6'. **SPREAD:** 4'–6'. **SPACING:** 3'–4'. **BLOOM/FRUIT:** Clusters of off-white flowers in fall, followed by small, shiny black fruit. **PROPAGATION:** Cuttings. **HABITS/CULTURE:** Large, single-stem 12" tropical-looking leaves, rounded overall shape. Needs well-prepared soil, good drainage, and protection from freezing weather. **USES:** Shade gardens, Oriental gardens, tropical effects, coarse texture. **PROBLEMS:** Aphids on new growth and freeze damage. **TIPS/NOTES:** Severe winter can kill this plant. Best used in the southern half of the state. Native to Japan.

FERN, HOLLY—see *Cyrtomium falcatum*

FERN, WOOD—see *Dryopteris* spp.

FESCUE, TALL—see *Festuca arundinacea*

FESTUCA

Festuca arundinacea (fess-TOO-cah ah-run-dah-NAY-see-ah). **COMMON NAME:** TALL FESCUE. **TYPE:** Cool-season perennial grass. **LOCATION:** Sun or light shade. **HEIGHT:** 2"–4" (mown). **SPACING:** Sow 8–10 lbs. seed per thousand sq. ft. **BLOOM/FRUIT:** Panicled 4"–12" seed head on a stiff stem. **PROPAGATION:** Seed. **HABITS/CULTURE:** Bunch-type grass. Used as a winter overseeding or as the primary grass in shady lawn areas. Used as a permanent grass in the cooler parts of the state. Needs fertile, well-drained soil. September is the ideal time for planting, but can be planted through November. Mow at 3"–4". Grows to 3' when unmowed. **USES:** Lawn grass in shade, overseeding. **PROBLEMS:** Must be mown all winter. **TIPS/NOTES:** Best of the winter grasses for home use. Some people don't recommend it for overseeding since it won't completely die out in the summer. I'm not too concerned about that. It blends well with rye and white clover for overseeding. Native to Europe.

Festuca ovina 'Glauca' blue glaucagrass

Fatshedera lizei fatshedera

Fatsia japonica aralia

Festuca arundinacea tall fescue

Festuca ovina 'Glauca' (fess-TOO-kah oh-VEEN-ah GLAH-kah). **COMMON NAME:** GLAUCAGRASS, BLUE GLAUCAGRASS, BLUE FESCUEGRASS. **TYPE:** Evergreen grass. **LOCATION:** Sun. **HEIGHT:** 4"–10". **SPREAD:** Ground cover, border. **SPACING:** 9"–12". **BLOOM/FRUIT:** Insignificant. **PROPAGATION:** Seed, division. **HABITS/CULTURE:** Slender, bristly, powdery blue-gray hairlike leaves in distinct clumps. Light-colored flowers on thin stalks in early spring. Easy to grow in any soil, drought tolerant, low fertilization needs. Clip away flowers after blooms have faded. **USES:** Ground cover, low border. **PROBLEMS:** Never forms a solid mass, so mulching is important to prevent weeds. **TIPS/NOTES:** Native to southeast Asia and Japan.

FICUS

Ficus carica (FIE-cus CAR-ih-ka). **COMMON NAME:** EDIBLE FIG. **TYPE:** Deciduous tree. **LOCATION:** Sun to part shade. **HEIGHT:** 8'–10'. **SPREAD:** 8'–10'. **SPACING:** 6'–8'. **PROPAGATION:** Cuttings. **HABITS/CULTURE:** 'Celeste' is a large-production tree with a small fig that has a tightly closed eye and a very sweet taste. 'Texas Everbearing' or 'Southern Brown Turkey' is a large-production tree with medium-size fruit; it bears two crops—the largest, on last year's wood and a medium-sized one, on the current season's wood. Neither should be pruned heavily, and both do best in the warmer half of the state. Self-pollinating.

Ficus pumila (FIE-cus PEW-mi-lah). **COMMON NAME:** FIG IVY, CREEPING FIG. **TYPE:** Evergreen vine. **LOCATION:** Sun to part shade. **HEIGHT:** 20'–30'. **SPREAD:** Wide-spreading vine. **SPACING:** 3'–5'. **BLOOM/FRUIT:** Insignificant flowers. Large oblong fruit on large mature vines. **PROPAGATION:** Cuttings. **HABITS/CULTURE:** Small-leafed climbing vine, needs no support. Climbs by aerial roots. Leaves become much larger on older plants. Prefers a moist, well-drained soil and high humidity. Needs protection from winter winds. Sunny southern exposure is best. **USES:** Climbing vine for protected courtyards, conservatories, and garden rooms. **PROBLEMS:** Freeze damage during severe winters in northern part of the state. **TIPS/NOTES:** Native to southeast Asia and Japan.

Ficus pumila fig ivy

Firmiana simplex parasol tree

FIG, CREEPING—see *Ficus pumila*

FIG, EDIBLE—see *Ficus carica*

FIG IVY—see *Ficus pumila*

FILBERT, WALKING STICK—see *Corylus avellana*

FIREBUSH, MEXICAN—see *Hamelia* spp.

FIRETHORN—see *Pyracantha* spp.

FIRMIANA

Firmiana simplex (fir-me-AHN-ah sim-plex). **COMMON NAME:** PARASOL TREE, CHINESE PARASOL TREE, CHINESE VARNISH TREE. **TYPE:** Deciduous tree. **LOCATION:** Sun. **HEIGHT:** 30'–50'. **SPREAD:** 50'. **SPACING:** 20'–50'. **BLOOM/FRUIT:** Yellowish green flowers in June or July, followed by showy brown fruit. **PROPAGATION:** Seed, cuttings. **HABITS/CULTURE:** Fast-growing and upright, with smooth green bark, huge leaves, thick stems. Easy to grow in any soil, relatively drought tolerant, average water and fertilizer needs. **USES:** Shade tree, conversation piece. **PROBLEMS:** Coarse-looking, weak wood, short-lived. **TIPS/NOTES:** Native to China and Japan.

FLAG—see *Iris* spp.

FLAME ACANTHUS—see *Anisacanthus quadrifidus*

FLAMINGO PLANT—see *Justicia* spp.

FLOSS FLOWER—see *Ageratum houstonianum*

FLOWERING QUINCE—*Chaenomeles japonica*

FLOWERING TOBACCO—see *Nicotiana alata*

FORESTIERA

Forestiera pubescens (for-est-tea-ERE-ah pew-BESS-enz). **COMMON NAME:** ELBOW BUSH, TEXAS ELBOW BUSH. **TYPE:** Deciduous shrub. **LOCATION:** Sun to part shade. **HEIGHT:** 8'–10'. **SPREAD:** 8'–10'. **SPACING:** 4'–6'. **BLOOM/FRUIT:** Small yellowish flowers in clusters. Dark purple berries. **PROPAGATION:** Seed. **HABITS/CULTURE:** One of the first plants to flower and leaf out in the spring. Leaves are opposite and alternate, giving a very angular but interesting appearance. Forms thickets by self-layering. Looks similar to yaupon holly. **USES:** Natural shrub, wildlife food, screen. **PROBLEMS:** Caterpillars. **TIPS/NOTES:** Good to attract wildlife.

FORSYTHIA

Forsythia intermedia (for-SITH-ee-ah in-ter-ME-dee-ah). **COMMON NAME:** FORSYTHIA. **TYPE:** Deciduous shrub. **LOCATION:** Sun to part shade. **HEIGHT:** 6'–7'. **SPREAD:** 5'–6'. **SPACING:** 3'–4'. **BLOOM/FRUIT:** Yellow or white spring flowers, insignificant fruit. **PROPAGATION:** Cuttings. **HABITS/CULTURE:** Fountainlike growth, bare branches covered with bright yellow bell-shaped flowers in early spring. Flowers last about two weeks. Grows well in any soil, sun or shade. Better flower production in full sun. Good drainage is important. Prune after blooms fade. **USES:** Specimen, background plant, yellow spring color, cut flowers. **PROBLEMS:** None serious. **TIPS/NOTES:** Best to use

Forsythia intermedia forsythia

with evergreen plants since winter look is bare and uninteresting. Should at least be planted in the utility area or cutting garden for its flowers. Cuttings can be forced into bloom indoors. Native to China.

FOSTER HOLLY—see *Ilex × attenuata*

FOUNTAINGRASS—see *Pennisetum* spp.

FOUR-NERVE DAISY—see *Hymenoxys scaposa*

FOUR O'CLOCK—see *Mirabilis jalapa*

FOXGLOVE—see *Digitalis* spp.

FRAGARIA
Fragaria virginiana (fra-GAH-ree-a ver-gin-ee-AN-ah). **COMMON NAME:** STRAWBERRY. **TYPE:** Short-lived perennial berry. **LOCATION:** Sun. **HEIGHT:** 6"–8". **SPREAD:** 12"–18". **SPACING:** 12"–18". **BLOOM/FRUIT:** White flowers in spring, edible fruit in summer. **PROPAGATION:** Seed, division. **HABITS/CULTURE:** Plant in well-prepared, highly organic, very well drained raised beds. Matted row or perennial beds should be planted in December through February. Fruit is harvested about 16 months later in April or May. **TIPS/NOTES:** Varieties for this approach include 'Sunrise,' 'Pocahontas,' 'Cardinal,' and 'Allstar.' With the annual approach, planting is in early November and harvesting the next February through April. Good varieties for this technique include 'Sequoia,' 'Chandler,' 'Fresno,' 'Tioga,' 'Tangi,' and 'Douglas.' Self-pollinating.

FRANGIPANI—see *Plumeria* spp.

FRAXINUS
Fraxinus pennsylvanica (FRAK-suh-nus pen-cil-VAN-ik-a). **COMMON NAME:** GREEN ASH. **TYPE:** Deciduous tree. **LOCATION:** Sun. **HEIGHT:** 50'. **SPREAD:** 40'. **SPACING:** 20'–30'. **BLOOM/FRUIT:** Puny flowers and winged seed. **PROPAGATION:** Seed or cuttings. **HABITS/CULTURE:** Fast-growing, large compound leaves, dark green foliage, yellow fall color. Smooth, mottled bark when young, rougher with age. Easy to grow when young in any soil. Needs more water than Texas ash. **USES:** Shade tree, fall color, background tree, mass tree planting. **PROBLEMS:** Aphids in early summer. Not a long-lived tree. **TIPS/NOTES:** Native to

Fraxinus pennsylvanica green ash

Fraxinus texensis Texas ash

Fraxinus texensis Texas ash, fall

North America. *Fraxinus pennsylvanica* 'Marshalli' is a seedless form of green ash and even less adapted than the parent.

Fraxinus texensis (FRAK-suh-nus tex-EN-sis). **COMMON NAME:** TEXAS ASH. **TYPE:** Deciduous tree. **LOCATION:** Sun. **HEIGHT:** 50'. **SPREAD:** 40'. **SPACING:** 20'–30'. **BLOOM/FRUIT:** Small greenish yellow flowers and dry-winged samora containing a single seed. **PROPAGATION:** Cuttings or seed. **HABITS/CULTURE:** Medium growth, large compound leaves. Rounded leaflets on young growth. White splotches on trunk and limbs. Orange to purple fall color. Easy to grow in any well-drained soil, grows readily in alkaline soil on rock or steep slopes. Low water and fertilizer needs. Needs excellent drainage. Easy to transplant. **USES:** Shade tree, fall color. **PROBLEMS:** Poor drainage, borers. **TIPS/ NOTES:** One of Texas' best-kept secrets. *Fraxinus americana,* kin to the white ash, is also a good tree and should be used much more. Excellent white ash cultivars are 'Autumn Purple' and 'Rosehill.' *Fraxinus cuspidata,* fragrant ash, is another good native tree.

Fraxinus texensis Texas ash   *Fraxinus velutina* 'Arizona' Arizona ash

Gaillardia pulchella Indian Blanket

Fraxinus velutina 'Arizona' (FRAK-suh-nus vel-you-TEE-na). **COMMON NAME:** ARIZONA ASH. **TYPE:** Deciduous tree. **LOCATION:** Sun. **HEIGHT:** 30'. **SPREAD:** 30'. **SPACING:** Do not plant! **BLOOM/FRUIT:** Ugly flowers and lots of winged fruit. **PROPAGATION:** Cuttings. **HABITS/CULTURE:** Fast-growing junk tree. Brittle wood, yellow fall color, smooth bark. Grows in any soil, heavy water and light fertilization needs. **USES:** Fast-growing temporary shade tree. **PROBLEMS:** Borers, aphids, brittle wood, short-lived, destructive roots. **TIPS/NOTES:** This ash was introduced as a drought-tolerant, low-maintenance tree, but it is far from it. I once thought all ash trees were bad because of this one. Native to waterways in Arizona and New Mexico.

FRINGE TREE—see *Chionanthus virginica*

FROG FRUIT—see *Phyla nodiflora*

GAILLARDIA
Gaillardia pulchella (ga-LAR-dee-ah pul-KELL-ah). **COMMON NAME:** INDIAN BLANKET, MEXICAN BLANKET, FIREWHEEL. **TYPE:** Annual wildflower. **LOCATION:** Sun. **HEIGHT:** 6"–12". **SPREAD:** 12"–18". **SPACING:** 12"–18" or 10 lbs. seed per acre. **BLOOM/FRUIT:** 2" red and yellow flowers. **PROPAGATION:** Seed. **HABITS/CULTURE:** Easy to grow from seed in any soil type. *Gaillardia amblyodon* grows only in sandy soil and is pure red. **USES:** Wildflower for meadows, low-maintenance bedding plant. **PROBLEMS:** Few if any.

GARDENIA
Gardenia jasminoides (gar-DEEN-ee-ah jas-mi-NOID-ease). **COMMON NAME:** GARDENIA. **TYPE:** Evergreen shrub. **LOCATION:** Shade to part shade. **HEIGHT:** 4'–6'. **SPREAD:** 3'–5'. **SPACING:** 3'. **BLOOM/FRUIT:** Showy, fragrant white summer flowers. **PROPAGATION:** Cuttings. **HABITS/CULTURE:** Glossy foliage, large white flowers in early summer. Needs highly organic soil with good drainage. Even moisture is important. Organic feeding in winter is a good idea. Chelated iron and soil acidifiers are often needed. **USES:** Specimen, accent, flower fragrance, container plant. **PROBLEMS:** Aphids, scale, whiteflies, chlorosis. **TIPS/ NOTES:** A dwarf variety exists, but it has the same problem as the full-size plant. Native to China.

Gardenia jasminoides gardenia

GARLIC—see *Allium* spp.

GARLIC CHIVES—see *Allium* spp.

GAYFEATHER—see *Liatris* spp.

GAZANIA

Gazania hybrids (ga-ZANE-ee-ah). **COMMON NAME:** GAZANIA. **TYPE:** Perennial bedding plant. **LOCATION:** Morning sun. **HEIGHT:** 6"–12". **SPREAD:** 12"–18". **SPACING:** 9"–12". **BLOOM/FRUIT:** Colorful, daisylike flowers in yellow, orange, white, and bronze from spring through fall. **PROPAGATION:** Seed, division. **HABITS/CULTURE:** Clump-forming summer flower. Mostly yellows and oranges. Plant in afternoon shade, with morning sun, in any soil with good drainage. Drought tolerant, low fertilization requirements. **USES:** Summer color, drought-tolerant gardens. **PROBLEMS:** None. **TIPS/NOTES:** Native to South Africa. Plant from containers in spring.

GELSEMIUM

Gelsemium sempervirens (jel-SEE-mee-um sem-per-VYE-rens). **COMMON NAME:** CAROLINA JESSAMINE. **TYPE:** Evergreen vine. **LOCATION:** Sun. **HEIGHT:** High-climbing. **SPREAD:** Wide-spreading. **SPACING:** 4'–8'. **BLOOM/FRUIT:** Bright yellow tubular flowers in spring. **PROPAGATION:** Seed. **HABITS/CULTURE:** Climbing vine that needs support to start. Profuse yellow flowers in the early spring. Will

Gazania gazania

Gelsemium sempervirens Carolina jessamine

sometimes bloom during winter warm spells. Needs well-prepared soil, good drainage, moderate water and fertilizer. Top of plant sometimes needs thinning to prevent a large mass from forming and shading out the lower foliage. Will grow in shade but will not bloom well. **USES:** Climbing vine in full sun for arbors, fences, walls, screens. Early spring color. Should not be used as a ground cover. **PROBLEMS:** None. **TIPS/NOTES:** Not a jasmine. All parts of plant are poisonous but not to the touch. Native to East Texas, Florida, and Virginia.

GERANIUM—see *Pelargonium hortorum*

GERBERA

Gerbera jamesonii (GER-ba-ra jaym-SON-ee-eye). **COMMON NAME:** GERBERA DAISY. **TYPE:** Annual bedding plant. **LOCATION:** Morning sun. **HEIGHT:** 12"–18". **SPREAD:** 12"–15". **SPACING:** 12". **BLOOM/FRUIT:** Showy, daisylike flower in many colors on long stems. **PROPAGATION:** Seed. **HABITS/CULTURE:** Large lettuce-looking foliage and very showy flowers in various shades of reds, pinks, and yellows. Mulch heavily. Plant in moist but well-drained soil and fertilize every two weeks. **USES:** Color for cooler parts of the growing season. Container plant. **PROBLEMS:** Whiteflies, slugs, and snails. Doesn't like hot weather. **TIPS/NOTES:** Use a few in the early spring for a splash of color, but don't invest a lot of money in these plants.

Gerbera jamesonii Gerbera daisy

GERMANDER—see *Teucrium* spp.

GILL IVY—see *Glechoma hederacea*

GINGER—see *Zingiber officinale*

GINKGO

Ginkgo biloba (GINK-oh bye-LOBE-ah). **COMMON NAME:** GINKGO, MAIDENHAIR TREE. **TYPE:** Deciduous tree. **LOCATION:** Sun. **HEIGHT:** 50'–70'. **SPREAD:** 30'. **SPACING:** 20'–40'. **BLOOM/FRUIT:** Puny waxy flowers, awful-smelling 1" fruit on mature female trees. **PROPAGATION:** Cuttings, grafts. **HABITS/CULTURE:** Unique, open-branching tree with vibrant yellow fall color. Foliage is medium green, fan-shaped, and beautiful. Light-color bark and slow growth. Grows in any well-drained soil, but doesn't like solid rock. Moderate water and fertilizer needs. **USES:**

Ginkgo biloba ginkgo

Ginkgo biloba ginkgo, fall

Ginkgo biloba ginkgo, winter

Shade tree, fall color, distinctive foliage. Leaves are medicinal and used in teas to improve memory. **PROBLEMS:** Fruit on female trees stinks. Sometimes a slow grower. **TIPS/NOTES:** Darwin called it "a living fossil." Also called "The Tree of Life." Buddhist monks believe the ginkgo tree could restore youth and vitality. One of the oldest trees on earth, can be found on every continent in the world. Largest I've seen is in Frank Lloyd Wright's office garden in Chicago. Ginkgo can ultimately reach a height of over 120'. First identified from fossil records in China. Ginkgo has the reputation of being a slow grower, but I have discovered a secret. Under an organic program, the tree's root system will have natural beneficial fungi on its root system. The result is a larger, healthier root system and faster growth. My ginkgo puts on 20"–24" of new growth each year. The cultivar 'Autumn Gold' is available.

GLADIOLA—see *Gladiolus hortulanus*

GLADIOLUS

Gladiolus hortulanus (glad-ee-oh-lus hort-ew-LAH-nus). **COMMON NAME:** GLADIOLA. **TYPE:** Perennial bedding plant. **LOCATION:** Morning sun with afternoon shade. **HEIGHT:** 24"–48". **SPREAD:** 12"–15". **SPACING:** 6"–12". **BLOOM/FRUIT:** Thin vertical spikes with flowers of many colors from late spring through summer. Various shades of red, pink, salmon, orange, lavender, yellow, and white. **PROPAGATION:** Corms. **HABITS/CULTURE:** Plant the bulb-like corms in the spring in well-prepared, highly organic soil. Tall types need to be staked. Miniature types are available. **USES:** Summer color, cut flowers. **PROBLEMS:** Chewing insects and thrips. **TIPS/NOTES:** Corms can be dug, dried, dusted with diatomaceous earth and sulfur, and stored for replanting in the spring. Best to plant new ones each year. Some will return if left in the ground.

GLAUCAGRASS—see *Festuca ovina* 'Glauca'

GLECHOMA

Glechoma hederacea (glay-KO-ma he-de-RAH-kee-a). **COMMON NAME:** GROUND IVY, GILL IVY. **TYPE:** Perennial ground cover. **LOCATION:** Shade. **HEIGHT:** 3"–6". **SPREAD:** Unlimited. **SPACING:** 6"–18". **BLOOM/FRUIT:** Small trumpet-shaped blue flowers from spring to fall. **PROPAGATION:** Division. **HABITS/CULTURE:** Low-growing, aggressive ground cover, evergreen in the southern half of the state. Round leaves resembling dichondra, but larger and with scalloped edges. Spreads freely and roots at joints. Fragrant when crushed. Very easy to transplant and grow. Needs little to no bed preparation. **USES:** Ground cover in shade. **PROBLEMS:** Spreads easily and can be very invasive. **TIPS/NOTES:** Be careful where you plant it—you'll have it forever.

GLEDITSIA

Gleditsia triacanthos (glad-IT-see-ah try-ah-CAN-thos). **COMMON NAME:** HONEY LOCUST. **TYPE:** Deciduous tree. **LOCATION:** Sun. **HEIGHT:** 50'. **SPREAD:** 30'. **SPACING:** 20'–30'. **BLOOM/FRUIT:** Inconspicuous flowers, followed by long, broad, inch-wide pods with hard black seeds. **PROPAGATION:** Seed. **HABITS/CULTURE:** Narrow, upright, open, with lacy foliage, yellow fall color. The native plants have huge thorns on the limbs with clusters on the trunk. Large dark brown beans in fall and winter. Grows in any soil, drought tolerant, tough. **USES:** Shade tree. **PROBLEMS:** Big nasty thorns, borers. Tend to die back. **TIPS/NOTES:** If nice specimens exist on your property, try to use them, but I don't recommend planting new ones. Native from the eastern United States to Texas. The thornless hybrids do not seem healthy here.

GLOBE AMARANTH—see *Gomphrena globosa*

GLOVE THISTLE—see *Echinops exaltatus*

GOLDENBALL LEADTREE—see *Leucaena retusa*

Glechoma hederacea gill ivy

GOLDEN LEAD BALL—see *Leucaena retusa*

GOLDENRAIN TREE—see *Koelreuteria paniculata*

GOLDENROD—see *Solidago* spp.

Gomphrena globosa globe amaranth

GOMPHRENA

Gomphrena globosa (gom-FREE-na glo-BO-sa). **COMMON NAME:** GLOBE AMARANTH. **TYPE:** Annual bedding plant. **LOCATION:** Sun. **HEIGHT:** 12"–24". **SPREAD:** 18"–24" **SPACING:** 12". **BLOOM/FRUIT:** Long-lasting summer flowers in several colors, including purple, orange, and off-white. **HABITS/CULTURE:** Likes hot weather and well-drained soil. Plant after risk of frost. Can be planted as late as midsummer for color through fall. **USES:** Annual color. **PROBLEMS:** Poor drainage. **TIPS/NOTES:** Cut flowers can be dried and will last all winter.

GOSSYPIUM

Gossypium spp. (go-SIP-ee-um). **COMMON NAME:** COTTON. **TYPE:** Annual fiber crop and ornamental bedding plant. **LOCATION:** Full sun. **HEIGHT:** 3'–9'. **SPREAD:** 3'. **SPACING:** 12"–36". **BLOOM/FRUIT:** White, yellow, red, purple, or pink summer flowers. **PROPAGATION:** Seed. **HABITS/CULTURE:** Needs a long, hot growing season for best results. Needs moisture, but too much water is fatal. **USES:** Cotton crop, annual ornamental garden color. **PROBLEMS:** Boll weevil, aphids, cotton root rot. **TIPS/NOTES:** The acreage of organically grown cotton and colored cotton is growing steadily in Texas. These organic farmers have been very successful and are making excellent profits. Several interesting ornamental hybrids are available.

GOURD—see *Luffa* spp.

GRAPE—see *Vitis* spp.

GRAPE HYACINTH—see *Hyacinthus* spp.

GRASSES—see specific grass names

GREENBRIAR—see *Smilax* spp.

GROUND IVY—see *Glechoma hederacea*

GUM, BLACK—see *Nyssa sylvatica* var. *sylvatica*

GUM, SWEET—see *Liquidambar styraciflua*

GYMNOCLADUS

Gymnocladus dioica (jim-NO-kla-dus dee-oh-EE-ka). **COMMON NAME:** KENTUCKY COFFEE TREE. **TYPE:** Deciduous tree. **LOCATION:** Sun. **HEIGHT:** 50'–60'. **SPREAD:** 30'–40'. **SPACING:** 20'–30'. Insignificant greenish flowers appear May or June, followed by 6"–10" flat reddish brown pods with hard black seeds. **PROPAGATION:** Seed. **HABITS/CULTURE:** Thick, blunt branches tend to get twisted and interesting-looking. 1"–3" leaves with many small pointed leaflets. Yellow fall color. **USES:** Interesting shade tree. **PROBLEMS:** Not that thrilled with calcareous Texas soils. **TIPS/NOTES:** It's a legume, so it fixes nitrogen in the soil. Raw seeds are poisonous. Roasting supposedly removes the poison and makes a fair coffee substitute, but I don't recommend trying this. Just use it as shade tree.

Gleditsia triacanthos honey locust

HACKBERRY—see *Celtis occidentalis*

HAIRY VETCH—see *Vicia*

HAMELIA

Hamelia spp. (ham-EEL-yah). **COMMON NAME:** MEXICAN FIREBUSH. **TYPE:** Tropical used as annual bedding plant. **LOCATION:** Sun. **HEIGHT:** 2'. **SPREAD:** 2'. **SPACING:** 18". **BLOOM/FRUIT:** Coral-red flowers. **PROPAGATION:** Cuttings. **HABITS/CULTURE:** Drought tolerant, easy to grow in loose, well-drained soils. Dies from a hard freeze. **USES:** Summer color, hummingbird attractant, pot plant. **PROBLEMS:** Few if any. **TIPS/NOTES:** Perennializes in the southern half of the state.

Hamelia Mexican firebush

HARRY LAUDER'S WALKING STICK—see *Corylus avellana* 'Contorta'

HAWTHORN, INDIAN—see *Rhapiolepis indica*

HAWTHORN, NATIVE—see *Crataegus mollis*

HAWTHORN, PARSLEY—see *Crataegus mollis*

HAWTHORN, TEXAS—see *Crataegus mollis*

HAWTHORN, WASHINGTON—see *Crataegus phaenopyrum*

HEATHER, MEXICAN—see *Cuphea* spp.

HEAVENLY BAMBOO—see *Nandina domestica*

HEDERA

Hedera helix (HEAD-eh-rah HE-lix). **COMMON NAME:** ENGLISH IVY. **TYPE:** Evergreen vine and ground cover. **LOCATION:** Shade to part shade. **HEIGHT:** 1'–50'. **SPREAD:** Unlimited. **SPACING:** 9"–12" for ground cover, 4' for vine. **BLOOM/FRUIT:** Round clusters of small greenish flowers, followed by small black berries. Flowering only happens on tall vines. Mature vines will usually climb trees or buildings. **PROPAGATION:** Cuttings. **HABITS/CULTURE:** Relatively fast-growing vine for northern exposure or other shady spots. Excellent ground cover for shade or partial shade. Will climb any surface. Needs good bed prepara-

tion, good drainage, and mulch for establishment. Keep trimmed from windows, eaves, and canopy of trees. **USES:** Ground cover for shade and part sun, vine for shade. **PROBLEMS:** Aphids, cotton root rot, leaf spot, root and stem fungus. **TIPS/NOTES:** As a ground cover, should be trimmed back in late winter or early spring like all ground covers but with more care. 'Needlepoint' and 'Hahns' are smaller-leafed cultivars. 'Wilsoni' is a crinkled-leaf choice. Native to Europe, Asia, and Africa. *Fatshedera* is a vine cross between English ivy and *Fatsia japonica*. Persian ivy is *Hedera colchica* and has large egg-shaped or heart-shaped leaves. Very tough, good-looking ivy. *Hedera helix* 'Hahni' is a smaller-leafed version of the species.

Hedera helix English ivy

Helianthus maximiliani Maximilian sunflower

HELIANTHUS

Helianthus spp. (hee-lee-AN-thus). **COMMON NAME:** SUNFLOWER. **TYPE:** Annual and perennial wildflowers. **LOCATION:** Sun. **HEIGHT:** 3'–12'. **SPREAD:** Annuals make single plants, perennials spread readily. **SPACING:** Varies with type. **BLOOM/FRUIT:** Yellow or red. **PROPAGATION:** Seed for annuals, tubers for perennials. **HABITS/CULTURE:** Plant seed or tubers in any well-drained soil in full sun. Fertilize monthly for the largest flower heads. **USES:** Food, summer color, bird attractant. **PROBLEMS:** Too large and coarse-textured for many small gardens. **TIPS/NOTES:** *Helianthus annuus* is the annual common sunflower. *Helianthus multiflorus* is a perennial. *Helianthus angustifolius*, swamp sunflower, likes wet soil. *Helianthus maximiliani* is Maximilian sunflower, a beautiful clumping perennial that blooms from August to October. *Helianthus tuberosus*, Jerusalem artichoke or sunchoke, is a 6'–8' perennial grown for its edible underground tubers that taste like water chestnuts and are used as a potato substitute. Make sure you want it before you plant it—it spreads easily. I recommend it for the lazy gardener's garden. Dig the tubers in the fall after the tops have died. Mexican sunflower is *Tithonia rotundifolia.*

Heliopsis scabra yellow coneflower

Hemerocallis daylily

HELIOPSIS

Heliopsis scabra (hee-lee-OP-sis SCAB-ra). **COMMON NAME:** YELLOW CONEFLOWER. **TYPE:** Perennial wildflower. **LOCATION:** Sun. **HEIGHT:** 3'–5'. **SPREAD:** 4'–5'. **SPACING:** 3'. **BLOOM/FRUIT:** Large yellow sunflower-like summer flowers. **PROPAGATION:** Seeds. **HABITS/CULTURE:** Dark green foliage, upright growth. Easy to grow in any well-drained soil. **USES:** Background summer color. **PROBLEMS:** Few if any. **TIPS/NOTES:** This is a sunflower relative and a little more refined.

HEMEROCALLIS

Hemerocallis spp. (him-er-oh-CALL-us). **COMMON NAME:** DAYLILY, POOR MAN'S ORCHID. **TYPE:** Perennial bedding plant. **LOCATION:** Sun to part shade. **HEIGHT:** 8"–36". **SPREAD:** 24"–36". **SPACING:** 18"–24". **BLOOM/FRUIT:** Lilylike flowers in many colors. **PROPAGATION:** Division. **HABITS/CULTURE:** Foliage resembles large-leafed grass. Many colors, shapes of blooms, and heights of plants available. Blooms from late May to September with diameters of 2"–8". Each bloom lasts only one day, but others follow. Easy to grow, likes any well-prepared, well-drained soil. Average water and heavy fertilizer needs. Divide in October or November every few years. Plant from containers year round. **USES:** Summer flowers, background or accent plant, cut flowers. **PROBLEMS:** Few serious. **TIPS/NOTES:** Plant divisions in the fall. Container plants can actually be planted any time of the year. Native to Europe, China, and Japan. Daylily flowers are a gourmet vegetable.

HENBIT—see *Lamium amplexicaule*

HERBS

Aloe vera—see *Aloe vera*

Arugula—*Eruca vesicara*. Annual herb that likes cool weather and is used as a salad ingredient for a peppery and nutty taste.

Basil—see *Ocimum basilicum*

Bay—see *Laurus nobilis*

Borage—see *Borago officinalis*

Catnip—see *Nepeta* spp.

Chamomile—see *Chamaemelum* spp.

Comfrey—see *Symphytum officinale*

Coriander—see *Coriandrum sativum*

Dandelion—see *Taraxacum officinale*

Dill—see *Anethum graveolens*

Elderberry—see *Sambucus canadensis*

Epazote—see *Chenopodium* spp.

Fennel—*Foeniculum vulgare*. Semihardy perennial, usually used as an annual. Grows to 4' and has yellow flowers. Leaves, stems, and seeds are used to flavor food.

Ginger—see *Zingiber* spp.

Garlic—see *Allium* spp.

Ginseng—*Panax quinquefolius.* Herb with a single stem, compound leaves, green flowers, and red berries. Difficult to grow. The roots are the medicinal part of the plant and are taken internally to cure many ills and increase energy.

Gotu kola—*Centella asiatica.* A ground-cover herb with rounded leaves. Used medicinally to increase mental processes.

Hojo santa—see *Piper auritum*

Horehound—*Marrubium vulgare.* A bushy ground-cover herb with wooly stems and leaves. Used in cough syrup and other remedies. The leaves, which are square, are good in lemonade.

Hyssop—see *Hyssopus officinalis*

Hyssop, anise (*Agastache foeniculum*)—see *Hyssopus officinalis*

Lamb's ear—see *Stachys byzantina*

Lavender—see *Lavandula* spp.

Lemon balm—see *Melissa officinalis*

Lemongrass—see *Cymbopogon citratus*

Lemon verbena—see *Aloysia triphylla*

Marjoram—see *Origanum* spp.

Mint—see *Mentha* spp.

Onion—see *Allium* spp.

Oregano—see *Origanum* spp.

Rosemary—see *Rosmarinus officinale*

Saffron—see *Crocus* spp.

Sage—see *Salvia greggii*

Salad burnet—*Poterium sanguisorba.* Perennial herb that grows in a rosette; its rounded, toothed leaflets taste like cucumber and are excellent in salads and other dishes.

Savory—*Satureja* spp. Summer savory, *Satureja hortensis,* is an annual; winter savory, *Satureja montana,* is a perennial. Both are used to flavor foods, especially beans.

Sorrel—*Rumex acetosa.* A weedy-looking herb with leaves that are delicious in salads.

Tansy—see *Tanacetum vulgare*

Tarragon, French—see *Artemisia dracunculus*

Tarragon, Texas—see *Tagetes* spp.

Thyme—see *Thymus* spp.

Wormwood—see *Artemisia absinthium*

Yarrow—see *Achillea* spp.

HESPERALOE

Hesperaloe parviflora (hes-per-AH-low par-vi-FLOR-ah). **COMMON NAME:** RED YUCCA. **TYPE:** Evergreen accent plant. **LOCATION:** Sun. **HEIGHT:** 3'. **SPREAD:** 3'–5'. **SPACING:** 3'–4'. **BLOOM/FRUIT:** 3'–4' clusters of reddish pink flowers that bloom almost all summer. **PROPAGATION:** Seed, division. **HABITS/CULTURE:** Slender, fountainlike blue-green foliage, fairly slow-growing. Extremely drought tolerant, grows in any well-drained soil. Low fertilizer needs. **USES:** Specimen, accent, summer color. **PROBLEMS:** None. **TIPS/NOTES:** Native to West Texas.

Hesperaloe parviflora red yucca

Hibiscus moscheutos hardy hibiscus

HIBISCUS

Hibiscus spp. (hi-BIS-kus). **COMMON NAME:** HIBISCUS. **TYPE:** Tropical shrubs used as annuals and perennials. **LOCATION:** Sun to part shade. **HEIGHT:** 5'–6'. **SPREAD:** 3'–6'. **SPACING:** 2'–3'. **BLOOM/FRUIT:** Single or double flowers in bright shades of pink, white, yellow, orange, purple, and many combinations. Annual hibiscus has smaller, brighter colors; the huge subtle-colored flowers are the perennial forms. **PROPAGATION:** Cuttings. **HABITS/CULTURE:** Upright, thick succulent stems. Many colors and characteristics available. Blooms all summer. Easy to grow in any well-drained soil, moderate water and fertilizer requirements. Native to the southern United States. **USES:** Summer flower color, specimen, pots. Flowers are edible. **PROB-**

LEMS: Whiteflies, aphids, leaf-chewing beetles. **TIPS/NOTES:** There are many other hibiscus that are wonderful plants. The tropicals, which act as annuals in most of Texas, are the most colorful. The hearty perennials like *Hibiscus moscheutos*, hardy hibiscus or rose mallow, are beautiful and will die to the ground in winter but return each spring. 'Frisbee,' 'Southern Belle,' 'Confederate,' and 'Marsh' are excellent perennial cultivars. *Hibiscus rosa-sinensis* is the Chinese or tropical hibiscus. *Hibiscus coccineus* is the perennial Texas star hibiscus.

Hibiscus esculentus (hi-BIS-kus es-kew-LEN-tus). **COMMON NAME:** OKRA. **TYPE:** Annual vegetable. **LOCATION:** Sun. **HEIGHT:** 8'–15'. **SPREAD:** 5'–6'. **SPACING:** 6"–9". **BLOOM/FRUIT:** Yellow flowers, followed by edible pods. **PROPAGATION:** Seed. **HABITS/CULTURE:** Upright growth after soil temperature is warm. Likes temperatures of 75–90 degrees. Germinates in 4–14 days in warm soil. **USES:** Vegetable. **PROBLEMS:** Won't germinate in cool soil. Hates "wet feet." Ants, aphids, nematodes, cutworms, and fungus. **TIPS/NOTES:** Harvest pods when young and tender.

Hibiscus syriacus (hi-BIS-kus si-ri-AH-kus). **COMMON NAME:** ALTHEA, ROSE OF SHARON. **TYPE:** Deciduous shrub. **LOCATION:** Sun to shade. **HEIGHT:** 10'–15'. **SPREAD:** 8'–10'. **SPACING:** 8'–10'. **BLOOM/FRUIT:** Summer flowers of primarily white, pink, or purple shades. **PROPAGATION:** Cuttings. **HABITS/CULTURE:** Summer-flowering shrub, upright growth. Bare branches in winter. Yellow fall color. Easy to grow in any soil, fairly drought tolerant. **USES:** Summer flowers. **PROBLEMS:** Cotton root rot, aphids. **TIPS/NOTES:** Should always be used with evergreens since it is so homely in the winter. Native to Asia.

HICKORY—see *Carya* spp.

HIPPEASTRUM

Hippeastrum spp. (hip-ee-ASS-trum). **COMMON NAME:** CHRISTMAS AMARYLLIS. **TYPE:** Tropical perennial flower. **LOCATION:** Part shade. **HEIGHT:** 30". **SPREAD:** 30". **SPACING:** 15". **BLOOM/FRUIT:** Large colorful blooms forced in winter for decorative purposes. **PROPAGATION:** Bulbs. **HABITS/CULTURE:** Tropical and native to dry climates. **USES:** Winter color. **PROBLEMS:** Freezes outdoors. Poisonous. **TIPS/NOTES:** Can be brought back into bloom by allowing to dry out after blooming. Dry summer is its normal dormant period. *Hippeastrum* × *johnsonii*, hardy amaryllis, is the tough red-flowering perennial. Almost all members of the amaryllis family are highly toxic, including jonquil, daffodil, narcissus, Atamasco lily, spider lily, crinum lily, snowflake, snowdrop, rain lily, and stargrass.

HOJO SANTA—see *Piper auritum*

HOLLY, BURFORD—see *Ilex cornuta* 'Burfordii'

HOLLY, DECIDUOUS YAUPON—see *Ilex decidua*

HOLLY, DWARF BURFORD—see *Ilex cornuta* 'Burfordii Nana'

HOLLY, DWARF CHINESE—see *Ilex cornuta* 'Rotunda'

HOLLY, DWARF YAUPON—see *Ilex vomitoria* 'Nana'

HOLLY, EAST PALATKA—see *Ilex* × *attenuata* 'East Palatka'

HOLLY, FERN—see *Cyrtomium falcatum*

HOLLY, FOSTER—see *Ilex* × *attenuata* 'Foster'

HOLLY, LUSTER LEAF—see *Ilex cornuta* 'Burfordii'

HOLLY, NELLIE R. STEVENS—see *Ilex* × 'Nellie R. Stevens'

Hibiscus rosa-sinensis tropical hibiscus

Hibiscus coccineus Texas star hibiscus

Hibiscus syriacus althea

H

HOLLY, POSSUMHAW—see *Ilex decidua*

HOLLY, SAVANNAH—see *Ilex opaca* (× *attenuata*) 'Savannah'

HOLLY, WEEPING YAUPON—see *Ilex vomitoria* 'Pendula'

HOLLY, YAUPON—see *Ilex vomitoria*

HOLLYHOCK—see *Alcea rosea*

HONEY LOCUST—see *Gleditsia triacanthos*

HONEYSUCKLE—see *Lonicera japonica* 'Atropurpurea'

HONEYSUCKLE, CORAL—see *Lonicera sempervirens*

HONEYSUCKLE, WHITE—see *Lonicera albiflora*

HONEYSUCKLE, WINTER—see *Lonicera albiflora*

HORSEHERB—see *Calyptocarpus vialis*

HORSEMINT—see *Monarda citriodora*

HORSETAIL REED—see *Equisetum hyemale*

HOSTA

Hosta spp. (HOSS-tah). **COMMON NAME:** HOSTA, PLANTAIN LILY, SHADE LILY. **TYPE:** Perennial bedding plant or ground cover. **LOCATION:** Shade to part shade. **HEIGHT:** 1'–3'. **SPREAD:** 2'–3'. **SPACING:** 1'–3'. **BLOOM/FRUIT:** White or light-blue trumpet flowers atop thin stems in late summer. **PROPAGATION:** Division. **HABITS/CULTURE:** Tufted, leafy plants with fragrant white, lilac, or blue spiked flowers in late summer. Green or blue foliage. Many varieties and cultivars available. Relatively easy to grow. Likes moist, well-drained, highly organic soil. Can be divided in fall. Moderate fertilizer needs. **USES:** Mass or border for shade gardens. Used more for foliage than flowers. **PROB-**

LEMS: Slugs, snails, summer heat. **TIPS/NOTES:** Native to Korea, China, and Japan. Those varieties with blue foliage like shade best, the variegated varieties like a little more sun; all do best with some shade. 'Royal Standard' has large white flowers, 'Sieboldii' has lavender flowers; both are excellent and immune to sunburn. No transplanting or division necessary.

Hosta hosta

HOUTTUYNIA

Houttuynia cordata 'Variegata' (hoo-TIE-nee-a core-DAH-tah). **COMMON NAME:** HOUTTUYNIA. **TYPE:** Perennial ground-cover herb. **LOCATION:** Sun to shade. **HEIGHT:** 1'. **SPREAD:** Ground cover. **SPACING:** 1'–2'. **BLOOM/FRUIT:** Small white flowers in summer. **PROPAGATION:** Division. **HABITS/CULTURE:** Colorful ground cover that spreads aggressively and has yellow, rosy, and red foliage in full sun.

Houttuynia cordata 'Variegata' houttuynia

Tolerates any soil condition but does best in wet or boggy soil. **USES:** Ground cover for poorly drained areas. Herb used especially in Oriental cooking. **PROBLEMS:** Invasive, should be contained. **TIPS/NOTES:** Loves wet feet—a nice surprise. Bruised foliage smells like strong citrus. Native to Japan. Dies completely to the ground in winter but returns aggressively each spring.

HUISACHE—see *Acacia* spp.

HYACINTH BEAN—see *Dolichos lablab*

HYACINTHUS

Hyacinthus spp. (HI-ah-sinth-us). **COMMON NAME:** HYACINTH. **TYPE:** Perennial bulb. **LOCATION:** Sun. **HEIGHT:** 3"–12". **SPREAD:** 3"–12". **SPACING:** 6"–9". **BLOOM/FRUIT:** Vertical foliage in spring, followed by dramatic flower spike of most any color. **PROPAGATION:** Bulbs. **HABITS/CULTURE:** Extremely fragrant. Likes well-prepared, well-drained soil; moderate water and fertilizer requirements. Add bone meal or soft rock phosphate to soil when planting. **USES:** Spring color, fragrance. **PROBLEMS:** Expensive for the show. **TIPS/NOTES:** Plant bulbs in December for early spring flowers. Plants will return but will be quite weak. Better to plant new ones again. *Muscari* is the small grape hyacinth. It is much better at returning each year and should be planted 3"–6" apart.

HYDRANGEA

Hydrangea macrophylla (hi-DRAN-ja mac-crow-FILE-ah). **COMMON NAME:** HYDRANGEA. **TYPE:** Deciduous shrub. **LOCATION:** Sun to part shade. **HEIGHT:** 3'–5'. **SPREAD:** 3'–5'. **SPACING:** 3'–4'. **BLOOM/FRUIT:** Blue or pink false flowers through the summer. **PROPAGATION:** Cuttings. **HABITS/CULTURE:** Big, bold-textured foliage and long-lasting flowers in summer, completely bare in winter. Although shade-loving, it will produce more and larger flowers in bright places. Needs plenty of water and rich, organic soil for best results. Prune immediately after blooms fade away. Add soil acidifiers for blue flowers if you want to, but you may get dark, muddy-colored pink. **USES:** Summer leaf texture and flower color. **PROBLEMS:** None serious. Likes a lot of water. **TIPS/NOTES:** Should be used in association with evergreen plants. Native to Japan and China.

Hyacinthus hyacinth

Muscari grape hyacinth

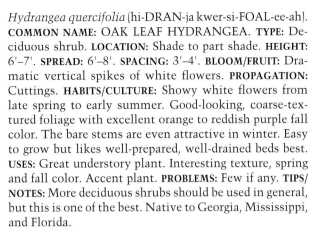

Hydrangea quercifolia (hi-DRAN-ja kwer-si-FOAL-ee-ah). **COMMON NAME:** OAK LEAF HYDRANGEA. **TYPE:** Deciduous shrub. **LOCATION:** Shade to part shade. **HEIGHT:** 6'–7'. **SPREAD:** 6'–8'. **SPACING:** 3'–4'. **BLOOM/FRUIT:** Dramatic vertical spikes of white flowers. **PROPAGATION:** Cuttings. **HABITS/CULTURE:** Showy white flowers from late spring to early summer. Good-looking, coarse-textured foliage with excellent orange to reddish purple fall color. The bare stems are even attractive in winter. Easy to grow but likes well-prepared, well-drained beds best. **USES:** Great understory plant. Interesting texture, spring and fall color. Accent plant. **PROBLEMS:** Few if any. **TIPS/NOTES:** More deciduous shrubs should be used in general, but this is one of the best. Native to Georgia, Mississippi, and Florida.

HYMENOCALLIS
Hymenocallis spp. (high-men-oh-KAH-lis). **COMMON NAME:** SPIDER LILY. **TYPE:** Perennial flower. **LOCATION:** Sun to part shade. **HEIGHT:** 3'–5'. **SPREAD:** 4'–6'. **SPACING:** 2'–3'. **BLOOM/FRUIT:** Large white flowers in summer. **PROPAGATION:** Division. **HABITS/CULTURE:** Large, dark green foliage and dramatic, spiderlike white flowers in midsummer. **USES:** Accent, summer color. **PROBLEMS:** Needs plenty of space. **TIPS/NOTES:** 'Tropical Giant' is used mostly in the Gulf Coast region but adapted to much of Texas.

HYMENOXYS
Hymenoxys scaposa (hye-men-OX-iss skay-POH-sah). **COMMON NAME:** FOUR-NERVE DAISY. **TYPE:** Perennial wildflower. **LOCATION:** Sun to part shade. **HEIGHT:** 12". **SPREAD:** 6"–9". **SPACING:** 9". **BLOOM/FRUIT:** Solitary yellow 1"–2" daisylike flowers from March to October. **PROPAGATION:** Seed. **HABITS/CULTURE:** Small, easy-to-grow, native perennial with pale gray-green leaves, furry or shiny

Hydrangea macrophylla hydrangea

Hydrangea quercifolia oak leaf hydrangea

Hymenocallis spider lily

bare stems. Foliage has strong, bitter fragrance when crushed. **USES:** Rock gardens, xeriscapes. **PROBLEMS:** Too much water will rot the plant. **TIPS/NOTES:** Name comes from the four veins on each flower petal.

Hymenoxys scaposa four-nerve daisy

Hypericum hypericum

HYPERICUM

Hypericum spp. (hi-PEAR-eh-cum). **COMMON NAME:** HYPERICUM, ST. JOHN'S WORT. **TYPE:** Perennial bedding plant. **LOCATION:** Sun to part shade. **HEIGHT:** 2'–3'. **SPREAD:** 3'–4'. **SPACING:** 18"–24". **BLOOM/FRUIT:** 2"–3" yellow flowers from late spring through summer. **PROPAGATION:** Cuttings. **HABITS/CULTURE:** Evergreen or semievergreen. Showy yellow flowers in summer. Low-growing, attractive foliage, sometimes reddish in fall. Grows in any soil, sun or part shade. Likes prepared beds, moderate water and fertilizer. **USES:** Mass, accent, summer color. **PROBLEMS:** Few if any. **TIPS/NOTES:** Native to Europe. Several good varieties are available. *Hypericum patulum henryi* is the most commonly sold here. *Hypericum beanii* is apparently the correct name.

HYSSOPUS

Hyssopus officinalis (hi-SOP-us oh-fis-ih-NAH-lis). **COMMON NAME:** HYSSOP. **TYPE:** Perennial herb. **LOCATION:** Sun. **HEIGHT:** 18"–24". **SPACING:** 18"–24". **BLOOM/FRUIT:**

Blue, pink, or white flower spikes. **PROPAGATION:** Seed, division, or cuttings. **HABITS/CULTURE:** Slow-growing, upright, small flowers that are attractive to bees and butterflies. Well adapted to alkaline soils. **TIPS/NOTES:** The 3' perennial *Agastache foeniculum*, anise hyssop, is easy to grow and has pale lavender or blue flower spikes. Dried leaves are used to flavor teas and foods. Flowers of both plants are edible.

Agastache foeniculum anise hyssop

IBERIS

Iberis sempervirens (eye-BER-is sem-per-VIE-rens). **COMMON NAME:** CANDYTUFT. **TYPE:** Perennial bedding plant. **LOCATION:** Sun to part shade. **HEIGHT:** 8"–12". **SPREAD:** 12'–15'. **SPACING:** 9"–12". **BLOOM/FRUIT:** Pure white flower clusters in early spring. **PROPAGATION:** Cuttings. **HABITS/CULTURE:** Low, compact, neat perennial that produces white flowers in spring. Will usually return for a few years. Plant in sun or partial shade in well-prepared soil that drains well. Moderate water and fertilizer requirements. **USES:** Small gardens, rock walls, small containers. **PROBLEMS:** Few if any. **TIPS/NOTES:** I find this plant a short-lived perennial.

Iberis sempervirens candytuft

ICE PLANT—see *Mesembryanthemum* spp.

ILEX

Ilex cornuta 'Burfordii' (EYE-lex cor-NUTE-ah). **COMMON NAME:** BURFORD HOLLY. **TYPE:** Evergreen shrub. **LOCATION:** Sun to shade. **HEIGHT:** 15'. **SPREAD:** 15'. **SPACING:** 4'–8'. **BLOOM/FRUIT:** Small white flowers in spring, red berries from fall through winter. **PROPAGATION:** Cuttings. **HABITS/CULTURE:** Upright, hard, single-spined leaves and red berries in winter. Grows in any soil and any exposure with good drainage. Should not be sheared into hedge. **USES:** Specimen shrub or small tree, background, screen, or tall border. **PROBLEMS:** Scale, chlorosis. **TIPS/NOTES:** Native to China and Korea. Always buy full, bushy plants. Leggy bargains never fill in well. An interesting large-leafed holly is luster leaf holly, *Ilex latifolia.* Other large-growing hollies that do well in Texas are 'Emily Brunner' and 'Mary Nell,' which has 3"–4" leaves with toothed edges. It grows 8'–10' tall, does well in sun or shade. 'Nasa' grows 6'–8' tall and has thinner leaves.

growing. Grows in sun or shade in any soil with good drainage. Moderate water and fertilization requirements. **USES:** Medium-height border, mass, screen, or background. **PROBLEMS:** Scale, chlorosis. **TIPS/NOTES:** The excellent 'Willowleaf' and 'Needlepoint' are closely kin, but with narrower leaves. 'Dazzler' is a good heavy-berried holly. Despite what you might have heard, 'Berries Jubilee' is a coarse plant and a poor choice. 'Carissa' is a compact, single-pointed, wavy-leaf holly that has few if any berries in winter. Cultivated.

Ilex cornuta 'Burfordii Nana' dwarf Burford holly

Ilex cornuta 'Willowleaf' willowleaf holly

Ilex cornuta 'Burfordii' Burford holly

Ilex latifolia luster leaf holly

Ilex cornuta 'Carissa' Carissa holly

Ilex 'Mary Nell' Mary Nell holly

Ilex cornuta 'Burfordii Nana' (EYE-lex cor-NUTE-ah). **COMMON NAME:** DWARF BURFORD HOLLY. **TYPE:** Evergreen shrub. **LOCATION:** Sun to shade. **HEIGHT:** 3'–5'. **SPREAD:** 3'–5'. **SPACING:** 2'–3'. **BLOOM/FRUIT:** Small white flowers in spring, red berries in fall and winter. **PROPAGATION:** Cuttings. **HABITS/CULTURE:** Same characteristics as Burford holly but smaller, more compact, and lower-

Ilex cornuta 'Rotunda' dwarf Chinese holly

Ilex cornuta 'Rotunda' (EYE-lex cor-NUTE-ah row-TUN-dah). **COMMON NAME:** DWARF CHINESE HOLLY. **TYPE:** Evergreen shrub. **LOCATION:** Sun to shade. **HEIGHT:** 18"–36". **SPREAD:** 24"–36". **SPACING:** 18"–24". **BLOOM/FRUIT:** Small white spring flowers, no berries normally. **PROPAGATION:** Cuttings. **HABITS/CULTURE:** Low-growing, rounded, compact, with very dense, spiny foliage. Grows in any well-drained soil, but a good organically prepared bed is best. Moderate water and fertilizer needs. Best to prune in late February or early March just before new growth. **USES:** Low border, mass, or barrier. People and pets won't walk through this plant but once. One of the best low-growing evergreens for commercial use. **PROBLEMS:** Scale but not serious. **TIPS/NOTES:** Avoid if you like to work in your garden barefoot. The parent is the large Chinese holly, a coarse, undesirable plant. Originally from China; the dwarf forms have been hybridized.

Ilex decidua (EYE-lex dee-SID-you-ah). **COMMON NAME:** DECIDUOUS YAUPON HOLLY, POSSUMHAW HOLLY. **TYPE:** Deciduous tree. **LOCATION:** Sun to shade. **HEIGHT:** 20'. **SPREAD:** 15'. **SPACING:** 12'–15'. **BLOOM/FRUIT:** Small white flowers in spring, orange or red berries in fall and winter on female plants. **PROPAGATION:** Cuttings. **HABITS/CULTURE:** Bushy growth if not trimmed, small leaves, red berries on bare branches all winter long. Easy to grow in any soil, drought tolerant. **USES:** Winter color, understory tree, specimen garden tree. **PROBLEMS:** Suckers from base, buying male plants accidentally. **TIPS/NOTES:** I had a deciduous Christmas tree one year using this plant. Best to purchase when the berries can be seen on the plant. 'Warren's Red' has bright red berries. The male is not worth much. Native from the southeastern United States to Texas.

Ilex decidua possumhaw holly

Ilex decidua possumhaw holly, winter

Ilex opaca (× *attenuata*) 'Savannah' (EYE-lex o-PAY-kuh). **COMMON NAME:** SAVANNAH HOLLY. **TYPE:** Evergreen tree. **LOCATION:** Sun to shade. **HEIGHT:** 15'–30'. **SPREAD:** 10'–15'. **SPACING:** 8'–12'. **BLOOM/FRUIT:** Small white flowers in spring, red berries in fall and winter. **PROPAGATION:** Cuttings. **HABITS/CULTURE:** Moderate upright, pyramidal growth, with medium-green spiny leaves, lots of red berries in winter. Easy to grow in any well-drained soil. **USES:** Small specimen garden tree, border, or evergreen background. **PROBLEMS:** Few. Leaf miners occasionally. **TIPS/NOTES:** Good small evergreen cultivar.

Ilex opaca (× *attenuata*) 'Savannah' Savannah holly

Ilex vomitoria yaupon holly, winter

Ilex vomitoria (EYE-lex vom-ee-TORE-ee-ah). **COMMON NAME:** YAUPON HOLLY. **TYPE:** Evergreen tree. **LOCATION:** Sun to shade. **HEIGHT:** 20'. **SPREAD:** 20'. **SPACING:** 10'–15'. **BLOOM/FRUIT:** Small white flowers in spring, red berries in fall and winter on female plants. **PROPAGATION:** Cuttings. **HABITS/CULTURE:** Bushy unless trimmed into tree form. Light-color bark, interesting branching. Easy to grow in all soils. Drought tolerant, but grows much faster when irrigated regularly. Can stand fairly wet soil. **USES:** Ornamental understory or specimen tree. Good for courtyards and small garden spaces. **PROBLEMS:** Leaf miners occasionally in summer—nothing serious. **TIPS/NOTES:** Native to Central Texas.

Ilex vomitoria yaupon holly

Ilex vomitoria 'Pendula' (EYE-lex vom-ee-TORE-ee-ah PEN-due-lah). **COMMON NAME:** WEEPING YAUPON HOLLY. **TYPE:** Evergreen tree. **LOCATION:** Sun to shade. **HEIGHT:** 15'–20'. **SPREAD:** 8'–10'. **SPACING:** 5'–10'. **BLOOM/FRUIT:** Small white flowers in spring; red berries in fall and winter on female plants. **PROPAGATION:** Cuttings. **HABITS/CULTURE:** Upright with sharply drooping limbs. Leaves are smaller than those of regular yaupon holly. Easy to grow in any well-drained soil. **USES:** Specimen garden ornamental, border, background plant, container tree, Oriental gardens. **PROBLEMS:** Few if any. **TIPS/NOTES:** Very interesting and unusual plant.

Ilex vomitoria 'Nana' (EYE-lex vom-ee-TORE-ee-ah). **COMMON NAME:** DWARF YAUPON HOLLY. **TYPE:** Evergreen shrub. **LOCATION:** Sun to shade. **HEIGHT:** 18"–36". **SPREAD:** 24"–36". **SPACING:** 18"–24". **BLOOM/FRUIT:** Insignificant white flowers in spring, no berries. **PROPAGATION:** Cuttings. **HABITS/CULTURE:** Rounded, compact, and dense, with small, shiny oval leaves. A very tidy plant. Grows in any soil, but likes well-prepared beds best. Tolerates fairly wet soils but prefers good drainage. **USES:** Low border or mass planting. **PROBLEMS:** Leaf rollers occasionally. **TIPS/NOTES:** This is the dwarf form of the Texas native yaupon holly tree.

Ilex × attenuata 'East Palatka' (EYE-lex ah-ten-you-AH-tah). **COMMON NAME:** EAST PALATKA HOLLY. **TYPE:** Evergreen tree. **LOCATION:** Sun to part shade. **HEIGHT:** 15'–30'. **SPREAD:** 10'–15'. **SPACING:** 8'–10'. **BLOOM/FRUIT:** Small white flowers in spring, red berries in fall and winter. **PROPAGATION:** Cuttings. **HABITS/CULTURE:** Large bush or small tree with upright, moderate growth, rather open branching. Smooth light bark. Grows in any soil except solid rock, needs good drainage. **USES:** Specimen ornamental, evergreen border, small garden tree. **PROBLEMS:** Scale, mealybugs, iron deficiency, although none are serious. **TIPS/NOTES:** Distinguished by one spine on end of leaf rather than several, as with 'Savannah' and 'Foster.' All are hybrids of *Ilex opaca*, American holly.

Ilex × attenuata 'Foster' (EYE-lex ah-ten-you-AH-tah). **COMMON NAME:** FOSTER HOLLY. **TYPE:** Evergreen shrub. **LOCATION:** Sun to shade. **HEIGHT:** 20'. **SPREAD:** 10'. **SPACING:** 3'–10'. **BLOOM/FRUIT:** Small white flowers in spring, red berries in fall and winter. **PROPAGATION:** Cuttings. **HABITS/CULTURE:** Small, spiny dark green leaves, upright pyramidal growth, many small red berries in winter. Fairly slow growth. Relatively easy to grow in any well-drained soil, prefers slightly acid soil but adapts well to alkaline clays. **USES:** Specimen evergreen tree, border or background plant. Berry color in winter. **PROBLEMS:** Leaf miners occasionally. **TIPS/NOTES:** Excellent plant for dark green color. Cultivated.

Ilex vomitoria 'Nana'
dwarf yaupon holly

Ilex vomitoria 'Pendula'
weeping yaupon holly

Ilex × attenuata 'East Palatka'
East Palatka holly

Ilex × attenuata 'Foster'
Foster holly

Ilex × 'Nellie R. Stevens' (EYE-lex). **COMMON NAME:** NELLIE R. STEVENS HOLLY. **TYPE:** Evergreen shrub or small tree. **LOCATION:** Sun to shade. **HEIGHT:** 10'–20'. **SPREAD:** 10'–20'. **SPACING:** 4'–14'. **BLOOM/FRUIT:** Insignificant white flowers in spring, large, showy red berries in fall and winter. **PROPAGATION:** Cuttings. **HABITS/CULTURE:** Large, dark green leaves. Extremely durable. More compact and healthy in full sun but can tolerate fairly heavy shade. Tolerates severe weather conditions. **USES:** Screen or specimen plant. Can be trimmed into ornamental tree. Good in containers. **PROBLEMS:** None, one of the most durable plants available. **TIPS/NOTES:** 'Nellie R. Stevens' is a cross between *Ilex aquifolium*, English holly, and *Ilex cornuta*, Chinese holly.

Ilex × 'Nellie R. Stevens'
Nellie R. Stevens holly

IMPATIENS

Impatiens balsamina (im-PAY-shunz bal-SAM-eh-nah). **COMMON NAME:** IMPATIENS, BALSAM, SHADY LADY. **TYPE:** Annual bedding plant. **LOCATION:** Shade. **HEIGHT:** 10"–24". **SPREAD:** 18"–24". **SPACING:** 9"–12". **BLOOM/FRUIT:** Orange, white, pink, salmon, red, and purple flowers in summer. **PROPAGATION:** Seed, cuttings. **HABITS/CULTURE:** Colorful low-spreading annual with tender stems, foliage, and flowers. Plant in well-prepared beds in shade after the last frost. Must have excellent drainage. **USES:** Annual beds, pots, hanging baskets. One of the best flowers for shady areas. **PROBLEMS:** Cutworms, red spider mites, slugs. **TIPS/NOTES:** Native to India and China. 'New Guinea' has showy foliage and can take much more sun. All varieties are very susceptible to freezing.

Impatiens balsamina impatiens

INCENSE CEDAR—see *Calocedrus decurrens*

INDIAN BEAN—see *Catalpa bignonioides*

INDIAN BLANKET—see *Gaillardia pulchella*

INDIAN-CURRANT SNOWBERRY—see *Symphoricarpos orbiculatus*

INDIAN HAWTHORN—see *Rhapiolepis indica*

INDIAN PAINTBRUSH—see *Castilleja* spp.

INDIGOBUSH—see *Amorpha fruticosa*

INLAND SEAOATS—see *Chasmanthium latifolium*

IPOMOEA

Ipomoea spp. (eye-po-MAY-ah). **COMMON NAME:** MORNING GLORY, MOON VINE. **TYPE:** Annual vines and perennials. **LOCATION:** Sun to part shade. **HEIGHT/SPREAD:** Tall-growing, wide-spreading vine. **SPACING:** 4'–8'. **BLOOM/FRUIT:** Summer flowers in many colors. **PROPAGATION:** Seeds, tubers. **HABITS/CULTURE:** Fast-growing annuals, grow easily in any soil with very little maintenance. **USES:** Summer color. **PROBLEMS:** Caterpillars. **TIPS/NOTES:** *Ipomoea leptophylla* is the native bush morning glory. *Ipomoea alba* is the night-blooming moon flower. *Ipomoea tricolor* is the common morning glory. *Ipomoea quamoclit* is the cypress vine or cardinal climber. Morning glory is a kissing cousin to field bindweed and can grow to 16', depending on the species. Control by increasing organic matter in the soil.

Ipomoea tricolor morning glory

Ipomoea batatas (eye-po-MAY-ah ba-TAH-tas). **COMMON NAME:** SWEET POTATO. **TYPE:** Annual vine. **LOCATION:** Sun. **HEIGHT/SPREAD:** High-climbing and widely spreading. **SPACING:** 12"–16". **PROPAGATION:** Slips. **HABITS/CULTURE:** Warm-season annual. Plant slips 12"–16" apart at a depth of 2"–3" after soil is warm in the spring. Germination occurs at 77 degrees. Harvest in the fall and store in a cool, dry place. Does best in sandy soil, but grows in any loose, well-drained soil. **USES:** Food. **PROBLEMS:** Sweet potato weevil, nematodes. **TIPS/NOTES:** Dig sweet potatoes when the soil is dry.

Ipomoea quamoclit cypress vine   *Ipomopsis rubra* standing cypress

IPOMOPSIS

Ipomopsis rubra (eye-po-MOP-sis ROO-bra). **COMMON NAME:** STANDING CYPRESS, RED GILIA. **TYPE:** Biennial wildflower. **LOCATION:** Sun. **HEIGHT:** 2'-6'. **SPREAD:** 6'-12". **SPACING:** 6"-9". **BLOOM/FRUIT:** Red or yellow spires of 1" flowers in May and June. **PROPAGATION:** Seed. **HABITS/CULTURE:** Requires sandy or gravelly soil with excellent drainage, prefers fertile soil. Plant seed for at least two years since blooms come the second season. **USES:** Wildflower. **PROBLEMS:** Few if any. **TIPS/NOTES:** Let plants go to seed before cutting back. Rosettes can be transplanted in the fall.

Iris Louisiana iris

IRIS

Iris spp. (EYE-ris). **COMMON NAME:** IRIS, FLAG. **TYPE:** Perennial bedding plant. **LOCATION:** Sun. **HEIGHT:** 10"-40". **SPREAD:** 3'-4'. **SPACING:** 6"-24". **BLOOM/FRUIT:** Showy spring flowers in many colors. **PROPAGATION:** Division. **HABITS/CULTURE:** Vertical swordlike leaves, spreads by underground rhizomes, available in any color. Beardless and bearded are the major groups. Iris culture varies greatly—some of the beardless irises (Japanese and Louisiana) can grow in or at the edge of water. Others, like Siberian iris, need to be continually moist. Others, like the tall bearded kinds, need relatively dry, well-drained soil. When clumps get too thick, dig with turning fork, cut leaves to 6"-8", and replant. Place bearded iris rhi-

zomes even with the soil surface and beardless 1"-2" below the surface. **USES:** Spring flowers, perennial gardens, cut flowers. **PROBLEMS:** None serious. **TIPS/NOTES:** Iris means "rainbow" in Greek, so I like to plant mixed color masses. Louisianas and spurias grow the tallest. Intermediates are a good choice for a landscape iris.

IRONCROSS—see *Bignonia capreolata*

IVY, BOSTON—see *Parthenocissus tricuspidata* 'Lowii'

IVY, ENGLISH—see *Hedera helix*

IVY, FIG—see *Ficus pumila*

IVY, HAHN'S—see *Hedera helix*

IVY, PERSIAN—see *Hedera colchica*

IXORA

Ixora coccinea (icks-OH-rah kok-SIN-ee uh). **COMMON NAME:** IXORA, FLAME OF THE WOODS. **TYPE:** Tropical used as an annual. **LOCATION:** Sun. **HEIGHT:** 2'-3'. **SPREAD:** 2'-3'. **SPACING:** 18"-24". **BLOOM/FRUIT:** Clusters of red, yellow, orange, or white flowers all summer. **PROPAGATION:** Cuttings. **HABITS/CULTURE:** Tropical, tender plant. Cross-shaped flowers and glossy green crossed foliage, grows into a mounded form covered with long-lasting flowers. Best in healthy, well-drained soil. Blooms best with regular fertilizer applications. **USES:** Summer color, potted plants, hummingbird attractant. **PROBLEMS:** Freezes easily. Use as an annual. **TIPS/NOTES:** Add vinegar, seaweed, and fish emulsion to the watering can at every watering for best results. This is an excellent summer-color container plant.

Ixora coccinea ixora

88 Jacobina–Joseph's coat

JACOBINA—see *Justicia* spp.

JAPANESE ANEMONE—see *Anemone hupehensis*

JAPANESE ARALIA—see *Fatsia japonica*

JAPANESE ARDISIA—see *Ardisia japonica*

JAPANESE SPURGE—see *Pachysandra terminalis*

JAPANESE WISTERIA—see *Wisteria floribunda*

JASMINE, ARABIAN—see *Jasminum sambac*

JASMINE, ASIAN—see *Trachelospermum asiaticum*

JASMINE, ASIATIC—see *Trachelospermum asiaticum*

JASMINE, CONFEDERATE—see *Trachelospermum jasminoides*

JASMINE, ITALIAN—see *Jasminum humile*

JASMINE, SAMBAC—see *Jasminum sambac*

JASMINE, YELLOW STAR—see *Trachelospermum asiaticum*

Jasminum sambac sambac jasmine

JASMINUM

Jasminum humile (JAS-min-um HUME-eh-lee). **COMMON NAME:** ITALIAN JASMINE. **TYPE:** Semi-evergreen shrub. **LOCATION:** Sun. **HEIGHT:** 5'–6'. **SPREAD:** 5'–6'. **SPACING:** 3'–4'. **BLOOM/FRUIT:** Clusters of fragrant yellow flowers in summer. **PROPAGATION:** Cuttings. **HABITS/CULTURE:** Gracefully arching shrub with willowy green stems and small yellow flowers in early summer. Loses one-half to two-thirds of its foliage in winter. Likes well-prepared, well-drained soil. Moderate water and fertilization needs. Little pruning needed. In fact, heavy clipping or shearing will ruin this plant. **USES:** Border, hedge, or specimen plant. **PROBLEMS:** Freeze damage in harsh winters. **TIPS/NOTES:** Native to China. *Jasminum nudiflorum,* a close kin, is completely deciduous. Best suited to the southern half of the state.

Jasminum humile Italian jasmine

Jasminum sambac (JAS-min-um SAM-back). **COMMON NAME:** SAMBAC JASMINE, ARABIAN JASMINE. **TYPE:** Tender evergreen shrub. **LOCATION:** Sun. **HEIGHT:** 2'–3'. **SPREAD:** 3'. **SPACING:** 2'. **BLOOM/FRUIT:** White 3/4"–1" flowers, extremely fragrant. New flowers are produced every day during the summer. **PROPAGATION:** Cuttings. **HABITS/CULTURE:** Spreading to upright with age. Shiny leaves and beautiful white flowers. **USES:** Flowers are used for leis and in perfume. I use the flowers for jasmine tea—so do other people, I suppose. **PROBLEMS:** Freezes in the northern part of the state, perennializes in the southern half.

Jatropha integerima jatropha

JATROPHA

Jatropha integerima (ja-TRO-fa in-TEG-eh-ree-mah). **COMMON NAME:** JATROPHA. **TYPE:** Tender perennial shrub. **LOCATION:** Sun. **HEIGHT:** 3'–8'. **SPREAD:** 3'–4'. **SPACING:** 2'–4'. **BLOOM/FRUIT:** Showy red flowers from spring through fall. **PROPAGATION:** Seed, cuttings. **HABITS/CULTURE:** Easy to grow in most any soil. **USES:** Summer annual color. **PROBLEMS:** Very poisonous. Used for poisonous darts in South America. **TIPS/NOTES:** Available in dwarf forms. Freezes easily in Texas. Best used as an annual.

JERUSALEM ARTICHOKE—see *Helianthus* spp.

JERUSALEM THORN—see *Parkinsonia aculeata*

JESSAMINE, CAROLINA—see *Gelsemium sempervirens*

JEW, PURPLE—see *Setcreasea pallida*

JEW, WANDERING—see *Tradescantia* spp.

JIMSONWEED—see *Datura wrightii*

JOHNNY JUMP-UP—see *Viola wittrockiana*

JOHNSONGRASS—see *Sorghum halepense*

JONQUIL—see *Narcissus* spp.

JOSEPH'S COAT—see *Amaranthus tricolor*

JUGLANS

Juglans nigra (JEW-gluns NI-gra). **COMMON NAME:** BLACK WALNUT. **TYPE:** Deciduous tree. **LOCATION:** Sun. **HEIGHT:** 50'. **SPREAD:** 50'. **SPACING:** 20'–50'. **BLOOM/FRUIT:** Male flowers are slender, green, drooping catkins. Female flowers occur in short terminal spikes. Fruit is the walnut. **PROPAGATION:** Seed, grafting. **HABITS/CULTURE:** Open, branching character, large distinctive leaves with evenly sized and arranged leaflets on each side of stem. Yellow fall color. Dark bark. Moderate to slow growth. Likes deep soil and good drainage. Tolerates alkaline soil, but likes a more neutral soil. **USES:** Shade tree. **PROBLEMS:** Roots and leaves give off a toxin harmful to some other plants. Nut is not edible, almost all structure and no meat. Native to the southern United States. *Juglans regia* is the English walnut, native to Poland, Russia, Czechoslovakia, and Germany. This species is often called Persian or Carpathian walnut, not well adapted here due to disease. Does much better under an organic program. Likes sandy acid soil better than alkaline soil. *Juglans major* is the Texas walnut. *Juglans microcarpa* is the little walnut.

Juglans nigra black walnut

JUJUBE—see *Ziziphus* spp.

JUNIPER, CREEPING—see *Juniperus horizontalis*

JUNIPER, PFITZER—see *Juniperus sabina* 'Tamariscifolia'

JUNIPER, SHORE—see *Juniperus horizontalis*

JUNIPER, TAM—see *Juniperus sabina* 'Tamariscifolia'

JUNIPERUS

Juniperus horizontalis (joo-NIP-er-us hor-eh-zon-TALL-us). **COMMON NAME:** CREEPING JUNIPER. **TYPE:** Evergreen shrub. **LOCATION:** Sun. **HEIGHT:** 1'–2'. **SPREAD:** 3'–6'. **SPACING:** 18"–24". **BLOOM/FRUIT:** Insignificant. **PROPAGATION:** Cuttings. **HABITS/CULTURE:** Low-spreading juniper that acts as a ground cover. Likes well-prepared, well-drained soil. Drought tolerant, but responds well to even moisture and regular fertilization. **USES:** Ground cover for hot areas, raised planters. **PROBLEMS:** Red spider mites, juniper blight. **TIPS/NOTES:** Dozens of varieties. 'Bar Harbour' is 4' tall, blue-green in summer, a nice purple color in winter. 'Wiltoni' (Blue Rug) is 4"–6" tall, silver-blue in summer, a light purple cast in winter. 'Blue Pacific' is 12"–15" tall. *Juniperus conferta*, shore juniper, is a low-growing juniper, 6" tall, with soft, light green foliage. Native to Nova Scotia, Canada, and the northern United States.

Juniperus conferta shore juniper

Juniperus sabina 'Tamariscifolia' (joo-NIP-er-us sa-BEAN-ah tam-ah-RISK-ih-foe-lee-ah). **COMMON NAME:** TAM JUNIPER. **TYPE:** Evergreen shrub. **LOCATION:** Sun. **HEIGHT:** 5'. **SPREAD:** 6'. **SPACING:** 36". **BLOOM/FRUIT:** Insignificant. **PROPAGATION:** Cuttings. **HABITS/CULTURE:** Medium height, dark green foliage, dense to the ground. Needs full sun in well-drained area, grows in any soil with average water and fertilizer. **USES:** Evergreen mass, tall ground cover. Good cold tolerance. **PROBLEMS:** Red spider mites and bagworms. **TIPS/NOTES:** I prefer leafy shrubs that are more insect resistant. *Juniperus chinensis* 'Pfitzeriana,' Pfitzer juniper, grows to 5' but spreads to 12'. One of the better junipers, it has dark green arching branches. 'Pfitzeriana glauca' has gray-green or bluish foliage.

Juniperus virginiana
Eastern red cedar

Juniperus virginiana (joo-NIP-er-us vir-gin-ee-AN-ah). **COMMON NAME:** EASTERN RED CEDAR. **TYPE:** Evergreen tree. **LOCATION:** Sun. **HEIGHT:** 40'. **SPREAD:** 20'. **SPACING:** 20'–30'. **BLOOM/FRUIT:** Very small unimpressive flowers in spring; small blue-purple berries in the fall on female plants. **PROPAGATION:** Seed, cuttings. **HABITS/CULTURE:** Single trunk, upright and conical when young, spreading with age. Dark green juniper-like foliage, hard fragrant wood. *Juniperus ashei*, mountain cedar, is similar but usually has multiple-stem trunk and does not suffer cedar apple rust fungus. Drought tolerant, easy to grow in any soil—even solid rock. **USES:** Shade tree, screen for bad views, evergreen backdrop. **PROBLEMS:** Bagworms, red spider mites. **TIPS/NOTES:** Becoming more available as a nursery-grown tree. Many are allergic to the pollen, but it's in the air already from the wild trees. Native from the eastern United States to Texas.

Juniperus virginiana Eastern red cedar

Juniperus ashei mountain cedar

JUSTICIA

Justicia spp. (jus-TIS-ee-a). **COMMON NAME:** SHRIMP PLANT, BRAZIL PLUME, JACOBINA. **TYPE:** Tropical used as an annual. **LOCATION:** Sun to part shade. **HEIGHT:** 2'–3'. **SPREAD:** 2'–3'. **SPACING:** 18". **BLOOM/FRUIT:** Summer flowers. **PROPAGATION:** Seed, cuttings. **HABITS/CULTURE:** Needs healthy, highly organic, well-drained soil for best results. **USES:** Tropical plant used as tender summer annual in Texas. Good for pots. Used strictly for summer flower color. **PROBLEMS:** Freezes easily. **TIPS/NOTES:** *Justicia carnea* is jacobina or Brazilian plume flower or flamingo plant. *Justicia brandegeana*, the shrimp plant, can be used as a tender perennial in the southern part of the state.

KALE—see *Brassica oleracea*

KATSURA—see *Cercidiphyllum japonicum*

KENTUCKY COFFEE TREE—see *Gymnocladus dioica*

KIDNEYWOOD, TEXAS—see *Eysenhardtia texana*

Koelreuteria paniculata goldenrain tree

KOELREUTERIA

Koelreuteria paniculata (cole-roo-TEH-ree-ah pa-nik-ew-LAH-ta). **COMMON NAME:** GOLDENRAIN TREE. **TYPE:** Deciduous tree. **LOCATION:** Sun. **HEIGHT:** 30'. **SPREAD:** 20'. **SPACING:** 15'–20'. **BLOOM/FRUIT:** Yellow flowers in summer, followed by decorative pods. **PROPAGATION:** Seed, cuttings. **HABITS/CULTURE:** Upright and open branching. Easy to grow in any soil, moderately drought tolerant. Does not like heavy fertilization. **USES:** Medium-size shade tree, summer color. Good for hot spots. **PROBLEMS:** Few if any, but relatively short-lived. **TIPS/NOTES:** Ugly duckling when small but develops into a beautiful tree. Native to the Orient. *Koelreuteria bipinnata*, a close kin, is not as cold hardy in the northern half of the state.

KUDZU—see *Pueraria lobata*

LACEBARK ELM—see *Ulmus parvifolia sempervirens*

LACEVINE, SILVER—see *Polygonum aubertii*

LACEY OAK—see *Quercus virginiana*

LACTUCA

Lactuca sativa (lak-TOO-ka sa-TEE-va). **COMMON NAME:** LETTUCE. **TYPE:** Annual vegetable. **LOCATION:** Sun to part shade. **HEIGHT:** 12"–18". **SPREAD:** 12"–18". **SPACING:** 6"–12". **BLOOM/FRUIT:** Insignificant. **PROPAGATION:** Seed, transplants. **HABITS/CULTURE:** Cool-season veggie. Easy to grow in healthy soil. Germinates in temperatures from freezing to 85 degrees. Key to success is lots of compost and even soil moisture. **USES:** Food. **PROBLEMS:** Cutworms, high temperature, acid soil, crowded growing conditions, loopers, aphids, slugs, downy mildew, flea beetles, and garden flea hoppers. **TIPS/NOTES:** Different types include leaf lettuce, butterhead, romaine, and iceberg. The leaf types are easiest to grow here. Plant in spring 2–4 weeks before the last average killing frost, in fall 8–10 weeks before the first killing frost.

LADY BANKS ROSE—see *Rosa banksiae*

LAGERSTROEMIA

Lagerstroemia indica (lah-ger-STROH-me-ah IN-dik-kah). **COMMON NAME:** CRAPE MYRTLE. **TYPE:** Deciduous tree. **LOCATION:** Sun. **HEIGHT:** 25'. **SPREAD:** 15'. **SPACING:** 15'–20'. **BLOOM/FRUIT:** Lacy, multicolored summer flowers and decorative winter seed pods on terminal growth. **PROPAGATION:** Seed, cuttings. **HABITS/CULTURE:** Slow-growing, with light smooth bark and small oval leaflets on compound leaves. Red, purple, pink, or white blooms all summer. Fall color is red on all except white-flowering varieties, which have yellow fall color. Easy to grow in any soil. Top pruning can be done after flowers fade for second burst of blooms. **USES:** Ornamental tree, summer color, fall color, beautiful bare branches in winter. **PROBLEMS:** Aphids, mildew, suckers. **TIPS/NOTES:** Do not trim back in winter—it does not increase flower production. Besides, the seed pods are decorative. Native to China.

Lagerstroemia indica (lah-ger-STROH-me-ah IN-dik-ah). **COMMON NAME:** DWARF CRAPE MYRTLE. **TYPE:** Deciduous shrub. **LOCATION:** Sun. **HEIGHT:** 5'–8'. **SPREAD:** 6'–8'. **SPACING:** 3'–8'. **BLOOM/FRUIT:** Lacy multicolored summer flowers and decorative winter seed pods on terminal growth. **PROPAGATION:** Cuttings. **HABITS/CULTURE:** Small version of the crape myrtle tree. Blooms all summer in colors of red, pink, white, and lavender. White variety has yellow fall color, others have red. Easy to grow in any soil in full sun. Do not prune back—let it grow! Can be pick-pruned lightly to maintain miniature size. **USES:** Specimen, summer color, container plant. **PROBLEMS:** Aphids on new growth, powdery mildew. **TIPS/NOTES:** Fantastic plant! Native to China.

LAMB'S EAR—see *Stachys byzantina*

LAMB'S-QUARTER—see *Chenopodium* spp.

Lagerstroemia indica crape myrtle

Lagerstroemia indica dwarf crape myrtle

LAMIUM

Lamium amplexicaule (LAM-ee-um am-plex-ih-CALL-ee). **COMMON NAME:** HENBIT. **TYPE:** Annual wildflower. **LOCATION:** Sun. **HEIGHT:** 6"–8". **SPREAD:** 8"–10". **BLOOM/FRUIT:** Small purple flowers in late winter or early spring. **PROPAGATION:** Seed. **HABITS/CULTURE:** Square stem, round scalloped leaves. Germinates in the fall. Plant can be controlled by applying corn gluten meal at a rate of 20 lbs. per thousand sq. ft. just before the germination period. **USES:** Wildflower. **PROBLEMS:** Usually develops powdery mildew in humid areas. Yes, it can be killed with a broadleaf weed killer, but that would be a dopey thing to do. Control if you must by mowing it. Healthy soil is rarely infested. **TIPS/NOTES:** Considered a weed by many. I like the plant. If you don't, mow it down.

Lantana Dallas red lantana

Lamium amplexicaule henbit

Lamium maculatum dead nettle

Lantana horrida native Texas lantana

Lamium maculatum (LAM-ee-um mac-you-LAY-tum). **COMMON NAME:** LAMIUM, DEAD NETTLE, SPOTTED DEAD NETTLE. **TYPE:** Perennial ground cover. **LOCATION:** Shade to part shade. **HEIGHT:** 9"–12". **SPREAD:** Ground cover. **SPACING:** 9"–12". **BLOOM/FRUIT:** Purple, red, or white flowers in summer, nothing to get excited about. **PROPAGATION:** Cuttings. **HABITS/CULTURE:** Low-growing, silver-leafed ground cover. Spreads easily. Easy to grow in any well-drained soil. Likes moderate water and fertilizer. Needs afternoon shade. Does best in moist soil. **USES:** Ground cover, containers. **PROBLEMS:** Fairly carefree. **TIPS/NOTES:** 'White Nancy' is a nice white-flowering cultivar. Several other improved cultivars exist.

LANTANA

Lantana spp. (lan-TAN-ah). **COMMON NAME:** LANTANA. **TYPE:** Perennial bedding plant. **LOCATION:** Sun. **HEIGHT:** 1'–3'. **SPREAD:** 2'–4'. **SPACING:** 12"–18". **BLOOM/FRUIT:** Clusters of small flowers that bloom from spring to the first hard frost. **PROPAGATION:** Cuttings. **HABITS/CULTURE:** Bushy growth all summer with flowers of yellow, white, orange, pink, blue, and purple. Trailing varieties are available. The tough varieties will return every year. Easy to grow in any well-drained soil, likes good bed preparation. Drought tolerant. Regular fertilization will produce more blooms. **USES:** Summer color, pots, hanging baskets, hummingbird attractant. **PROBLEMS:** Whiteflies, but no big deal. Gets woody with age. **TIPS/NOTES:** Berries are said to be poisonous. Plant in the spring. Used as an annual in the northern part of the state. Native Texas lantana is *Lantana horrida*.

LARKSPUR—see *Consolida ambigua*

LATHYRUS
Lathyrus odoratus (LA-thi-rus o-do-RAH-tus). **COMMON NAME:** SWEET PEA. **TYPE:** Annual vine. **LOCATION:** Sun or afternoon shade. **HEIGHT:** 6' or more. **SPREAD:** 3'–6'. **SPACING:** 3'–4'. **BLOOM/FRUIT:** Fragrant pink, red, purple, and white flowers. **PROPAGATION:** Seed. **HABITS/CULTURE:** Plant seeds in late fall or winter 2" deep in rich, healthy, well-drained soil. Mulch heavily as the plant grows. Needs to be trained on a support. **USES:** Vining plant for color in early spring. **PROBLEMS:** Heat. **TIPS/NOTES:** More common in cooler climates.

LAUREL, CHERRY—see *Prunus caroliniana*

LAUREL, TEXAS MOUNTAIN—see *Sophora secundiflora*

LAUREL OAK—see *Quercus virginiana*

LAURUS
Laurus nobilis (LAR-us NO-bi-lis). **COMMON NAME:** BAY, SWEET BAY. **TYPE:** Evergreen herb. **LOCATION:** Sun to part shade. **HEIGHT:** 3'–8'. **SPREAD:** 4'–6'. **SPACING:** 3'–4'. **BLOOM/FRUIT:** Unimpressive. **PROPAGATION:** Cuttings. **HABITS/CULTURE:** Hardy to about 15 degrees. **USES:** Fresh leaves make excellent flavoring agent for all kinds of foods, such as soups, stews, sauces, and vegetables. Leaves should be removed from food before serving. Excellent flavor in teas. Leaves are also used to repel insects in stored grain. Container plant, potpourri. **PROBLEMS:** Freeze damage in the northern half of the state. **TIPS/NOTES:** Easy to grow. Protect from strong, drying winds.

LAVANDULA
Lavandula spp. (la-VAN-dew-la). **COMMON NAME:** LAVENDER. **TYPE:** Evergreen perennial herb. **LOCATION:** Sun. **HEIGHT:** 8"–4'. **SPREAD:** 12"–36". **SPACING:** 12"–24". **BLOOM/FRUIT:** Lavender-blue flowers on narrow stalks in spring or intermittently throughout the summer. Pink- and white-flowering varieties are also available. **PROPAGATION:** Cuttings, seed. **HABITS/CULTURE:** Aromatic, narrow gray-green foliage, lavender-blue flowers. Can be grown by putting seed on top of the ground when it's hot. **USES:** Antiseptic, sedative. Tea for headaches. Substitute for rosemary in cooking. Used in potpourri. Beautiful perennial for landscape. **PROBLEMS:** Overwatering, damp weather. **TIPS/NOTES:** *Lavandula angustifolia* is English lavender. *Lavandula dentata*, French lavender, has a serrated leaf in either green or gray. *Lavandula stoechas*, Spanish lavender, has flat purple blooms. All need perfect drainage and full sun. Can be grown from seed but plants may not come true to parent plant. Slow to germinate. Gray varieties seem to be tougher.

LAVENDER—see *Lavandula* spp.

LAVENDER COTTON—see *Santolina chamaecyparissus*

LEAD BALL, GOLDEN—see *Leucaena retusa*

LEADTREE, GOLDENBALL—see *Leucaena retusa*

LEEK—see *Allium* spp.

LEMON BALM—see *Melissa officinalis*

LEMONGRASS—see *Cymbopogon citratus*

LEMON MINT—see *Monarda citriodora*

LEMON VERBENA—see *Aloysia triphylla*

LETTUCE—see *Lactuca sativa*

Lathyrus odoratus sweet pea

Lavandula lavender

Leucaena retusa goldenball leadtree

L

LEUCAENA

Leucaena retusa (loo-SEE-nah reh-TOO-sah). **COMMON NAME:** GOLDENBALL LEADTREE, GOLDEN LEAD BALL. **TYPE:** Deciduous tree. **LOCATION:** Sun to part shade. **HEIGHT:** 12'–20'. **SPREAD:** 10'–15'. **SPACING:** 12'–15'. **BLOOM/FRUIT:** Gold 1" fragrant globes from April to October. **PROPAGATION:** Seed, cuttings. **HABITS/CULTURE:** Needs well-drained soil, rocky soil is okay. Native to dry canyons in West Texas. Open-branching with lacy foliage. Naturally multitrunked. Moderate growth, brittle wood. **USES:** Ornamental tree with yellow summer color. Does well in most areas of Texas if given excellent drainage. Best in arid areas. **PROBLEMS:** Wind damage, root rot if overwatered. Freeze tolerant. Few if any pest problems. **TIPS/NOTES:** Hardest part is getting it established.

LEUCOJUM

Leucojum aestivum (loo-KO-jum EES-ti-vum). **COMMON NAME:** SUMMER SNOWFLAKE. **TYPE:** Perennial bulb. **LOCATION:** Sun or part shade. **HEIGHT:** 14"–16". **SPREAD:** 18"–24". **SPACING:** 12"–18". **BLOOM/FRUIT:** Tiny white bell-shaped flowers from spring to early summer. **PROPAGATION:** Division, seed. **HABITS/CULTURE:** Attractive upright foliage. Easy to establish and maintain. Divide in the fall if planting becomes crowded. **USES:** Borders, spring and early summer color.

Leucojum aestivum summer snowflake

LEUCOPHYLLUM

Leucophyllum frutescens (lew-co-FI-lum FRU-tes-sens). **COMMON NAME:** TEXAS SAGE, CENIZO, PURPLE SAGE. **TYPE:** Evergreen shrub. **LOCATION:** Sun. **HEIGHT:** 5'–7'. **SPREAD:** 5'–7'. **SPACING:** 3'. **BLOOM/FRUIT:** Primarily purple 1" flowers from mid through late summer, also in pink and white. **PROPAGATION:** Cuttings, seed. **HABITS/CULTURE:** Compact, soft, and slow-growing. Silver-gray foliage. Purple, pink, or white flowers in summer. Grows better if not overwatered, tolerates any soil with good drainage. Drought and heat tolerant. **USES:** Specimen, mass, summer color, gray foliage. **PROBLEMS:** Too much water. **TIPS/NOTES:** 'Compactum' is the dwarf form, 'Green Cloud' has darker foliage, and 'White Cloud' has white flowers. Native to Texas and Mexico.

Leucophyllum frutescens Texas sage

LIATRIS

Liatris spp. (lee-AT-tris). **COMMON NAME:** GAYFEATHER. **TYPE:** Perennial wildflower. **LOCATION:** Sun. **HEIGHT:** 1'–2'. **SPREAD:** 1'–3'. **SPACING:** 1'–2'. **BLOOM/FRUIT:** Tufts of narrow stems topped by narrow plumes of fluffy purple flowers. **PROPAGATION:** Seed, division. **HABITS/CULTURE:** Tough, drought-tolerant wildflowers that respond fairly well to maintained gardens. Cut to the ground in winter. Can be planted from pots or seed. Sow seed in the fall. **USES:** Perennial gardens, borders, summer flowers. **PROBLEMS:** Too much water. **TIPS/NOTES:** Makes a wonderful cut flower—the purple color lasts indefinitely in a dry arrangement. Several good species exist. Our most common native is *Liatris punctata.* Native to Texas and Oklahoma. Another common species is *Liatris pycnostachya.*

Liatris gayfeather

LIBOCEDRUS—see *Calocedrus decurrens*

LIGUSTRUM

Ligustrum japonicum (li-GUS-trum ja-PON-eh-cum). **COMMON NAME:** WAX LIGUSTRUM. **TYPE:** Evergreen shrub or small tree. **LOCATION:** Sun to part shade. **HEIGHT:** 10'–15' **SPREAD:** 8'–10'. **SPACING:** 3'–4'. **BLOOM/FRUIT:** Fragrant white flower clusters in late spring to early summer. **PROPAGATION:** Cuttings. **HABITS/CULTURE:** Glossy leaves, blue berries in winter. Usually multitrunked, but single-stem plants are available at nurseries. Grows in any soil as long as drainage is good. Light shearing or pick-pruning in March and July is helpful to keep the plant compact. **USES:** Ornamental tree, screen, tall border, background plant. Not a high-quality plant. **PROBLEMS:** White-flies, cotton root rot. Freeze damage in severe winters. **TIPS/NOTES:** Wax ligustrum has been grossly misused as a foundation planting or low hedge. I also think pyramid-, poodle-, and globe-shaped pruning is a silly thing to do with this plant, but it is done a lot. Native to the Orient.

Ligustrum lucidum (li-GUS-trum loo-SEE-dum). **COM-MON NAME:** JAPANESE LIGUSTRUM. **TYPE:** Evergreen shrub or small tree. **LOCATION:** Sun to part shade. **HEIGHT:** 15'–20'. **SPREAD:** 8'–10'. **SPACING:** 4'–8'. **BLOOM/FRUIT:** Fragrant white flower clusters from late spring to early summer. **PROPAGATION:** Cuttings. **HABITS/CULTURE:** Very large, vigorous shrub with larger, duller leaves than those of wax ligustrum. Clusters of blue berries in winter. Grows in any soil in sun or part shade. Low water and fertilizer requirements. **USES:** Tall screen, ornamental tree. **PROBLEMS:** Cotton root rot, whiteflies, and ice storm damage. **TIPS/NOTES:** The 1983 freeze killed or severely damaged many of these plants. Native to the Orient. I sometimes try to keep existing plants but seldom plant new ones. A low-quality plant. The small-leaf privet, *Ligustrum vulgare,* is a close relative.

Ligustrum lucidum 'Variegata' (li-GUS-trum loo-SEE-dum). **COMMON NAME:** VARIEGATED LIGUSTRUM, VARIEGATED PRIVET. **TYPE:** Evergreen shrub. **LOCATION:** Sun to part shade. **HEIGHT:** 6'–10'. **SPREAD:** 6'–8'. **SPACING:** 3'–4'. **BLOOM/FRUIT:** Fragrant white flowers in late spring. **PROPAGATION:** Cuttings. **HABITS/CULTURE:** Small rounded leaves, dense branching. Light, variegated foliage. Easy to grow in any soil in sun or part shade. Drought tolerant. **USES:** Color contrast, hedge or screen. **PROBLEMS:** Few if any. **TIPS/NOTES:** Native to China and Korea.

LILAC—see *Syringa* spp.

LILAC CHASTE TREE—see *Vitex agnus-castus*

LILIUM

Lilium spp. (LEE-lee-um). **COMMON NAME:** LILY, TRUE LILY. **TYPE:** Perennial bulb. **LOCATION:** Sun to light shade. **HEIGHT:** 24"–60". **SPREAD:** 20"–40". **SPACING:** 18"–24". **BLOOM/FRUIT:** Dramatic summer flowers in white, pink, orange, rose, salmon, red, and many blends. **PROPAGATION:** Bulbs. **HABITS/CULTURE:** Plant fleshy bulbs 5"–6" deep in the fall in well-prepared and well-drained beds. Use moderate amounts of water and fertilizer. **USES:** Summer color. **PROBLEMS:** Heat. **TIPS/NOTES:** Not reliable repeat bloomers in most of Texas. Like a cooler climate. Madonna lily is *Lilium candidum. Lilium tigrinum,* the tiger lily, is good in Texas, especially the orange hybrid called 'Enchantment.' Oxblood lily is *Rhodophiala bifida.*

LILY—see *Lilium* spp.

LILY, CRINUM—see *Crinum* spp.

LILY, OXBLOOD—see *Rhodophiala bifida*

LILY, SCHOOLHOUSE—see *Rhodophiala bifida*

LILY, SPIDER—see *Hymenocallis* spp. and *Lycoris* spp.

LILYTURF—see *Liriope muscari*

TOP TO BOTTOM:
Ligustrum japonicum wax ligustrum
Ligustrum lucidum Japanese ligustrum
Ligustrum lucidum 'Variegata' variegated ligustrum

LIMONIUM

Limonium sinuatum (lee-MO-nee-um sin-ew-AH-tum). **COMMON NAME:** STATICE. **TYPE:** Annual bedding plant. **LOCATION:** Sun. **HEIGHT:** 18"–24". **SPREAD:** 12"–18". **SPACING:** 12". **BLOOM/FRUIT:** Clusters of small spring flowers of white, yellow, rose, purple, and blue. **PROPAGATION:** Cuttings. **HABITS/CULTURE:** Set out transplants in early spring. Beautiful, easy-to-grow annual flower that should be used more often. Tolerates drought as well as moist soils. **USES:** Excellent cut flower. **PROBLEMS:** Slugs and snails. **TIPS/NOTES:** Cut when fully open, hang upside down to dry.

LINDEN—see *Tilia* spp.

LIPPIA

Lippia dulcis (LIP-ee-ah DOOL-sis). **COMMON NAME:** SWEET HERB. **TYPE:** Tender perennial herb. **LOCATION:** Sun to part shade. **HEIGHT:** 3"–6". **SPREAD:** 12"–18". **SPACING:** 12". **BLOOM/FRUIT:** Small white cylindrical summer flowers. **PROPAGATION:** Cuttings. **HABITS/CULTURE:** Very easy to grow. Perennializes in the southern half of the state. **USES:** Ground cover, sugar substitute in food and beverages. **PROBLEMS:** Chlorosis, freeze damage. **TIPS/NOTES:** Use as an annual in most of the state. The correct name is *Lippia graveolens*, but the plant is usually sold as *Lippia dulcis*.

Lippia dulcis sweet herb

Liquidambar styraciflua sweet gum

LIPPIA CITRIODORA—see *Aloysia triphylla*

LIQUIDAMBAR

Liquidambar styraciflua (lick-wid-AM-bar sty-rah-SIFF-flu-ah). **COMMON NAME:** SWEET GUM. **TYPE:** Deciduous tree. **LOCATION:** Sun to part shade. **HEIGHT:** 70'. **SPREAD:** 30'. **SPACING:** 20'–30'. **BLOOM/FRUIT:** Nondescript flowers, round spiny fall fruit. **PROPAGATION:** Seed, cuttings. **HABITS/CULTURE:** Vertical, cone-shaped, stiff-branching. Spreads with age. Star-shaped leaves with 5–7 lobes. Red, salmon, orange, and yellow fall foliage color. Round spiny seed pods. **CULTURE:** Needs deep soil, prefers sandy acid conditions, hates solid rock. Quite easy to transplant if given ample water. **USES:** Shade tree, great fall color. **PROBLEMS:** Chlorosis in dry, rocky soil. **TIPS/NOTES:** Native to East Texas and other sandy areas. Grows much larger in sandy acid soils. Improved cultivars include 'Palo Alto' and 'Burgundy.' Excellent fall color but seem to be much less durable.

LIRIODENDRON

Liriodendron tulipifera (lir-ee-ah-DEN-dron too-li-PIF-err-ah). **COMMON NAME:** TULIP TREE, YELLOW POPLAR, WHITEWOOD. **TYPE:** Deciduous tree. **LOCATION:** Sun. **HEIGHT:** 70'. **SPREAD:** 40'. **SPACING:** 30'–40'. **BLOOM/FRUIT:** 2" tulip-shaped greenish yellow flowers in late spring. Not showy from a distance. Usually do not form until the tree

Liriodendron tulipifera tulip tree

is 10–12 years old. **PROPAGATION:** Seed, cuttings. **HABITS/CULTURE:** Straight trunk, smooth bark, leaves shaped like tulips, yellow fall color. Interesting flowers in late spring but sometimes hard to see. Grows in any deep, well-drained soil. Does not like rock. Needs lots of water in heat of summer. **USES:** Shade tree. **PROBLEMS:** Leaf drop in mid to late summer. **TIPS/NOTES:** Native to midwestern, northeastern, and southeastern United States.

LIRIOPE

Liriope muscari (li-RYE-oh-pee mus-KAH-ree). **COMMON NAME:** LIRIOPE, MONKEYGRASS, LILYTURF. **TYPE:** Evergreen ground cover. **LOCATION:** Sun to shade. **HEIGHT:** 9"–15". **SPREAD:** Unlimited. **SPACING:** 12". **BLOOM/FRUIT:** White or lavender spikelike flowers in mid to late summer. **PROPAGATION:** Division. **HABITS/CULTURE:** Grasslike clumps that spread by underground stems to form a solid mass planting. Has primarily one flush of growth in the spring. Blue flowers on stalks in early summer. Easy to grow in well-prepared beds that drain well. Does best in shade or partial shade. Mow or clip to a height of 3" in late winter just before new spring growth. Easy to divide and transplant anytime. **USES:** Ground cover of low bor-

Liriope muscari liriope

der. Good for texture change. **PROBLEMS:** Snails and slugs sometimes, usually not a big problem. **TIPS/NOTES:** Variegated form is called 'Silvery Sunproof.' My favorite is the dark green 'Big Blue.' The giant forms *Liriope gigantea* and *Liriope muscari* 'Evergreen Giant' are also good. Native to China and Japan. Flowers last well in cut-flower arrangements.

LISIANTHUS—see *Eustoma grandiflorum*

LIVE OAK—see *Quercus virginiana*

LOBELIA
Lobelia cardinalis (low-BEAL-yah card-en-AL-is). **COMMON NAME:** CARDINAL FLOWER. **TYPE:** Perennial wildflower. **LOCATION:** Sun to part shade. **HEIGHT:** 2'–4'. **SPREAD:** 2'–3'. **SPACING:** 18". **BLOOM/FRUIT:** Flame-red 1" flowers in summer. **PROPAGATION:** Seed. **HABITS/CULTURE:** Erect, single-stem, summer-blooming. Saw-edged on stem. Likes moist healthy soil but can stand wet soil. **USES:** Perennial color. **PROBLEMS:** Slugs and snails. **TIPS/NOTES:** *Lobelia erinus* is a compact annual with blue to violet flowers that have white or yellowish throats. Best in morning sun, afternoon shade. Likes the cooler parts of Texas best. A bog plant in nature. The more moisture it gets, the longer it will bloom. Useful in shallow pools.

Lobularia maritima alyssum

LOBULARIA
Lobularia maritima (lob-ew-LAR-ee-ah ma-ri-time-ah). **COMMON NAME:** ALYSSUM. **TYPE:** Annual bedding plant. **LOCATION:** Sun. **HEIGHT:** 3"–4". **SPREAD:** 9"–12". **SPACING:** 6". **BLOOM/FRUIT:** Clusters of small white or lavender flowers that bloom best in the cooler months. **PROPAGATION:** Seed. **HABITS/CULTURE:** Low-growing bedding plant. Requires little

care but easily damaged by foot traffic and pets. Grows in any well-prepared soil, relatively drought tolerant. **USES:** Borders, rock gardens, pockets in stone walls, small accent areas of annual color. **PROBLEMS:** Few if any. **TIPS/NOTES:** Native to Turkey.

LOCUST, BLACK—see *Robinia pseudo-acacia*

LOCUST, HONEY—see *Gleditsia triacanthos*

LOLIUM
Lolium spp. (LOW-lee-um). **COMMON NAME:** RYEGRASS. **TYPE:** Annual and perennial lawn grass. **LOCATION:** Sun to part shade. **HEIGHT:** 2"–4" (mown). **SPACING:** 10 lbs. seed per thousand sq. ft. **BLOOM/FRUIT:** 5–12 flowers on a spike, followed by seed. **PROPAGATION:** Seed. **HABITS/CULTURE:** Cool-season clumping grass. **USES:** Fall overseeding of warm-season grasses. **PROBLEMS:** Competition with permanent lawn grasses. Can become a pest. **TIPS/NOTES:** The annual *Lolium multiflorum* is less expensive and very aggressive. *Lolium perenne*, the perennial choice, is a better-quality grass although more expensive.

LONDON PLANE TREE—see *Platanus occidentalis*

Lonicera albiflora winter honeysuckle

LONICERA
Lonicera albiflora (lon-ISS-er-ah al-bah-FLOR-ah). **COMMON NAME:** WINTER HONEYSUCKLE, BUSH HONEYSUCKLE. **TYPE:** Deciduous shrub. **LOCATION:** Sun to part shade. **HEIGHT:** 8'–10'. **SPREAD:** 8'–10'. **SPACING:** 6'–8'. **BLOOM/FRUIT:** Fragrant white late-winter flowers. **PROPAGATION:** Cuttings. **HABITS/CULTURE:** Many stems grow up from the ground and arch over to form a loosely shaped shrub. White flowers in late winter, showy red berries in late summer, yellow fall color. Bare branches most of winter. Easy to grow in any soil, drought tolerant. **USES:** Shrub mass for soft, natural effect. **PROBLEMS:** A little wild-looking in formal gardens. Winter dieback of entire branches. **TIPS/NOTES:** *Lonicera fragrantissima*, white honeysuckle, has sharp-pointed leaves and flowers in spring. It's an import but has naturalized in Texas.

Lonicera japonica honeysuckle

Lonicera japonica (lon-ISS-er-ah ja-PON-ih-kah). **COMMON NAME:** HONEYSUCKLE. **TYPE:** Evergreen vine and ground cover. **LOCATION:** Sun to part shade. **HEIGHT:** 12'–20'. **SPREAD:** Unlimited. **SPACING:** 12" for ground cover, 6' for vine. **BLOOM/FRUIT:** Fragrant white summer flowers. **PROPAGATION:** Cuttings. **HABITS/CULTURE:** Aggressive climbing vine or ground cover. Needs support at first to climb. Fragrant white and yellow blooms. Tends to get leggy. Grows in any soil and any location. Very drought tolerant. **USES:** Unrefined ground cover areas. Erosion control of slopes. **PROBLEMS:** Too aggressive and invasive, chokes out more desirable native plants. I don't recommend it. Control by physical removal. **TIPS/NOTES:** There are several choices better than honeysuckle, but it exists in many places, so we have to deal with it. Native to Asia and the Orient.

Lonicera sempervirens (lon-ISS-er-ah sem-per-VYE-rens). **COMMON NAME:** CORAL HONEYSUCKLE. **TYPE:** Evergreen vine. **LOCATION:** Sun. **HEIGHT:** High-climbing. **SPREAD:** 8'–15'. **SPACING:** 6'–8'. **BLOOM/FRUIT:** Red 2" overblooming summer flowers. **PROPAGATION:** Cuttings. **HABITS/CULTURE:** Climbing vine that needs support to

start. Coral-red flowers all summer. Grows easily in any well-drained soil, drought tolerant but does better with irrigation. **USES:** Climbing vine for fences, walls, arbors, and decorative screens. **PROBLEMS:** Few if any. **TIPS/NOTES:** Good plant for attracting hummingbirds. *Lonicera sempervirens* 'Sulphurea' is a beautiful yellow-flowering variety. Native from the eastern United States to Texas.

Lonicera sempervirens
coral honeysuckle

LOOSESTRIFE—see *Lythrum salicaria*

LOQUAT—see *Eriobotrya japonica*

LUFFA

Luffa spp. (loof-ah). **COMMON NAME:** GOURD. **TYPE:** Annual vine. **LOCATION:** Sun. **HEIGHT:** Vine. **SPACING:** 5'–10'. **BLOOM/FRUIT:** Most gourds have yellow flowers, some have white. The gourds are the fruit. **PROPAGATION:** Seed. **HABITS/CULTURE:** Fast-growing vine for a hot, sunny location on a fence or arbor. **USES:** Decorative items, bird houses, dippers. **PROBLEMS:** Grows very large. **TIPS/NOTES:** *Luffa aegyptiaca* and two other species are the bath sponge gourds. *Cucurbita pepo ovifera* is the very common yellow-flowered gourd. *Lagenaria siceraria (Luffa vulgaris)* is the white-flowered gourd that produces gourds in sizes from 3" to 3' and in many shapes. Harvest the gourds when the vines have died.

Lupinus texensis bluebonnet

LUPINUS

Lupinus texensis (loo-PYE-nus tex-IN-sis). **COMMON NAME:** BLUEBONNET. **TYPE:** Annual perennial. **LOCATION:** Sun. **HEIGHT:** 9"–12". **SPREAD:** 12"–15". **SPACING:** 35 lbs. of seed per acre. **BLOOM/FRUIT:** Blue 2"–4" spikes of fragrant flowers in spring. **PROPAGATION:** Plant seeds in late summer or early fall. **HABITS/CULTURE:** Upright to sprawling spring wildflower. Germinates from seed in fall. Leaves and stems are hairy. Flowers have wonderful fragrance. Sometimes hard to start. Once established, reliable in returning each year. **USES:** Wildflower. **PROBLEMS:** Seed is sometimes hard to germinate, may germinate the second or third year. **TIPS/NOTES:** Do not fertilize this or other wildflowers. Nurseries are now selling 2 1/4" pots for planting small garden areas in the spring. Many people recommend scarified seed, which germinates the first year. But it's more natural to plant untreated seed and have some sprouting for several years. Native to Texas and our state flower.

LYCOPERSICON

Lycopersicon esculentum (ly-ko-PER-si-kun es-kew-LENT-um). **COMMON NAME:** TOMATO. **TYPE:** Annual vegetable. **LOCATION:** Sun. **HEIGHT:** 3'–15'. **SPREAD:** 3"–15'. **SPACING:** 24"–36". **BLOOM/FRUIT:** Yellow flowers followed by red, pink, or yellow edible fruit. **PROPAGATION:** Seed or transplants. Germinates in 5–14 days at 68–86 degrees.

L

Lysimachia nummularia moneywort

LYSIMACHIA

Lysimachia nummularia (liz-se-MACH-ee-ah num-mew-LARR-ee-ah). **COMMON NAME:** MONEYWORT, CREEPING JENNIE. **TYPE:** Evergreen ground cover. **LOCATION:** Shade to part shade. **HEIGHT:** 3". **SPREAD:** Unlimited. **SPACING:** 9"–12". **BLOOM/FRUIT:** Insignificant. **PROPAGATION:** Cuttings, division. **HABITS/CULTURE:** Very low-growing, with soft round leaves. Spreads by runners, roots easily where stem touches ground. Grows best in shade or part shade in moist, well-prepared beds. **USES:** Ground cover for small shady places. **PROBLEMS:** Starts easily from broken pieces in areas where it may not be wanted. **TIPS/NOTES:** Native to Europe.

LYTHRUM

Lythrum salicaria (LITH-rum sal-eh-CARE-ee-ah). **COMMON NAME:** LYTHRUM, LOOSESTRIFE. **TYPE:** Perennial bedding plant. **LOCATION:** Sun to light shade. **HEIGHT:** 2'–4'. **SPREAD:** 3'–4'. **SPACING:** 3'. **BLOOM/FRUIT:** Pink or lavender flowers on terminal spikes. **PROPAGATION:** Cuttings. **HABITS/CULTURE:** Plant is fairly woody and upright. Mother plants are somewhat invasive—cultivars are not as bad. Tough and very adaptable. Grow easily in damp, normal, or dry soils of various pH. **USES:** Perennial garden, color accent, cutting garden. **PROBLEMS:** None. **TIPS/NOTES:** 'Happy,' 'Morden's Gleam,' 'Firecandle,' and 'Morden's Pink' are good cultivars.

Lythrum salicaria lythrum

Lycoris radiata spider lily

HABITS/CULTURE: Tender perennial grown as an annual. Set out transplants after there is no danger of frost. To cheat and start earlier, cover the plants with a "wall of water" or floating row cover. Plant tomatoes in metal cages for best production. **USES:** Food. **PROBLEMS:** Wet feet, aphids, red spider mites, early blight, blossom end rot, pinworms, tomato hornworms, southern blight, viruses. **TIPS/NOTES:** Excellent Texas varieties include Celebrity, Carnival, Salsa, Better Boy, Porter, Viva Italia, Jackpot, Roma, Super Fantastic, Supersonic, Brandywine, and Whopper. *Physalis philadelphica* is the tomatillo.

LYCORIS

Lycoris spp. (li-KO-ris). **COMMON NAME:** SPIDER LILY. **TYPE:** Perennial bedding plant. **LOCATION:** Sun to part shade. **HEIGHT:** 15"–24". **SPREAD:** 6"–12". **SPACING:** 6"–12". **BLOOM/FRUIT:** Clusters of purple, red, pink, white, or yellow summer flowers. **PROPAGATION:** Bulbs, division. **HABITS/CULTURE:** Plant bulbs from spring through late summer. May not bloom the first fall. Narrow leaves appear in spring but die down before the plant blooms. **USES:** Perennial summer color. **PROBLEMS:** Cutworms, loopers, and other caterpillars. **TIPS/NOTES:** *Lycoris radiata* is the red spider lily. *Lycoris squamigera* is the trumpet-shaped pink belladonna lily that blooms in late summer to early fall. *Lycoris africana* is bright yellow. *Lycoris × albiflora* is the white fall spider lily.

MACLURA

Maclura pomifera (ma-CLUE-ra puh-MIFF-er-ah). **COM-MON NAME:** BOIS D'ARC, OSAGE ORANGE, HORSE-APPLE. **TYPE:** Deciduous tree. **LOCATION:** Sun. **HEIGHT:** 40'. **SPREAD:** 40'. **SPACING:** Do not plant! **BLOOM/FRUIT:** Insignificant flowers, huge yellow-green fruits on female plants. **PROPAGATION:** Seed, cuttings. **HABITS/CULTURE:** Fast-growing, spreading dense foliage, thorny branches,

"horse apples" on female trees, wood like iron. Yellow fall color. Needs full sun, grows in any soil with good drainage, drought tolerant, low fertilization needs. **USES:** Shade, background, fence rows. **PROBLEMS:** Messy, hard to grow anything beneath it, weak root system. **TIPS/NOTES:** Bois d'arc trees should be removed to favor more desirable plants. Native from Texas to Arkansas.

Maclura pomifera bois d'arc

MADRONE—see *Arbutus texana*

MAGNOLIA

Magnolia grandiflora (mag-NOLE-ee-ah gran-dee-FLORE-ah). **COMMON NAME:** MAGNOLIA. **TYPE:** Evergreen tree. **LOCATION:** Sun. **HEIGHT:** 60'. **SPREAD:** 30'. **SPACING:** 30'–50'. **BLOOM/FRUIT:** Large summer-blooming white flowers. Conelike fruit full of bright red seeds opens in fall. **PROPAGATION:** Seed, cuttings. **HABITS/CULTURE:** Straight central stem, foliage to ground unless trimmed up. Dense, fibrous, shallow root system. Large white flowers bloom a few at a time in summer. Relatively easy to grow in any soil, likes sandy acid soils best. Grows to 100' in deep sandy soils. Needs lots of room. **USES:** Specimen tree for large area. **PROBLEMS:** Chlorosis. Messy—almost continuous leaf drop. Difficult to grow anything beneath it. **TIPS/NOTES:** Native from the southeastern United States to East Texas. The deciduous *Magnolia soulangiana*, saucer magnolia or tulip magnolia, has pink flowers in spring and grows to 20'. Another deciduous species, *Magnolia stellata*, star magnolia, has white spring flowers and grows to 12'. Both do better with some shade. Many cultivars exist. A wonderful dwarf variety is *Magnolia grandiflora* 'Little Gem.' *Magnolia virginiana*, bay magnolia, is deciduous or semi-evergreen and has fragrant creamy white flowers from summer to fall. Leaves are grayish-green and almost white underneath. Native to deep East Texas.

Magnolia grandiflora southern magnolia

Magnolia virginiana bay magnolia

Magnolia grandiflora magnolia flower

Magnolia stellata star magnolia

Magnolia grandiflora 'Little Gem'
Little Gem magnolia

Magnolia soulangiana deciduous magnolia

Magnolia virginiana bay magnolia

MAHONIA

Mahonia bealei (mah-HONE-ee-ah BEAL-ee-eye). **COMMON NAME:** LEATHER LEAF MAHONIA. **TYPE:** Evergreen shrub. **LOCATION:** Shade. **HEIGHT:** 5'–7'. **SPREAD:** 3'–5'. **SPACING:** 3'. **BLOOM/FRUIT:** Erect, spikelike clusters of yellow flowers in very early spring and often in winter during warm spells, followed by powder-blue berries. **PROPAGATION:** Seed, cuttings. **HABITS/CULTURE:** Unique shrub with vertical stems that tend to get a leggy, dramatic character. Thick spiny leaves, yellow early-spring flowers, blue berries. Easy to grow in prepared beds in shade. Moderate water and food requirements. Remove one-third of the canes each year for a bushier effect. **USES:** Accent, distinctive foliage and character, Oriental gardens. **PROBLEMS:** None. **TIPS/NOTES:** Native to China. The closely kin *Mahonia aquifolium*, Oregon grape, is unsuccessful in heavy Texas soils. It needs sandy soil and a cooler climate—like that of its native home, the Pacific Northwest.

Mahonia bealei
leather leaf mahonia

Mahonia aquifolium Oregon grape

MAIDENGRASS—see *Miscanthus* spp.

MAIDENHAIRGRASS—see *Miscanthus* spp.

MAIDENHAIR TREE—see *Ginkgo biloba*

MALABAR SPINACH—see *Spinacia oleracea*

MALUS

Malus floribunda (MAH-lus flor-ih-BUND-ah). **COMMON NAME:** CRABAPPLE. **TYPE:** Deciduous tree. **LOCATION:** Sun to part shade. **HEIGHT:** 25'. **SPREAD:** 25'. **SPACING:** 15'–20'. **BLOOM/FRUIT:** White, red, and pink flowers in spring, half-inch fruit matures in fall. **PROPAGATION:** Cuttings. **HABITS/CULTURE:** Easy to grow in any well-drained soil, fall color is usually yellow but red in some varieties. **USES:** Ornamental tree, spring flowers. **PROBLEMS:** Aphids, scale, red spider, webworms, rust, apple scab, fire blight, short-lived. **TIPS/NOTES:** Flowers are usually white with a pink tinge. 'Snowdrift' has white flowers, dark red fruit. 'Callaway' has light pink flowers, large red fruit. 'Radiant' has single red flowers, red fruit. Native to China and Japan. *Malus ioensis* is the prairie or Blanco crabapple, a Texas native.

Malus floribunda crabapple blooms

Malus pumila (MAH-lus PEW-me-lah). **COMMON NAME:** APPLE. **TYPE:** Deciduous tree. **LOCATION:** Sun. **HEIGHT:** 8'–20'. **SPREAD:** 15'–30'. **SPACING:** 15'–30'. **BLOOM/FRUIT:** Pink and white spring blooms after new foliage has emerged. Fruit ripens from summer through fall, depending on the variety. **PROPAGATION:** Cuttings, graphs. **HABITS/CULTURE:** Long-lived, productive fruit tree. **USES:** Food. **PROBLEMS:** Cotton root rot (the main concern in Texas), brown rot. **TIPS/NOTES:** Dwarf trees can be grown on trellises and planted as close together as 3'. Good choices for Texas include Molly's Delicious, Granny Smith, Gala, Fugi, Braeburn, and Dorsett Golden. Check your local extension service for the best varieties for your specific area.

MALVAVISCUS

Malvaviscus arboreus (mal-vah-VISS-kus ar-BOR-ee-us). **COMMON NAME:** TURK'S CAP. **TYPE:** Deciduous perennial shrub. **LOCATION:** Part shade. **HEIGHT:** 5-10'. **SPREAD:** 5'–8'. **SPACING:** 3'–5'. **BLOOM/FRUIT:** Red fezlike flowers in summer, red berrylike fruit in fall. **PROPAGATION:** Seed, cuttings, transplants. **HABITS/CULTURE:** Many stems grow from the ground. Likes moist soil in partial shade. **PROBLEMS:** Caterpillars. **USES:** Perennial color. **TIPS/NOTES:** Good choice. Give it a try.

MANDEVILLA

Mandevilla × 'Alice du Pont' (man-da-VEE-yah). **COMMON NAME:** MANDEVILLA. **TYPE:** Tropical vine used as an annual. **LOCATION:** Sun. **HEIGHT:** High-climbing. **SPREAD:** 8'–12'. **SPACING:** 3'–7'. **BLOOM/FRUIT:** Pure pink 2"–4" flowers all summer. **PROPAGATION:** Cuttings. **HABITS/CULTURE:** Fast-growing, climbing vine with large oval leaves and pink trumpetlike flowers that bloom from early summer until the first hard freeze. Needs wire or support structure to get started. There's also a lovely white-flowering variety. Treat this tropical vine as an annual—when it freezes, throw it away. Likes well-prepared soil, moisture, and regular fertilization. **USES:** Summer color. Good in pots set by a post or arbor. **PROBLEMS:** Few if any. Red spider mites and aphids if in stress. **TIPS/NOTES:** Tough and dramatic annual color. I highly recommend it. Native to Central and South America.

Malus floribunda crabapple fruit

Malvaviscus arboreus Turk's Cap

Mandevilla × 'Alice du Pont' mandevilla

MAPLE, ASH LEAF—see *Acer negundo*

MAPLE, BIGTOOTH—see *Acer saccharum*

MAPLE, BOX ELDER—see *Acer negundo*

MAPLE, CADDO—see *Acer saccharum*

MAPLE, CHALK—see *Acer saccharum*

MAPLE, JAPANESE—see *Acer palmatum*

MAPLE, RED—see *Acer rubrum*

MAPLE, RED RIVER—see *Acer negundo*

MAPLE, SILVER—see *Acer saccharinum*

MAPLE, SUGAR—see *Acer saccharum*

MARIGOLD—see *Tagetes* spp.

MARIGOLD, ENGLISH—see *Calendula officinalis*

MARIGOLD, POT—see *Calendula officinalis*

MARJORAM, SWEET—see *Origanum* spp.

MATTHIOLA

Matthiola incana (matt-ee-OH-la in-KAH-na). **COMMON NAME:** STOCK. **TYPE:** Annual bedding plant. **LOCATION:** Morning sun, afternoon shade. **HEIGHT:** 12"–18". **SPREAD:** 18". **SPACING:** 12". **BLOOM/FRUIT:** Upright spikes of fragrant white, rose, pink, or lavender flowers. **PROPAGATION:** Seed, cuttings. **HABITS/CULTURE:** Set out transplants in late winter or early spring, fall okay in South Texas. Needs healthy, well-drained soil and even moisture. Cutting back to stimulate additional flowers is not recommended. **USES:** Cut flowers, cool-season flower display, fragrance. **PROBLEMS:** Hot weather. **TIPS/NOTES:** Likes cooler weather best.

MAXIMILIAN SUNFLOWER—see *Helianthus* spp.

MAY APPLE—see *Podophyllum peltatum*

MAYHAW—see *Crataegus mollis*

MAYPOP—see *Passiflora incarnata*

Melampodium yellow melampodium

MELAMPODIUM

Melampodium leucanthum (mel-lam-PODE-ee-um loo-KAN-thum). **COMMON NAME:** BLACKFOOT DAISY. **TYPE:** Perennial wildflower or bedding plant. **LOCATION:** Sun to part shade. **HEIGHT:** 12". **SPREAD:** 12"–15". **SPACING:** 9"–12". **BLOOM/FRUIT:** White daisylike 1" flowers with yellow centers. **PROPAGATION:** Seed, cuttings. **HABITS/CULTURE:** Low-growing, compact daisy. White blossoms throughout the growing season. Dies to the ground in winter, returns each year unless it rots in the ground. Fairly easy to grow in any soil. **USES:** Perennial garden, border. Spring, summer, and fall flowers. **PROBLEMS:** Overwatering. Often rots during our cool moist winters, especially in clay soil. **TIPS/NOTES:** Easy to transplant or plant any time of the year. This is one of my favorites. A taller-growing, yellow-flowering annual variety is also quite good.

MELIA

Melia azedarach (ME-lee-ah ah-ZED-ah-rack). **COMMON NAME:** CHINABERRY, UMBRELLA TREE. **TYPE:** Deciduous tree. **LOCATION:** Sun. **HEIGHT:** 30'–50'. **SPREAD:** 20'–30'. **SPACING:** 15'–20'. **PROPAGATION:** Seed, cuttings. **HABITS/CULTURE:** A fast-growing junk tree to many, but it has delicate dark green foliage and strongly fragrant lilac flowers in spring. Grows easily in any soil. Yellow fall color. **USES:** Shade tree, spring color and fragrance. **PROBLEMS:** Fast growth but short life. Brittle wood and suckers. **TIPS/NOTES:** One of the better fast-growing trees.

Matthiola incana stock

Melampodium leucanthum
blackfoot daisy

Melia azedarach chinaberry

MELISSA

Melissa officinalis (me-LISS-a oh-fis-ih-NAH-lis). **COMMON NAME:** LEMON BALM. **TYPE:** Perennial herb. **LOCATION:** Sun to partial shade. **HEIGHT:** 18"–24". **SPREAD:** 24"–36". **SPACING:** 18"–24". **BLOOM/FRUIT:** Delicate white flowers in clusters along stems in summer. **PROPAGATION:** Seed, division, cuttings. **HABITS/CULTURE:** Likes partial shade best. Bushy, spreading, lemon-scented herb. Easy to grow in most soils, prefers healthy, well-drained soil. Slightly heart-shaped, mintlike leaves with scalloped edges. **USES:** Lemon-flavor herb for many foods, teas, cool beverages. Contains lots of vitamin C, excellent for attracting bees. **PROBLEMS:** Spider mites during hot, humid summers, pill bugs, worms, aphids. Can become invasive. **TIPS/NOTES:** Excellent for deterring pests in the vegetable garden.

MENTHA

Mentha spp. (MEN-tha). **COMMON NAME:** MINT. **TYPE:** Perennial herb. **LOCATION:** Sun to shade. **HEIGHT:** 1'–3'. **SPREAD:** 24". **SPACING:** 12"–24". **BLOOM/FRUIT:** Small purple or white flowers, should be kept cut off. **PROPAGATION:** Seed; stem cuttings most common. **HABITS/CULTURE:** Aggressively spreading plants. Best in loose, well-drained soil. Develops best flavor in full sun, but tolerates much shade. Needs to be trimmed back frequently. **USES:** Herbal remedies for coughs, colds, respiratory problems, and sinus headaches. Sedative. Flavoring for all kinds of foods, especially green peas, salads, desserts, good in teas and cool drinks. Repels fleas and sometimes aphids as well as rodents; dried mint in drawers may repel moths and cockroaches. **PROBLEMS:** Some chewing insects but none serious. Whiteflies and aphids occasionally. Tends to take over a garden, so be careful where you plant it. Susceptible to rust when kept too damp. **TIPS/NOTES:** Mints are very broadly divided into two groups according to fragrance: *Mentha spicata*, the spearmints, and *Mentha piperita*, the peppermints. There are hundreds of varieties. *Mentha pulegium* is pennyroyal mint. Highly aromatic leaves may be roundish, oval, or slightly pointed, smooth or wrinkly, with slightly serrated edges, square stems. Whorls of small flowers bloom throughout summer in shades from white to lavender. It's best to plant mint where it can be contained.

MESEMBRYANTHEMUM

Mesembryanthemum spp. (mes-em-bree-ANTH-ee-mum). **COMMON NAME:** ICE PLANT. **TYPE:** Annual and perennial bedding plant. **LOCATION:** Sun. **HEIGHT:** 6"–9". **SPREAD:** 9"–12". **SPACING:** 6"–9". **BLOOM/FRUIT:** White, pink, or purple summer flowers. **PROPAGATION:** Seed. **HABITS/CULTURE:** Low-growing, summer-flowering succulents. Need little to no water once established, but do better with some water during dry spells. **USES:** Summer color, rock gardens. Good for niches in natural stone walls. **PROBLEMS:** Tender foliage is easily damaged. Can be quickly drowned with too much water. **TIPS/NOTES:** Should be used as an annual in Texas.

MESCAL BEAN—see *Sophora secundiflora*

MESQUITE—see *Prosopis glandulosa*

METASEQUOIA

Metasequoia glyptostroboides (met-ah-see-KWOY-ah glip-toe-stro-BOY-dis). **COMMON NAME:** DAWN REDWOOD. **TYPE:** Deciduous tree. **LOCATION:** Sun. **HEIGHT:** 80'. **SPREAD:** 30'. **SPACING:** 20'–40'. **BLOOM/FRUIT:** Insignificant spring flowers, cones in the fall. **PROPAGATION:** Seed. **HABITS/CULTURE:** Deciduous conifer. Narrow and pyramidal, upward-pointing branches rather than perpendicular like those of bald cypress. Fine-textured, lacy foliage, reddish brown fall color. Likes deep, slightly acid soils best, but adapts to our alkaline soils quite well. Doesn't turn brown in late summer like bald cypress. **USES:** Specimen garden tree, shade tree, backdrop. **PROBLEMS:** Chlorosis and foliage burn in shallow soils. **TIPS/NOTES:** Ancient tree native to China and Japan. Distinctive and worth trying.

Mentha top, orange mint;
bottom, variegated pineapple mint
Agricultural Research Magazine, USDA

Metasequoia glyptostroboides
dawn redwood

Metasequoia glyptostroboides dawn redwood

Millettia reticulata evergreen wisteria

Mirabilis jalapa four o'clock

Miscanthus maidengrass

MEXICAN BLANKET—see *Gaillardia pulchella*

MEXICAN BLUE OAK—see *Quercus virginiana*

MEXICAN BUCKEYE—see *Ungnadia speciosa*

MEXICAN FIREBUSH—see *Hamelia* spp.

MEXICAN HAT—see *Ratibida columnaris*

MEXICAN HEATHER—see *Cuphea* spp.

MEXICAN OREGANO—see *Origanum* spp.

MEXICAN PLUM—see *Prunus mexicana*

MEXICAN POINCIANA—see *Caesalpinia* spp.

MEXICAN SUNFLOWER—see *Tithonia rotundifolia*

MILLETTIA
Millettia reticulata (mill-LEE-she-ah re-ti-cue-LA-tah). **COMMON NAME:** EVERGREEN WISTERIA. **TYPE:** Evergreen vine. **LOCATION:** Sun to part shade. **HEIGHT:** 8'–15'. **SPACING:** 5'–8'. **BLOOM/FRUIT:** Sparse purple orchidlike flowers in summer. **PROPAGATION:** Cuttings. **HABITS/CULTURE:** Climbing vine with lighter and more refined growth and texture than that of regular wisteria. Needs loose, well-drained soil, moderate water and fertilizer. **USES:** Evergreen climbing vine, fences, arbors. **PROBLEMS:** Freeze damage in northern half of the state. **TIPS/NOTES:** Relatively new to Texas. Use with caution for a while. I think it will be a winner. Native to China.

MIMOSA—see *Albizia julibrissin*

MINT—see *Mentha* spp.

MIRABILIS
Mirabilis jalapa (mee-RAH-bi-lis ha-LAH-pa). **COMMON NAME:** FOUR O'CLOCK. **TYPE:** Perennial bedding plant. **LOCATION:** Shade to part shade. **HEIGHT:** 2'–4'. **SPREAD:** 2'–3'. **SPACING:** 18"–24". **BLOOM/FRUIT:** Fragrant trumpet-shaped red, pink, yellow, and white flowers that open in midafternoon. **PROPAGATION:** Seed. **HABITS/CULTURE:** Upright-growing, summer-flowering perennial. Sow seed in full sun in early spring for color from midsummer to fall. Reseeds readily. As name implies, flowers open in late afternoon and last into the evening. Drought tolerant. **USES:** Summer color. **PROBLEMS:** Can develop into a weedy pest. **TIPS/NOTES:** Tuberous roots can be dug and stored if needed, transplants easily. Very tough perennial, can survive lots of abuse.

MISCANTHUS
Miscanthus spp. (miss-CAN-thus). **COMMON NAME:** MAIDENGRASS, MAIDENHAIRGRASS, ZEBRAGRASS. **TYPE:** Perennial grass. **LOCATION:** Sun. **HEIGHT:** 5'–8'. **SPREAD:** 3'–4'. **SPACING:** 3'–4'. **BLOOM/FRUIT:** Showy fall flower spikes on long stems, usually white or off-white. **PROPAGATION:** Division. **HABITS/CULTURE:** Large grass plants, some green, some variegated. Similar in character to pampas grass but smaller and more delicate-looking.

USES: Specimen, summer color, texture change. Flowers are great for indoor arrangements. **PROBLEMS:** Few if any. **TIPS/NOTES:** Good ornamentals, should be used more often. *Miscanthus sinensis* 'Gracillimus,' maidengrass, has slender weeping leaves and feathery beige flowers. 'Variegatus' is variegated Japanese silvergrass. 'Zebrinus' is zebragrass.

Miscanthus sinensis 'Zebrinus' zebragrass

Monarda citriodora horsemint

Monarda fistulosa wild bergamot

Monarda didyma red monarda

MOCK ORANGE—see *Philadelphus* spp.

MOHR OAK—see *Quercus virginiana*

MONARDA
Monarda citriodora (mo-NAR-da sit-ree-oh-DOR-ah). **COMMON NAME:** HORSEMINT, LEMON MINT, BERGAMOT. **TYPE:** Perennial herb. **LOCATION:** Full sun. **HEIGHT:** 12"–18". **SPREAD:** 3'. **SPACING:** 6"–12" or 3 lbs. of seed per acre. **BLOOM/FRUIT:** Purple flowers in late summer. **PROPAGATION:** Seed, transplants, stolons. **HABITS/CULTURE:** Upright and slow-spreading, sturdy and tough. **USES:** Teas for colds, fevers, and respiratory problems. Similar to mints. Excellent bee plant, repels fleas and chiggers. **PROBLEMS:** None serious. **TIPS/NOTES:** Nothing browses any of the monardas—not even deer. The *Monarda* genus comprises a number of fragrant herbs with especially beautiful flowers. Most are native plants, such as *Monarda fistulosa*, wild bergamot; *Monarda punctata*, spotted bee balm; and *Monarda citriodora*, lemon mint. *Monarda didyma* is the red-flowering variety. Seeds are increasingly available in mail-order catalogs, and small plants are being seen more often in retail nurseries.

MONDOGRASS—see *Ophiopogon japonicus*

MONEYWORT—see *Lysimachia nummularia*

MONKEYGRASS—see *Liriope muscari*

MONTERREY OAK—see *Quercus virginiana*

MOON VINE—see *Ipomoea* spp.

MORNING GLORY—see *Ipomoea* spp.

MOSS ROSE—see *Portulaca grandiflora*

MORUS
Morus alba (MORE-us AL-bah). **COMMON NAME:** MULBERRY. **TYPE:** Deciduous tree. **LOCATION:** Sun. **HEIGHT:** 30'. **SPREAD:** 40'. **SPACING:** 20'–30'. **BLOOM/FRUIT:** Inconspicuous flowers, followed by very sweet, delicious fruit. **PROPAGATION:** Cuttings, seed. **HABITS/CULTURE:** The hybrid fruitless form is a fast-growing junk tree with large various-shaped leaves and very shallow and destructive root systems. Uses large quantities of water. The native, fruiting mulberry has smaller leaves that are not as shiny. It is the better choice unless the tree will be located over your patio or car. **USES:** The fruitless form has no redeeming value. Fruiting tree is good for wildlife and has edible fruit. **PROBLEMS:** Webworms, cotton root rot, destructive roots, ugly. **TIPS/NOTES:** Fruitless type is an undesirable tree. Do not plant! This is the most overplanted junk tree in the United States. The fruiting mulberries are messy if planted by your drive or patio, but they are excellent sources of food for birds. The fruit is also delicious for people. Small weeping forms are available that are quite effective in Oriental gardens.

MOSSY OAK—see *Quercus macrocarpa*

MULBERRY—see *Morus alba*

MULLEIN—see *Verbascum* spp.

Ensete red banana

Morus alba fruitless mulberry

Myrica cerifera wax myrtle

Myrica cerifera wax myrtle

Myrica pusilla dwarf wax myrtle

MUSA

Musa spp. (MEW-sa). **COMMON NAME:** BANANA. **TYPE:**
Perennial tree. **LOCATION:** Sun. **HEIGHT:** 5'–20'. **SPREAD:**
5'–10'. **SPACING:** 5'–10'. **BLOOM/FRUIT:** Large, heavy red or
purple flower clusters, followed by edible bananas. **PROPA-
GATION:** Division. **HABITS/CULTURE:** All species have thick
stems and spread by suckers to form clumps. Will set fruit
in the warmer parts of the state where the growing season is longer. Also grows in greenhouses. **USES:** Food, tropical effect. **PROBLEMS:** Freeze damage in the northern half
of the state. Huge leaves are easily torn by the wind. **TIPS/
NOTES:** In cooler parts of the state, protect in winter by
cutting off the top and putting a thick mulch layer over
the stump. If the roots don't stay too wet and rot, the
plant will return in the spring. Pieces of banana leaves
and stalk are said to repel fleas. The decorative red-leaf
varieties *Ensete* are not true bananas.

MYRICA

Myrica cerifera (MY-ruh-kuh sir-RIFF-eh-ruh). **COMMON
NAME:** WAX MYRTLE. **TYPE:** Evergreen tree. **LOCATION:**
Sun to part shade. **HEIGHT:** 15'. **SPREAD:** 10'. **SPACING:** 8'–
12'. **BLOOM/FRUIT:** Golden yellow and green male and female flowers on different plants. Flowers from March
through April. Fruit of the female plants are small blue
drupes clustered along the stems. **PROPAGATION:** Seed,
cuttings, transplants. **HABITS/CULTURE:** Moderately fast-
growing and spreading, with many small medium-green
leaves, blue-gray berries in fall. Aromatic foliage dotted
above and below. Easy to grow in any soil, drought tolerant. **USES:** Specimen garden tree, evergreen background.
Good alternative to yaupon holly. **PROBLEMS:** Brittle wood,
suckers. **TIPS/NOTES:** Birds like the berries. *Myrica pusilla,*
dwarf wax myrtle, is an excellent dwarf form that works
as a shrub. Native to the southern states and the eastern
half of United States.

MYRTLE, DWARF WAX—see *Myrica cerifera*

MYRTLE, WAX—see *Myrica cerifera*

NANDINA

Nandina domestica (nan-DEEN-ah doe-MESS-ti-ka). **COM-MON NAME:** NANDINA, HEAVENLY BAMBOO. **TYPE:** Evergreen shrub. **LOCATION:** Sun to shade. **HEIGHT:** 12"–8'. **SPREAD:** 2'–6'. **SPACING:** 2'–4'. **BLOOM/FRUIT:** Pinkish or purplish white flowers in clusters at branch ends in early spring. Red berries in winter. **PROPAGATION:** Cuttings, seed. **HABITS/CULTURE:** Vertical unbranching shoots, leggy but distinctive. Soft, delicate red-orange foliage. Regular Nandina is 5'–8' tall, compact 3'–4', 'Harbour Dwarf' 1'–2', and 'Nana' 1'–2'. Grows in any soil, any location. Drought tolerant. Do not shear or box—ever! Withstands an unbelievable amount of neglect. To lower height of plant, cut the tallest shoots off at ground level. **USES:** Specimen, container, accent, screen, hedge, Oriental gardens, mass, border. **PROBLEMS:** None. **TIPS/NOTES:** Nandinas, native to China, are wonderful plants, but they have a curious negative connotation with many people—probably because they are often seen growing wild around abandoned properties. This just shows how tough they really are. All varieties are good except 'Nana,' which looks like a chlorotic basketball all summer. Nandina 'San Gabriel' has distinctively thin foliage.

Nandina domestica compact nandina

Nandina domestica 'Harbour Dwarf' dwarf nandina

Nandina domestica nandina

Narcissus daffodil

Nandina domestica 'San Gabriel' San Gabriel nandina

NARCISSUS

Narcissus spp. (narr-SIS-us). **COMMON NAME:** DAFFODIL, JONQUIL. **TYPE:** Perennial bulb. **LOCATION:** Sun. **HEIGHT:** 9"–18" **SPREAD:** 12"–18". **SPACING:** 6"–12". **BLOOM/FRUIT:** Lovely bell-shaped flowers in early spring in white, yellow, orange, and combinations. **PROPAGATION:** Bulbs. **HABITS/CULTURE:** Vertical blades of foliage grow from the ground. Plant bulbs in loose organic beds with good drainage. Add 1 tablespoon bone meal or soft rock phosphate to each hole before planting. Foliage must be left to turn brown on the plant before removing it; otherwise blooms won't form the next year. The foliage can be pinned to the ground to look better. **USES:** Spring flowers, naturalized area, cutting garden. **PROBLEMS:** Snails, slugs. **TIPS/NOTES:** Flowers last about two weeks or less. Don't invest a lot of money in daffodils. The smaller-flowering narcissus has the same basic characteristics but returns more dependably each year.

Nerium oleander oleander   *Nicotiana alata* flowering tobacco

Nierembergia cup flower

NASTURTIUM—see *Tropaeolum*

NATAL PLUM—see *Carissa macrocarpa*

NEPETA

Nepeta spp. (NAY-pah-tah). **COMMON NAME:** CATMINT,
CATNIP. **TYPE:** Perennial herb. **LOCATION:** Sun to part
shade. **HEIGHT:** 18"–24". **SPREAD:** Wide-spreading. **SPAC-
ING:** 12"–18". **BLOOM/FRUIT:** Blue, mauve, and white flower
spikes. **PROPAGATION:** Seed, cuttings. **HABITS/CULTURE:**
Nepeta cataria, catnip, has pinkish flowers and a strong
odor. *Nepeta mussinii*, catmint, has lilac-colored flowers
and is more controlled in its growth. Both have round,
serrated, gray-green leaves. Need moist, well-drained soil.
Very easy to grow. **USES:** Herb garden, medicinal, teas with
a peppery flower. **PROBLEMS:** Spread by seed. **INSIGHT:**
Catnip tea is the tea for children. It reduces fever. The
chemical that is so intoxicating to cats is *nepetalactone.*

NERIUM

Nerium oleander (NEER-ee-um oh-lee-ANN-der). **COM-
MON NAME:** OLEANDER. **TYPE:** Evergreen. **LOCATION:**
Sun. **HEIGHT:** 8'–12'. **SPREAD:** 8'–12'. **SPACING:** 5'–8'.
BLOOM/FRUIT: Red, white, or pink 2"–3" flowers clustered
at branch ends from early summer to fall. **PROPAGATION:**
Cuttings. **HABITS/CULTURE:** Upright shrub with many as-
cending stems that are bare below. Long thin leaves,

flowers all summer long. Plant in well-prepared beds with
protection from the winter winds. **USES:** Screen, background, summer color. **PROBLEMS:** Very poisonous plant
parts, freeze damage. **TIPS/NOTES:** Red and pink are the
most cold hardy. 'Mrs. Roeding' is a gorgeous salmon-color
cultivar. It needs protection in harsh winters. Native to
the Mediterranean.

NICOTIANA

Nicotiana alata (nee-KO-she-ah-na a-LAY-tah). **COMMON
NAME:** FLOWERING TOBACCO. **TYPE:** Annual bedding
plant. **LOCATION:** Morning sun, afternoon shade. **HEIGHT:**
12"–24". **SPREAD:** 12"–18". **SPACING:** 10"–12". **BLOOM/
FRUIT:** Fragrant star-shaped flowers in red, rose, pink,
purple, white, yellow, or green in late spring and summer. **PROPAGATION:** Transplants, seed. **HABITS/CULTURE:**
Grows best in healthy, well-drained soil in dappled shade
or morning sun with afternoon shade. **USES:** Summer color,
fragrance. **PROBLEMS:** Slugs and snails. **TIPS/NOTES:** Flowering tobacco is fairly difficult to grow from seed; transplants are better.

NIEREMBERGIA

Nierembergia spp. (near-im-BERG-ee-ah). **COMMON NAME:**
CUP FLOWER, NIEREMBERGIA. **TYPE:** Perennial bedding plant. **LOCATION:** Sun to part shade. **HEIGHT:** 6"–12".
SPREAD: 12"–18". **SPACING:** 9"–12". **BLOOM/FRUIT:** Blue or
white 2"–3" summer flowers clustered at branch ends.
PROPAGATION: Cuttings. **HABITS/CULTURE:** Low-bunching
growth. Well-drained organic soil is best. Moderate water
and fertilization needs. Loves hot weather. **USES:** Colorful
border, rock gardens, perennial gardens, stone walls. **PROB-
LEMS:** Few if any. **TIPS/NOTES:** Native to Argentina. Plant
from containers in spring or fall.

NUTGRASS—see *Cyperus alternifolius*

NYSSA

Nyssa sylvatica var. *sylvatica* (NI-sa sil-VA-ti-ka). **COM-
MON NAME:** BLACK GUM. **TYPE:** Deciduous tree. **LOCA-
TION:** Sun. **HEIGHT:** 50'–100'. **SPREAD:** 30'. **SPACING:** 30'.
BLOOM/FRUIT: Clusters of shiny blue-black fruit enjoyed
by many wild animals. **PROPAGATION:** Seed. **HABITS/CUL-
TURE:** Foliage is shiny green in the summer and scarlet
in the fall. A few leaves will sometimes turn red in the
late summer. One of the best Texas trees for fall color.
Unfortunately, it won't grow in alkaline soils. Prefers East
Texas acid sand or Houston-area clays. Likes moist to wet

soils best. Relatively slow-
growing. **USES:** Shade tree,
fall color. **PROBLEMS:** Needs
acid soil. **TIPS/NOTES:** *Nyssa*
also includes the East Texas
tupelo tree. *Nyssa aquatica*
is water tupelo. *Nyssa sylvatica* var. *biflora* is the swamp
tupelo. All these trees can
grow well over 100' tall in
the right conditions.

Nyssa sylvatica var. *sylvatica*
black gum

Ocimum basilicum basil

Ophiopogon japonicus mondograss

OAK, BIGELOW—see *Quercus sinuata* var. *sinuata*

OAK, BLACKJACK—see *Quercus virginiana*

OAK, BUR—see *Quercus macrocarpa*

OAK, CHINKAPIN—see *Quercus muhlenbergii*

OAK, CHISOS—see *Quercus shumardii* or *texana*

OAK, CUP—see *Quercus macrocarpa*

OAK, DURRAND—see *Quercus sinuata* var. *sinuata*

OAK, EVERGREEN—see *Quercus virginiana*

OAK, LACEY—see *Quercus virginiana*

OAK, LAUREL—see *Quercus virginiana*

OAK, LIVE—see *Quercus virginiana*

OAK, MEXICAN BLUE—see *Quercus virginiana*

OAK, MOHR—see *Quercus virginiana*

OAK, MONTERREY—see *Quercus virginiana*

OAK, MOSSY—see *Quercus macrocarpa*

OAK, PIN—see *Quercus shumardii* or *texana* and *Quercus virginiana*

OAK, POST—see *Quercus virginiana*

OAK, SANDPAPER—see *Quercus virginiana*

OAK, SAWTOOTH—see *Quercus acutissima*

OAK, SHUMARD—see *Quercus shumardii* or *texana*

OAK, SOUTHERN RED—see *Quercus shumardii* or *texana* and *Quercus virginiana*

OAK, SPANISH—see *Quercus virginiana*

OAK, SWAMP CHESTNUT—see *Quercus muhlenbergii* and *Quercus virginiana*

OAK, TEXAS RED—see *Quercus shumardii* or *texana*

OAK, VASEY—see *Quercus virginiana*

OAK, WATER—see *Quercus nigra*

OAK, WHITE—see *Quercus virginiana*

OAK, WILLOW—see *Quercus nigra* and *Quercus virginiana*

OATS—see Cover Crops

OBEDIENT PLANT—see *Physostegia virginiana*

OCIMUM
Ocimum basilicum (o-SEE-mum ba-SI-li-kum). **COMMON NAME:** BASIL. **TYPE:** Annual herb. **LOCATION:** Sun to part shade. **HEIGHT:** 12"–24". **SPREAD:** 12"–18". **SPACING:** 12"–18". **BLOOM/FRUIT:** Whorls ranging from white to purple. **PROPAGATION:** Seed, transplants. **HABITS/CULTURE:** Easy to grow from seed or transplants. Usually reseeds easily. Soft, very fragrant leaves ranging from dark purple to pale green. May be serrated or smooth, glossy or dull. Keep basil pinched back for bushy growth. **USES:** Flavoring for many foods, including salads, vegetables, vinegars, teas, oils, and butter. Good companion plant for tomatoes. **PROBLEMS:** Worms and grasshoppers. **TIPS/NOTES:** Be sure to freeze leaves to provide a winter supply of basil. Basil picked at the end of the day will keep twice as long as basil picked early in the morning. Builds up sugars during the day. Stores best in perforated plastic bags at 60 degrees.

OENOTHERA
Oenothera spp. (ee-NOTH-er-ah). **COMMON NAME:** EVENING PRIMROSE, TEXAS BUTTERCUP. **TYPE:** Perennial wildflower. **LOCATION:** Sun. **HEIGHT:** 12"–18". **SPREAD:** 2'–3'. **SPACING:** 12"–18". **BLOOM/FRUIT:** Pink or white 2" blooms in spring. **PROPAGATION:** Seed. **HABITS/CULTURE:** Sprawling perennial with showy, long-lasting flower display in the spring, not for the well-groomed garden. Plant from containers in the spring or seeds in the fall. **USES:** Wildflowers in grassy areas, carefree perennial garden. **PROBLEMS:** Ragged-looking when not in bloom. Attracts beneficial ground beetles. **TIPS/NOTES:** Native from Missouri to Texas. Do not fertilize wildflowers.

O

Origanum oregano

ture and regular fertilization. To remove brown tips, mow down in late winter just before new growth appears. **USES:** Low ground cover for small to medium-size areas. **PROBLEMS:** Nematodes, rabbits. **TIPS/NOTES:** A dwarf form, *Ophiopogon japonicus* 'Nana,' is very compact, dark green, and slow-growing. It should be planted at least 6" apart. Native to Japan and Korea.

OPUNTIA

Opuntia spp. (o-PUN-tee-ah). **COMMON NAME:** PRICKLY PEAR CACTUS. **TYPE:** Evergreen cactus. **LOCATION:** Sun. **HEIGHT:** 2'–6'. **SPREAD:** 4'–6'. **SPACING:** 2'–4'. **BLOOM/FRUIT:** Yellow to red flowers in spring, red to purple edible fruit in fall. **PROPAGATION:** Seed, division. **HABITS/CULTURE:** Flat pads covered with tufts of spines. **USES:** Maintenance-free spring flowers. **PROBLEMS:** Spines can be a nuisance. **TIPS/NOTES:** Texas prickly pear is *Opuntia lindheimeri*. *Opuntia imbricata* is the native cholla or walking stick.

OLEANDER—see *Nerium oleander*

OLIVE, RUSSIAN—see *Elaeagnus angustifolia*

ONION—see *Allium* spp.

OPHIOPOGON

Ophiopogon japonicus (oh-fee-oh-POE-gon ja-PON-eh-cum). **COMMON NAME:** OPHIOPOGON, MONDOGRASS, MONKEYGRASS. **TYPE:** Evergreen ground cover. **LOCATION:** Shade to part shade. **HEIGHT:** 8"–10". **SPREAD:** Unlimited. **SPACING:** 9". **BLOOM/FRUIT:** Subtle off-white summer flowers. **PROPAGATION:** Division. **HABITS/CULTURE:** Low-growing, grasslike ground cover. Grows in clumps but spreads by rhizomes to form solid mass. Best in shade or partial shade but will grow in sun. Needs even mois-

ORANGE—see *Citrus* spp.

ORANGE, HARDY—see *Poncirus trifoliata*

ORANGE, MOCK—see *Philadelphus* spp.

OREGANO—see *Origanum* spp.

OREGON GRAPE—see *Mahonia bealei*

ORIGANUM

Origanum spp. (o-ree-GAH-num). **COMMON NAME:** OREGANO. **TYPE:** Perennial herb. **LOCATION:** Sun to part shade. **HEIGHT:** 10"–24". **SPREAD:** 18"–24". **SPACING:** 12"–18". **BLOOM/FRUIT:** White to mauvish purple flowers in spring. **PROPAGATION:** Cuttings, seed, division. **HABITS/CULTURE:** Sprawling woody-stemmed plants with creep-

Oenothera speciosa evening primrose

Opuntia prickly pear cactus

Poliomintha longiflora Mexican oregano

ing roots. Some species are very winter hardy and drought resistant. Easily grown in well-drained garden soil, baskets, or containers. Tolerate shade but have better flavor when grown in sun. **USES:** Herb in Greek and Italian food—the pizza herb. **PROBLEMS:** None. **TIPS/NOTES:** There are about 25 species of *Origanum*. Some oreganos have green leaves, some have hairy white leaves. Greek and Italian oregano are very similar, but Greek oregano is lower-growing and the toughest. Seems to deter insects with its strong odor. The popular seasoning *Origanum vulgare*, Spanish oregano, is a green-leaf variety. The next most popular for cooking is *Origanum vulgare* var. *prismaticum*, Greek oregano. *Origanum marjorana* is sweet marjoram. *Poliomintha longiflora* is Mexican oregano, primarily a decorative herb with tubelike lavender flowers.

OSAGE ORANGE—see *Maclura pomifera*

OSMANTHUS

Osmanthus spp. (oss-MAN-thus). **COMMON NAME:** SWEET OLIVE, FALSE HOLLY. **TYPE:** Evergreen shrub. **LOCATION:** Sun or shade. **HEIGHT:** 4'–10'. **SPREAD:** 5'–8'. **SPACING:** 3'–4'. **BLOOM/FRUIT:** Small fragrant flowers that bloom mostly in spring but sporadically all summer. **PROPAGATION:** Cuttings. **HABITS/CULTURE:** Spiny, holly-like leaves. Needs moist, well-drained soil and more care than hollies. *Osmanthus* 'Variegatus' is variegated with white edges on spiny leaves. *Osmanthus fragrans*, sweet olive, has larger leaves and grows into a bigger plant than other varieties. Extremely fragrant flowers. Careful bed preparation is imperative. **USES:** Hedge, specimen, garden fragrance. **PROBLEMS:** Possible freeze damage.

OXALIS

Oxalis spp. (ox-AL-iss). **COMMON NAME:** OXALIS, WOOD SORREL. **TYPE:** Perennial bedding plant. **LOCATION:** Part shade. **HEIGHT:** 6"–12". **SPREAD:** 12"–15". **SPACING:** 9"–12". **BLOOM/FRUIT:** Pink, white, rose, or yellow flowers in spring. **PROPAGATION:** Division, seed. **HABITS/CULTURE:** Tough, low-growing perennial. Available in several colors. Foliage looks like clover. Easy to grow in light to fairly heavy shade. Can grow in full sun but prefers afternoon shade. Needs normal bed preparation, water, and fertilizer. **USES:** Low border, perennial gardens. **PROBLEMS:** Red spider mites. **TIPS/NOTES:** *Oxalis bowiei* has pink blooms in spring and fall. *Oxalis stricta*, yellow wood sorrel or sheep sorrel, has yellow flowers and small seed capsules that resemble okra pods. Considered a weed by some, it can be removed by hand.

OXBLOOD LILY—see *Rhodophiala bifida*

OXEYE DAISY—see *Chrysanthemum leucanthemum*

TOP TO BOTTOM:
Osmanthus fragrans sweet olive
Osmanthus 'Variegatus' variegated osmanthus
Oxalis bowiei oxalis

PACHYSANDRA

Pachysandra terminalis (pack-eh-SAN-drah term-eh-NAH-lus). **COMMON NAME:** PACHYSANDRA, JAPANESE SPURGE. **TYPE:** Evergreen ground cover. **LOCATION:** Shade. **HEIGHT:** 6"–8". **SPREAD:** 18"–36". **SPACING:** 9"–12". **BLOOM/FRUIT:** White fragrant flowers in summer, followed by white fruit. **PROPAGATION:** Seed, division. **HABITS/CULTURE:** Low-growing ground cover, spreads by underground rhizomes. Does best in highly organic soils in deep shade. Plant in well-prepared, shaded area. Needs lots of organic material, good drainage, ample water and fertilizer. **USES:** Ground cover for small areas in heavy shade, interesting foliage texture. **PROBLEMS:** Summer heat, alkaline soils, leaf blight, scale, nematodes. **TIPS/NOTES:** Native to Japan.

Pachysandra terminalis pachysandra

Paeonia tree peony

PAEONIA

Paeonia hybrids (pie-ON-ee-ah). **COMMON NAME:** PEONY. **TYPE:** Perennial bedding plant. **LOCATION:** Sun to part shade. **HEIGHT:** 24"–36". **SPREAD:** 20"–30". **SPACING:** 18"–24". **BLOOM/FRUIT:** Large, showy, bowl-shaped flowers in mid-spring, single and double blooms in white, pink, rose, salmon, and red. **PROPAGATION:** Roots. **HABITS/CULTURE:** Need morning sun, afternoon shade. Like deep, rich organic soil and areas with cold winters best. Plant the roots 2" deep in fall. Cut foliage to the ground in fall and cover with mulch. Do not overfertilize. **USES:** Cut flowers, perennial beds, borders. **PROBLEMS:** Peonies like cooler weather than most of Texas has to offer. Leaf diseases can be a problem. Peonies have to be considered high-maintenance plants. Tree peonies are easier to grow.

PAINTED DAISY—see *Chrysanthemum cinerariifolium*

PALM, RIO GRANDE—see *Sabal texana*

PALM, TEXAS—see *Sabal texana*

PALM, WINDMILL—see *Sabal texana*

PALMETTO—see *Sabal texana*

PAMPAS GRASS—see *Cortaderia selloana*

PANSY—see *Viola wittrockiana*

PAPAVER

Papaver spp. (pa-PAY-ver). **COMMON NAME:** POPPY. **TYPE:** Annual wildflower or bedding plant. **LOCATION:** Sun. **HEIGHT:** 12"–4'. **SPREAD:** 12"–3'. **SPACING:** 9"–15". **BLOOM/FRUIT:** Mostly annual flower in many colors but reseeds to return each spring. Lovely flowers on long slender stems. **PROPAGATION:** Seeds, transplants. **HABITS/CULTURE:** Lacy, hairy stems and foliage. Blooms usually from late April to early May. Some varieties will perennialize. Plant seeds directly in beds in September. Likes cool weather. **USES:** Spring flowers. **PROBLEMS:** Heat. **TIPS/NOTES:** *Papaver orientale* is the Oriental poppy, *Papaver nudicaule* is the Iceland poppy, *Papaver rhoeas* is the corn poppy, *Papaver somniferum* is the opium poppy. Native to Greece and the Orient.

Papaver somniferum opium poppy

PAPAYA—see *Carica papaya*

PAPYRUS—see *Cyperus alternifolius*

PARASOL TREE—see *Firmiana simplex*

PARKINSONIA

Parkinsonia aculeata (par-kin-SOH-nee-ah ak-you-lee-AH-tah). **COMMON NAME:** JERUSALEM THORN, RETAMA. **TYPE:** Deciduous tree. **LOCATION:** Sun. **HEIGHT:** 12'–30'. **SPREAD:** 15'–20'. **SPACING:** 12'–15'. **BLOOM/FRUIT:** Fragrant yellow clusters from spring to fall. On older blooms one petal turns orange. **PROPAGATION:** Seed, cuttings. **HABITS/CULTURE:** Native to the Rio Grande Valley. Light, lacy foliage, green trunk and limbs. Grows in any soil. Drought tolerant but tolerates moist soil. Leaf stem is thicker than the leaflets. Leaflets are very small but almost all parts of the plant are photosynthetic and will manufacture food. **USES:** Ornamental tree, summer flowers. It's a legume, so it helps improve the soil. **PROBLEMS:** Freeze damage in the northern two-thirds of the state. Seedlings can become a problem by sprouting up everywhere. **TIPS/NOTES:** Don't even think of using it north of Austin. Well, you can think about it, but don't do it! *Parkinsonia texana*, paloverde, is more drought tolerant and has a smoother, greener trunk.

Parkinsonia aculeata Jerusalem thorn

PARSLEY—see *Petroselinum crispum*

PARTHENOCISSUS

Parthenocissus quinquefolia (par-thuh-no-SIS-us kwin-kuh-FOLE-ee-ah). **COMMON NAME:** VIRGINIA CREEPER. **TYPE:** Deciduous vine. **LOCATION:** Sun to shade. **HEIGHT:** High-climbing. **SPACING:** 3'–8'. **BLOOM/FRUIT:** Insignificant blooms, blue-black berries in fall. **PROPAGATION:** Cuttings, seed. **HABITS/CULTURE:** Vigorous climbing vine. Looser growth and larger leaves than Boston Ivy. Red foliage in fall. Needs pruning to keep under control. Grows in any soil in sun or shade. Responds to well-prepared beds and moderate water and fertilizer. **USES:** Interesting texture and good fall color. Good for arbor, fence, or large building. **PROBLEMS:** None serious. **TIPS/NOTES:** Often confused with poison ivy. Virginia creeper has five leaflets instead of poison ivy's three. Native to Texas and the eastern United States.

Parthenocissus quinquefolia Virginia creeper

Parthenocissus tricuspidata Boston ivy

Parthenocissus tricuspidata (par-then-oh-SIS-us try-cus-pi-DA-tah). **COMMON NAME:** BOSTON IVY. **TYPE:** Deciduous vine. **LOCATION:** Sun to shade. **SPREAD:** High-climbing, wide-spreading. **SPACING:** 6'–8'. **BLOOM/FRUIT:** Insignificant. **PROPAGATION:** Cuttings. **HABITS/CULTURE:** Fast-growing, clinging vine. Fall color ranges from weak, reddish brown to bright scarlet. Easy to grow almost anywhere. Likes good bed preparation and partial shade best. **USES:** Vine for brick, wood, or other slick surfaces. **PROBLEMS:** Black caterpillars in spring. **TIPS/NOTES:** Native to China and Japan. 'Beverly Brooks' is the large-leaf plant, and 'Lowii' is the small-leafed plant that I prefer.

PASPALUM

Paspalum dilatatum (pass-PALE-um dill-ah-TOT-tum). **COMMON NAME:** DALLISGRASS. **TYPE:** Perennial grass. **LOCATION:** Sun. **BLOOM/FRUIT:** Seed pods on tall, fast-growing stalks look like 12" hockey sticks, lots of black pepperlike seed. **PROPAGATION:** Seed. **HABITS/CULTURE:** Long-lived, warm-season, deep-rooted perennial bunchgrass, considered a noxious weed. Dark green foliage forms low, flat clumps about the size of a dinner plate, with dead-looking centers. **USES:** Good forage for livestock but one of the worst weed pests in turf. **TIPS/NOTES:** Hard to control, physical removal is the only sure solution.

PASSIFLORA

Passiflora incarnata (pass-sih-FLO-ruh in-kar-NAY-tuh). **COMMON NAME:** PASSIONFLOWER, PASSION VINE, MAYPOP. **TYPE:** Perennial vine. **LOCATION:** Sun. **HEIGHT:** High-climbing. **SPREAD:** Unlimited. **SPACING:** 3'–6'. **BLOOM/FRUIT:** Gorgeous, intricately detailed summer flower in many colors, usually whites, pinks, and purples, although red, yellows, and oranges are available. The edible fruit, which comes in many sizes and colors, is reported to have aphrodisiac qualities. **PROPAGATION:** Cuttings. **HABITS/CULTURE:** Large, deeply cut leaves. Climbs quickly by tendrils. Blooms almost all summer with spectacular purple and white flowers. Easy to grow in any soil, drought tolerant. Dies to the ground each winter but returns in spring. **USES:** Summer climbing vine, flower display. **PROBLEMS:** Butterfly caterpillars. **TIPS/NOTES:** Native from Florida to East Texas. The introduced varieties also have dramatic flowers, but most are not winter hardy. There are over a hundred varieties. An entire book has been written on this beautiful vine, *Passion Flowers* by John Vanderplank (MIT Press).

PASSIONFLOWER—see *Passiflora incarnata*

PASSION VINE—see *Passiflora incarnata*

PAVONIA

Pavonia lasiopetala (pa-VOH-nee-ah lass-ee-oh-PET-ah-lah). **COMMON NAME:** ROCK ROSE. **TYPE:** Perennial shrub. **LOCATION:** Sun to part shade. **HEIGHT:** 3'–4'. **SPREAD:** 3'–4'. **SPACING:** 2'–3'. **BLOOM/FRUIT:** Pink, five-petaled 2" blooms from late spring until frost. Hibiscus-like flowers open in the morning and close in the afternoon. **PROPAGATION:** Seed, cuttings. **HABITS/CULTURE:** Evergreen to almost evergreen in the southern part of the state. Freezes easily north of Waco if not protected. Usually lives three to four years but reseeds freely. Velvety leaves. Best location is morning sun and afternoon shade. Shrubby. Occasional shearing keeps plant compact and blooming. **USES:** Summer color, perennial gardens, borders and masses. **PROBLEMS:** Freeze damage. **TIPS/NOTES:** Best to treat as an annual in most of the state.

PAWPAW—see *Asimina triloba*

PEA—see *Pisum sativum*

PEACH—see *Prunus persica*

PEAR—see *Pyrus pyrifolia*

PEAR, BRADFORD—see *Pyrus calleryana* 'Bradford'

PEAR, CALLERY—see *Pyrus calleryana*

PEAR, ORNAMENTAL—see *Pyrus calleryana*

Pelargonium hortorum geranium

PECAN—see *Carya illinoinensis*

PELARGONIUM

Pelargonium hortorum (pell-ar-GO-nee-um hor-TORE-um). **COMMON NAME:** GERANIUM. **TYPE:** Annual bedding plant. **LOCATION:** Sun to part shade. **HEIGHT:** 18"–24". **SPREAD:** 18"–24". **SPACING:** 12". **BLOOM/FRUIT:** Clusters of red, orange, pink, or white flowers. **PROPAGATION:** Cuttings. **HABITS/CULTURE:** Upright or trailing. Flowers bloom best in the cooler months. Grows well in prepared beds with good drainage. Plant in late winter from containers. **USES:** Annual gardens, pots, hanging baskets. **PROBLEMS:** Cutworms, caterpillars, summer heat. **TIPS/NOTES:** A little cold weather is good for them. Native to South Africa. The true geraniums are members of the genus *Geranium*. They are smaller, perennial plants. Scented geraniums bloom only once a year and are grown mostly for their wonderfully varied fragrances. Fresh leaves can be used in desserts, salads, soups, and cakes.

Passiflora incarnata passionflower

Pavonia lasiopetala rock rose

Pennisetum fountaingrass

PENNISETUM

Pennisetum spp. (pen-eh-SEE-tum). **COMMON NAME:** FOUNTAINGRASS. **TYPE:** Perennial grasses. **LOCATION:** Sun to part shade. **HEIGHT:** 3'–4'. **SPREAD:** 3'–4'. **SPACING:** 3'–4'. **BLOOM/FRUIT:** Fluffy, summer-blooming flower spikes on long stems. Colors range from white to pale purple. **PROPAGATION:** Division. **HABITS/CULTURE:** Showy ornamental grasses, with slender leaves and flower plumes from July to October. Easy to grow in any well-drained soil in sun to light shade. Moderate water and fertilizer requirements. **USES:** Specimen, medium-height border, summer flowers. **PROBLEMS:** None. **TIPS/NOTES:** Several similar varieties are available in different heights and flower colors. *Pennisetum setaceum* 'Rubrum,' purple fountaingrass, is pretty but will freeze and must be treated as an annual in northern half of the state. Native to Central America.

PENNYROYAL—see *Mentha* spp.

PENSTEMON

Penstemon spp. (PEN-sta-men). **COMMON NAME:** PENSTEMON. **TYPE:** Perennial flower. **LOCATION:** Sun to part shade. **HEIGHT:** 1'–4'. **SPREAD:** 1'–3'. **SPACING:** 9"–18". **BLOOM/FRUIT:** Several species with many colors and blooming periods, mostly spring through fall. **PROPAGATION:** Seed, root division, cuttings. **HABITS/CULTURE:** Most species are very upright and light in appearance. All need good drainage. Most species grow to about 2', some will reach 6'. Cut back brown or unattractive flower stalks for additional flower display. **USES:** Perennial garden color. **PROBLEMS:** Root rot, aphids. **TIPS/NOTES:** *Penstemon triflorus*, Hill Country penstemon, has dark pink to red blooms and is one of the best choices, but there are many other good choices. *Penstemon cobaea*, prairie or wild foxglove, is an excellent wildflower. Penstemon hybridizes readily.

Penstemon cobaea wild foxglove

PENTAS

Pentas lanceolata (PEN-tas lan-see-oh-LAY-tah). **COMMON NAME:** PENTA, EGYPTIAN STAR CLUSTER. **TYPE:** Annual flower. **LOCATION:** Sun to part shade. **HEIGHT:** 24". **SPREAD:** 18"–24". **SPACING:** 12"–18". **BLOOM/FRUIT:** Clusters of summer-blooming star-shaped flowers in white, pink, red, lilac, and candy stripe. **PROPAGATION:** Seed, cuttings. **HABITS/CULTURE:** Easy to grow. Plant after there is no danger of frost in well-drained soil. Moderate water and fertilizer needs. Best to allow for afternoon shade. **USES:** Summer annual. Great for true red color. Attracts butterflies and hummingbirds. **PROBLEMS:** None serious. **TIPS/NOTES:** Not widely used but should be.

PEONY—see *Paeonia* hybrids

PEPPER, RED—see *Capsicum* spp.

PEPPERMINT—see *Mentha* spp.

PERIWINKLE—see *Catharanthus roseus*

Pentas lanceolata penta   *Perovskia atriplicifolia* Russian sage

PEROVSKIA

Perovskia atriplicifolia (per-OVS-key-ah at-tre-plick-ih-FOLE-ee-ah). **COMMON NAME:** RUSSIAN SAGE. **TYPE:** Perennial bedding plant. **LOCATION:** Sun. **HEIGHT:** 3'–4'. **SPREAD:** 3'–4'. **SPACING:** 2'–3'. **BLOOM/FRUIT:** Small light blue to lavender flowers in whorls along stem. **PROPAGATION:** Seed, cuttings. **HABITS/CULTURE:** Colorful flower spikes from July through October. Silver-gray foliage. Likes sunny, dry locations. Very heat tolerant and drought resistant. Needs well-drained soil. **USES:** Accent plant, summer color, perennial gardens. Good cut flower. **PROBLEMS:** Few if any. **TIPS/NOTES:** Foliage smells like sage when crushed. Several cultivars are available: 'Blue Mist,' 'Blue Haze,' 'Blue Spire,' and 'Longin.'

Petunia × *hybrida* petunia

PERSEA

Persea americana (PER-see-ah ah-mer-ih-KAN-ah). **COMMON NAME:** AVOCADO. Avocados are very cold tender and are limited to the extreme southern part of Texas. They produce quickly, in as little as four years but are also sensitive to anthracnose disease. Avocados will ripen quickly after harvesting. They can be grown easily indoors as an ornamental plant by planting the large seed half submerged in potting soil. Will freeze in 95 percent of the state.

PERSIAN IVY—see *Hedera helix*

PERSIMMON, COMMON—see *Diospyros virginiana*

PERSIMMON, EASTERN—see *Diospyros virginiana*

PERSIMMON, TEXAS—see *Diospyros texana*

PETROSELINUM

Petroselinum crispum (pet-ro-se-LEEN-um KRIS-pum). **COMMON NAME:** PARSLEY, CURLY FRENCH PARSLEY. **TYPE:** Biennial herb. **LOCATION:** Sun to part shade. **HEIGHT:** 12"–18". **SPREAD:** 15"–18". **SPACING:** 12". **BLOOM/FRUIT:** Unimportant, remove to maintain a healthy plant. **PROPAGATION:** Seed. **HABITS/CULTURE:** Easy to grow in loose, well-drained soil. Parsley grows best in the cool months of the year. Germination in 11–28 days at 68–86 degrees. **USES:** Food, flavoring agent, breath freshener. High in vitamins A, B, C, rich in iron. **PROBLEMS:** Caterpillars, especially the black and yellow larva of the gorgeous swallowtail butterfly—don't kill them all. **TIPS/NOTES:** Pinch off bloom stalk as it emerges. To aid seed germination, soak seed in hot water or a 1 percent seaweed solution. The curly French variety is the most common sold. *Petroselinum crispum* var. *neapolitanum*, Italian parsley, has a flat leaf and is known for its superior flavor.

PETUNIA

Petunia × *hybrida* (pe-TUNE-ee-ah HI-brid-ah). **COMMON NAME:** PETUNIA. **TYPE:** Annual bedding plant. **LOCATION:** Sun. **HEIGHT:** 12"–24". **SPREAD:** 18"–24". **SPACING:** 9"–12". **BLOOM/FRUIT:** Available in many colors: white, pink, red, blue, purple, and yellow, singles and doubles. **PROPAGATION:** Seed, transplants. **HABITS/CULTURE:** Tender summer-flowering annual with thick leaves, sticky to the touch. Plant before last frost in well-prepared beds with good drainage. Needs large amounts of fertilizer for best blooms. **USES:** Summer flowers, pots, hanging baskets. **PROBLEMS:** Cutworms, caterpillars, summer heat. **TIPS/NOTES:** Do not plant as a summer annual—it likes the cool parts of the growing seasons. 'Madness' and 'Cherry Blossom' are more heat tolerant. Old petunias or species petunias have softer shades of pink and lavender and reseed easily. Native to South America.

PETUNIA, MEXICAN—see *Ruellia* spp.

PETUNIA, WILD—see *Ruellia* spp.

PHASEOLUS

Phaseolus vulgaris (fa-see-OH-lus vu-GAH-ris). **COMMON NAME:** BEAN. **TYPE:** Annual vegetable. **LOCATION:** Sun. **HEIGHT/SPREAD:** Low bush types to high-climbing types. **SPACING:** 6"–36". **BLOOM/FRUIT:** Small spring flowers, edible fruit. **PROPAGATION:** Seed. **HABITS/CULTURE:** Warm-season annual legume vegetable, needs little fertilization and care. Plant beans in single raised rows. Germination in 5–8 days at 68–86 degrees. Needs warm soil. **USES:** Edible vegetable. **PROBLEMS:** Planting too early. Beans, especially limas, should not be planted until the soil is at least 65 degrees. Various diseases in unhealthy soil. Nematodes, spider mites, grubs, cutworms. **TIPS/NOTES:** Best variety in Texas is the plain ole pinto bean. Lima beans are also excellent and one of the most nutritious foods of all.

PHILADELPHUS

Philadelphus spp. (fil-ah-DEL-fus). **COMMON NAME:** MOCK ORANGE. **TYPE:** Deciduous shrub. **LOCATION:** Sun to shade. **HEIGHT:** 8'–15'. **SPREAD:** 8'–10'. **SPACING:** 4'–6'. **BLOOM/FRUIT:** Fragrant white flowers in late spring or early

summer. **PROPAGATION:** Cuttings. **HABITS/CULTURE:** Large-growing fountain-like shrubs, medium-green foliage. Normal soil and maintenance requirements. Prune immediately after blooms fade, cut oldest shoots all the way back to the ground. **USES:** Background shrub, late-spring color, garden fragrance, specimen. **TIPS/NOTES:** Should be used more.

Philadelphus mock orange

Phlox divaricata blue phlox

PHLOX

Phlox paniculata (FLOCKS pa-nik-ew-LAH-ta). **COMMON NAME:** SUMMER PHLOX. **TYPE:** Perennial bedding plant. **LOCATION:** Sun to part shade. **HEIGHT:** 15"–30". **SPREAD:** 15"–30". **SPACING:** 12"–15". **BLOOM/FRUIT:** Early summer flowers on long stalks. Colors include pink, rose, red, white, lavender. Hot pink is the easiest to grow in Texas. 'Mt. Fuji' is a lovely white selection. **PROPAGATION:** Seed, transplants. **HABITS/CULTURE:** Plant transplants in spring. Needs healthy, well-drained organic soil. **USES:** Summer color, perennial beds, background color. **PROBLEMS:** Powdery mildew. **TIPS/NOTES:** *Phlox divaricata* is the spring-blooming blue phlox, which grows 12" high and likes shady areas best. Morning sun and afternoon shade is the best location.

Phlox subulata (FLOCKS sub-you-LAY-tah). **COMMON NAME:** THRIFT, MOSS PHLOX. **TYPE:** Perennial bedding plant. **LOCATION:** Sun. **HEIGHT:** 6"–8". **SPREAD:** 10"–12". **SPACING:** 10"–12". **BLOOM/FRUIT:** Blooms in spring in pink, blue, and white. Hot pink is the most common color. **HABITS/CULTURE:** Low-growing, spreading perennial that acts like an evergreen in mild winters. Easy to grow in any well-drained soil, moderate water and fertilizer needs. **USES:** Dwarf border, spring color, stone walls. **PROBLEMS:** None. **TIPS/NOTES:** Blooms reliably year after year. Plant in fall or spring. Native to North America. 'Blue Emerald' is the best, with lush, dark green foliage all summer.

PHOTINIA

Photinia serrulata (foe-TIN-ee-ah sir-roo-LA-ta). **COMMON NAME:** CHINESE PHOTINIA. **TYPE:** Evergreen shrub or small tree. **LOCATION:** Sun to part shade. **HEIGHT:** 15'–20'. **SPREAD:** 15'–20'. **SPACING:** 5'–10'. **BLOOM/FRUIT:** Clusters of white flowers in spring and red berries in winter. **PROPAGATION:** Cuttings, seed. **HABITS/CULTURE:** Massive, spreading evergreen shrub. Can be trimmed into small tree. Easy to grow in any soil, low water and food requirements. **USES:** Background, screen, small garden tree. **PROBLEMS:** Poisonous, powdery mildew, aphids, borers, leaf spot and fire blight. **TIPS/NOTES:** Native to China and Asia. Larger growing than Fraser's photinia. This is a superior plant to the overused red tip hybrid photinia.

Photinia × 'Fraseri' (foe-TIN-ee-ah FRAY-ser-eye). **COMMON NAME:** FRASER'S PHOTINIA. **TYPE:** Evergreen shrub. **LOCATION:** Sun to part shade. **HEIGHT:** 10'–15'. **SPREAD:** 8'–10'. **SPACING:** 4'–6'. **BLOOM/FRUIT:** Stinky white flowers in spring, no berries. **PROPAGATION:** Cuttings. **HABITS/CULTURE:** Very colorful, multistemmed, upright oval in shape. New growth in spring is red. Likes well-drained, prepared beds. Drainage is critical—avoid wet soils. **USES:** Screen, background, spring color. Foliage makes good cut-flower material. **PROBLEMS:** Poisonous, root fungus, nitrogen deficiency. Grossly overused. When the wax ligustrums froze in 1983, everyone replaced them with photinia. **TIPS/NOTES:** Also called red tip photinia, a cross

Phlox subulata thrift

Photinia serrulata Chinese photinia

Photinia × 'Fraseri' Fraser's photinia

Physostegia virginiana obedient plant

Phytolacca americana poke

between *Photinia serrulata*, Chinese photinia, and *Photinia glabra*, Japanese photinia, a smaller plant. Root fungus problems are quite significant and sometimes strike after the plant has been healthy for 7 or 8 years. Tends to come down with a lot of diseases—a poor choice.

PHYLA

Phyla nodiflora (FYE-lah no-deh-FLOR-ah). **COMMON NAME:** FROG FRUIT. **TYPE:** Perennial ground cover. **LOCATION:** Sun to shade. **HEIGHT:** 3"–4". **SPREAD:** 18"–24". **SPACING:** 12". **BLOOM/FRUIT:** Tiny white verbena-like flowers from spring until fall. **PROPAGATION:** Division. **HABITS/CULTURE:** Very low-growing, spreading native ground cover for sun or shade. Spreads by stolons. Very low maintenance. **PROBLEMS:** Dies out if mowed or overwatered. **TIPS/NOTES:** Delicate flowering plant that many would consider a weed.

PHYSOSTEGIA

Physostegia virginiana (fi-so-STEEG-ee-ah vir-gin-ee-AN-ah). **COMMON NAME:** OBEDIENT PLANT, FALSE DRAGONHEAD. **TYPE:** Perennial bedding plant. **LOCATION:** Sun to part shade. **HEIGHT:** 2'–4'. **SPREAD:** 12". **SPACING:** 9"–12". **BLOOM/FRUIT:** Pink, white, and lavender blooms from late summer to frost. **PROPAGATION:** Seed, division. **HABITS/CULTURE:** When flowers are twisted on the stem, they remain in that position. Slender, upright square stems with long pointed leaves. Drought tolerant, can grow in most any soil. **USES:** Perennial fall color, background flowers. **PROBLEMS:** Invasive, spreads by roots. **TIPS/NOTES:** *Physostegia angustifolia* is the spring-blooming obedient plant.

PHYTOLACCA

Phytolacca americana (FYE-toe-lac-ah ah-mer-ih-KAN-ah). **COMMON NAME:** POKE SALAD, POKE SALET, POKEWEED, POKE. **TYPE:** Perennial herb. **LOCATION:** Sun to part shade. **HEIGHT:** 4'–8'. **SPREAD:** 4'–8'. **SPACING:** Grows wild. **BLOOM/FRUIT:** White flowers on a large raceme from summer to fall. Drooping berry clusters from late summer through fall. **PROPAGATION:** Seeds, division. **HABITS/CULTURE:** Several stalks, with smooth bright red to purple bark. Large smooth green leaves. Small red berries turn purple when ripe; their juice leaves a red stain. Likes rich moist soil but will grow anywhere in Texas except the far west. **USES:** Bird attractant. Pot herb that tastes likes spinach. **PROBLEMS:** Deadly poisonous if not carefully prepared. **TIPS/NOTES:** The berries, bark, and older leaves contain a very toxic alkaloid. The berries are particularly poisonous to children. Although cooking apparently inactivates the toxins in young leaves, they can enter the body through the skin during harvesting. The young leaves, cooked properly, taste great and are good for you, but they shouldn't be eaten unless the first boil water is poured off. None of the plant should ever be eaten raw.

PIGEONBERRY—see *Rivina humilis*

PINE, AFGHAN—see *Pinus eldarica*

PINE, AUSTRIAN—see *Pinus nigra*

PINE, CROSS—see *Pinus nigra*

PINE, JAPANESE BLACK—see *Pinus thunbergii*

PINE, LOBLOLLY—see *Pinus palustris*

PINE, LONGLEAF—*Pinus palustris*

PINE, MONDELL—see *Pinus eldarica*

PINE, MUGHO—see *Pinus mugo* 'Mughus'

PINE, PONDEROSA—see *Pinus palustris*

PINE, SLASH—see *Pinus palustris*

PINK—see *Dianthus* spp.

PIN OAK—see *Quercus shumardii* or *texana* and *Quercus virginiana*

PINUS

Pinus eldarica (PIE-nus ell-DAR-eh-kah). **COMMON NAME:** ELDARICA PINE, MONDELL PINE, AFGHAN PINE. **TYPE:** Evergreen tree. **LOCATION:** Sun. **HEIGHT:** 40'. **SPREAD:** 20'. **SPACING:** 12'–20'. **BLOOM/FRUIT:** Inconspicuous flowers, followed by seed-bearing cones. **PROPAGATION:** Seed. **HABITS/CULTURE:** Fast-growing, upright, medium-green needles, foliage to the ground. Grows in any soil, drought tolerant. **USES:** Shade tree. **PROBLEMS:** Pine tip moth. **TIPS/NOTES:** Seemed to be especially good in alkaline clay soils but has now developed some problems and is dying out in some areas. Has done very well in the drier parts of the state.

Pinus eldarica eldarica pine

Pinus nigra Austrian pine

Pinus mugo 'Mughus' (PIE-nus MEW-go MEW-gus). **COMMON NAME:** MUGHO PINE. **TYPE:** Evergreen shrub. **LOCATION:** Sun. **HEIGHT:** 4'. **SPREAD:** 4'. **SPACING:** 3'–4'. **BLOOM/FRUIT:** No showy flowers or cones. **PROPAGATION:** Seed, cuttings. **HABITS/CULTURE:** Shrubby, symmetrical little pine, spreads out with age. Needs loose, well-drained soil. Likes sandy, acid soil best. Seems to adapt to alkaline soil fairly well. **USES:** Specimen, accent, Oriental gardens, containers. **PROBLEMS:** Heat, chlorosis, pine tip moth. **TIPS/NOTES:** Chelated iron and Epsom salts help greatly to keep mugho pine healthy. Native to central and southern Europe.

Pinus nigra (PIE-nus NI-gra). **COMMON NAME:** AUSTRIAN PINE. **TYPE:** Evergreen tree. **LOCATION:** Sun. **HEIGHT:** 30' **SPREAD:** 30'. **SPACING:** 10'–15'. **BLOOM/FRUIT:** Ugly flowers, followed by cones. **PROPAGATION:** Seed. **HABITS/CULTURE:** Slow growth, thick foliage to the ground. Easy to grow in any soil except solid rock. **USES:** Ornamental evergreen tree, background, evergreen screen. **PROBLEMS:** Chlorosis occasionally. **TIPS/NOTES:** This tree and the cross pine, *Pinus nigra* × *thunbergii* (a cross between the Japanese black pine and Austrian pine), are the best pines for the alkaline soils of Texas. *Pinus leucodermis* 'Heldreki,' the red cone pine, is a good small pine that grows to 15'. Native to Europe and Asia.

Pinus palustris (PIE-nus puh-LUS-tris). **COMMON NAME:** LONGLEAF PINE. **TYPE:** Evergreen tree. **LOCATION:** Sun. **HEIGHT:** 80'–100'. **SPREAD:** 20'. **SPACING:** 20'–30'. **BLOOM/FRUIT:** Insignificant flowers. **PROPAGATION:** Seed. **HABITS/CULTURE:** Native to the deep, sandy, acid soils of East Texas. Looks like a clump of evergreen grass for three or more years while the young tree builds a root system. Long needles hang like pompoms. **USES:** Specimen shade tree, lumber. **PROBLEMS:** Ice storm damage. **TIPS/NOTES:** Other pines in this category include *Pinus ponderosa*, ponderosa pine, which is much more tolerant of clay and alkaline soils. Its needles are blue-green and it grows to 50' and taller. *Pinus taeda* is loblolly pine; *Pinus elliottii* is slash pine. Both are very similar to longleaf pine but more common in Texas.

Pinus elliottii slash pine

Pinus ponderosa ponderosa pine

Pinus thunbergii Japanese black pine

Pinus thunbergii (PIE-nus thun-BERG-ee-eye). **COMMON NAME:** JAPANESE BLACK PINE. **TYPE:** Evergreen tree. **LOCATION:** Sun. **HEIGHT:** 30'. **SPREAD:** 20'. **SPACING:** 15'–20'. **BLOOM/FRUIT:** Ugly flowers, followed by cones. **PROPAGATION:** Seed. **HABITS/CULTURE:** Irregular form, foliage to ground. Central stem is not well defined. Grows in any soil except solid rock, likes neutral to slightly acid soil best. **USES:** Evergreen ornamental, background, Oriental gardens. **PROBLEMS:** Chlorosis. **TIPS/NOTES:** Not quite as good as Austrian and cross pines. Native to Japan.

PIPER

Piper auritum (PIE-per aw-REE-tum). **COMMON NAME:** HOJO SANTA. **TYPE:** Perennial herb. **LOCATION:** Sun to part shade. **HEIGHT:** 4'–8'. **SPREAD:** 6'–8'. **SPACING:** 3'. **BLOOM/FRUIT:** Cylindrical white 4" flower spikes. **PROPAGATION:** Division. **HABITS/CULTURE:** Semi-woody herb with many new shoots from the ground. Large, velvety, heart-shaped leaves sometimes 10" or more. Likes morning sun and afternoon shade in healthy soil. **USES:** Big pots, distinctive bold foliage, tropical look. Leaves are used in cooking to flavor dishes and to wrap various fillers of meat and fish. Distinctive root beer taste. **TIPS/NOTES:** Freezes in the northern part of the state. Worth replanting if it freezes, although it will usually return each spring. *Piper nigrum* is black pepper.

Piper auritum hojo santa

Pistacia chinensis Chinese pistachio

Pistacia chinensis Chinese pistachio

Pistacia texana Texas pistache

PISTACHE, TEXAS—see *Pistacia chinensis*

PISTACHIO, CHINESE—see *Pistacia chinensis*

PISTACIA

Pistacia chinensis (pis-TA-see-ah chi-NEN-sis). **COMMON NAME:** CHINESE PISTACHIO. **TYPE:** Deciduous tree. **LOCATION:** Sun. **HEIGHT:** 50'–70'. **SPREAD:** 50'. **SPACING:** 20'–50'. **BLOOM/FRUIT:** Inconspicuous flowers in spring, red berries on female trees in late summer. **PROPAGATION:** Seed, cuttings. **HABITS/CULTURE:** Fast-growing shade tree with open structure; yellow, red, and orange fall color—sometimes all at once. Compound leaves with 10–16 paired leaflets. Light, smooth bark when young. Branching structure is poor when young but quickly fills out. Easy to grow in any well-drained soil, drought tolerant. **USES:** Shade tree, fall color. **PROBLEMS:** Tip growth sometimes burns in early summer from too much water. **TIPS/NOTES:** Incorrectly called Chinese pistache. One of the best fast-growing trees. Native to China but acts like a native Texan. *Pistacia texana,* the evergreen Texas pistache, is native to South Texas. Has some freeze problems in North Texas. Looks more like a big shrub than a tree. Normal height is 15'–20' but can grow to 30' or more. It has small glossy green leaves that are reddish in the spring. Female plants have small red berries in the fall. The pistachio that produces the delicious nut is *Pistacia vera,* a desert plant that can't take much water at all.

PISUM

Pisum sativum (PEE-sum sa-TEE-vum). **COMMON NAME:** PEA. **TYPE:** Annual vegetable. **LOCATION:** Sun. **HEIGHT:** 3'–6'. **SPREAD:** 3'–6'. **SPACING:** 1'–2'. **BLOOM/FRUIT:** Small orchidlike flowers, followed by beans. **PROPAGATION:** Seed. **HABITS/CULTURE:** Most peas need support to climb. Use a lot of compost in the soil and mulch on the ground. Cool-season annual, likes cool soil. Germination in 5–8 days at 68 degrees. **USES:** Food, cover crop. **PROBLEMS:** Powdery mildew, aphids, viruses, cutworms, heat. **TIPS/NOTES:** Good choices include 'Sugar Snap,' 'Sugar Baby,' and other sugar this-and-thats. Southern peas (buckeye, crowder, and purple hull) are actually beans and members of the genus *Vigna.* For a cover crop, plant at a rate of 20 lbs. seed per acre after the last killing frost in spring.

PITTOSPORUM

Pittosporum tobira 'Variegata' (pit-tos-SPOR-um toe-BY-rah). **COMMON NAME:** VARIEGATED PITTOSPORUM. **TYPE:** Evergreen shrub. **LOCATION:** Sun to part shade. **HEIGHT:** 6'–7'. **SPREAD:** 5'–6'. **SPACING:** 36". **BLOOM/FRUIT:** Small off-white flowers in spring. **PROPAGATION:** Cuttings. **HABITS/CULTURE:** Soft, billowy-shaped shrub. Gray-green foliage edged in white. Can be kept trimmed to a height of 36" but will grow much taller. Plant in well-prepared, well-drained beds with protection against winter winds. Moderate water and food needs. **USES:** Foun-

Pittosporum tobira 'Variegata' variegated pittosporum

Pittosporum tobira 'Wheeler's Dwarf' Wheeler's dwarf pittosporum

Platanus occidentalis sycamore

Ceratostigma plumbaginoides blue plumbago

dation plant, mass, tall border, cut-flower foliage. **PROB-LEMS:** Severe freeze damage. **TIPS/NOTES:** Although the 1983 freeze killed almost every pittosporum in North Texas, people are still planting them. I do not advise using them north of Austin. The solid green form has the same characteristics.

Pittosporum tobira 'Wheeler's Dwarf' (pit-tos-SPOR-um toe-BY-rah). **COMMON NAME:** WHEELER'S DWARF PITTOSPORUM. **TYPE:** Evergreen shrub. **LOCATION:** Sun to part shade. **HEIGHT:** 3'–4'. **SPREAD:** 3'–4'. **SPACING:** 24". **BLOOM/FRUIT:** Very small off-white flowers in spring. **PROPAGATION:** Cuttings. **HABITS/CULTURE:** Very low, dense, and compact. Available in green or variegated form. Same soft foliage as the full-size varieties. Plant in well-prepared, well-drained beds with good protection from north winds. **USES:** Low border, mass, or foundation plant. **PROBLEMS:** Pittosporums can freeze easily. **TIPS/NOTES:** Limbs are easily broken by pets and kids.

PLANETREE—see *Platanus occidentalis*

PLATANUS

Platanus occidentalis (PLAT-ta-nus ox-eye-den-TAL-is). **COMMON NAME:** SYCAMORE, PLANETREE. **TYPE:** Deciduous tree. **LOCATION:** Sun. **HEIGHT:** 90'. **SPREAD:** 70'. **SPACING:** Do not plant! **BLOOM/FRUIT:** Insignificant flowers. Fruits are round brown balls. **PROPAGATION:** Seed. **HABITS/CULTURE:** Fast-growing, with large fuzzy leaves, white and gray flaky bark, yellow-brown fall color. Easy to grow in any soil the first few years. **USES:** Shade. The white trunks and limbs are lovely. **PROBLEMS:** Messy, anthracnose, leafspot, aphids, scale, bagworms, borers. Leaves are a nuisance, but they don't break down quickly. **TIPS/NOTES:** Poor choice. The London plane tree (*Platanus* × *acerifolia*) and other hybrids are supposed to be healthier, but I don't recommend any of them.

PLUM, MEXICAN—see *Prunus mexicana*

PLUM, NATAL—see *Carissa macrocarpa*

PLUM, PURPLE—see *Prunus cerasifera*

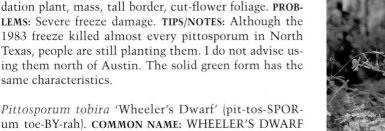

Plumbago capensis plumbago

PLUMBAGO

Plumbago spp. (plum-BAY-go). **COMMON NAME:** PLUMBAGO. **TYPE:** Perennial bedding plant. **LOCATION:** Sun to part shade. **HEIGHT:** 1'–3'. **SPREAD:** 2'–5'. **SPACING:** 12"–18". **BLOOM/FRUIT:** Blue or white summer blooms. **PROPAGATION:** Cuttings, seed. **HABITS/CULTURE:** Sprawling, fast-growing, drought-tolerant perennial. Dies to ground in fall, returns in spring in the southern half of the state. Likes well-prepared beds. **USES:** Summer flowers, stone walls, natural settings. **PROBLEMS:** Few if any. **TIPS/NOTES:** Native to South Africa. *Ceratostigma plumbaginoides* has dark blue flowers. *Plumbago capensis* has baby blue flowers and is larger-growing. *Plumbago auriculata* 'Alba' has white flowers.

PLUMERIA

Plumeria spp. (ploo-ME-ree-ah). **COMMON NAME:** FRANGIPANI. **TYPE:** Tropical shrub or small tree. **LOCATION:** Sun to part shade. **BLOOM/FRUIT:** Fragrant summer flowers in red, pink, purple, rose, salmon, yellow, and white. **PROPAGATION:** Stem cuttings. **HABITS/CULTURE:** Open growth habit, thick succulent stems. Clusters of long, pointed, leathery leaves, clusters of very showy and very fragrant flowers. Easy to grow in warm to hot weather. Keep fairly dry in winter, moist during the growing season. Needs rich potting soil. **USES:** Great plant for pots outdoors in summer. **PROBLEMS:** Hates cold, wet soil.

Podocarpus macrophyllus podocarpus

POA

Poa arachnifera (PO-ah a-rak-NIF-er-a). **COMMON NAME:** TEXAS BLUEGRASS. **TYPE:** Cool-season grass. **LOCATION:** Sun. **HEIGHT:** 18"–24". **SPREAD:** 36" or more. **SPACING:** Plant clumps 18" apart. Seed rate unknown at this time. **BLOOM/ FRUIT:** Off-white 36" plumes in summer. **PROPAGATION:** Division, seed. **HABITS/CULTURE:** Blue-green forage plant with decorative flower plumes. Spreads by rhizomes. **USES:** Pasture forage. **PROBLEMS:** Availability. **TIPS/NOTES:** Dr. James Reed at Texas A&M University is working on cross breeds between Texas bluegrass and several other blue-grass species. The goal is a drought-tolerant evergreen forage and lawn grass. *Poa annua* is annual bluegrass, a cool-season lawn grass usually considered a weed. *Poa trivilias* is roughstalk bluegrass, used as an overseeding grass on golf courses.

PODOCARPUS

Podocarpus macrophyllus (po-doe-CAR-pus mac-crow-FILE-us). **COMMON NAME:** PODOCARPUS, FALSE JAPANESE YEW. **TYPE:** Evergreen shrub. **LOCATION:** Shade to part shade. **HEIGHT:** 10'–15'. **SPREAD:** 4'–6'. **SPACING:** 3'–

4'. **BLOOM/FRUIT:** Insignificant. **PROPAGATION:** Cuttings. **HABITS/CULTURE:** Vertical-growing shrub with dark green foliage and blue berries in winter. Plant in well-prepared bed. Needs excellent drainage, moderate fertilizer. **USES:** Specimen, background plant, screen. **PROBLEMS:** Root rot, nematodes. **TIPS/NOTES:** *Podocarpus sinensis* is short and bushy and very cold hardy.

PODOPHYLLUM

Podophyllum peltatum (po-DOF-eh-lum pell-TAY-tum). **COMMON NAME:** MAY APPLE. **TYPE:** Perennial foliage plant. **LOCATION:** Shade. **HEIGHT:** 12"–24". **SPREAD:** 24"–36". **SPACING:** 24". **BLOOM/FRUIT:** White flowers in April, pale yellow fruit (May apples) in May. **PROPAGATION:** Seed, division. **HABITS/CULTURE:** Vigorous spreader that can become invasive. Very large umbrella-looking leaves. **USES:** Woodsy, forest-floor effect. **PROBLEMS:** Hard to find and somewhat difficult to establish.

POINSETTIA—see *Euphorbia* spp.

POISON IVY—see Weeds

POKE SALAD—see *Phytolacca americana*

POLYGONUM

Polygonum aubertii (poe-LIG-eh-num awe-BERT-ee-eye). **COMMON NAME:** SILVER LACEVINE. **TYPE:** Deciduous vine. **LOCATION:** Sun. **HEIGHT:** High-climbing. **SPREAD:** Wide-spreading. **SPACING:** 4'–8'. **BLOOM/FRUIT:** Masses of small white flowers in summer. **PROPAGATION:** Cuttings. **HABITS/CULTURE:** Fast-growing, climbing vine, spreads by rhizomes. Twining character. Easy to grow in most soils, drought tolerant, low fertilizer requirements. **USES:** Climbing vine for hot dry areas, summer flower color. **PROBLEMS:** Can be aggressive and weedlike. **TIPS/NOTES:** Native to China.

POMEGRANATE—see *Punica granatum*

Plumeria frangipani

Poa arachnifera Texas bluegrass

Polygonum aubertii silver lacevine

Poncirus trifoliata hardy orange

PONCIRUS

Poncirus trifoliata (pon-SI-rus tri-fo-lee-AH-ta). **COMMON NAME:** TRIFOLIATE ORANGE, HARDY ORANGE. **TYPE:** Deciduous tree. **LOCATION:** Sun. **HEIGHT:** 15'. **SPREAD:** 15'. **SPACING:** 10'–15'. **BLOOM/FRUIT:** Fragrant spring flowers. Hard, bitter, inedible yellow-orange fruit. **PROPAGATION:** Cuttings, seed. **HABITS/CULTURE:** Easy to grow just about anywhere. **USES:** Impenetrable hedge, root stock for other citrus trees. **PROBLEMS:** Ugly and thorny. **TIPS/NOTES:** A false orange with nasty thorns. Makes a great barrier plant. Provides the root stock of most citrus production in Texas.

POPLAR, LOMBARDY—see *Populus nigra italica*

POPLAR, SILVER—see *Populus deltoides*

POPPY—see *Papaver* spp.

POPULUS

Populus deltoides (POP-ewe-lus dell-TOY-des). **COMMON NAME:** COTTONWOOD. **TYPE:** Deciduous tree. **LOCATION:** Sun. **HEIGHT:** 100'. **SPREAD:** 50'. **SPACING:** Do not plant! **BLOOM/FRUIT:** Very messy white cottonlike seeds on female trees. **PROPAGATION:** Seed, cuttings. **HABITS/CULTURE:** Very fast-growing, upright character, light-color bark, brittle wood, yellow fall color. Very easy to grow. **USES:** Shade tree. **PROBLEMS:** Short-lived, destructive root system, cotton from females, wind damage, borers, cotton root rot. This is a very dangerous tree because large limbs or the entire tree can fall on cars, houses, and people. **TIPS/NOTES:** Cotton from female

Populus deltoides cottonwood

Populus nigra 'Italica' Lombardy poplar

plants not only is ugly but can damage air conditioners. This is one tree I almost always recommend removing in urban landscapes. Native from the eastern United States to New Mexico. *Populus alba*, the silver poplar, is kind of pretty but sprouts up everywhere and becomes a huge pest by spreading from root suckers.

Populus nigra 'Italica' (POP-ewe-lus NI-gra eh-TAL-eh-kuh). **COMMON NAME:** LOMBARDY POPLAR. **TYPE:** Deciduous tree. **LOCATION:** Sun. **HEIGHT:** 70'. **SPREAD:** 10'. **SPACING:** Do not plant! **BLOOM/FRUIT:** Who cares? **PROPAGATION:** Don't! **HABITS/CULTURE:** Slender and extremely fast-growing junk tree. Very short-lived. Grows anywhere for a while. **USES:** None. **PROBLEMS:** Borers, root rot, short life, trunk canker, scale. **TIPS/NOTES:** Usually not healthy and never desirable—do not plant! Native to Europe and Asia.

Portulaca grandiflora purslane

Prosopis glandulosa mesquite

Prunus caroliniana cherry laurel

PORTULACA

Portulaca grandiflora (por-chew-LAC-ah gran-dee-FLORE-ah). **COMMON NAME:** PORTULACA, MOSS ROSE, PURSLANE. **TYPE:** Annual bedding plant. **LOCATION:** Sun. **HEIGHT:** 6". **SPREAD:** 12"–18". **SPACING:** 9"–12". **BLOOM/ FRUIT:** Roselike flowers throughout summer; many colors are available. Flowers open in the morning and close in the heat of the day. **PROPAGATION:** Seed, vegetative. **HABITS/CULTURE:** Low-growing annual with succulent stems and new flowers every day. Easy to grow in any well-drained soil. Low water and fertilizer requirements. **USES:** Colorful ground cover, summer flowers, pots, hanging baskets. **PROBLEMS:** Afternoon heat closes flowers; snails, slugs, and cutworms. **TIPS/NOTES:** Hippocrates used it as a medicine.Henry David Thoreau found it in a cornfield, boiled it, and called it a satisfactory dinner. *Portulaca oleracea*, the common purslane, comes up wild, so most people consider it a weed. Don't be so fast to pull it up, though—it's great for salads and contains high levels of Omega-3 fatty acids, vitamin E, and beta-carotene. Both are native to South America.

Potentilla verna potentilla

POSSUMHAW HOLLY—see *Ilex decidua*

POST OAK—see *Quercus virginiana*

POTATO—see *Solanum tuberosum*

POTENTILLA

Potentilla verna (poe-ten-TEE-ah VER-na). **COMMON NAME:** POTENTILLA. **TYPE:** Evergreen ground cover. **LOCATION:** Sun to shade. **HEIGHT:** 2"–6". **SPACING:** 6"–9". **BLOOM/ FRUIT:** Very small yellow flowers in summer. **PROPAGATION:** Seed, division. **HABITS/CULTURE:** Light-textured, low-growing. Resembles tiny strawberry plants. Grows in any soil, responds best to well-prepared, well-drained beds in partial shade. Moderate water and fertilizer needs. **USES:** Ground cover for small to medium-size areas. **PROBLEMS:** Red spider, rust. **TIPS/NOTES:** Plant gets a little weedy. Avoid using in large areas. Native to Europe.

POT MARIGOLD—see *Calendula officinalis*

PRICKLY ASH—See *Zanthoxylum clava-herculis*

PRICKLY PEAR CACTUS—see *Opuntia* spp.

PRIMROSE—see *Primula vulgaris*

PRIMROSE, EVENING—see *Oenothera* spp.

PRIMULA

Primula vulgaris (PRIM-you-la vul-GAH-ris). **COMMON NAME:** PRIMROSE, ENGLISH PRIMROSE. **TYPE:** Annual bedding plant. **LOCATION:** Sun to shade. **HEIGHT:** 8"–10". **SPREAD:** 8"–10". **SPACING:** 6"–8". **BLOOM/FRUIT:** Red, pink, yellow, blue, or white flowers in late winter and spring. **PROPAGATION:** Seed. **HABITS/CULTURE:** Cool-weather annual. Plant in the fall in loose, well-prepared beds. Needs good drainage. Perennializes in cooler climates. **USES:** Winter color. One of the few plants that will bloom in the shade in winter, but without the dramatic overall color display as pansies.

PROSOPIS

Prosopis glandulosa (pruh-SO-pis glan-due-LO-suh). **COMMON NAME:** MESQUITE. **TYPE:** Deciduous tree. **LOCATION:** Sun. **HEIGHT:** 25'. **SPREAD:** 30'. **SPACING:** 20'–40'. **BLOOM/FRUIT:** Subtle yellow flowers in spring, hard beanlike seed pods in fall. **PROPAGATION:** Seed. **HABITS/CULTURE:** Interesting branching, spreading character with age. Delicate, fine-textured foliage and thorns. Easy to grow in any well-drained soil. Extremely drought tolerant. Can be killed by overwatering. **USES:** Shade tree for xeriscape gardens. **PROBLEMS:** Borers, too much water. **TIPS/NOTES:** Not as hard to transplant as once thought. Nursery-grown plants are probably easier to keep alive. Best collected trees are from Corpus Christi and other high-rainfall areas. Mesquite is a legume, thus a nitrogen-fixing plant. Millions of dollars have been wasted trying to eradicate this helpful tree. Large mesquite trees are beneficial on ranches. Livestock like the shade and the quality of the grass beneath them. Mesquites become a problem only when they bush out into a thicket after being cut off at the ground. When the soil is improved, mesquite trees die out like most pioneer plants. Native from Kansas to Mexico.

PRUNUS

Prunus amygdalus (PROO-nus a-MIG-da-lus). **COMMON NAME:** ALMOND. **TYPE:** Deciduous fruit tree. **LOCATION:** Sun. **HEIGHT:** 15'–20'. **SPREAD:** 15'–20'. **SPACING:** 15'–20'. **BLOOM/FRUIT:** Blooms in late winter or early spring, often damaged by late frost. **PROPAGATION:** Seed, grafts. **HABITS/CULTURE:** Good nut production requires an extremely long, hot, dry summer. **USES:** Food. **PROBLEMS:** Quite susceptible to several diseases. Early-blooming habit. **TIPS/NOTES:** Almonds are not suited to Texas, according to the experts, because they bloom too early, so a freeze often ruins the entire crop. Flowering almond is *Prunus triloba.*

Prunus armeniaca (PROO-nus ar-MEN-ee-ah-ka). **COMMON NAME:** APRICOT. **TYPE:** Deciduous fruit tree. **LOCATION:** Sun. **HEIGHT:** 15'–20'. **SPREAD:** 15'–20'. **SPACING:** 20'–25'. **BLOOM/FRUIT:** White to light pink flowers in spring, followed by summer fruit. **PROPAGATION:** Seed, grafts. **HABITS/CULTURE:** Open-growing fruit tree with small leaves and fruit. Easy to grow in Texas but hard to get good fruit production due to early-blooming habit. **USES:** Food, ornamental. **PROBLEMS:** Brown rot, plum curculio, birds. Don't expect a crop every year—or every other year, for that matter. **TIPS/NOTES:** Probably the best varieties for Texas are 'Bryan,' 'Hungarian,' 'Bleinheim,' 'Royal,' and 'Moorepark.'

Prunus caroliniana (PROO-nus ka-ro-lin-ee-AA-nah). **COMMON NAME:** CHERRY LAUREL. **TYPE:** Evergreen tree. **LOCATION:** Sun to shade. **HEIGHT:** 25'. **SPREAD:** 15'. **SPACING:** 8'–15'. **BLOOM/FRUIT:** Small white flowers along stems in spring, followed by black fruit. **PROPAGATION:** Cuttings, seed. **HABITS/CULTURE:** Upright bushy growth, can be trimmed into tree form. Will grow in any soil. **USES:** Evergreen screen, small ornamental tree. **PROBLEMS:** Borers, cotton root rot, crown gall, chlorosis, ice storms. Not long-lived. **TIPS/NOTES:** 'Bright and Tight' is an improved compact cultivar. There are much better choices. Native from the eastern United States to Texas.

Prunus cerasifera (PROO-nus ser-as-SIFF-eh-ruh). **COMMON NAME:** PURPLE PLUM. **TYPE:** Deciduous tree. **LOCATION:** Sun to shade. **HEIGHT:** 20'. **SPREAD:** 15'. **SPACING:** 12'–15'. **BLOOM/FRUIT:** Small but showy pink spring flowers. **PROPAGATION:** Cuttings. **HABITS/CULTURE:** Small ornamental tree with bronze or purple foliage after spring flowering. Grows in any soil with good drainage. Moderate maintenance. **USES:** Ornamental garden tree, summer color. **PROBLEMS:** Borers, possible freeze damage, not long-lived. **TIPS/NOTES:** 'Krauter Vesuvius' is the most colorful and my favorite. Native to Asia.

Prunus cerasus (PROO-nus ker-RA-sus). **COMMON NAME:** SOUR CHERRY. **TYPE:** Deciduous fruit tree. **LOCATION:** Sun. **HEIGHT:** 15'–20'. **SPREAD:** 15'–20'. **SPACING:** 20'–25'. **PROPAGATION:** Cuttings. **HABITS/CULTURE:** Can be grown in the far northern part of the state. 'Montmorency' is about the only decent choice for Texas. Fruit is large, white fleshed, and tart. Not a good eating cherry although it is large-growing and quite productive. Best to use, if at all, as an ornamental tree. **USES:** Fruit and ornamental tree. **PROBLEMS:** Typical fruit tree pests.

Prunus cerasifera purple plum

Prunus mexicana Mexican plum, fall

Prunus mexicana Mexican plum, spring

Prunus mexicana
Mexican plum, summer

Prunus serotina
wild black cherry

Prunus mexicana (PROO-nus mex-ee-KAHN-ah). **COMMON NAME**: MEXICAN PLUM. **TYPE**: Deciduous tree. **LOCATION**: Sun to shade. **HEIGHT**: 25'. **SPREAD**: 25'. **SPACING**: 12'–20'. **BLOOM/FRUIT**: Fragrant white 1" flowers in spring, edible reddish purple fruit in late summer. **PROPAGATION**: Seed, cuttings. **HABITS/CULTURE**: White spring flowers and orange fall color. Exfoliating bark, graceful branching structure, thorns. Easy to grow in any soil, drought tolerant. **USES**: Specimen garden tree, understory tree, spring and fall color. **PROBLEMS**: Insects chew on the leaves occasionally but no major problems. **TIPS/NOTES**: Wonderful tree that is being used more and more. Native from Oklahoma to Mexico. Fairly difficult to transplant from the wild, best to buy container-grown plants. Another native is the low-growing *Prunus rivularis*, the hog plum.

Prunus persica (PROO-nus PURR-si-cah). **COMMON NAME**: PEACH. **TYPE**: Deciduous fruit tree. **LOCATION**: Sun. **HEIGHT**: 15'. **SPREAD**: 15'. **SPACING**: 25'–30'. **BLOOM/FRUIT**: Early spring flowers of all colors. Large fuzz-covered fruit in summer. **PROPAGATION**: Cuttings. **HABITS/CULTURE**: This is one of the fruit trees that are harder to grow in Texas, but it can be done—especially in sandy soils. **USES**: Food. **PROBLEMS**: Borers, leaf rollers, crown gall, brown rot, bacterial stem canker, stink bugs, nematodes, scale insects, plum curculio. **TIPS/NOTES**: Flowers appear on year-old red growth, so prune carefully when removing the two-year-old gray shoots. Peaches should be thinned by 50 percent in late winter for best production of large fruit. Food crop varieties for Texas include 'Demman,' 'Harvester,' 'Redskin,' 'Ranger,' 'Sentinel,' 'Spring Gold,' 'Loring,' 'Majestic,' and 'Bicentennial.' Cultivated. Check with your local extension agent or commercial producers for the best choices in your area. Ignore those who say the young trees need to be cut back to 24". Pruning to form an open-branching structure is good for fruit production but unnecessary for the health of the tree. The flowering peach is spectacular and much easier to grow than the fruiting peach.

Prunus salicina (PROO-nus sa-LICK-ih-nah). **COMMON NAME**: PLUM. **TYPE**: Deciduous fruit tree. **LOCATION**: Sun. **HEIGHT**: 20'. **SPREAD**: 15'–20' **SPACING**: 20'–25'. **BLOOM/FRUIT**: Pink flowers in spring, followed by summer fruit. **PROPAGATION**: Cuttings. **HABITS/CULTURE**: Good-looking fruit tree that can be used as an ornamental. Easy to grow in most soils. **USES**: Fruit, ornamental tree. **PROBLEMS**: Bacterial stem canker, brown rot, peach tree borer, plum curculio. **TIPS/NOTES**: Best choices for Texas include 'Methley,' 'Morris,' and 'Bruce.'

P

Prunus serotina (PROO-nus ser-oh-TEN-ah). **COMMON NAME:** CHOKE CHERRY, WILD BLACK CHERRY. **TYPE:** Deciduous tree. **LOCATION:** Sun. **HEIGHT:** 25'–50'. **SPREAD:** 25'–30'. **SPACING:** 25'–30'. **BLOOM/FRUIT:** White drooping flowers when leaves have just emerged, followed by clusters of green, red, and black cherries, which can all be on the tree at the same time. Most of the fruit ripens in late summer. **PROPAGATION:** Seed, cuttings. **HABITS/CULTURE:** Upright growth habit, shiny leaves, yellow fall color. Needs moist, well-drained soil. **USES:** Ornamental tree, high-quality wood. Food for birds and other wildlife. **PROBLEMS:** Twigs and leaves can be toxic to animals and humans. **TIPS/NOTES:** Can grow to over 100' in the deep sandy soils of East Texas.

PUERARIA
Pueraria lobata (pew-RARE-ee-ah lo-BA-ta). **COMMON NAME:** KUDZU. **TYPE:** Deciduous vine. **LOCATION:** Sun to part shade. **HEIGHT/SPREAD:** Unlimited. **SPACING:** Do not plant! **BLOOM/FRUIT:** Purple pea-shaped flowers. **PROPAGATION:** Seed, rhizomes. **HABITS/CULTURE:** Extremely fast-growing, aggressive vine that spreads quickly by underground runners. Leaves 3"–6" long on hard, slender, hairy stems. Each leaf has three dark leaflets. **USES:** Nitrogen-fixing, protein source for livestock and compost pile. **PROBLEMS:** Spreads too aggressively. **TIPS/NOTES:** Japanese farmers are growing kudzu as a high-protein food crop.

PUMPKIN—see *Cucurbita* spp.

PUNICA
Punica granatum (PEW-ni-kah gran-NAY-tum). **COMMON NAME:** POMEGRANATE. **TYPE:** Deciduous shrub. **LOCATION:** Sun to part shade. **HEIGHT:** 10'–15'. **SPREAD:** 8'–10'. **SPACING:** 6'–8'. **BLOOM/FRUIT:** Showy red-orange flowers in summer, yellow fall color. The 2"–3" fruit has a thick red skin and is filled with hundreds of juicy seeds. **PROPAGATION:** Cuttings, seed. **HABITS/CULTURE:** Upright growth on many stems. Narrow glossy leaves, bronze new growth. Grows in any soil in any location, needs full sun for the best blooms. Quite tolerant of our soil and heat. Drought tolerant. **USES:** Specimen, barrier, summer color. **PROBLEMS:** Few if any. **TIPS/NOTES:** Like other deciduous flowering shrubs, the pomegranate has not been used enough. Several improved cultivars exist. 'Albescens' is a white-flowering selection. Native to Europe and Asia.

Punica granatum pomegranate

PURPLE CONEFLOWER—see *Echinacea angustifolia*

PURPLE FOUNTAINGRASS—see *Pennisetum setaceum* 'Rubrum'

PURPLE HEART—see *Setcreasea pallida*

PURPLE JEW—see *Setcreasea pallida*

PURSLANE—see *Portulaca grandiflora*

PYRACANTHA
Pyracantha spp. (pie-ra-CAN-thuh). **COMMON NAME:** PYRACANTHA, FIRETHORN. **TYPE:** Evergreen shrub. **LOCATION:** Sun. **HEIGHT:** 3'–15'. **SPREAD:** 3'–15'. **SPACING:** 4'–8'. **BLOOM/FRUIT:** Small white flowers in spring, red or orange berries in fall and winter. **PROPAGATION:** Cuttings. **HABITS/CULTURE:** Large sprawling, thorny, vinelike shrub. Can grow free-form as a shrub or be trained to wall or fence. Likes well-prepared, well-drained beds. Good positive drainage and consistent fertilization are critical. Needs careful pruning to control growth. **USES:** Barrier, screen, or mass planting. **PROBLEMS:** Aphids, scale, lacebugs, mealybugs, red spider mites, root rot. The thorns are lethal. **TIPS/NOTES:** Dwarf forms are better for mass planting. I don't really recommend any of them. Many have died out around the state. Native to Europe and Asia.

Pueraria lobata kudzu

Pyracantha pyracantha

Pyrus calleryana Callery pear

Pyrus calleryana 'Bradford'
Bradford pear

Pyrus calleryana 'Bradford' Bradford pear

PYRUS

Pyrus calleryana (PIE-rus cal-er-ee-AH-nah). **COMMON NAME:** CALLERY PEAR, ORNAMENTAL PEAR. **TYPE:** Deciduous tree. **LOCATION:** Sun. **HEIGHT:** 25'–30'. **SPREAD:** 25'. **SPACING:** 15'–20'. **BLOOM/FRUIT:** Pure white flower clusters in early spring, followed by small, hard, round inedible fruit. **PROPAGATION:** Seed, cuttings. **HABITS/CULTURE:** More open-branching than other ornamental pears, with limbs almost perpendicular to trunk. Red fall color. Easy to grow in any soil with average maintenance and water. **USES:** Specimen ornamental tree. **PROBLEMS:** Fire blight possible but rare. Some think the thorns are a problem—I don't. **TIPS/NOTES:** This is the mother plant of the 'Bradford' pear. I like this plant better because it is more treelike and much more graceful.

Pyrus calleryana 'Bradford' (PIE-rus cal-er-ee-AH-nah). **COMMON NAME:** BRADFORD PEAR. **TYPE:** Deciduous tree. **LOCATION:** Sun. **HEIGHT:** 25'–30'. **SPREAD:** 15'–20'. **SPACING:** 10'–20'. **BLOOM/FRUIT:** White early-spring flowers, red fall color. **PROPAGATION:** Cuttings. **HABITS/CULTURE:** Upright, very symmetrical, with stiff, candelabra-like branching. Short-lived. Easy to grow in any soil with normal water and fertilization. **USES:** Specimen ornamental tree, spring flower color. **PROBLEMS:** Overused, very weak branching structure, short-lived. **TIPS/NOTES:** 'Aristocrat' is an excellent cultivar that has a more open-branching structure and long, drooping leaves. It is much more graceful than 'Bradford.' 'Capital' is a good narrow-growing cultivar. 'Whitehouse' has not had good reviews.

Pyrus pyrifolia (PIE-rus pie-rah-FOL-ee-ah). **COMMON NAME:** PEAR, ASIAN PEAR. **TYPE:** Deciduous fruit tree. **LOCATION:** Sun. **HEIGHT:** 15'–25'. **SPREAD:** 15'. **SPACING:** 15'–20'. **BLOOM/FRUIT:** Early white spring flowers, followed by summer fruit. **PROPAGATION:** Cuttings, grafting. **HABITS/CULTURE:** Easy to grow compared with other fruit trees. **USES:** Food. **PROBLEMS:** Fire blight, bacterial leaf spot. **TIPS/NOTES:** Asian pears (often called "pear apples") have very juicy round fruit. Good varieties for regular pears include 'Orient,' 'Ayers,' 'Moonglow,' and 'Kieffer,' which has the texture of sand.

Pyrus calleryana 'Aristocrat' Aristocrat pear

Q

QUEEN'S WREATH—see *Antigonon leptopus*

QUERCUS

Quercus acutissima (KWER-kus ah-cue-TISS-eh-mah).
COMMON NAME: SAWTOOTH OAK. **TYPE:** Deciduous
tree. **LOCATION:** Sun. **HEIGHT:** 50'. **SPREAD:** 40'. **SPACING:**
20'–40'. **BLOOM/FRUIT:** Rust-color male flowers hang from
terminal growth in early spring. Female flowers bloom
singly or in small clusters. Fruits are acorns. **PROPAGA-
TION:** Seed, cuttings. **HABITS/CULTURE:** Very fast-growing
oak with golden brown fall color. Leaves stay on tree all
winter. Long, narrow, serrated leaves. Excellent in deep
soils. Tends to develop iron deficiency and turn yellow in
alkaline soils, especially if rock is near the surface. **USES:**
Shade tree. **PROBLEMS:** Chlorosis in highly alkaline areas.
Wet feet. **TIPS/NOTES:** Excellent fast-growing shade tree
in deep-soil areas. Native to the Orient.

Quercus macrocarpa bur oak

Quercus acutissima sawtooth oak   *Quercus macrocarpa* bur oak

Quercus macrocarpa (KWER-kus mack-row-CAR-puh).
COMMON NAME: BUR OAK, MOSSY OAK, CUP OAK.
TYPE: Deciduous tree. **LOCATION:** Sun. **HEIGHT:** 80'.
SPREAD: 80'. **SPACING:** 20'–50'. **BLOOM/FRUIT:** Rust-color
male flowers hang from terminal growth in early spring.
Female flowers bloom singly or in small clusters. Fruits
are large golf-ball-size acorns. **PROPAGATION:** Seed, cuttings. **HABITS/CULTURE:** Spreading, branching structure,
with large leaves, large acorns, yellow fall color. Thick,
corklike stems, branches, and trunk. Fast-growing oak.
Can grow to 150' in deep soil. Easy to grow in any well-
drained soil, including extremely rocky soil. Drought
tolerant. Grows almost anywhere in the United States.
USES: Handsome and hardy shade tree. **PROBLEMS:** Few if
any. **TIPS/NOTES:** Possibly my favorite shade tree. One of
the longest-lived oaks. Native to Texas, Oklahoma, and
the eastern United States.

Quercus muhlenbergii (KWER-kus mew-lin-BERG-ee-
eye). **COMMON NAME:** CHINKAPIN OAK. **TYPE:** Deciduous tree. **LOCATION:** Sun. **HEIGHT:** 80'. **SPREAD:** 80'. **SPAC-
ING:** 20'–50'. **BLOOM/FRUIT:** Rust-color male flowers hang
from terminal growth in early spring. Female flowers
bloom singly or in small clusters. Fruits are dark purple

Quercus muhlenbergii chinkapin oak

Quercus muhlenbergii
chinkapin oak

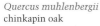
Quercus nigra water oak

Quercus phellos willow oak

Quercus texana Texas red oak

one-seeded acorns. **PROPAGATION:** Seed, cuttings. **HABITS/CULTURE:** Irregularly spreading, relatively fast growth, yellow-brown fall color. Grows in any soil, sensitive to poor drainage, drought tolerant. **USES:** Shade tree. **PROBLEMS:** Wet feet, transplant difficulties. **TIPS/NOTES:** Easily confused with *Quercus michauxii,* swamp chestnut oak, which does not do well in alkaline soils and has rounded lobes in contrast to the chinkapin's sharp-pointed edges. Buy nursery-grown rather than field-collected trees. Native to Texas, Oklahoma, and the eastern United States.

Quercus nigra water oak

Quercus nigra (KWER-kus NI-gra). **COMMON NAME:** WATER OAK. **TYPE:** Deciduous tree. **LOCATION:** Sun. **HEIGHT:** 50'–80'. **SPREAD:** 30'–50'. **SPACING:** 20'–50'. **BLOOM/FRUIT:** Dull-looking spring flowers, followed by acorns that mature in the fall. **PROPAGATION:** Seed. **HABITS/CULTURE:** Grows best in moist, deep, acid soils. Dark green spoon-shaped leaves are almost evergreen in the southern half of the state. **USES:** Shade tree. **PROBLEMS:** Doesn't like alkaline soil, hates soil in white-rock areas. **TIPS/NOTES:** *Quercus phellos,* willow oak, requires almost the exact same conditions. Both are beautiful trees. Native to East Texas.

Quercus shumardii or *texana* (KWER-kus shoe-MARD-ee-eye tex-AN-ah). **COMMON NAME:** SHUMARD OAK, TEXAS RED OAK. **TYPE:** Deciduous tree. **LOCATION:** Sun. **HEIGHT:** 80'. **SPREAD:** 80'. **SPACING:** 20'–50'. **BLOOM/FRUIT:** Rust-color male flowers hang from terminal growth in early spring. Female flowers bloom singly or in small clusters. Fruits are one-seeded acorns. **PROPAGATION:** Seed, cuttings. **HABITS/CULTURE:** Fast-growing, graceful, upright, and spreading, typically with no central stem. Fall color varies from brown to yellow to red. Sometimes hard to establish. Must have excellent drainage in any soil. Drought tolerant. **USES:** Shade tree, fall color. **PROBLEMS:** Borers, scale, wet feet. **TIPS/NOTES:** Red oak has always been one of my favorite trees, but it's the subject of a multimillion dollar tree problem. The problem is buying the right plant. Only two kinds of red oak will work in alkaline soils, *Quercus shumardii* and *Quercus texana.* Pin oak (*Quercus palustris*) and crossbreeds of southern red oak (*Quercus falcata*) and others are being sold in great quantities and will not survive here. Chisos oak (*Quercus gravesii*) is the smallest of the native Texas red oaks and grows wild in Big Bend. Its fall color is not outstanding when grown in other parts of Texas. Texas red oak is also sold as *Quercus buckleyii.*

Quercus shumardii Shumard oak

Quercus gravesii Chisos oak

Quercus falcata Southern red oak

Quercus stellata post oak

Quercus palustris pin oak

Quercus sinuata var. *sinuata* Durrand oak

Quercus virginiana live oak

Quercus sinuata var. *sinuata* (KWER-kus sin-you-AH-tah). **COMMON NAME:** DURRAND OAK. **TYPE:** Deciduous tree. **LOCATION:** Sun. **HEIGHT:** 60'. **SPREAD:** 40'. **SPACING:** 20'–50'. **BLOOM/FRUIT:** Rust-color male flowers hang from terminal growth in early spring. Female flowers bloom singly or in small clusters. Fruits are one-seeded acorns. **PROPAGATION:** Seed, cuttings. **HABITS/CULTURE:** Upright, open-branching structure with dense rounded top, smallish leaves with rounded lobes. Handsome tree. Reddish fall color. Easy to grow in any well-drained soil. Drought tolerant, doesn't mind rocky soil. **USES:** Shade tree. **PROBLEMS:** Few if any. Not widely available in the nursery trade at this time. **TIPS/NOTES:** The close relative *Quercus sinuata* var. *breviloba*, Bigelow oak, is a small-growing 12'–15' tree with pale flaky bark, orange fall color, and interesting branching. Bigelow is native to the north-central area of Texas. Durrand is native to Waco and Central Texas.

Quercus virginiana (KWER-kus ver-gin-ee-AN-ah). **COMMON NAME:** LIVE OAK. **TYPE:** Evergreen tree. **LOCATION:** Sun. **HEIGHT:** 50'. **SPREAD:** 60'. **SPACING:** 20'–60'. **BLOOM/FRUIT:** Rust-color male flowers hang from terminal growth in early spring. Female flowers bloom singly or in small clusters. Fruits are one-seeded black acorns. **PROPAGATION:** Seed, cuttings. **HABITS/CULTURE:** Spreading ever-

Quercus sinuata var. *sinuata* Durrand oak

Q

Quercus marilandica blackjack oak

Quercus graciliformis evergreen oak

Quercus virginiana live oak

Quercus mohriana Mohr oak

green shade tree. Small glossy leaves vary in shape and size. Single and multitrunk structure. Easy to establish, hard to maintain—needs regular pruning. Grows in any soil. Relatively drought tolerant. Needs thinning when transplanted from the wild. **USES:** Shade tree, evergreen background. **PROBLEMS:** Aphids, ice damage, galls, oak wilt, high maintenance, almost continuous leaf drop. **TIPS/ NOTES:** Freezes during severe winters in North Texas. Looks its worst in spring when new leaves are kicking off the old leaves. Native to South, Central, and West Texas and the southeastern United States. *Quercus fusiformis* is the drought-tolerant and cold-hardy native live oak. Other Texas oaks include the following:

Blackjack oak—*Quercus marilandica.* Native that resents people's intrusions. Leaves look like clubs, bark is almost black and deeply fissured.

Evergreen oak—*Quercus graciliformis.* Lovely trees with shiny leaves. Sometimes called graceful oak or slender oak. Should be used more often. These are true evergreens, but not as evergreen as the live oak.

Lacey oak—*Quercus glaucoides.* Blue-green mature foliage, deciduous, native, grows to 30', drought tolerant, peach-colored new growth and fall color, likes all soils, easy to grow, very narrow willowlike leaves.

Quercus glaucoides Lacey oak

Quercus polymorpha
Monterrey oak

Quercus pungens var. pungens
sandpaper oak

Quercus pungens var. vaseyana Vasey oak

Laurel oak—*Quercus laurifolia.* Also called Darlington oak. Evergreen, native to southeast Texas. Best in East Texas sandy soils.

Mexican blue oak—*Quercus oblongifolia.* Native to far West Texas. Deep blue evergreen foliage. Sounds like a great tree if we can get some growers interested.

Mohr oak—*Quercus mohriana.* A shin oak that grows to about 20'. Leaves are shiny green on top, fuzzy white on the underside. Drought tolerant, tends to sucker into groves. Beautiful small tree.

Monterrey oak—*Quercus polymorpha.* Leather-leafed, native from Mexico into South Texas. Freeze damage is the only worry, but mine lived in Dallas through several hard winters.

Pin oak—*Quercus palustris.* When planted in Texas, it usually turns bright yellow unless in acid soil. It has a very straight trunk, a pointed top, limbs that grow horizontally, and lower limbs that droop. Often confused with red oak, can be a very expensive mistake to plant in alkaline soils. When it cross-breeds with reds, the hybrids are also a problem.

Post oak—*Quercus stellata.* Slow-growing native oak that hates people—well, their activities, anyway. Thousands of these die every year in new developments because they can't stand to have their environment changed. To keep them alive, don't water, don't fertilize, don't thin out, don't change the grade under them, and don't remove the native undergrowth.

Sandpaper oak—*Quercus pungens* var. *pungens.* Very similar to the Vasey oak. Gray-green leaves slightly larger than those of Vasey oak. Native to far West Texas. One of the shin oaks.

Shin oak. Generic name for all the small-scale oaks like Vasey, Lacey, Mohr, and sandpaper.

Southern red oak—*Quercus falcata.* A large-growing, graceful oak that is often confused with Shumard red oak. The southern red oak has long droopy leaves, not much fall color, and will not grow in alkaline soil. It must have sandy acid soil.

Spanish oak—Common name for the Texas, southern, or Shumard red oak.

Swamp chestnut oak—*Quercus michauxii.* Tall-growing shade tree for deep, sandy, acid soils. Its leaves are similar to but wider than those of the chestnut oak. Unlike chestnut oak, it will not grow well in high-calcium, alkaline soils.

Vasey Oak—*Quercus pungens* var. *vaseyana.* Compact, scaly-bark native oak with small leaves that are gently lobed and wavy-edged. Almost evergreen, has the smallest leaf of all the shin oaks.

White oak—*Quercus alba.* Light gray flaky bark. Grows to 80' or more in deep soils, dislikes the white rock of North Texas. Rounded lobes on leaves that otherwise look like those of red oaks. Grows best in the sandy acid soil of East Texas. Beautiful red-orange fall color.

Willow oak—*Quercus phellos.* Will grow well in North Texas only in deep acid soils. Likes East Texas and Houston soils best.

QUINCE, FLOWERING—see *Chaenomeles japonica*

RABBITEYE BLUEBERRIES—see *Vaccinium ashei*

RAIN LILY—see *Zephyranthes* spp.

RANUNCULUS
Ranunculus asiaticus (rah-NUN-kew-lus a-she-AT-ti-kus). **COMMON NAME:** RANUNCULUS, ASIATIC BUT-TERCUP. **TYPE:** Perennial tuber used as an annual. **LOCA-TION:** Sun. **HEIGHT:** 12"–15". **SPREAD:** 6"–8". **SPACING:** 5"–6". **BLOOM/FRUIT:** White, pink, red, and yellow flowers. **PROPAGATION:** Tubers. **HABITS/CULTURE:** Strong upright stems, with extremely colorful flowers in early spring. Tubers should be planted 2" deep in the fall in South Texas, in the late winter in North Texas. Doesn't return well, best planted each year and treated as an annual. **USES:** Early spring color. **PROBLEMS:** Aphids. **TIPS/NOTES:** Plant the pointed end of the tubers down.

Ranunculus asiaticus ranunculus   Photograph by August A. DeHertogh

RAPHANUS
Raphanus sativus (RAY-fa-nus sa-TEEV-us). **COMMON NAME:** RADISH. **TYPE:** Annual vegetable. **LOCATION:** Sun. **HEIGHT:** 4"–8". **SPREAD:** 4". **SPACING:** 1"–2". **BLOOM/FRUIT:** Insignificant. **PROPAGATION:** Seed. **HABITS/CULTURE:** Ger-mination in 4–6 days at 68 degrees. Likes cool soil. Plant 1/2" deep. Swollen root is the edible part of the plant. **USES:** Food. **PROBLEMS:** Slugs, wireworms, cutworms. **TIPS/NOTES:** Fastest of all vegetables to grow into edible size. Excellent for children to grow.

RATIBIDA
Ratibida columnaris (rah-TIB-eh-dah kahl-um-NARE-us). **COMMON NAME:** MEXICAN HAT. **TYPE:** Perennial wild-flower. **LOCATION:** Sun to part shade. **HEIGHT:** 18"–36". **SPREAD:** 18"–24". **SPACING:** 12"–18". **BLOOM/FRUIT:** Red, yellow, or orange 2" flowers from May until frost. **PROPA-GATION:** Seed, transplants. **HABITS/CULTURE:** Taprooted perennial wildflower, evergreen in mild winters. Easy to grow in most soils. Seems to adapt to dry, rocky slopes as well as moist, low areas. Flowers emerge from rosettes of fernlike foliage. **USES:** Wildflower. **PROBLEMS:** Can become a pest, especially on grazing land. Once established, it's hard to get rid of. **TIPS/NOTES:** Good landscape wildflower. Usually doesn't bloom until the second year.

Ratibida columnaris Mexican hat

REDBUD, EASTERN—see *Cercis canadensis*

RED GILIA—see *Ipomopsis rubra*

RED OAK—see *Quercus shumardii* or *texana* and *Quercus virginiana*

REDWOOD, DAWN—see *Metasequoia glyptostroboides*

RED YUCCA—see *Yucca parviflora*

RETAMA—see *Parkinsonia aculeata*

RHAMNUS
Rhamnus caroliniana (RAM-nus care-oh-lin-ee-AN-ah). **COMMON NAME:** CAROLINA BUCKTHORN, INDIAN CHERRY. **TYPE:** Deciduous shrub or small tree. **LOCATION:** Sun to shade. **HEIGHT:** 15'. **SPREAD:** 15'. **SPACING:** 4'–10'. **BLOOM/FRUIT:** Small inconspicuous blooms in late spring or early summer. Red berries in late summer, ripening to blue-black in the fall. **PROPAGATION:** Seed, cuttings. **HAB-ITS/CULTURE:** Bushy shrub or small tree. Large glossy leaves, yellow-orange fall color. Can grow to 30'. Easy to grow in any soil with good drainage. Drought tolerant. **USES:** Specimen understory plant, ornamental tree, back-ground plant. **PROBLEMS:** Few if any. **TIPS/NOTES:** This is a beautiful plant that should be used more.

Rhamnus caroliniana Carolina buckthorn

Rhapiolepis indica Indian hawthorn

Rhododendron azalea

Rhapiolepis indica
Indian hawthorn

RHAPIOLEPIS

Rhapiolepis indica (rah-pee-oh-LEP-is IN-dee-kah). **COMMON NAME:** INDIAN HAWTHORN. **TYPE:** Evergreen shrub. **LOCATION:** Sun to light shade. **HEIGHT:** 2'–5'. **SPREAD:** 3'–5'. **SPACING:** 2'–3'. **BLOOM/FRUIT:** Showy white or pink spring flowers. Blue-black berries in fall. **PROPAGATION:** Cuttings. **HABITS/CULTURE:** A small evergreen shrub, although varieties vary in size. New varieties seem to be healthier, but all like well-prepared, well-drained beds. **USES:** Mass foundation planting, low border, spring color. **PROBLEMS:** Leaf fungus, fire blight. **TIPS/NOTES:** *Rhapiolepis ovata*, roundleaf hawthorn, is a large white-flowering variety. 'Clara' and 'Snow' are compact white-flowering varieties. 'Spring Rapture' is a dark pink. 'Jack Evans' and 'Enchantress' are pink. Native to Korea and Japan.

RHODODENDRON

Rhododendron spp. (row-do-DEN-dron). **COMMON NAME:** AZALEA. **TYPE:** Evergreen shrub. **LOCATION:** Shade to part shade. **HEIGHT:** 3'–6' **SPREAD:** 3'–6'. **SPACING:** 3'–6'. **BLOOM/FRUIT:** Spectacular spring colors in red, white, pink, lavender, and all sorts of combinations. **PROPAGATION:** Cuttings. **HABITS/CULTURE:** Dramatic, showy, fibrous-rooted shrubs. Some varieties have attractive evergreen foliage, others are deciduous. Must be grown in special beds of mostly organic material—a 50-50 mix of shredded hardwood bark and compost is good. Add 1 lb. each of sulfur, copperas, and Epsom salts per cubic yard of mix. A small amount of native soil, 2–5 lbs. per cubic yard, should also be added. **USES:** Evergreen hedge or mass, spring color. **PROBLEMS:** Extremely costly, high-maintenance plant. Summer heat, chlorosis, poor drainage, scale, spider mites. **TIPS/NOTES:** Indica azaleas such as 'Fielder's White' and 'Pride of Mobile' can take more sun and are more open-

Rhododendron rhododendron

growing. Kurume azaleas such as 'Hino Crimson,' 'Snow,' and 'Coral Bells' are tighter-growing and need more shade. Gumpos are dwarf types and bloom later than other azaleas. Huge numbers of species, varieties, and cultivars are native to various parts of the world. The native Texas azaleas grow in the bogs and low woodlands of southeast Texas.

Rhododendron spp. (row-do-DEN-dron). **COMMON NAME:** RHODODENDRON. **TYPE:** Evergreen shrub. **LOCATION:** Shade to part shade. **HEIGHT:** 3'–8' **SPREAD:** 4'–8'. **SPACING:** 3'–7'. **BLOOM/FRUIT:** Large showy flowers of red, pink, white, purple, yellow, and orange in spring. **PROPAGATION:** Cuttings. **HABITS/CULTURE:** Leaves are larger and darker than those of azalea. There are at least 800 species and 5,000 hybrids of this long-lived shrub. Some are tiny plants just inches tall, others grow to be 50'–60' tall. Prefer highly organic acid soil and cool, moist climates. Growing them in most of Texas is tricky. Plant them in a 50-50 mix of compost and shredded bark or other coarse material. Drainage is critical. Shade, especially from afternoon sun, is also important. Avoid dense, heavy shade. Feed with organic fertilizer only. **USES:** Evergreen hedge, background plant, mass. Spring flower display. **PROBLEMS:** Heat, low humidity. Avoid hot locations with reflected light. Acid-treating the irrigation water is needed in some areas. **TIPS/**

NOTES: Do not plant near shallow-rooted trees. Root competition will be a problem. Native to Asia, North America, the East Indies, and the lowland bogs of southeast Texas.

RHODOPHIALA

Rhodophiala bifida (roe-doe-FEE-ah-luh BIF-ih-duh). **COMMON NAME:** OXBLOOD LILY, SCHOOLHOUSE LILY. **TYPE:** Perennial flower. **LOCATION:** Sun to part shade. **HEIGHT:** 10"–12". **SPREAD:** 24"–36". **SPACING:** 6"–8". **BLOOM/FRUIT:** Several trumpetlike flowers per stem in early fall. **PROPAGATION:** Bulbs. **HABITS/CULTURE:** Looks like a small red amaryllis. Well adapted and easy to grow in sandy or clay soils. Foliage growth and flowering are usually triggered by a good rain in August or September. Transplant bulbs in the fall. **USES:** Fall color in large drifts or borders.

RHUS

Rhus aromatica (RUSE err-oh-MAT-eh-kuh). **COMMON NAME:** AROMATIC SUMAC, FRAGRANT SUMAC, SKUNKBUSH. **TYPE:** Deciduous shrub. **LOCATION:** Sun to part shade. **HEIGHT:** 4'–6'. **SPREAD:** 5'–7'. **SPACING:** 3'–4'. **BLOOM/FRUIT:** Yellow flowers in early spring, followed by red berries in the fall. **PROPAGATION:** Cuttings, seeds. **HABITS/CULTURE:** Leaves have three leaflets, fragrant when crushed. Plant will sucker and spread but not excessively. Red-orange fall color. Can grow as high as 12'. **CULTURE:** Grows in any soil with good drainage, even in rock. Fibrous roots, easy to transplant. **USES:** Naturalizing an area, attracting birds. **PROBLEMS:** None. **TIPS/NOTES:** A good place to see this and other natives is the nature trail at Mountain View College in Dallas. 'Gro-Low' is a compact form. 'Green Glove' is a larger cultivar. Native from the eastern United States to Texas.

Rhus copallina (RUSE ko-pal-LINE-ah). **COMMON NAME:** FLAMELEAF SUMAC. **TYPE:** Deciduous shrub or small tree. **LOCATION:** Sun to shade. **HEIGHT:** 15'. **SPREAD:** 15'. **SPACING:** 5'–10'. **BLOOM/FRUIT:** Greenish white terminal flower clusters. Seed clusters in winter. **PROPAGATION:** Cuttings, seed. **HABITS/CULTURE:** Open-growing. The top of the leaf is dark. Leafy wings along stems. Brilliant red fall color. Spreads by suckers. Easy to grow in any soil with very little water. Can be bare-rooted. **USES:** Specimen garden tree or background mass. **PROBLEMS:** None except overwatering. Overwatering is sure to kill. **TIPS/NOTES:** *Rhus lanceolata* is prairie flameleaf sumac. Both are native to Texas.

Rhus glabra (RUSE GLA-bra). **COMMON NAME:** SMOOTH SUMAC. **TYPE:** Deciduous shrub. **LOCATION:** Sun to part shade. **HEIGHT:** 10'. **SPREAD:** 10'. **SPACING:** 4'–8'. **BLOOM/FRUIT:** Large, dense, greenish flower clusters in early summer, fruit matures by fall and remains on bare stems through the winter. **PROPAGATION:** Cuttings, seed. **HABITS/CULTURE:** Thick stems with foliage at ends, spreads by suckers from the mother plant. Excellent orange to red fall color. Unbelievably durable and widely adaptable. Can by transplanted easily—even bare-rooted. Can take more water than the other sumacs. **USES:** Background,

Rhus aromatica skunkbush

Rhus glabra smooth sumac

Rhus copallina flameleaf sumac

Rhus radicans poison ivy

Rhus virens evergreen sumac

Rivina humilis pigeonberry

mass, natural areas, fall color. **PROBLEMS:** Spreads aggressively, can become a pest. **TIPS/NOTES:** 'Lancinata' is a cutleaf cultivar that is almost fernlike. Native to Texas.

Rhus radicans (RUSE RAD-ih-cans). **COMMON NAME:** POISON IVY. **TYPE:** Deciduous vine. **LOCATION:** Sun or shade. **HEIGHT/SPREAD:** Unlimited. **PROPAGATION:** Seed. **HABITS/CULTURE:** Very tall-growing, spreading vine. Red berries, beautiful red fall color. **USES:** None—noxious weed. **PROBLEMS:** Contact causes severe skin rash. Breathing the smoke from burning plants can be extremely harmful and even cause death. **TIPS/NOTES:** Dig out to remove. The least toxic chemical that works is Finale. *Rhus diversiloba*, poison oak, is very similar but not common in Texas.

Rhus virens (RUSE VIE-rens). **COMMON NAME:** EVERGREEN SUMAC. **TYPE:** Evergreen shrub. **LOCATION:** Sun. **HEIGHT:** 7'–10'. **SPREAD:** 7'–10'. **BLOOM/FRUIT:** White or greenish flowers in summer. **PROPAGATION:** Cuttings, seed. **HABITS/CULTURE:** Bushy growth. Rounded leaves, unlike those of other sumacs. Red berries in summer. Reddish new leaves, green summer color, reddish purple fall color. Drought tolerant and carefree. May need some protection from winter winds in North Texas. Overwatering is sure to kill. **USES:** Specimen, mass planting, natural areas. **PROBLEMS:** Possible freeze damage. **TIPS/NOTES:** Native to Central Texas. Deer love this plant.

RICE-PAPER PLANT—see *Tetrapanax papyriferus*

RICINUS

Ricinus communis (RI-ki-nus kom-EW-nis). **COMMON NAME:** CASTOR BEAN. **TYPE:** Annual foliage plant. **LOCATION:** Sun. **HEIGHT:** 6'–15'. **SPACING:** 6'–8' **SPREAD:** 3'–4'. **BLOOM/FRUIT:** Clusters of small white flowers, followed by prickly husks with shiny black seeds. **PROPAGATION:** Seed. **HABITS/CULTURE:** Easy to grow in any soil, likes hot weather. Very large, tropical-looking foliage. **USES:** Bold texture, tall and quick-growing, inexpensive screen. **PROBLEMS:** Seeds are highly poisonous. Foliage and stems are also toxic and can cause severe skin irritation. **TIPS/NOTES:** Pinch off burrlike seed capsules to prevent seed from maturing.

Ricinus communis castor bean

Robinia pseudoacacia black locust

RIVINA

Rivina humilis (rah-VYE-nah HEW-muh-liss). **COMMON NAME:** PIGEONBERRY. **TYPE:** Perennial ground cover. **LOCATION:** Shade. **HEIGHT:** 1'–2'. **SPREAD:** 3'. **SPACING:** 12". **BLOOM/FRUIT:** Pink and white 2" spikes during warm weather. Red berries from spring though fall. **PROPAGATION:** Seed, cuttings. **HABITS/CULTURE:** Easy to grow in shade in well-drained soil. Excellent tall ground cover for otherwise hard-to-grow spots. Pink and white flowers and red berries are on the plant at the same time throughout the summer. **USES:** Birds love the fruit. Colorful ground cover in shade. **PROBLEMS:** Few if any. **TIPS/NOTES:** Looks like miniature poke salad.

ROADSIDE ASTER—see Weeds

ROBINIA

Robinia pseudoacacia (row-BIN-ee-ah SUE-doe-ah-KAY-see-ah). **COMMON NAME:** BLACK LOCUST. **TYPE:** Deciduous tree. **LOCATION:** Sun. **HEIGHT:** 40'. **SPREAD:** 40'. **SPACING:** 20'–30'. **BLOOM/FRUIT:** White flowers in spring. **PROPAGATION:** Seed. **HABITS/CULTURE:** Upright and spreading, with small oval leaflets on large compound leaves. Yellow fall color. Fast-growing and drought tolerant. Easy to grow in any soil. **USES:** Shade tree. **PROBLEMS:** Few if any but not extremely long-lived. **TIPS/NOTES:** Black locust is a beautiful tree that should be used in more small gardens and courtyards. Native to Texas and central United States.

R

Rosa antique rose

Rosa wild rose

Rosa banksiae Lady Banks rose

ROCK ROSE—see *Pavonia lasiopetala*

ROSA

Rosa spp. (ROW-sa). **COMMON NAME:** ANTIQUE ROSE, OLD ROSE, HERITAGE ROSE. **TYPE:** Perennial shrub. **LOCATION:** Sun. **HEIGHT:** 12"–12'. **SPREAD:** 24"–8'. **SPACING:** 36"–8'. **BLOOM/FRUIT:** Smaller and more fragrant summer flowers than most of the modern hybrid roses. Usually in pastel colors of white, rose, pink, and lavender. **PROPAGATION:** Cuttings. **HABITS/CULTURE:** Old roses vary from big bushes and low ground covers to large climbing vines. They are better for landscape use than the modern hybrids because they are prettier plants, more fragrant, and much easier to maintain. Use lots of organic material as well as sulphur and magnesium in the bed preparation. Use the same watering and fertilization program as for your other plantings. **USES:** Vines, perennial color, mass, fragrance, nostalgia. **PROBLEMS:** Black spot, powdery mildew, thrips, aphids. **TIPS/NOTES:** Many great choices are available. *Rosa wichuraiana* 'Porteriifolia' is an almost indestructible low-growing, ground-cover type. 'Cecile Brunner,' 'Betty Prior,' 'Marie Pavié,' 'Old Blush,' and 'Elsie Poulsen' are carefree choices. 'Petite Pink Scotch,' a miniature rose with lovely, delicate foliage, forms a symmetrical 3' mound. In general, species roses have Latin names, usually bloom only in spring, and are exceptionally vigorous and healthy. China roses are the parents of the hybrid tea roses, bloom in the fall as well as the spring, and have a fruity fragrance, peppery leaves, and a bushy shape. Noisettes are fragrantly scented hybrid climbers, developed in Charleston, South Carolina, about 1810. Bourbons were developed on the island of Réunion (once known as Ile de Bourbon) off the coast of Madagascar. They are shrubby and have heavy, intensely fragrant flowers full of lots of petals. Polyanthas are from a cross between *Rosa multiflora* and a China rose. They are bushy and ever-blooming but not strongly scented. Wichuraiana roses are native to China, Korea, and Japan. They were introduced into North America in 1891. Wild native Texas roses can be used for the most carefree, drought-tolerant, and pest-resistant rose choice. The 'Music Rose' is a very fragrant old rose that is now commercially available.

Rosa banksiae (ROW-sa BANK-see-ee). **COMMON NAME:** LADY BANKS ROSE. **TYPE:** Semi-evergreen vine. **LOCATION:** Sun. **HEIGHT:** 10'–15'. **SPREAD:** 10'–15'. **SPACING:** 8'–10'. **BLOOM/FRUIT:** Small yellow or white flowers in spring. **PROPAGATION:** Cuttings. **HABITS/CULTURE:** Massive, free-flowing, bushy vine with arching shoots. Small yellow or white flowers. Likes even moisture but is fairly drought tolerant. Tough, grows in any soil, likes well-prepared soil best. Low maintenance. **USES:** Vining rose for walls, fences, overhead structures. **PROBLEMS:** Very fast-growing, regular pruning needed to control aggressive growth. **TIPS/NOTES:** This plant needs plenty of room—not good for small garden spaces. Native to China. 'Alba Plena,' the white-flowering cultivar, is not as cold tolerant as the yellow variety.

ROSE, MOSS—see *Portulaca* spp.

ROSE MALLOW—see *Hibiscus* spp.

ROSMARINUS

Rosmarinus officinalis (roz-mah-RINE-us oh-fis-ih-NAH-lis). **COMMON NAME:** ROSEMARY. **TYPE:** Evergreen herb. **LOCATION:** Sun to part shade. **HEIGHT:** 1'–4'. **SPREAD:** 4'. **SPACING:** 12"–24". **BLOOM/FRUIT:** Light blue, white, or pink flowers in early spring, then intermittently all season. Blooms all winter in a mild season. **PROPAGATION:** Stem cuttings, transplants. Seeds are difficult. **HABITS/CULTURE:** Upright and creeping varieties available. Low-growing, spreading herb. Leaves are velvety and similar to thick pine needles, fragrantly resinous to the touch. Light blue flowers. Likes well-drained, slightly alkaline soil. Drought tolerant once established. Plant in a well-prepared bed with excellent drainage. The safest place is at the base of a south-facing wall in a spot protected from winter winds. Full sun is ideal, will tolerate some shade. **USES:** Ground cover, ornamental shrub, summer flowers, herb for cooking. Rosemary, like garlic, announces its presence with a bold fragrance. To use, first cut young branches with soft growth. Remove the needlelike leaves from the woody stems. If any liquid is in your recipe, you may blend the leaves in the liquid. Or you may cut the leaves with scissors or a knife and mix them thoroughly into oil, butter,

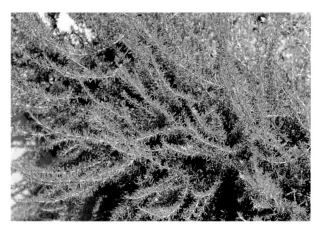

Rosmarinus officinalis rosemary

or other ingredients. **PROBLEMS:** Freeze damage in the northern part of the state. **TIPS/NOTES:** *Rosemary officinalis* 'Arp' is said to be the most cold-hardy shrub type. Some herbalists are skeptical, however. 'Lockwood de Forest' and 'Prostratus' are low-growing forms. Native to the Mediterranean. Rosemary is a traditional symbol of remembrance, friendship, and love. Oil of rosemary is reputed to benefit rheumatism, sores, eczema, bruises, and wounds. Rosemary in bathwater stimulates blood circulation. It's a wonderful flavor in many foods and stimulates digestion as well as the liver and gall bladder.

ROSEMARY—see *Rosmarinus officinalis*

ROSE OF SHARON—see *Hibiscus syriacus*

RUBUS
Rubus spp. (ROO-bus). **COMMON NAME:** BLACKBERRY. **TYPE:** Perennial berry. **LOCATION:** Sun. **HEIGHT:** 6'–8'. **SPREAD:** 3'–8' or more. **SPACING:** 3'. **BLOOM/FRUIT:** White flowers in early spring, followed by red and then purple-black fruit. **PROPAGATION:** Root division. **HABITS/CULTURE:** Easy-to-grow fruit crop for Texas, although the berries will not have a good flavor in unbalanced alkaline soils. Self-pollinating. **USES:** Food. **PROBLEMS:** Anthracnose, redneck cane borer. Can spread and become a pest, can also form double blossoms or rosettes. **TIPS/NOTES:** Good varieties for Texas include 'Brazos,' 'Cheyenne,' 'Rosborough,' 'Womack,' 'Choctaw,' and the thornless 'Navajo.' Raspberries (*Rubus idaeus*), which are also self-pollinating, are very difficult to grow in Texas. They need sandy acid soil and don't like hot summers. 'Dorman Red' is the best choice.

RUDBECKIA
Rudbeckia hirta (rude-BECK-ee-ah HIR-ta). **COMMON NAME:** GLORIOSA DAISY, CONEFLOWER, BLACK-EYED SUSAN. **TYPE:** Perennial wildflower. **LOCATION:** Sun to part shade. **HEIGHT:** 18"–3'. **SPREAD:** 18"–24". **SPACING:** 12"–18". **BLOOM/FRUIT:** Fuzzy foliage, yellow daisy-like flowers with dark brown centers from June into September. **PROPAGATION:** Seed. **HABITS/CULTURE:** Grows well in dry soil but responds more favorably to moist,

well-prepared beds. Needs good drainage. **USES:** Summer flowers, perennial garden, low water areas. **PROBLEMS:** Few if any. **TIPS/NOTES:** Native to Texas. *Rudbeckia* 'Goldstrum' is an improved variety that perennializes very well. *Rudbeckia nitida* is a dramatic taller-growing species that can be planted from seed or pots.

RUELLIA
Ruellia spp. (roo-ELL-ee-a). **COMMON NAME:** WILD PETUNIA, MEXICAN PETUNIA. **TYPE:** Perennial bedding plant. **LOCATION:** Sun to part shade. **HEIGHT:** 18"–30". **SPREAD:** 36" and more. **SPACING:** 12"–18". **BLOOM/FRUIT:** Lavender petunia-like summer flowers. **PROPAGATION:** Seed, division. Seeds explode when watered. **HABITS/CULTURE:** Invasive, easy-to-grow perennial. Needs moisture, but will grow in almost any soil. **USES:** Large informal settings, perennial color. **PROBLEMS:** Invasive. **TIPS/NOTES:** Wilts easily without ample moisture. *Ruellia nudiflora* is the Texas native. *Ruellia brittoniana* 'Katie's' is a low-growing strap-leafed variety. It freezes more frequently in the northern part of the state.

RYEGRASS—see *Lolium* spp.

Rudbeckia hirta gloriosa daisy

Ruellia wild petunia

Sabal mexicana Texas palm

Salix matsudana 'Tortuosa' corkscrew willow

SABAL

Sabal mexicana (SAY-bahl mex-ee-CAN-ah). **COMMON NAME:** TEXAS PALM. **TYPE:** Evergreen tree. **LOCATION:** Sun. **HEIGHT:** 40'–50'. **SPACING:** 10'–15'. **BLOOM/FRUIT:** Large clusters of showy flowers on mature trees. **PROPAGATION:** Seed. **HABITS/CULTURE:** Single straight trunk, large fan-shaped leaves, large root system. Hard to transplant, new plants need plenty of water to get established. **USES:** Specimen tree, accent plant. **PROBLEMS:** Freeze damage in the northern half of the state. *Trachycarpus fortunei,* windmill palm, is a fairly hardy introduction to Texas. **TIPS/NOTES:** *Sabal minor* is the palmetto, a trunkless shrub that grows 4'–6' tall. *Sabal mexicana* is the Rio Grande palm.

SAGE, AUTUMN—see *Salvia greggii*

SAGE, BLUE—see *Salvia farinacea*

SAGE, PINEAPPLE—see *Salvia greggii*

SAGE, RUSSIAN—see *Perovskia atriplicifolia*

SAGE, TEXAS—see *Leucophyllum frutescens*

ST. AUGUSTINEGRASS—see *Stenotaphrum secundatum*

ST. JOHN'S WORT—see *Hypericum* spp.

SALIX

Salix babylonica (SAY-lix bab-eh-LON-eh-kah). **COMMON NAME:** WEEPING WILLOW. **TYPE:** Deciduous tree. **LOCATION:** Sun. **HEIGHT:** 40'. **SPREAD:** 30'. **SPACING:** 20'–40'. **BLOOM/FRUIT:** Many-flowered catkins precede the new foliage. Fruit is a light brown capsule. **PROPAGATION:** Cuttings. **HABITS/CULTURE:** Graceful, fast-growing. First tree with leaves in spring, the last to lose them in fall—almost evergreen. Dense, fibrous root system. Easy to grow in any deep soil, needs lots of water. **USES:** Softening effect, edges of lakes and streams, temporary tree. **PROBLEMS:** Brittle wood, borers, cotton root rot, short-lived. **NOTES:** *Salix matsudana* 'Tortuosa,' the corkscrew willow, is more upright, with twisted limbs and branches. Root problems are actually worse on other trees, such as mulberry and sycamore. *Salix nigra,* the native black willow, is not a very good landscape tree. *Salix alba,* white weeping willow, has yellow stems. *Salix blanda,* blue weeping willow, is supposed to be a healthier variety.

SALT CEDAR—see *Tamarix* spp.

Salix babylonica weeping willow

Salvia farinacea mealy blue salvia

Salvia 'Indigo Spires' Indigo Spires salvia

SALVIA

Salvia farinacea (SAL-vee-ah far-eh-NAY-see-ah). COM-
MON NAME: MEALY BLUE SALVIA, BLUE SAGE. TYPE:
Perennial bedding plant. LOCATION: Sun to part shade.
HEIGHT: 2'–3'. SPREAD: 2'–3'. SPACING: 1'–2'. BLOOM/FRUIT:
Light blue or white flowers in summer. PROPAGATION:
Cuttings. HABITS/CULTURE: Gray-green foliage, long blue
flowers on vertical stems. Easy to grow in any well-drained
soil, drought tolerant, low fertilizer requirements. USES:
Summer flowers, perennial garden, blue color. PROBLEMS:
None. TIPS/NOTES: Native to Central and West Texas and
New Mexico. Plant in fall or spring. A compact cultivar
is now available. 'Indigo Spires' is another tough blue
flowering salvia. Native to Texas.

Salvia greggii (SAL-vee-ah GREG-ee-eye). COMMON NAME:
GREGG SALVIA, AUTUMN SAGE. TYPE: Perennial
shrub. LOCATION: Sun. HEIGHT: 2'–3'. SPREAD: 3'–4'. SPAC-
ING: 2'. BLOOM/FRUIT: Showy spring to fall flowers in colors of red, pink, orange, salmon, and white. PROPAGATION:
Cuttings. HABITS/CULTURE: Shrubby perennial with long-
lasting summer color. Grows in any well-drained soil,
extremely drought tolerant. USES: Spring, summer, and
fall color, perennial gardens. PROBLEMS: None. TIPS/NOTES:
Native to Texas. *Salvia splendens,* annual salvia (also
called scarlet sage), likes plenty of water and fertilizer.
Salvia coccinea, scarlet sage, is a native perennial that
grows 1'–2' high and looks like the annual salvia. *Salvia
regla,* mountain sage, blooms in the fall. *Salvia guaran-
itica,* anise sage, which has intense blue flowers and
grows 3'–4' tall, is not quite as winter hearty as *Salvia
greggii. Salvia leucantha,* Mexican bush salvia, is a large-
growing perennial with beautiful foliage and purple
flowers in late summer. *Salvia elegans,* pineapple sage,
has bright red flowers in late summer. *Salvia officinalis*
is common garden sage.

SAMBAC JASMINE—see *Jasminum sambac*

Salvia greggii Gregg salvia

Salvia officinalis garden sage

Salvia leucantha
Mexican bush salvia

Salvia elegans pineapple sage

Sambucus canadensis elderberry

Santolina chamaecyparissus gray santolina

SAMBUCUS

Sambucus canadensis (sam-BEW-cus can-ah-DEN-sis). **COMMON NAME:** ELDERBERRY. **TYPE:** Perennial herb. **LOCATION:** Sun to part shade. **HEIGHT:** 10'–12'. **SPREAD:** 8'–10'. **SPACING:** 6'–8'. **BLOOM/FRUIT:** White flower clusters in spring. Edible purple-black berries ripen in August. **PROPAGATION:** Cuttings. **HABITS/CULTURE:** Shrubby, tall, and multitrunked. Grows easily to 12'. **USES:** Excellent for attracting birds. Diuretic. Flower heads and berries are used for wines, jellies, pies, and excellent fritters. Good landscape plant. **PROBLEMS:** Invasive. **TIPS/NOTES:** Known for its ability to produce humus quickly. Plant and stay out of the way.

SANDPAPER OAK—see *Quercus virginiana*

SANTOLINA

Santolina chamaecyparissus (san-toe-LINE-ah kam-ah-sip-eh-RIS-us). **COMMON NAME:** GRAY SANTOLINA, LAVENDER COTTON. **TYPE:** Evergreen shrub. **LOCATION:** Sun. **HEIGHT:** 12'–18'. **SPREAD:** 24'. **SPACING:** 18'–24'. **BLOOM/FRUIT:** Small yellow button flowers in late spring. **PROPAGATION:** Cuttings. **HABITS/CULTURE:** Low, compact, and spreading. Herblike foliage is fragrant when crushed. Drought tolerant and undemanding but needs excellent drainage. **USES:** Low border, mass, rock gardens, extremely hot, dry places. **PROBLEMS:** Poor drainage, too much water, red spider mites. **TIPS/NOTES:** *Santolina virens*, a dark green variety, has the same characteristics. Native to Europe.

SAPINDUS

Sapindus drummondii (sap-IN-dus druh-MUN-dee-eye) WESTERN SOAPBERRY, INDIAN LILAC. **TYPE:** Deciduous tree. **LOCATION:** Sun to part shade. **HEIGHT:** 40'. **SPREAD:** 30'. **SPACING:** 20'–40'. **BLOOM/FRUIT:** Cone-shaped creamy white flowers in vertical clusters in spring. Fruit

Sapindus drummondii Western soapberry

Sapindus drummondii Western soapberry

Sapium sebiferum Chinese Tallow

is round, golden, translucent, flesh-covered hard seed. **PROPAGATION:** Seed, cuttings. **HABITS/CULTURE:** Foliage resembles that of Chinese pistachio. Golden fall color and winter berries, light gray bark, brittle wood. Easy to grow anywhere, drought tolerant, low fertilization requirements. **USES:** Shade tree. **PROBLEMS:** Brittle and short lived. **TIPS/NOTES:** Berries are used as a soap in Mexico. Native to the west-central and southwestern United States.

SAPIUM

Sapium sebiferum (SAY-pee-um seb-eh-FARE-um). **COMMON NAME:** CHINESE TALLOW. **TYPE:** Deciduous tree. **LOCATION:** Sun. **HEIGHT:** 30'. **SPREAD:** 30'. **SPACING:** Do not plant! **BLOOM/FRUIT:** Tiny yellow flowers in spikes at branch tips. Distinctive clusters of hard white seeds remain attached after foliage has fallen. **PROPAGATION:** Seed. **HABITS/CULTURE:** Fast-growing, short-lived, poor-quality shade tree. Yellow to red fall color and white berries in winter. Easy to grow anywhere. Branch tips freeze back every winter. **USES:** Temporary tree. **PROBLEMS:** Freeze damage, borers, cotton root rot, short-lived. **TIPS/NOTES:** I used to recommend this tree, but it is not a good choice. Native to China and Japan. Seeds are poisonous.

SAPONARIA

Saponaria officinalis (sap-oh-NAR-ee-ah oh-fis-ih-NAH-lis). **COMMON NAME:** BOUNCING BET, SOAPWORT. **TYPE:** Perennial bedding plant. **LOCATION:** Sun to part shade. **HEIGHT:** 1'–2'. **SPREAD:** 2'–3'. **SPACING:** 12"–18". **BLOOM/FRUIT:** Fragrant double pink and white phloxlike flowers from late spring until fall. **PROPAGATION:** Division, cuttings. **HABITS/CULTURE:** Easy-to-grow, drought-tolerant perennial with 3"–4" leaves, prefers morning sun and afternoon shade. **USES:** Perennial garden. Roots contain a cleansing agent that substitutes for soap. **PROBLEMS:** Few if any. **TIPS/NOTES:** Cut back to encourage a second round of flowers.

Saponaria officinalis bouncing bet

SASSAFRAS

Sassafras albidum (SASS-ah-frass al-BEE-dum). **COMMON NAME:** SASSAFRAS. **TYPE:** Deciduous tree. **LOCATION:** Sun to part shade. **HEIGHT:** 20'–40'. **SPREAD:** 20'–25'. **SPACING:** 15'–20'. **BLOOM/FRUIT:** Yellow 1"–2" flowers in spring. Male and female flowers on separate trees, female flowers are larger. Small blue fruit on bright red stalk in fall, quickly eaten by birds. **PROPAGATION:** Seed, root division. **HABITS/CULTURE:** Needs sandy, acid soil. Spreads by rhizomes to create groves. Very hard to transplant. Leaves

have many shapes, some lobed and some not. Beautiful yellow, orange, and red fall color. **USES:** Tea from the roots, fall color, flavoring agent. The dried and crushed leaves are the only ingredient in the Cajun seasoning filé. **PROBLEMS:** Poor drainage, alkaline soils. **TIPS/NOTES:** Native to East Texas.

Sassafras albidum sassafras

SAWTOOTH OAK—see *Quercus acutissima*

SCARLET SAGE—see *Salvia greggii*

SCAEVOLA

Scaevola 'Mauve Clusters' (ska-VO-la). **COMMON NAME:** FAN FLOWER, BLUE FAN, BLUE HAZE. **TYPE:** Tender perennial, used as an annual in most of Texas. **LOCATION:** Full sun. **HEIGHT:** 4"–6". **SPREAD:** 2'–3'. **SPACING:** 12"–18". **BLOOM/FRUIT:** Bluish or lilac flowers in 1 1/2" clusters. Flowers are fan-shaped, with petals all on one side. **PROPAGATION:** Seed, transplants. **HABITS/CULTURE:** Ever-blooming bedding plant that forms a mat, evergreen in South Texas. Moderately drought tolerant. **USES:** Summer bedding plant, excellent for hanging baskets. **PROBLEMS:** Chlorosis unless iron and magnesium amendments are used. **TIPS/NOTES:** Good plant for summer color, should be used more.

SCHOOLHOUSE LILY—see *Rhodophiala bifida*

SCUTELLARIA

Scutellaria drummondii (sku-te-LAH-ree-ah druh-MUN-dee-eye). **COMMON NAME:** SKULLCAP. **TYPE:** Annual wildflower. **LOCATION:** Sun. **HEIGHT:** 8"–12". **SPREAD:** 12". **SPACING:** 6"–9". **BLOOM/FRUIT:** Bluish purple spring flowers with two white marks in leaf axils of upper leaves. Fruit is a tiny black nutlet. **PROPAGATION:** Seed. **HABITS/CULTURE:** Soft, hairy stems, grows in clumps opposite hairy leaves. Easy to grow in various soils. **USES:** Wildflower. **TIPS/NOTES:** This is one mint that is not safe to use as a tea.

Scaevola 'Mauve Clusters' blue haze

Setcreasea pallida purple heart

Scutellaria drummondii skullcap

Sedum sedum

SEAOATS—see *Chasmanthium latifolium*

SEDUM

Sedum spp. (SEE-dum). **COMMON NAME:** SEDUM, STONECROP. **TYPE:** Evergreen ground cover. **LOCATION:** Sun to part shade. **HEIGHT:** 2"–6". **SPREAD:** 8"–24". **SPACING:** 6"–9". **BLOOM/FRUIT:** White, pink, rose, yellow, or red flowers. **PROPAGATION:** Division. **HABITS/CULTURE:** Finely textured, succulent ground cover. Easily damaged by foot traffic or pets. Easy to grow in any soil, prefers well-prepared and well-drained beds. Best exposure is partial shade. **USES:** Ground cover for small areas, Oriental gardens, rock gardens, stone walls, small accent areas. **PROBLEMS:** Damage from foot traffic. **TIPS/NOTES:** Native to Europe and Asia. *Sedum* 'Autumn Joy' is a tall-growing perennial with dramatic flowers—they are white in the summer and become red in the fall. 'Ruby Glow' is lower-growing and blooms all summer.

SETCREASEA

Setcreasea pallida (set-KRESS-ee-ah PA-li-da). **COMMON NAME:** PURPLE HEART, PURPLE JEW. **TYPE:** Perennial vine or ground cover. **LOCATION:** Sun to part shade. **HEIGHT:** 12"–18". **SPREAD:** 24" and more. **SPACING:** 12"–18". **BLOOM/FRUIT:** White, pink, or light purple flower in spring and summer. **PROPAGATION:** Cuttings. **HABITS/CULTURE:** Easy to grow in well-drained soil. **USES:** Pots, hanging baskets, colorful ground cover, effective annual color. Looks great when used with pink verbena.

SHRIMP PLANT—see *Justicia* spp.

SHUMARD OAK—see *Quercus shumardii* or *texana*

SIBERIAN ELM—see *Ulmus pumila*

SIDEOATS GRAMA—see *Bouteloua curtipendula*

SILVER LACEVINE—see *Polygonum aubertii*

SILVERBERRY—see *Elaeagnus* spp.

SISYRINCHIUM

Sisyrinchium spp. (siss-ee-RINK-ee-um). **COMMON NAME:** BLUE-EYED GRASS. **TYPE:** Perennial herb. **LOCATION:** Sun. **HEIGHT:** 6"–12". **SPREAD:** 12". **SPACING:** 9". **BLOOM/FRUIT:** Purple-blue 1/2" flower with yellow center in spring. **PROPAGATION:** Seed. **HABITS/CULTURE:** Bulb member of the iris family, grasslike foliage, beautiful light blue flowers in spring. Goes dormant and looks pretty ratty in the summer. Don't mow it down until it has gone dormant. **USES:** Beautiful wildflower that should be used more. **PROBLEMS:** Looks rough in the summer.

SKULLCAP—see *Scutellaria drummondii*

SKUNKBUSH—see *Rhus aromatica*

SMILAX

Smilax spp. (SMIL-laks). **COMMON NAME:** GREENBRIAR. **TYPE:** Perennial vine. **LOCATION:** Sun to shade. **HEIGHT:** High-climbing. **SPREAD:** 25' or more. **BLOOM/FRUIT:** Flowers from February to June. Black berries in September and October. **PROPAGATION:** Seed. **HABITS/CULTURE:** Woody vine with strong thorny stems from large underground tubers. Leaves are tardily deciduous and sometimes white-blotched. **USES:** Deer like it. The new tender growth is delicious in salads. **PROBLEMS:** A weedy pest for most folks. Control by digging out the woody underground tubers.

SMOKETREE—see *Cotinus* spp.

SNAPDRAGON—see *Antirrhinum* spp.

SNOWBALL BUSH—see *Viburnam* spp.

SNOWBERRY, INDIAN-CURRANT—see *Symphoricarpos orbiculatus*

SNOWFLAKE, SUMMER—see *Leucojum aestivum*

SNOW-ON-THE-MOUNTAIN—see *Euphorbia marginata*

SOAPBERRY, WESTERN—see *Sapindus drummondii*

SOCIETY GARLIC—see *Allium* spp.

SOLANUM

Solanum tuberosum (so-LAH-num tew-be-RO-sum). **COMMON NAME:** POTATO. **TYPE:** Annual vegetable. **LOCATION:** Sun. **HEIGHT:** 18"–24". **SPREAD:** 24"–36". **SPACING:** 8"–12". **BLOOM/FRUIT:** Insignificant. Root tubers are the food crop. **PROPAGATION:** Potato pieces. **HABITS/CULTURE:** Plant in January or February for best results. Plant whole potatoes or cut pieces the size of golf balls after coating with fireplace ashes. Whole potatoes are the best choice. It's best to fertilize fairly heavily in the beginning rather than sidedressing after the plants are growing. Germinates at 68 degrees. **USES:** Food. **PROBLEMS:** Colorado potato beetle, flea beetles, garden flea hopper, aphids, nematodes, wireworms, leaf and root fungus. **TIPS/NOTES:** Unfortunately, most commercially grown seed potatoes have been chemically treated and should not be eaten. For best results, cover potatoes with a very thick layer of natural

Sophora affinis Eve's necklace

Smilax greenbriar

Solidago goldenrod

Sophora affinis Eve's necklace

Sophora secundiflora Texas mountain laurel

mulch. Harvest when foliage first starts to turn brown or before. Don't wait until it turns completely brown. S*olanum melongena* is eggplant. My favorites are the small Japanese varieties.

SOLIDAGO

Solidago spp. (sal-eh-DAY-go). **COMMON NAME:** GOLD-ENROD. **TYPE:** Perennial wildflower. **LOCATION:** Sun to part shade. **HEIGHT:** 2'–7'. **SPREAD:** Wide-spreading. **SPAC-ING:** One is enough. **BLOOM/FRUIT:** Striking yellow fall pyramids of flowers on tall stems. **PROPAGATION:** Seed, root division. **HABITS/CULTURE:** Upright perennial with beautiful fall color. **USES:** Low-maintenance perennial. Looks terrific with asters, wallflowers, or other purple flowers. Attracts ladybugs. **PROBLEMS:** Very aggressive and can sometimes get out of control. **TIPS/NOTES:** It has a reputation for causing hay fever, but this is inaccurate—the pollen is too heavy. Ragweed is the allergy plant. Gold-enrod is in my perennial garden and should be in more gardens. Dwarf goldenrod only grows 24"–36" high. 'Fire-works' is a dwarf that doesn't spread badly by suckers.

SOPHORA

Sophora affinis (so-FORE-ah af-FIN-is). **COMMON NAME:** EVE'S NECKLACE, TEXAS SOPHORA. **TYPE:** Deciduous tree. **LOCATION:** Sun to shade. **HEIGHT:** 30'. **SPREAD:** 20'.

SPACING: 10'–15'. **BLOOM/FRUIT:** Pink wisteria-like flow-ers, black beadlike seed pods in fall. **PROPAGATION:** Seed, cuttings. **HABITS/CULTURE:** Moderately fast-growing, up-right, usually found in the wild as an understory tree. Bark, especially on young growth, is greenish. Easy to grow in any soil, drought tolerant. **USES:** Small garden tree, speci-men, natural settings. **PROBLEMS:** Few if any. **TIPS/NOTES:** Excellent small tree for residential gardens. Native to Texas, Arkansas, Oklahoma, and Louisiana.

Sophora secundiflora (so-FORE-ah se-kune-di-FLOR-ah). **COMMON NAME:** TEXAS MOUNTAIN LAUREL, MES-CAL BEAN. **TYPE:** Evergreen shrub. **LOCATION:** Sun to part shade. **HEIGHT:** 20'. **SPREAD:** 10'. **SPACING:** 8'–15'. **BLOOM/FRUIT:** Fragrant, wisteria-like purple flowers in spring. **PROPAGATION:** Seed, cuttings. **HABITS/CULTURE:** Slow-growing, with dense foliage. Bushy unless trimmed into tree form. Grows in any well-drained soil, drought toler-ant. **USES:** Specimen ornamental tree or large shrub, xeriscape gardens. **PROBLEMS:** Winter damage in the north-ern parts of the state. Seeds are very poisonous. **TIPS/NOTES:** Great in Central Texas but not so hot in North Texas. Native to the southwestern United States, Texas, and Mexico. All *sophora* are legumes and fix nitrogen in the soil.

SORGHUM

Sorghum halepense (SOR-gum HAL-a-pence). **COMMON NAME:** JOHNSONGRASS. **TYPE:** Perennial grass. **LOCATION:** Sun. **HEIGHT:** 3'–6'. **PROPAGATION:** Seed, rhizomes. **HABITS/CULTURE:** Wide leaves up to 3/4", with light-colored mid-vein. Tall flower plumes and millions of tiny black seed. **USES:** Cattle forage. **PROBLEMS:** Hard-to-control weed in cultivated crops. Prussic acid in the plant can be poisonous to cattle during dry summers, after an application of excess nitrogen fertilizer, or just after the first frost. **TIPS/NOTES:** Native to Africa and India. Introduced to the United States in 1830 as a high-quality pasture and hay grass but has become a noxious weed. Control in lawns by mowing.

SORREL, WOOD—see *Oxalis* spp.

SOUTHERN RED OAK—see *Quercus shumardii* or *texana* and *Quercus virginiana*

SOUTHERNWOOD—see *Artemisia abrotanum*

SPANISH BAYONET—see *Yucca aloifolia*

SPANISH DAGGER—see *Yucca aloifolia*

SPANISH OAK—see *Quercus virginiana*

SPEARMINT—see *Mentha* spp.

SPEEDWELL—see *Veronica* spp.

SPIDER LILY—see *Hymenocallis* spp. and *Lycoris* spp.

SPIDERWORT—see *Tradescantia* spp.

SPINACIA

Spinacia oleracea (spee-NAH-kee-a o-le-RAH-see-ah). **COMMON NAME:** SPINACH. **TYPE:** Annual vegetable. **LOCATION:** Sun to part shade. **HEIGHT:** 8"–12". **SPREAD:** 8"–12". **SPACING:** 3"–6". **BLOOM/FRUIT:** Bolting to seed ruins the foliage of the plant. **PROPAGATION:** Seed. **HABITS/CULTURE:** Cool-season leafy vegetable. Smooth and crinkled-leaf varieties available. Can be planted in late winter or fall. Sow seed 1/2"–1" apart, 1/8" below surface. Thin to at least 3" apart. Germination in 7–21 days at 59 degrees. **USES:** Food. **PROBLEMS:** Bolting in hot weather, flea beetles, cutworms, loopers, green worms, rust, aphids. **TIPS/NOTES:** For acid soils, add limestone or soft rock phosphate. New Zealand spinach is a bush. *Basella alba*, Malabar spinach, is a climber. Both do well in the heat of summer and are very sensitive to frost.

SPIRAEA

Spiraea spp. (spy-REE-ah). **COMMON NAME:** SPIRAEA, BRIDAL WREATH. **TYPE:** Deciduous shrub. **LOCATION:** Sun to part shade. **HEIGHT:** 5'–7'. **SPREAD:** 6'–8'. **SPACING:** 3'–5'. **BLOOM/FRUIT:** Showy white or coral flowers in spring. **PROPAGATION:** Cuttings. **HABITS/CULTURE:** Rounded overall form, with many stems growing from the ground. Minimal fall color. Many good species and cultivars. Extremely tough plant that will grow anywhere. **USES:** Specimen, accent, screen, spring color. **PROBLEMS:** None. **TIPS/NOTES:** Landscape snobs think spiraea is old-fashioned. I think they're missing out on a great plant.

Spiraea bumalda
'Anthony Waterer'
Anthony Waterer spiraea

Spiraea bridal wreath

'Vanhouttei' spiraea is a cross between two spiraeas from China. *Spiraea bumalda* 'Anthony Waterer' has a beautiful coral flower that blooms later in the spring. *Spiraea cantoniensis* 'Lanceata,' double Reeves spiraea, is another excellent choice. Native to Asia.

SPURGE—see *Euphorbia* spp.

SQUASH—see *Cucurbita* spp.

STACHYS

Stachys byzantina (STACK-is biz-an-TEEN-yah). **COMMON NAME:** LAMB'S EAR. **TYPE:** Evergreen herb and ground cover. **LOCATION:** Sun to light shade. **HEIGHT:** 6"–12". **SPREAD:** 36" and more. **SPACING:** 12"–18". **BLOOM/FRUIT:** Purple summer blooms. **PROPAGATION:** Seed, division, transplants. **HABITS/CULTURE:** Needs loose, well-drained, organic soil. Light-colored, low-growing, ground spreader. Drought tolerant. **USES:** Ground cover, antiseptic and styptic, teas. **PROBLEMS:** Too much water, poorly drained soil. Develops crown rot if kept too wet. **TIPS/NOTES:** Propagates and spreads easily by seeds and rhizomes. Cut back the flower spikes to maintain compact appearance. Flowers are good in dried arrangements. This is a hardy plant with feltlike white leaves as soft as a lamb's ear. It must be grown in dry, sunny conditions. Hard rains beat it down and turn it mushy, but it usually

Stachys byzantina lamb's ear

Stachys coccinea Texas betony

Stenotaphrum secundatum St. Augustinegrass

snaps back. Start it from purchased plants or seeds. Cut it back in early spring. The native *Stachys coccinea,* Texas betony, is a tough, good-looking perennial for shady areas and has red-orange blooms.

STANDING CYPRESS—see *Ipomopsis rubra*

STAR JASMINE, JAPANESE—see *Trachelospermum asiaticum*

STATICE—see *Limonium sinuatum*

STENOTAPHRUM
Stenotaphrum secundatum (sten-no-TAY-frum seh-coon-DAY-tum). **COMMON NAME:** ST. AUGUSTINEGRASS. **TYPE:** Warm-season lawn grass. **LOCATION:** Sun to moderate shade. **HEIGHT:** 2" (mown). **SPACING:** Solid sod is the only recommended planting method—from me anyway. **BLOOM/FRUIT:** Unimportant. **PROPAGATION:** Plugs, solid sod. **HABITS/CULTURE:** Wide-bladed grass, spreads by stolons. The most shade tolerant of our warm-season grasses. The hybrid 'Raleigh' is resistant to St. Augustine decline (SAD) and is more cold hardy than other hybrids. Grows in any well-drained soil that is fairly fertile. Not as tough as Bermudagrass. **USES:** Lawn grass for full sun and partially shaded areas. **PROBLEMS:** Chinch bugs, grub worms, diseases. Requires moderate to heavy irrigation. **TIPS/NOTES:** Native to Africa and the Gulf Coast.

STOCK—see *Matthiola incana*

STOKESIA
Stokesia laevis (STOKES-ee-ah LAY-vis). **COMMON NAME:** STOKES ASTER. **TYPE:** Perennial bedding plant. **LOCATION:** Sun to part shade. **HEIGHT:** 2'. Spread 2'–3'. **SPACING:** 1"–18". **BLOOM/FRUIT:** Daisylike flowers from midsummer through fall. **PROPAGATION:** Seeds, cuttings. **HABITS/CULTURE:** Long narrow leaves. Likes loose, moist soil and light fertilization. Tolerant of heat and a fair amount of neglect. Easy to grow. **USES:** Perennial garden, summer flowers. **PROBLEMS:** Not long-lived. **TIPS/NOTES:** Larger, more intricate than the real aster.

STONECROP—see *Sedum* spp.

STRAWBERRY—see *Fragaria virginiana*

STRAWBERRY, FALSE—*Duchesnea indica*

SUMAC, AROMATIC—see *Rhus aromatica*

SUMAC, EVERGREEN—see *Rhus virens*

SUMAC, FLAMELEAF—see *Rhus copallina*

SUMAC, SMOOTH—see *Rhus glabra*

SUMMER PHLOX—see *Phlox paniculata*

SUMMER SNOWFLAKE—see *Leucojum aestivum*

SUNFLOWER—see *Helianthus* spp.

SUNFLOWER, MEXICAN—*Tithonia rotundifolia*

SWAMP CHESTNUT OAK—see *Quercus muhlenbergii* and *Quercus virginiana*

S

SWEET BAY—see *Laurus nobilis*

SWEET GUM—see *Liquidambar styraciflua*

SWEET HERB—see *Lippia dulcis*

SWEET MARIGOLD—see *Tagetes* spp.

SWEET OLIVE—see *Osmanthus* spp.

SWEET PEA—see *Lathyrus odoratus*

SWISS CHARD—see *Beta vulgaris*

SYCAMORE—see *Platanus occidentalis*

SYMPHORICARPOS

Symphoricarpos orbiculatus (sim-for-eh-CAR-pus or-bic-cue-LAY-tus). **COMMON NAME:** CORALBERRY, INDIAN-CURRANT SNOWBERRY. **TYPE:** Deciduous shrub. **LOCA-TION:** Sun to shade. **HEIGHT:** 2'–3'. **SPREAD:** 5'. **SPACING:** 2'–3'. **BLOOM/FRUIT:** Small greenish white to pinkish flower spikes in spring. Coral red, purple, or pink berrylike drupes form along the stems and remain on bare stems most of the winter. **PROPAGATION:** Cuttings, seed. **HAB-ITS/CULTURE:** Blue-green foliage, low-growing, spreads by root suckers to form a shrubby thicket. Can grow as tall as 6'. Easy to grow in any soil, drought tolerant. Cut to the ground in late winter. **USES:** Naturalizing shrub, winter berry color, tall ground cover. **PROBLEMS:** Mildew sometimes. **TIPS/NOTES:** Too many people mow the plant down. If it exists on a site, try to save it. Native from the eastern United States to Texas and Mexico.

SYMPHYTUM

Symphytum officinale (SIM-fi-tum oh-fis-ih-NAH-lee). **COMMON NAME:** COMFREY, BONESET. **TYPE:** Perennial herb. **LOCATION:** Sun to part shade. **HEIGHT:** 24"–36". **SPREAD:** 24"–48" or more. **SPACING:** 18"–24". **BLOOM/FRUIT:** Light blue or white bell-like flowers in spring and summer. **PROPAGATION:** Seed, root division. **HABITS/CULTURE:** Deep-rooted, wide-spreading, with large bristly leaves 8"–18" long. **USES:** Coarse texture, bee attractant. Juice from leaves and stems is good for topical treatment of cuts, scrapes, and insect bites and stings. **PROBLEMS:** Can be invasive but worth the risk. **TIPS/NOTES:** Not recommended for internal use.

SYRINGA

Syringa spp. (si-RING-ga). **COMMON NAME:** LILAC. **TYPE:** Deciduous shrub. **LOCATION:** Sun to light shade. **HEIGHT:** 8'–10'. **SPREAD:** 8'–10'. **SPACING:** 4'–6'. **BLOOM/FRUIT:** Very fragrant lavender flower spikes in April and May. **PROPA-GATION:** Cuttings. **HABITS/CULTURE:** Light green foliage, purple as it emerges in the spring. Best adapted to the cooler parts of Texas. Needs winter chilling to set strong blooms. **USES:** Summer color. **PROBLEMS:** Leaf miners, scale insects, borers, several diseases. **TIPS/NOTES:** There are about 30 species of lilac from Asia and southern Europe, but none of them do very well in the southern two-thirds of Texas. *Syringa persica*, Persian lilac, is the best species for Texas. Under an organic program, it does better than most people would think.

Symphoricarpos orbiculatus coralberry

Symphytum officinale comfrey

Syringa lilac

TAGETES

Tagetes spp. (ta-JET-teez). **COMMON NAME:** MARIGOLD. **TYPE:** Annual bedding plant. **LOCATION:** Sun. **HEIGHT:** 1'–2'. **SPREAD:** 1'–2'. **SPACING:** 12"–36." **BLOOM/FRUIT:** Yellow or orange flowers throughout summer. **PROPAGATION:** Seed. **HABITS/CULTURE:** Fast-growing, with lacy foliage. Would last until frost if it weren't for the red spider. Grows in any soil, best in well-drained soil in full sun. It will reseed and come up the following year, but the plants will be weaker than the original ones. Can be planted in mid-summer for fall flowers, which have fewer spider mite problems than spring plants. **USES:** Summer color, cut flowers, border, mass planting. **PROBLEMS:** Red spider mites, short-lived. **TIPS/NOTES:** *Tagetes lucida,* Mexican mint marigold (also called sweet marigold, anise marigold, or Texas tarragon), is a perennial herb with yellow flowers in late summer. The foliage has a very strong tarragon flavor. Available in many container sizes. Native to Central America.

Tanacetum vulgare tansy

Tagetes marigold

Tagetes lucida
Mexican mint marigold

TAHOKA DAISY—see *Chrysanthemum leucanthemum*

TALLOW, CHINESE—see *Sapium sebiferum*

TAMARIX

Tamarix spp. (ta-ma-RICKS). **COMMON NAME:** SALT CEDAR. **TYPE:** Deciduous shrub. **LOCATION:** Sun. **HEIGHT:** 40'. **SPREAD:** 25'. **SPACING:** 10'–15'. **BLOOM/FRUIT:** Pink flowers in summer. **PROPAGATION:** Cuttings, seed. **HABITS/CULTURE:** Large, bushy, windproof, drought-resistant introduction from Asia that has become naturalized in Texas. Likes moist, salty soils. Small leaves. Grows like a big weed—which it is. **USES:** Erosion control. **PROBLEMS:** Heavy, aggressive invasive roots. **TIPS/NOTES:** Likes the seashore but prefers good healthy soil.

TANACETUM

Tanacetum vulgare (tan-ah-SET-um vul-GAH-ree). **COMMON NAME:** TANSY. **TYPE:** Perennial herb. **LOCATION:** Sun to part shade. **HEIGHT:** 3'–4'. **SPREAD:** 3'–6'. **SPACING:** 18"–24". **BLOOM/FRUIT:** Yellow button flowers in late summer. **PROPAGATION:** Seed, division. **HABITS/CULTURE:** Lacy foliage, sprawling growth, drought tolerant. More compact in sun, more open-growing in shade. Needs good drainage. **USES:** Dye from the yellow flowers. Effective ant repellent. Tear or crush foliage and sprinkle on fire ant mounds. Perennial color, fernlike texture. **PROBLEMS:** Can become invasive. Said to be allopathic to nearby plants.

TANSY—see *Tanacetum vulgare*

TARAXACUM

Taraxacum officinale (ta-RAX-ah-cum oh-fis-ih-NAH-lee). **COMMON NAME:** DANDELION. **TYPE:** Perennial herb. **LOCATION:** Sun. **HEIGHT:** 8"–12". **SPREAD:** 8"–12". **BLOOM/FRUIT:** Yellow flowers and powder-puff seed heads. **PROPAGATION:** Seed. **HABITS/CULTURE:** Lettucelike foliage, deep tap root. **USES:** Flowers are used in cookies and wine, young foliage in salads, the root in tea. The aggressive root system brings minerals from the subsoil up to the surface. **PROBLEMS:** Considered a lawn weed. **TIPS/NOTES:** Aeration and proper use of organic fertilizers will greatly reduce the population. Easy to kill if necessary by spraying with full-strength vinegar or removing manually.

TARRAGON, FRENCH—see *Artemisia dracunculus*

TARRAGON, TEXAS—see *Tagetes* spp.

Taxodium ascendens pond cypress

Taxodium ascendens pond cypress

Taxodium distichum bald cypress

TAXODIUM

Taxodium ascendens (tax-OH-dee-um uh-SEND-enz).
COMMON NAME: POND CYPRESS. **TYPE:** Deciduous tree.
LOCATION: Sun. **HEIGHT:** 70'. **SPREAD:** 30'. **SPREAD:** 20'–
40'. **BLOOM/FRUIT:** Male and female flowers on the same
branches. Fruit is a round, resinous cone of thick scales
with seeds at the base. **PROPAGATION:** Seed. **HABITS/CUL-
TURE:** Rapid, upright growth, narrower than regular bald
cypress, green earlier in the spring and longer into the
fall. Doesn't turn brown in late summer as the regular
bald cypress does. Leaves spiral out from the stem and
leaflets do not open. Lovely, soft overall appearance. Rust
fall color. Easy to grow in any soil, normal water and nutrient requirements. Can tolerate wet soil. **USES:** Specimen, shade tree, mass planting, background tree. **PROB-
LEMS:** Availability. **TIPS/NOTES:** Also called *Taxodium
distichum* 'Nutans.' Native from the southeastern United
States to Alabama.

Taxodium distichum (tax-OH-dee-um DIS-tick-um). **COM-
MON NAME:** BALD CYPRESS. **TYPE:** Deciduous tree. **LO-
CATION:** Sun. **HEIGHT:** 80'. **SPREAD:** 50'. **SPACING:** 20'–40'.
BLOOM/FRUIT: Male and female flowers on the same
branches. Fruit is a round, resinous cone of thick scales
with seeds at the base. **PROPAGATION:** Seed. **HABITS/CUL-
TURE:** Moderately fast-growing, upright, pyramidal when
young but spreading with age. Light green lacy foliage,

reddish brown fall color. Branching structure is layered
and distinctive. Root "knees" will appear in wet soil. Easy
to grow in any soil except solid rock. Drought tolerant
but can grow in wet areas. Cannot take any shade—must
have full sun to avoid limb dieback. **USES:** Specimen, shade
tree, background tree, fall color, delicate foliage texture.
PROBLEMS: Chlorosis and crown gall occasionally, bagworms. **TIPS/NOTES:** Likes well-drained soils best. The
lake habitation often seen with this species results from
seed germination in wet conditions and a protection
against prairie fires through the years. Native from the
eastern United States to Texas. The evergreen *Taxodium*

mucronatum, Montezuma
bald cypress, is native to
far South Texas but can
grow easily through Cen-
tral Texas. It might do well
as far north as Dallas–Fort
Worth but will definitely be
deciduous in the northern
half of Texas. It differs
mainly in that its flowers
are in short clusters rather
than long racemes.

Taxodium distichum bald cypress

TERNSTROEMIA

Ternstroemia gymnanthera (tern-STROH-me-ah gym-NAN-tha-rah). **COMMON NAME:** CLEYERA. **TYPE:** Evergreen shrub. **LOCATION:** Sun to part shade. **HEIGHT:** 4'–10'. **SPREAD:** 4'–6'. **SPACING:** 3'. **BLOOM/FRUIT:** Small, fragrant, creamy white flowers in the early summer. Yellow to red-orange berries split open to reveal black seeds. **PROPAGATION:** Seed. **HABITS/CULTURE:** Soft, glossy foliage. Reddish color, especially in spring and fall. Insignificant flowers. Berries ripen in late summer. Needs good drainage to avoid root rot. Do not box or shear this plant. **USES:** Background, border, accent plant. Can be trimmed into a small ornamental tree, does well in containers. **PROBLEMS:** Aphids on new growth, root rot in wet soil. **TIPS/NOTES:** Native to the Orient. Sometimes incorrectly sold as *Cleyera japonica*.

TETRAPANAX

Tetrapanax papyriferus (teh-tra-PAN-nax pah-pa-RIF-er-us). **COMMON NAME:** RICE-PAPER PLANT. **TYPE:** Perennial to evergreen foliage plant. **LOCATION:** Shade. **HEIGHT:** 8'–10'. **SPREAD:** Unlimited. **SPACING:** 3'–5'. **BLOOM/FRUIT:** Clusters of creamy white flowers in fall. **PROPAGATION:** Division. **HABITS/CULTURE:** Shrubby but striking, with large 1'–2' leaves, dark green on top and whitish beneath, tan trunk. Spreads underground and can become invasive. **USES:** Dramatic texture. **PROBLEMS:** Fuzz on the leaves is irritating to eyes and tender skin.

TEUCRIUM

Teucrium spp. (TOO-kree-um). **COMMON NAME:** GERMANDER. **TYPE:** Perennial herb. **LOCATION:** Full sun. **HEIGHT:** 2'–4'. **SPREAD:** 6"–12". **BLOOM/FRUIT:** Rose-pink or creamy yellow blossoms in summer. **PROPAGATION:** Cuttings, transplants, seeds. **HABITS/CULTURE:** Can be clipped into borders or low perennial hedges. Easy to grow, no special requirements. **USES:** Border, pots. **PROBLEMS:** None. **TIPS/NOTES:** Should be used more. *Teucrium chamaedrys* has small leaves and rose-colored flowers. *Teucrium lucidum* has larger gray-green leaves, grows to 2', and produces creamy yellow blossoms. *Teucrium fruticans*, commonly called tutti-frutti, is a tender perennial container plant that grows 3'–4' tall and has beautiful gray leaves. *Teucrium canadense*, with rose-colored blossoms and a creeping growth habit, does well as a border. *Teucrium marum*, called cat thyme, is a small, aromatic, gray-leaf plant best grown in containers. Cats love it. Dwarf germanders are also available. *Teucrium laciniatum*, the native dwarf germander, grows only to a height of 3"–6".

TEXAS BLUEGRASS—see *Poa arachnifera*

TEXAS BLUEBELLS—see *Eustoma grandiflorum*

TEXAS BUCKEYE—see *Aesculus glabra*

TEXAS MOUNTAIN LAUREL—see *Sophora secundiflora*

Ternstroemia gymnanthera cleyera

Tetrapanax papyriferus rice-paper plant

Teucrium chamaedrys germander

TEXAS PALM—see *Sabal texana*

TEXAS RED OAK—see *Quercus shumardii* or *texana*

TEXAS TARRAGON—see *Tagetes* spp.

TEXAS WISTERIA—see *Wisteria frutescens*

T

THRIFT—see *Phlox subulata*

THUJA

Thuja occidentalis (thu-ya ok-si-den-TALL-is). **COMMON NAME:** ARBORVITAE. **TYPE:** Evergreen shrub. **LOCATION:** Sun. **HEIGHT:** 25'. **SPREAD:** 15'. **SPACING:** Do not plant! **BLOOM/FRUIT:** Insignificant flowers. Fruit is a small green cone. **PROPAGATION:** Seed, cuttings. **HABITS/CULTURE:** Upright, multitrunked shrub or small tree. Plated or juniper-like foliage. Tight, pearlike shape when young, opening with age. Grows anywhere. **USES:** Cemeteries are the primary habitat of this plant. **PROBLEMS:** Every insect known to man either eats or lives in this plant. **TIPS/NOTES:** The photo makes the plant look decent—it isn't! Native to the northeastern United States.

THYME—see *Thymus* spp.

THYMUS

Thymus spp. (TIME-us). **COMMON NAME:** CREEPING THYME. **TYPE:** Perennial herb. **LOCATION:** Sun. **HEIGHT:** 1"–18". **SPREAD:** Ground cover. **SPACING:** 6"–12". **BLOOM/FRUIT:** Flowers of white, pink, and lavender. **PROPAGATION:** Cuttings, seed. **HABITS/CULTURE:** Low-growing, spreading, in three groups: 12"–18" upright shrubs, 3"–6" creeping herbs, and 1"–2" flat creepers. The larger plants are the most common culinary forms. Must have well-drained soil. Protection from the strong afternoon sun is ideal. Moderate fertilizer and water needs. **USES:** Ground cover, perennial gardens, containers and baskets, fragrance. Excellent flavoring agent for meat, poultry, and egg dishes. **PROBLEMS:** Extreme weather fluctuations. **TIPS/NOTES:** Creeping thymes cross-pollinate freely, causing a mix of flower color, but that's nice. Coconut, Lemon, Caraway, and Mother of Thyme are good choices. Can be dried and frozen for later use. My favorite is the dark green and wonderfully fragrant Odena's Kitchen Thyme, named for my friend Odena Brannam. It was brought to this country from Turkey by Byron Terry.

Thymus creeping thyme

Tilia cordata little-leaf linden

Thuja occidentalis arborvitae

Tithonia rotundifolia Mexican sunflower

Trachelospermum asiaticum Asian jasmine

TIFGRASS—see *Cynodon dactylon*

TILIA

Tilia spp. (TILL-ee-ah). **COMMON NAME:** BASSWOOD, LINDEN. **TYPE:** Deciduous tree. **LOCATION:** Sun to part shade. **HEIGHT:** 30'–50'. **SPREAD:** 20'–30'. **SPACING:** 20'. **BLOOM/FRUIT:** Small, fragrant off-white flowers in drooping clusters attached to a leaflike bract. Fruit is a winged hard capsule with 1 or 2 seeds. **PROPAGATION:** Seed, cuttings. **HABITS/CULTURE:** Straight trunk, symmetrical growth, very neat appearance. Moderate growth rate. Grows much taller in deep, moist soils. Heart-shaped leaves. **USES:** Shade tree, fragrant flowers, lumber. The flowers make excellent honey. **PROBLEMS:** Aphids sometimes. **TIPS/NOTES:** *Tilia caroliniana*, Carolina basswood, is native to East Texas. It grows to 90' in deep, rich soils and flowers from April to June. *Tilia cordata*, the little-leaf linden, is adapted for all of Texas. Its leaves are silvery on the underside, and it flowers in summer. Very symmetrical growth.

TITHONIA

Tithonia rotundifolia (tee-THO-nee-a ro-tun-di-FO-lee-a). **COMMON NAME:** MEXICAN SUNFLOWER. **TYPE:** Annual wildflower. **LOCATION:** Sun. **HEIGHT:** 5'–8'. **SPREAD:** 3'–4'. **SPACING:** 2'–3'. **BLOOM/FRUIT:** Red-orange sunflower-like flowers in summer. **PROPAGATION:** Seed. **HABITS/CULTURE:** Grows quickly and easily from seed planted in spring after there is no danger of frost. Habit very similar to that of sunflowers. **USES:** Butterfly attractant, background summer color, cut flowers. **PROBLEMS:** Few if any.

TOADSTOOLS—see *Chlorophyllum* spp.

TOBACCO, FLOWERING—see *Nicotiana alata*

TOMATILLO—see *Lycopersicon esculentum*

TOMATO—see *Lycopersicon esculentum*

TRACHELOSPERMUM

Trachelospermum asiaticum (tray-kell-oh-SPER-mum a-she-AT-ti-cum). **COMMON NAME:** ASIAN JASMINE, JAPANESE STAR JASMINE, ASIATIC JASMINE. **TYPE:** Evergreen ground cover. **LOCATION:** Sun to shade. **HEIGHT:** 6"–12". **SPREAD:** Ground cover. **SPACING:** 12". **BLOOM/FRUIT:** No flowers or fruit. **PROPAGATION:** Cuttings. **HABITS/CULTURE:** Dense, low-growing ground cover with small oval leaves. Will climb but not readily. A variegated form and a dwarf called 'Elegans' now exist. Needs moist, well-drained, well-prepared soil for establishment. Once established, fairly drought tolerant. Mow at highest setting in late winter—again in July if you prefer. **USES:** Ground cover for large areas. **PROBLEMS:** Extreme winters can severely damage or kill this plant. Average winters will often turn the foliage brown, but it recovers in spring. **TIPS/NOTES:** Native to Japan and Korea. If your jasmine has flowers, it's either Confederate jasmine or yellow star jasmine—not Asian jasmine.

Trachelospermum asiaticum Asian jasmine 'Elegans'

Trachelospermum jasminoides (tray-kell-lo-SPER-mum jazz-min-OY-dees). **COMMON NAME:** CONFEDERATE JASMINE. **TYPE:** Evergreen vine. **LOCATION:** Sun to shade. **HEIGHT:** High-climbing. **SPREAD:** Wide-spreading. **SPACING:** 3'–5'. **BLOOM/FRUIT:** Very fragrant white flowers in early summer. **PROPAGATION:** Cuttings. **HABITS/CULTURE:** Fast, open-growing, climbing vine with dark green leaves. Blooms in sun or shade. Requires support to climb. Needs well-prepared, well-drained beds, moderate water and fertilizer. Freezes fairly often—best to treat as an annual. **USES:** Climbing vine for fence, trellis, pole, or decorative screen. **PROBLEMS:** Freeze damage. **TIPS/NOTES:** I usually treat this plant as an annual and just plant another if it freezes. *Trachelospermum mandaianum*, yellow jasmine, is lemon-scented and more cold tolerant.

Trachelospermum jasminoides Confederate jasmine

Tradescantia andersoniana spiderwort

TRADESCANTIA

Tradescantia spp. (tray-dess-KAN-shah). **COMMON NAME:** SPIDERWORT, WANDERING JEW. **TYPE:** Perennial bedding plant. **LOCATION:** Shade to dappled sunlight. **HEIGHT:** 6"–24". **SPREAD:** 12"–18". **SPACING:** 12"–18". **BLOOM/FRUIT:** White to deep purple 1/2"–1" flowers from spring until fall. **PROPAGATION:** Seed or root division. **HABITS/CULTURE:** Drought tolerant, easy to grow in shady perennial gardens. Grows best in well-prepared, well-drained soil.

Slow-growing. **USES:** Good for informal, natural settings. **PROBLEMS:** Will burn in full sun. **TIPS/NOTES:** *Tradescantia andersoniana* is spiderwort. *Tradescantia fluminensis* is wandering jew.

TREE OF HEAVEN—see *Ailanthus altissima*

TRIDENT RED MAPLE—see *Acer rubrum*

TRIFOLIATE ORANGE—see *Poncirus trifoliata*

TRIFOLIUM

Trifolium repens (tri-FO-lee-um RAY-pens). **COMMON NAME:** WHITE CLOVER. **TYPE:** Perennial ground cover. **LOCATION:** Sun to fairly heavy shade. **HEIGHT:** 6"–8". **SPREAD:** 12"–15". **SPACING:** 1 lb. of seed per thousand sq. ft. or 30–40 lbs. per acre. **BLOOM/FRUIT:** Round flower heads consisting of 20–40 white to pinkish white florets on long stems. **PROPAGATION:** Seed. **HABITS/CULTURE:** Creeping stems up to 15' long with dark green three-part leaves. Roots at the joints of the stems. Deeply rooted. Likes cool weather and clay soils. Evergreen when irrigated in the summer. Plant in September or October for best results. **USES:** Ground cover, cover crop, turf plant. One of the nation's most important pasture legumes. Great for soil-building because of its deep roots and nitrogen-fixing ability. **PROBLEMS:** Usually considered a weed, but it shouldn't be. I encourage it on my lawn. **TIPS/NOTES:**

Trifolium repens white clover

Tropaeolum majus nasturtium

For a cover crop, plant a clover mixture at a total rate of 30 lbs. seed per acre. White, crimson, and red are good choices. White clover is the best for landscape use because it is the shortest. Native of Europe and Asia Minor. Has naturalized across North America. Source of four-leaf clovers. *Trifolium incarnatum* is crimson clover.

TROPAEOLUM

Tropaeolum spp. (tro-PIE-oh-lum). **COMMON NAME:** NASTURTIUM. **TYPE:** Annual herb. **LOCATION:** Sun to part shade. **HEIGHT/SPREAD:** High-climbing and wide-spreading. **SPACING:** 1'–3'. **BLOOM/FRUIT:** Fragrant flowers of red, brown, maroon, yellow, gold, and orange. Available in both single and double forms. **PROPAGATION:** Seed. **HABITS/CULTURE:** Fast-growing annual flowering herb. Easy to grow during the cooler months. Climbing and dwarf bush types are available. Sow seed in late winter or early spring. **USES:** Annual beds, pots, hanging baskets. Leaves, flowers, and unripe seed pods have a delicious peppery flavor and are excellent in salads and other dishes. Source of vitamin C. All parts of the plant are edible. **PROBLEMS:** Hot weather, aphids. **TIPS/NOTES:** *Tropaeolum peregrinum*, canary bird flower, is a climbing vine with yellow flowers. *Tropaeolum majus* is the common garden nasturtium.

TRUMPET CREEPER—see *Campsis radicans*

TRUMPET VINE—see *Campsis radicans*

TULIPA

Tulipa spp. (TOO-lip-ah). **COMMON NAME:** TULIP. **TYPE:** Annual bulb. **LOCATION:** Sun. **HEIGHT:** 9"–12". **SPREAD:** 6"–9". **SPACING:** 6"–9". **BLOOM/FRUIT:** Single and double flowers on stems in spring. Many colors available. **PROPAGATION:** Bulbs. **HABITS/CULTURE:** Dwarf and tall-growing varieties available in all colors. Plant in well-prepared, well-drained beds after the weather turns cold. Pull up

Tulipa tulip

and discard after blooming. **USES:** Spring color. **PROBLEMS:** Expensive, will usually not return in this area—should be replanted each year. Some of the small-flowering species will return fairly well each year. **TIPS/NOTES:** Plant in pansy beds for dramatic display in the spring. Can be planted farther apart (12"–18") if planted in this fashion. Native to Asia.

TULIP TREE—see *Liriodendron tulipifera*

TUPELO—see *Nyssa sylvatica* var. *sylvatica*

TURK'S CAP—see *Malvaviscus arboreus*

Ulmus americana American elm

Ulmus crassifolia cedar elm

ULMUS

Ulmus americana (ULL-mus uh-mer-ee-KAHN-ah). **COMMON NAME:** AMERICAN ELM. **TYPE:** Deciduous tree. **LOCATION:** Sun. **HEIGHT:** 70'. **SPREAD:** 70'. **SPACING:** Do not plant! **BLOOM/FRUIT:** Small green flowers in early spring. Fruit is a winged nut that ripens just after flowering. **PROPAGATION:** Seed. **HABITS/CULTURE:** Fast-growing, gracefully spreading, with large leaves, yellow fall color. Easy to grow in any soil with normal water and nutrients. **USES:** Shade tree, large estate or park planting, yellow fall color. **PROBLEMS:** Dutch elm disease, elm leaf beetle, cotton root rot. **TIPS/NOTES:** Not recommended, although I would certainly save any existing ones. Native to the eastern half of the United States. *Zelkova serrata* is being used as an American elm substitute. It is a similar tree but has more upright growth. It's a poor choice for Texas also.

Ulmus americana American elm

Ulmus parvifolia sempervirens lacebark elm

Ulmus crassifolia (ULL-mus krass-ee-FOLE-ee-ah). **COMMON NAME:** CEDAR ELM. **TYPE:** Deciduous tree. **LOCATION:** Sun. **HEIGHT:** 80'. **SPREAD:** 60'. **SPACING:** 20'–40'. **BLOOM/FRUIT:** Small ugly flowers and many small winged seeds. **PROPAGATION:** Seed, cuttings. **HABITS/CULTURE:** Upright, moderate growth, yellow-gold fall color, irregular growth pattern, rough-textured leaves. Grows in any soil. Drought tolerant but can also stand fairly wet soil.

USES: Shade tree, street tree. **PROBLEMS:** Aphids, elm leaf beetle, mildew, mistletoe. **TIPS/NOTES:** Overused in North Texas. Referred to as "poor man's live oak." It is becoming more unhealthy every year. The closely related *Ulmus alata*, winged elm, has the same characteristics in addition to wings on the stems. Native from the southern United States to West Texas.

U

Ulmus crassifolia cedar elm

Ulmus pumila Siberian elm

Ulmus parvifolia sempervirens (ULL-mus par-vi-FOAL-ee-ah sem-per-VYE-rens). **COMMON NAME:** LACEBARK ELM, CHINESE ELM, EVERGREEN ELM, DRAKE ELM. **TYPE:** Deciduous tree. **LOCATION:** Sun. **HEIGHT:** 50'. **SPREAD:** 40'. **SPACING:** 20'–30'. **BLOOM/FRUIT:** Ugly flowers in spring, round fruit in late summer. **PROPAGATION:** Seed, cuttings. **HABITS/CULTURE:** Very fast upright and spreading growth, delicate foliage on limber stems, distinctively mottled trunk bark. Fall color is so-so yellow. Extremely easy to grow in any soil. Drought tolerant but can also stand moist soil. Easy to transplant. **USES:** Shade tree. **PROBLEMS:** None except very tender bark in early spring when leaves appear. Can contract cotton root rot if overwatered or located in poorly drained soil. **TIPS/NOTES:** Often confused with *Ulmus pumila*, Siberian elm, which is the ultimate trash tree. Lacebark elm is a perfect example of an introduced tree that is better than its native counterpart. Native to China.

Ulmus pumila (ULL-mus PEWM-ih-luh). **COMMON NAME:** SIBERIAN ELM. **TYPE:** Deciduous tree. **LOCATION:** Sun. **HEIGHT:** 50'. **SPREAD:** 50'. **SPACING:** Do not plant! **BLOOM/FRUIT:** Ugly and messy. **PROPAGATION:** Chop down. **HABITS/CULTURE:** Upright to spreading shade tree, leaves just smaller than American elm. Grows anywhere. **USES:** Shade tree. **PROBLEMS:** Elm leaf beetle, Dutch elm disease, brittle wood, mistakenly called Chinese elm. Often confused

with the excellent lacebark (*Ulmus parvifolia*). **TIPS/NOTES:** Extremely unhealthy. I recommend removing any existing ones. Some landscape people say there is no such thing as junk or weed trees. They're wrong! This is the ultimate trash tree. Native to Asia.

UMBRELLA PLANT—see *Cyperus alternifolius*

UMBRELLA TREE—see *Melia azedarach*

UNGNADIA

Ungnadia speciosa (oong-NAD-ee-ah spee-see-OH-sa). **COMMON NAME:** MEXICAN BUCKEYE. **TYPE:** Deciduous tree. **LOCATION:** Sun to shade. **HEIGHT:** 20'. **SPREAD:** 20'. **SPACING:** 10'–20'. **BLOOM/FRUIT:** Fragrant pink-purple flowers in spring. Decorative three-pod seeds on bare branches in winter. **PROPAGATION:** Seed. **HABITS/CULTURE:** Moderate growth. Brilliant yellow fall color. Easy to grow in any soil with little fertilization. Drought tolerant but can also stand moist soils. Grows in any soil, likes limestone alkaline soils best. **USES:** Spring and fall color, understory tree, specimen courtyard tree. **PROBLEMS:** Few if any. **TIPS/NOTES:** Easily grown from seed. The sweet seeds are toxic to humans. A great little tree that should be used more. Native to Texas and Mexico.

Ungnadia speciosa
Mexican buckeye

Ungnadia speciosa
Mexican buckeye

V

VACCINIUM

Vaccinium ashei (va-SIN-ee-um ASH-ee-eye). **COMMON NAME:** RABBITEYE BLUEBERRY. **TYPE:** Deciduous shrub. **LOCATION:** Sun. **HEIGHT:** 3'–4'. **SPREAD:** 3'. **SPACING:** 3'–6'. **BLOOM/FRUIT:** Small white spring flowers, followed by delicious blue berries. **PROPAGATION:** Cuttings. **HABITS/CULTURE:** Very demanding fruit crop for most of Texas. Needs sandy and very acid soil. Shallow, fibrous root system similar to that of azaleas. Cross-pollinating. Need large amounts of organic matter in the soil. Bushes mature in 7–8 years. **USES:** Food. **PROBLEMS:** Very particular about soil conditions. Will die in anything but sandy, acid soil. **TIPS/NOTES:** *Vaccinium ovatum* is the huckleberry, which loves sandy soil and has bell-shaped white flowers in spring like those of lily of the valley. Good bird food.

VASEY OAK—see *Quercus virginiana*

VERBENA

Verbena spp. (ver-BEAN-ah). **COMMON NAME:** VERBENA. **TYPE:** Perennial budding plant. **LOCATION:** Sun. **HEIGHT:** 9"–12". **SPREAD:** 12"–18". **SPACING:** 9"–12". **BLOOM/FRUIT:** Clusters of small summer-blooming flowers in red, pink, salmon, purple, blue, rose, and combinations. **PROPAGATION:** Cuttings, seed. **HABITS/CULTURE:** Low-spreading perennial. Easy to grow in well-drained beds, low water and fertilization requirements. **USES:** Summer color. **PROBLEMS:** Red spider mites occasionally. **TIPS/NOTES:** The natives are *Verbena bipinnatifida*, prairie verbena, and *Verbena tenuisecta*, moss verbena. 'Pink Parfait' is a beautiful, large-flowered evergreen. The cultivated varieties are good as well. Annual verbenas are available, but I don't recommend them.

VERBENA, LEMON—see *Aloysia triphylla*

Verbascum mullein

Veronica veronica

Verbena verbena

VERBASCUM

Verbascum spp. (ver-BAS-kum). **COMMON NAME:** MULLEIN, FLANNEL LEAF, CANDLEWICK PLANT. **TYPE:** Annual and biennial wildflowers. **LOCATION:** Full sun. **HEIGHT:** 1'–5'. **SPREAD:** 2'. **SPACING:** One here and one there. **BLOOM/FRUIT:** Yellow, white, or purple flowers. **PROPAGATION:** Seeds. **HABITS/CULTURE:** Large, fuzzy gray leaves. Tall, thin flower stalk. **USES:** Teas and ornamental specimen plants. **PROBLEMS:** Leaf-chewing insects, cosmetic damage only. **TIPS/NOTES:** Plant in fall or early spring in a well-drained area in full sun and forget it. **TIPS/NOTES:** *Verbascum thapsus*, common mullein, has yellow flowers and grows wild throughout Texas and much of the South. Several species are cultivated as summer-blooming annuals, biennials, or perennials. All have the tall (as high as 6'), striking bloom stalk that emerges from the center of the rosette of large leaves. Indians brewed a mullein tea for colds and inhaled the hot vapors for throat irritation.

VERONICA

Veronica spp. (ve-RON-ee-ka). **COMMON NAME:** VERONICA, SPEEDWELL. **TYPE:** Perennial bedding plant. **LOCATION:** Sun to part shade. **HEIGHT:** 6"–24". **SPREAD:** 12"–18". **SPACING:** 9"–12". **BLOOM/FRUIT:** Vertical flower stalks of white, rose, pink, blue, and purple in summer. **PROPAGATION:** Division. **HABITS/CULTURE:** Long-lasting colorful perennial blooms when planted in loose, well-drained beds. Gray-green leaves. **USES:** Borders, perennials gardens. **TIPS/NOTES:** Cut back after heavy flush of bloom for more bloom.

VETCH, CROWN—see *Coronilla varia*

VETCH, HAIRY—see *Vicia* spp.

Viburnum macrocephalum snowball bush

Viburnum plicatum var. *tomentosum* 'Shasta' Shasta viburnum

VIBURNUM

Viburnum spp. (vi-BURN-um). **COMMON NAME:** SNOWBALL BUSH. **TYPE:** Deciduous or evergreen shrub. **LOCATION:** Sun to fairly heavy shade. **HEIGHT:** 6'–15'. **SPREAD:** 5'–8'. **SPACING:** 4'–8'. **BLOOM/FRUIT:** Beautiful white or pink-tinged flowers in spring, sizes vary from small to huge and showy. **PROPAGATION:** Cuttings. **HABITS/CULTURE:** Full, rounded shrubs with a variety of leaf and flower sizes. Some are open-growing. Deciduous viburnums are the most cold hardy, evergreens are the most sensitive and are best used in the southern half of the state. **USES:** Background, screen, spring color, cut flowers. **PROBLEMS:** Very few, should be used more. **TIPS/NOTES:** *Viburnum macrocephalum* is the more showy-blooming Chinese snowball. *Viburnum burkwoodii* is an excellent semi-evergreen with gorgeous spring flowers. V*iburnum caricephalum* is the fragrant viburnum. 'Spring Bouquet' is a smaller evergreen cultivar. *Viburnum plicatum* var. *tomentosum* 'Shasta' is a gorgeous dogwood-like small tree.

Viburnum odoratissimum (vi-BURN-um oh-doe-ra-TISS-eh-mum). **COMMON NAME:** JAPANESE VIBURNUM. **TYPE:** Evergreen shrub. **LOCATION:** Sun to shade. **HEIGHT:** 10'. **SPREAD:** 5'–7'. **SPACING:** 4'–6'. **BLOOM/FRUIT:** Clusters of fragrant flowers, followed by clusters of colorful fruit. **PROPAGATION:** Cuttings. **HABITS/CULTURE:** Upright growth on thick stems. Large glossy leaves turn a slight bronze color in fall. Bushy but can be trimmed into a tree form. Needs well-prepared and well-drained beds, moderate water and food. **USES:** Specimen, screen, background. Foliage is wonderful, long-lasting cut-flower material. In fact, it will easily root in water. **PROBLEMS:** Freeze damage. **TIPS/NOTES:** The flowers are more subtle on this variety than on other viburnum. Often sold as *Viburnum macrophyllum*.

Viburnum 'Spring Bouquet'
Spring Bouquet viburnum

Viburnum odoratissimum
Japanese viburnum

Viburnum rufidulum rusty blackhaw, spring

V

Viburnum rufidulum rusty blackhaw, fall

Viburnum rufidulum (vi-BURN-um rue-FID-you-lum). **COMMON NAME:** RUSTY BLACKHAW. **TYPE:** Deciduous tree or shrub. **LOCATION:** Sun to shade. **HEIGHT:** 20'.

SPREAD: 20'. **SPACING:** 10'–20'. **BLOOM/FRUIT:** White flower clusters in spring, blue-black berries in late summer. **PROPAGATION:** Seed, cuttings. **HABITS/CULTURE:** Shrubby tree, glossy leaves, reddish fall color. Can grow to 40'. Easy to grow in any soil, extremely drought tolerant. **USES:** Specimen garden tree, understory tree, background mass planting. **PROBLEMS:** Few if any—practically maintenance free. **TIPS/NOTES:** Great shrub or little tree. Native to Texas and Oklahoma.

Viburnum rufidulum
rusty blackhaw, fall

VICIA

Vicia spp. (vi-KEY-ah). **COMMON NAME:** VETCH. **TYPE:** Annual ground cover. **LOCATION:** Sun. **HEIGHT:** 12"–36". **SPACING:** 20–30 lbs. of seed per acre. **BLOOM/FRUIT:** White or purple flowers. Seeds are round and inside hard, elongated pods. **PROPAGATION:** Seed. **HABITS/CULTURE:** Vine-like annuals with long stems, small leaves, and tendrils that attach to other plants. **USES:** Green manure, cover crop, forage. I use vetches sometimes as decorative plants. **PROBLEMS:** Can become invasive. **TIPS/NOTES:** *Vicia villosa*, hairy vetch, is one of the best choices for Texas. *Vicia sativa*, common vetch, is less cold hardy but will grow well in Texas. Crown vetch is the perennial *Coronilla varia*. Hairy vetch makes an attractive winter cover crop. It can be planted in October at a rate of 20–30 lbs. per acre. Higher rates can be used on home vegetable gardens and then tilled into the soil in the spring as a green manure. If the soil is healthy, the vetch can simply be mowed in the spring and tomatoes, peppers, and other plants can be planted through the mulch without any tilling. University tests on this technique show significant increased production, as much as 100 percent.

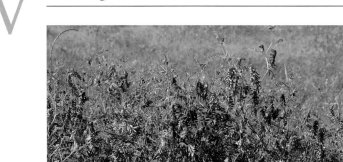
Vicia villosa hairy vetch

Viola missouriensis wood violet

Vinca minor vinca

Viola tricolor Johnny-jump-up

VIGNA

Vigna sinensis (VIG-na si-NEN-sis). **COMMON NAME:** SOUTHERN PEAS. **TYPE:** Annual vegetable. **LOCATION:** Sun. **HEIGHT/SPREAD:** High-climbing and wide-spreading. **SPACING:** 4"–8". **BLOOM/FRUIT:** White or purple flowers, followed by edible pods and peas. **PROPAGATION:** Seed. **HABITS/CULTURE:** Easy-to-grow legume that is fairly tolerant of high temperatures. Fairly drought tolerant. **USES:** Food, summer cover crop. **PROBLEMS:** Soil-borne fungi, garden flea hoppers, chlorosis, stink bugs, cutworms, nematodes, thrips, spider mites. **TIPS/NOTES:** This species includes cream peas, blackeyed peas, cowpeas, and purple hull peas. For a cover crop, plant 20 lbs. per acre after the last killing frost date in spring.

VINCA

Vinca spp. (VIN-cah). **COMMON NAME:** VINCA. **TYPE:** Evergreen ground cover. **LOCATION:** Shade to part shade. **HEIGHT:** 6"–18". **SPREAD:** Ground cover. **SPACING:** 12". **BLOOM/FRUIT:** Blue flowers in late spring. **PROPAGATION:** Cuttings. **HABITS/CULTURE:** Coarse ground cover for large areas in shade. Spreads quickly. Plant in any soil in shade. Relatively drought tolerant once established. **USES:** Good plant for a naturally wooded area. **PROBLEMS:** Leaf rollers, cutworms. **TIPS/NOTES:** Native to Europe and Asia. Not very good for residential property for close viewing. *Vinca major* is the large-leafed, more commonly used variety. *Vinca minor* has smaller, shinier leaves, is more refined in appearance, and can tolerate more sun.

Viola wittrockiana pansy

VIOLA

Viola wittrockiana (vie-OH-la we-trok-ee-AN-ah). **COMMON NAME:** PANSY. **TYPE:** Annual bedding plant. **LOCATION:** Sun. **HEIGHT:** 6"–8". **SPREAD:** 8"–12". **SPACING:** 6"–12". **BLOOM/FRUIT:** Winter and spring flowers in yellow, white, blue, purple, red, and combinations. **PROPAGATION:** Seed. **HABITS/CULTURE:** Low-growing annual. Needs well-prepared, well-drained beds, ample water and fertilizer. **USES:** Winter and cool-season flowers. **PROBLEMS:** Extreme freezes, aphids, cutworms. **TIPS/NOTES:** Plant in October or late winter. Will bloom from fall to spring in a mild winter. Giant flower varieties are available. Native to Europe. *Viola cornuta*, viola, is the small-flowering cousin. *Viola tricolor*, Johnny-jump-up, is an even smaller cousin with purple and yellow flowers. Both are more heat tolerant than pansies. The sweet violet is *Viola odorata*. The wood violet is *Viola missouriensis*. Some people treat them as weeds, but not me—I think they're beautiful. And of course the flowers of all violas are edible. The African violet, a houseplant, is not related and not edible.

VIOLET—see *Viola wittrockiana*

VIRGINIA CREEPER—see *Parthenocissus quinquefolia*

VITEX

Vitex agnus-castus (VIE-teks AG-nus CAST-us). **COMMON NAME:** VITEX, LILAC CHASTE TREE. **TYPE:** Deciduous tree. **LOCATION:** Sun. **HEIGHT:** 20'. **SPREAD:** 25'. **SPACING:** 15'–20'. **BLOOM/FRUIT:** Purple or white flowers in early summer. **PROPAGATION:** Seed, cuttings. **HABITS/CULTURE:** Spreading, usually multistemmed, brittle wood, not long-lived. Nicely textured foliage. Easy to grow in any soil, drought tolerant. **USES:** Summer flowers, foliage texture. **PROBLEMS:** Freeze damage in the northern part of the state, short-lived. **TIPS/NOTES:** Native to Europe and Asia. Should not be used as a primary tree but rather as a secondary tree for special interest.

Vitex agnus-castus vitex

VITIS

Vitis spp. (VIE-tis). **COMMON NAME:** GRAPE. **TYPE:** Deciduous vine. **LOCATION:** Sun. **HEIGHT:** High-climbing. **SPREAD:** Wide-spreading. **SPACING:** 8'–10'. **BLOOM/FRUIT:** Small spring flowers, followed by large, colorful, edible fruit. **PROPAGATION:** Cuttings, grafting. **HABITS/CULTURE:** Fast-growing climber for trellis or overhead structure. Needs support to get started. Grows in any well-drained soil, low water and fertilization requirements. Self-pollinating. **USES:** Food, good for quickly cooling a hot spot in summer. **PROBLEMS:** Grasshoppers, caterpillars, Pierce's disease. **TIPS/NOTES:** Some grape vines can get out of hand by growing so fast. Keep them out of trees. Native worldwide. The native *Vitis landicans* 'Wild Mustang' is great for jams and jellies. It is very sweet, acid, and tannic. Other recommended varieties for Texas include 'Reliance' (red), 'Flame' (red), 'Concord' (red), 'Fiesta' (white), 'Niagara' (white), 'Mustang' (red). *Vitis rotundifolia*, the muscadine grape, needs sandy, acid soil for best results.

Vitis grape

WALKING STICK FILBERT—see *Corylus avellana* 'Contorta'

WALLFLOWER—see *Cheiranthus cheiri*

WALNUT, BLACK—see *Juglans nigra*

WANDERING JEW—see *Tradescantia* spp.

WATERMELON—see *Citrullus vulgaris*

WATER OAK—see *Quercus nigra*

WAX MYRTLE—see *Myrica cerifera*

WEDELIA

Wedelia hispida (weh-DEEL-ee-ah HISS-peh-dah). **COMMON NAME:** ZEXMENIA. **TYPE:** Evergreen to perennial bedding plant. **LOCATION:** Sun to dappled shade. **HEIGHT:** 24"–36". **BLOOM/FRUIT:** Yellow 1" flowers from early summer to fall. **PROPAGATION:** Seed, cuttings. **HABITS/CULTURE:** Texas native with sticky foliage. Woody stems, rounded shape, yellow daisylike flowers all summer. Tends to sprawl in shaded locations. Evergreen in the southern half of the state. **USES:** Summer color, native perennial garden. **PROBLEMS:** Few if any. **TIPS/NOTES:** *Wedelia triloba* is a 12"–15" ground cover that is native to far South Texas and Mexico. Good in sun or part shade in natural settings. *Wedelia texana* is orange zexmenia.

Wedelia hispida zexmenia

WEEDS

Annual bluegrass—*Poa annua.* Annual low-growing, cool-season weed.

Aster, roadside—*Aster exilis.* Annual broad-leafed wildflower with white or light blue flowers in fall. Control by improving the moisture level and fertility of the soil.

Bermudagrass—see *Cynodon dactylon*

Bindweed—*Convolvulus arvensis.* Introduced from Eurasia. Ranked among the dozen worst perennial weeds in the world. Roots go 6' deep, can lie in the soil for 30 years and still germinate. Also called wild morning glory. Control by increasing organic matter in the soil.

Blue-eyed grass—see *Sisyrinchium* spp.

Brambles—*Rubus* spp. Various berry plants with sharp thorns, spread to form dense masses. Control by pulling up.

Bull nettle—*Cnidoscolus texanus.* Perennial problem weed in deep, sandy soils with low fertility. Leaves and stems are covered with stinging hairs. Huge underground storage tubers. Control by increasing organic matter in soil.

Bur clover—*Medicago hispida.* Very low-growing annual cool-weather legume. Small yellow pealike flowers. Seeds contained in a soft-spined bur.

Canada thistle—*Cirsium arvense.* Perennial weed, 1 1/2–4' in height. Very difficult to control because of its deep root system. Control by mowing when plant is in full bloom. Root system is exhausted when it is the prettiest.

Chickweed—*Stellaria media paronychia.* Annual broadleaf weed with small, bright green leaves. Low-growing benign weed. Just mow it.

Cocklebur—*Xanthium strumarium.* Tall, bushy, annual weed with prickly seeds and sandpaper-like leaves. Grows where excess phosphorous is available.

Crabgrass—see *Digitaria* spp.

Dallisgrass—see *Paspalum dilatatum*

Dandelion—see *Taraxacum officinale*

Dichondra (ponyfoot)—see *Dichondra micrantha*

Dodder—*Cuscuta* spp. Annual weed that reproduces by seed. It starts as an independent plant but establishes a parasitic relationship with the host crop. At this point it has no chlorophyll and looks like yellow string. Control by balancing the minerals in the soil.

Field bindweed—see Bindweed above

Goathead (puncture vine)—*Tribulus terrestris.* Hairy, low-growing annual with a taproot and several stems forming a rosette. Has yellow flowers and burs that will puncture tires.

mistletoe

Goosegrass (silver crabgrass)—*Eleusine indica.* Annual that reproduces by seed in unhealthy soil. Very similar to crabgrass.

Grassbur—see Sandbur below

Greenbriar—see *Smilax* spp.

Henbit—see *Lamium amplexicaule*

Honeysuckle—see *Lonicera japonica* 'Atropurpurea'

Johnsongrass—see *Sorghum halepense*

Lamb's-quarter—see *Chenopodium* spp.

Mistletoe—Plant parasite that primarily attaches to limbs and trunks of low quality and/or stressed trees, such as Arizona ash, hackberry, bois d'arc, locust, boxelder, and weak elms and ashes. Remove by cutting infected limbs off the tree. If that can't be done, knotch into the limb to remove the rooting structure of the mistletoe and paint with black pruning paint to prevent resprout. There are no magic chemical or organic sprays. Keeping the soil and trees healthy is the best preventative.

Morning glory—see *Ipomoea* spp.

Nutgrass—*Cyperus rotundus.* Perennial sedge introduced from Eurasia. Spreads by seed, nutlets, and creeping tendrils, likes wet soil. Remove with mechanical devices. Control in turf by planting ryegrass in the fall.

Oxalis—see *Oxalis* spp.

Pigweed—*Amaranthus* spp. Tagged by weed control specialists as one of the most troublesome. Likes healthy soil and grows about 5' tall. Control with cultural practices. No phosphorus or potassium is needed in these soils.

Poison ivy—see *Rhus radicans*

Purple nutsedge—see Nutgrass above

Purslane—see *Portulaca grandiflora*

Ragweed—*Ambrosia* spp. Annual broadleaf that indicates droughty soil. Releases a potent pollen that causes hay fever. Control by cultivation and mowing.

Rescuegrass—*Bromus catharticus.* Cool-season annual bromegrass. Control by broadcasting corn gluten meal in early October.

Sandbur—*Cenchrus pauciflorus.* Annual grass plant that produces a bur with strong, sharp spines. Seeds in the bur can lie dormant in the soil for years before germinating.

Sheep sorrel—see *Oxalis* spp.

Smilax—see *Smilax* spp.

Spurge—see *Euphorbia* spp.

Velvetleaf—*Abutilon theophrasti.* Annual weed with short, velvety hairs on its many branched stems. A problem in row crops, particularly soybeans, corn, and cotton. Chemical herbicides actually encourage this plant. Control by aerating soil and increasing organic matter in soil and general soil health.

White clover—see *Trifolium repens*

Wild carrot—see *Daucus carota*

Wood sorrel—see *Oxalis* spp.

WEIGELA
Weigela florida (WYE-ge-la FLO-ri-da). **COMMON NAME:** WEIGELA. **TYPE:** Deciduous shrub. **LOCATION:** Sun to part shade. **HEIGHT:** 8'. **SPREAD:** 6'–8'. **SPACING:** 4'–6'. **BLOOM/FRUIT:** Red, white, or pink summer flowers. **PROPAGATION:** Cuttings. **HABITS/CULTURE:** Upright to rounded overall growth. Summer flowers that resemble those of honeysuckle. Easy to grow in well-drained, healthy soil. Trim out old nonproductive wood annually. **USES:** Background, summer color, screen planting, perennial gardens. Good for attracting hummingbirds. **PROBLEMS:** Few if any, should be used more. **TIPS/NOTES:** Dwarf forms are available.

WHITE CLOVER—see *Trifolium repens*

WHITE OAK—see *Quercus virginiana*

WILD BANANA—see *Asimina triloba*

WILLOW, BLACK—see *Salix babylonica*

WILLOW, COCKSCREW—see *Salix babylonica*

WILLOW, DESERT—see *Chilopsis linearis*

WILLOW, WEEPING—see *Salix babylonica*

WILLOW OAK—see *Quercus nigra* and *Quercus virginiana*

WINECUP—see *Callirhoe involucrata*

WINGED ELM—see *Ulmus crassifolia*

WINTERCREEPER, PURPLE—see *Euonymus fortunei* 'Coloratus'

WISTERIA
Wisteria sinensis (wiss-TER-ee-ah sigh-NEN-sis). **COMMON NAME:** CHINESE WISTERIA. **TYPE:** Deciduous vine. **LOCATION:** Sun to part shade. **HEIGHT:** Vine. **SPACING:** 8'–10'. **BLOOM/FRUIT:** Purple spring flowers. 'Alba' has white flowers. Japanese wisteria (*Wisteria floribunda*) has longer flowers which don't open

Wisteria sinensis
Chinese wisteria

Wisteria floribunda Japanese wisteria

Yucca aloifolia Spanish bayonet

Yucca gloriosa soft yucca

until the foliage is on the plant. *Wisteria frutescens* var. *macrostachya* is the native Texas wisteria. **PROPAGATION:** Cuttings. **HABITS/CULTURE:** Fast-growing, twining vine that can grow to great heights. Easy to grow in any soil. **USES:** Spring-flowering climbing vine for arbor, fence, or wall. **PROBLEMS:** Can take over if not pruned to keep in shape. Grasshoppers, chlorosis. **TIPS/NOTES:** Most wisteria are native to China.

WISTERIA, EVERGREEN—see *Millettia reticulata*

WOOD SORREL—see *Oxalis* spp.

WRIGHT ACACIA—see *Acacia* spp.

YARROW—see *Achillea* spp.

YAUPON HOLLY—see *Ilex vomitoria*

YAUPON HOLLY, DECIDUOUS—see *Ilex decidua*

YESTERDAY, TODAY, AND TOMORROW—see *Brunfelsia australis*

YUCCA

Yucca aloifolia (YUCK-ah al-oh-eh-FOAL-ee-ah). **COMMON NAME:** HARD YUCCA, SPANISH BAYONET, SPANISH DAGGER. **TYPE:** Evergreen shrub. **LOCATION:** Sun. **HEIGHT:** 8'–10'. **SPREAD:** 8'–10'. **SPACING:** 6'–8'. **BLOOM/FRUIT:** Attractive white flower cluster in early summer. **PROPAGATION:** Seed, division. **HABITS/CULTURE:** Danger-

ously stiff leaves. Needs sun and drainage but very little water. Grows in any soil. **USES:** Desert gardens, specimen, accent. **PROBLEMS:** Sharp spiny leaves are very dangerous. **TIPS/NOTES:** Handle with care and do not use where children might be playing. Native to the southern United States.

Yucca gloriosa (YUCK-ah glor-ee-OH-sa). **COMMON NAME:** SOFT YUCCA. **TYPE:** Evergreen shrub. **LOCATION:** Sun. **HEIGHT:** 3'–8'. **SPREAD:** 3'–4'. **SPACING:** 3'–4'. **BLOOM/FRUIT:** White flower stalk in summer. **PROPAGATION:** Seed. **HABITS/CULTURE:** Single unbranching trunk. Has softer and larger leaves than Spanish bayonet. Spreads by offshoots to make new plants. Grows in any well-drained soil. **USES:** Accent, dramatic mass. **PROBLEMS:** None. **TIPS/NOTES:** Looks best at heights of 24"–36". When leggy, cut off the tall part and let the baby plants take over. Native to southern United States.

YUCCA, RED—see *Hesperaloe parviflora*

ZANTHOXYLUM

Zanthoxylum clava-herculis (zanth-OX-ih-lum CLA-va her-CUE-lis). **COMMON NAME:** PRICKLY ASH, HERCULES' CLUB, TOOTHACHE TREE, TICKLETONGUE TREE. **TYPE:** Deciduous tree. **LOCATION:** Sun. **HEIGHT:** 15'–30'. **SPREAD:** 15'–30'. **SPACING:** Seldom planted. **BLOOM/FRUIT:** Small yellowish-green flower clusters in spring.

Zanthoxylum clava-herculis prickly ash

Brown fruit contains a single seed that ripens in mid or late summer. **PROPAGATION:** Seed, cuttings. **HABITS/CULTURE:** Native to East Texas and the blackland prairie. Often found in fence rows. Grows in any soil. Compound leaves with 5–15 leaflets. Large, nasty spines on trunk and limbs. **USES:** Cover for wildlife, bee attractant. This is the favorite host of the giant swallowtail butterfly; the larva is hard to see because it looks like bird droppings. **PROBLEMS:** Caterpillars. **TIPS/NOTES:** All parts of the tree, including the bark, will numb the gums and tongue when chewed or sucked. Native Americans used it as a painkiller.

ZEA
Zea mays (ZEE-a MAYS). **COMMON NAME:** SWEET CORN. **TYPE:** Annual vegetable. **LOCATION:** Sun. **HEIGHT:** 6'–12'. **SPREAD:** 12"–18". **SPACING:** 10"–12". **BLOOM/FRUIT:** Male tassels and female silks protrude from the ends of ears. **PROPAGATION:** Seed. **HABITS/CULTURE:** Fast-growing grasslike food crop. Germination in 4–7 days at 68–86 degrees. Ready for harvest 18–24 days after silks first appear. **USES:** Food. **PROBLEMS:** Mildew, virus, corn earworm, raccoons, army worms. **TIPS/NOTES:** Plant in blocks rather than in long rows after soil is warm in the spring. Corn tastes better and is better for you if not overcooked.

ZEBRAGRASS— see *Miscanthus* spp.

ZELKOVA—see *Ulmus americana*

ZEPHYRANTHES
Zephyranthes spp. (ze-fi-RANTH-eez). **COMMON NAME:** RAIN LILY. **TYPE:** Perennial wildflower. **LOCATION:** Sun to part shade. **HEIGHT:** 12". **SPREAD:** 12". **SPACING:** 9"–12". **BLOOM/FRUIT:** Various colors of flowers on hollow stems in summer and fall, usually after rain or a climate change. White is the most common, also available in yellow, pink, and rose. **PROPAGATION:** Bulbs. **HABITS/CULTURE:** Bright green rushlike leaves. Plant in fall in masses for best results. Need some water but are fairly drought tolerant. Foliage looks like chives or thin liriope. **USES:** Wildflowers, summer color, interesting texture. **PROBLEMS:** Few if any. **TIPS/NOTES:** If plants are kept alternately wet and dry, they will bloom after rain or irrigation.

Zephyranthes rain lily

ZEXMENIA—see *Wedelia hispida*

ZINGIBER
Zingiber officinale (ZING-gi-ber oh-fis-ih-NAH-lee). **COMMON NAME:** GINGER. **TYPE:** Tender perennial herb. **LOCATION:** Semi-shade. **HEIGHT:** 3'–8'. **SPREAD:** 5'–8'. **SPACING:** 12"–36". **BLOOM/FRUIT:** Very fragrant yellow and purple flowers in late summer or early fall. **PROPAGATION:** Division of rhizomes. **HABITS/CULTURE:** Upright, jointed stems similar to bamboo. All gingers are heavy feeders. They need a rich, healthy soil, regular feeding with an organic fertilizer, and regular watering. Culinary ginger,

grown in containers, needs plenty of light and protection against freeze. Cut back gingers in the late fall and allow them to rest through the winter. Mature plants may be dug and divided. **USES:** Excellent container and greenhouse plant. Promotes blood circulation, good for respiratory problems. Flavoring agent in teas and many foods, including vegetables,

Zingiber officinale ginger

Z

Zinnia elegans zinnia

Zinnia linearis

Ziziphus jujube

ZIZIPHUS

Ziziphus spp. (ziz-ah-FUSE). **COMMON NAME:** JUJUBE, CHINESE JUJUBE, FALSE DATE. **TYPE:** Deciduous tree. **LOCATION:** Sun. **HEIGHT:** 25'–30'. **SPREAD:** 15'–30'. **SPACING:** 20'–30'. **BLOOM/ FRUIT:** Clusters of small yellow flowers in early summer. Shiny, edible, datelike brown fruit in fall. **PROPAGATION:** Seed. **HABITS/CULTURE:** Slow to moderate growth in almost any soil. Branches and twigs are spiny, gnarled, zigzagged (hence the name). Glossy, dark green leaves. **USES:** Unique shade tree. Food, although the taste of the fruit is nothing exciting. **PROBLEMS:** Can spread by root sprouts and seeds to become a rather annoying pest.

ZOYSIA

Zoysia japonica 'Meyer' (ZOY-sha jap-PON-eh-kah). **COMMON NAME:** ZOYSIAGRASS. **TYPE:** Warm-season grass. **LOCATION:** Sun to part shade. **HEIGHT:** 2"–4" (mown). **SPACING:** Solid sod. **BLOOM/FRUIT:** Insignificant. **PROPAGATION:** Solid sod only. **HABITS/CULTURE:** Thick, succulent-looking grass. Very slow to spread. Plant solid sod only, too slow growing for any other planting techniques. Low maintenance—can be mowed less often than other turf grasses and requires far less edging. **USES:** Lawn grass, small areas, Oriental gardens. **PROBLEMS:** Slow-growing, but this quality gives it its maintenance advantages. Thatch build-up when too much nitrogen fertilizer has been used. **TIPS/ NOTES:** Avoid using in high-traffic areas. 'Meyer Z-52' is wider-leafed and a better choice than the narrow-leafed 'Emerald.' Native to Japan.

Zoysia japonica 'Meyer' zoysiagrass

meats, and desserts. **PROBLEMS:** Subject to wind damage if not protected. **TIPS/NOTES:** Ornamental ginger has flowers in yellow, white, red, orange, and lavender and handsome tropical foliage. Freezes in the northern part of the state. The roots of all gingers are edible and have varying degrees of hotness, like peppers. Ginger root is used both fresh or dried and powdered. The rhizomes or roots are called "hands." To use fresh ginger, wash it, peel the thin paper skin, slice thin or chop fine.

ZINNIA

Zinnia spp. (ZEN-ee-ah). **COMMON NAME:** ZINNIA. **TYPE:** Annual bedding plant. **LOCATION:** Sun. **HEIGHT:** 8"–36". **SPREAD:** 12"–24". **SPACING:** 12". **BLOOM/FRUIT:** Flowers of all colors and sizes on long stems in summer. **PROPAGATION:** Seed, transplants. **HABITS/CULTURE:** Open, upright growth. Easy to grow from seed. Grows in any loose soil, fairly drought tolerant. Add superphosphate or soft rock phosphate for more blooms. **USES:** Summer flowers, cut flowers. **PROBLEMS:** Mildew, cutworms, red spider mites. Gets ragged toward the end of summer. **TIPS/NOTES:** Native to Mexico and Central America. Plant from seeds or pots in spring. *Zinnia elegans* 'Dreamland Mix' is a new low-growing hybrid that I really like. *Zinnea linearis* is an even lower-growing choice available in orange and white.